·2020·

何梁何利奖

HLHL PRIZE

何梁何利基金评选委员会　编

THE SELECTION BOARD OF HO LEUNG HO LEE FOUNDATION

中国科学技术出版社

·北京·

图书在版编目（CIP）数据

2020何梁何利奖 / 何梁何利基金评选委员会编. —
北京：中国科学技术出版社，2021.10
ISBN 978-7-5046-9173-6

Ⅰ.①2… Ⅱ.①何… Ⅲ.①自然科学—科学家—生
平事迹—中国—2020 Ⅳ.①K826.1

中国版本图书馆CIP数据核字（2021）第179394号

责任编辑	韩　颖	
责任校对	焦　宁　吕传新	
责任印制	李晓霖	

出　　版	中国科学技术出版社	
发　　行	中国科学技术出版社有限公司发行部	
地　　址	北京市海淀区中关村南大街 16 号	
邮　　编	100081	
发行电话	010-62173865	
传　　真	010-62173081	
网　　址	http://www.cspbooks.com.cn	

开　　本	787mm×1092mm　1/16	
字　　数	434 千字	
印　　张	19.75	
插　　页	4	
印　　数	1—3000 册	
版　　次	2021 年 10 月第 1 版	
印　　次	2021 年 10 月第 1 次印刷	
印　　刷	北京荣泰印刷有限公司	
书　　号	ISBN 978-7-5046-9173-6 / K·308	
定　　价	80.00 元	

编 辑 委 员 会

内 容 提 要

本书是何梁何利基金出版物——《何梁何利奖》的第二十七集。书中简要介绍了 2020 年度何梁何利基金 52 位获奖人的生平经历和主要科技成就。为了便于海内外人士了解本奖背景，书中同时收入了反映何梁何利基金及其科技奖励情况的资料，作为附录刊出。

This is the twenty-seven collection of the publications of Ho Leung Ho Lee Foundation—*Ho Leung Ho Lee Prize.* In this book, the biographical notes on the 52 awardees of the year 2020 and their main scientific and technological achievements are accounted briefly. This collection includes appendices concerning Ho Leung Ho Lee Foundation and its scientific and technological award in order to help the readers both in China and abroad to understand the background of this prize.

　　2020 年 11 月 3 日，何梁何利基金 2020 年度颁奖大会（第二十七届）在北京钓鱼台国宾馆举行。中共中央政治局委员、国务院副总理刘鹤出席大会并讲话。

　　On November 3, 2020, the 2020 Award Ceremony (27th) of HLHL Foundation is held at Diaoyutai State Guesthouse in Beijing. Liu He, a member of the Political Bureau of the Communist Party of China (CPC) Central Committee and Vice Premier of the State Council, attends and delivers a speech at the 2020 Award Ceremony of HLHL Foundation.

　　国家领导人、各界嘉宾、捐款人代表与何梁何利基金 2020 年度获奖人合影。

　　The state leaders, the honored guests and the representatives of the donors have a group photo taken with the winners of 2020 HLHL Prize.

何梁何利基金信托委员会主席、评选委员会主任朱丽兰在何梁何利基金2020年度颁奖大会上做评选委员会工作报告。

Zhu Lilan, Chairwoman of the Board of Trustees and Director of the Selection Board of HLHL Foundation, delivers a report on the work of the Selection Board at the 2020 Award Ceremony of HLHL Foundation.

何梁何利基金（北京）代表处首席代表、何梁何利基金评选委员会秘书长段瑞春主持大会。

Duan Ruichun, the chief representative of the Beijing Representative Office of the Ho Leung Ho Lee Foundation (Hong Kong)，and the Secretary-General of the Selection Board of HLHL Foundation，presides over the 2020 Award Ceremony of HLHL Foundation.

何梁何利基金 2020 年度科学与技术成就奖获得者钟南山院士在颁奖大会上发言。
Zhong Nanshan, the winner of 2020 HLHL Prize for Scientific and Technology Achievements and academician of the Chinese Academy of Engineering, delivers a speech at the 2020 Award Ceremony of HLHL Foundation.

何梁何利基金 2020 年度科学与技术成就奖获得者樊锦诗研究员在颁奖大会上发言。
Fan Jinshi, the winner of 2020 HLHL Prize for Scientific and Technology Achievements, delivers a speech at the 2020 Award Ceremony of HLHL Foundation.

中共中央政治局委员、国务院副总理刘鹤与何梁何利基金 2020 年度科学与技术成就奖获奖科学家钟南山、樊锦诗合影。

Liu He, member of the Political Bureau of the CPC Central Committee and Vice Premier of the State Council, has a photo taken with Zhong Nanshan and Fan Jinshi，the winners of 2020 HLHL Prize for Scientific and Technology Achievements.

何梁何利基金 2020 年度颁奖大会会场。
The meeting hall of the 2020 Award Ceremony of HLHL Foundation.

刘鹤出席何梁何利基金 2020 年度颁奖大会

　　新华社北京 11 月 3 日电　　11 月 3 日，何梁何利基金 2020 年度颁奖大会在京举行。中共中央政治局委员、国务院副总理刘鹤出席大会并讲话，全国人大常委会副委员长沈跃跃，全国政协副主席、中国科协主席万钢出席大会。

　　刘鹤指出，党中央、国务院高度重视科技工作。刚刚结束的五中全会，提出坚持创新在现代化建设全局中的核心地位，把科技自立自强作为国家发展战略支撑，摆在各项规划任务的首位，进行了全面部署，下一步将强化国家战略科技力量，提升企业技术创新能力，激发人才创新活力，完善科技创新体制机制。

　　刘鹤强调，科技发展最关键的是人才。要全方位培养、引进和用好人才，造就更多国际一流科技领军人才和创新团队。希望广大科技工作者扎根主业、潜心研究，将自己的科学追求融入社会主义现代化国家建设的伟大事业之中。

　　2020 年度何梁何利基金"科学与技术成就奖"授予国家呼吸系统疾病临床医学研究中心钟南山院士和敦煌研究院名誉院长樊锦诗研究员。另有 30 位和 20 位科技工作者荣获"科学与技术进步奖"和"科学与技术创新奖"。

　　何梁何利基金由香港爱国金融家何善衡、梁銶琚、何添、利国伟于 1994 年创立，旨在奖励中国杰出科学家，服务于国家现代化建设。26 年来，共遴选奖励 1414 位杰出科技工作者。

Liu He Attended the 2020 Award Ceremony of Ho Leung Ho Lee Foundation

On November 3, 2020, the 2020 Awarding Ceremony of the Ho Leung Ho Lee Foundation was held in Beijing. Liu He, member of the Political Bureau of the CPC Central Committee and vice premier of the State Council, attended the ceremony and delivered a speech. Shen Yueyue, vice chairperson of the Standing Committee of the National People's Congress, and Wan Gang, vice chairman of the Chinese People's Political Consultative Conference and chairman of China Association for Science and Technology, also attended the ceremony.

Liu He pointed out that the Central Committee of the CPC and the State Council attach high importance to the science and technology work. The Fifth Plenary Session of the 19th CPC Central Committee, which was recently concluded, proposes to continue to put innovation at the heart of China's modernization drive, regards self-reliance and self-improvement in science and technology as the strategic support for China's development, and makes an overall arrangement with scientific innovation as the top priority among all plans and tasks. Next, efforts will be intensified to improve the national strength in strategic science and technology, enhance the capacity of enterprises in technological innovation, unleash the innovation vitality of talents, and complete the building of the system and the mechanism for scientific and technological innovation.

Liu He stressed that talents are the key to realizing scientific and technological development. We should train, recruit and make good use of talents in a comprehensive way, and cultivate still more world-class leading talents in science and technology and a contingent of innovative talents. He hoped that scientists and engineers remain committed to their specialties, devote themselves to their research, and integrate their pursuit of scientific and technological achievements into the great undertaking of socialist modernization drive.

The 2020 "Prize for Scientific and Technological Achievements" of the Ho Leung Ho Lee Foundation was granted to Zhong Nanshan, academician of the Chinese Academy of Engineering and director of National Clinical Research Center for Respiratory Disease, and Fan Jinshi, research fellow and honorary director of Dunhuang Research Academy. The "Prize for Scientific and Technological Progress" was presented to 30 scientists and engineers, and the "Prize for Scientific and Technological Innovation" was given to 20 scientists and engineers.

The Ho Leung Ho Lee Foundation was established in 1994 by four Hong Kong–based patriotic financiers–Ho Sin–Hang, Leung Kau–kui, Ho Tim and Lee Quo–Wei for the purpose of awarding outstanding scientists in China and serving the national modernization drive. Over the past 26 years, it has selected and awarded 1,414 eminent scientists and engineers.

(Xinhua News Agency, November 3, 2020)

序

2020 年受到新冠病毒疫情肆虐的影响，全球工商业活动以至全球经济发展都受到严重影响，市民的生活模式也出现了重大的转变。即使面对新冠病毒疫情的挑战，何梁何利基金在信托委员会、投资委员会、评选委员会同人以及所有义务工作人员的努力下，能够继续畅顺运作，捐款人深表感谢和欣慰。

去年是基金北京代表处投入运作的第一年，也顺利完成了评选会议和颁奖大会，国务院刘鹤副总理更亲临担任主礼嘉宾和颁奖，并发表了重要讲话，基金同人都感到非常荣幸。遗憾的是，由于疫情关系，香港的代表不能亲自参与评选会议和颁奖大会，但这两个活动能够成功举行，充分反映基金信托委员会和评选委员会同人在面对挑战下展现的灵活性和能力，捐款人再一次衷心感谢。

疫情亦令环球金融市场变得波动，但在投资委员会成员的努力下，基金的财务状况继续保持稳健，有助基金的长远运作。虽然疫情依然反复，但随着疫苗接种大规模展开，以及各国社会共同努力抗疫下，相信疫情很快可以纾缓，令经济重回正轨。

国家在 2020 年 10 月召开的十九届五中全会中强调，"坚持创新在我国现代化建设全局中的核心地位，把科技自立自强作为国家发展的战略支撑，面向世界科技前沿、面向经济主战场、面向国家重大需求、面向人民生命健康，深入实施科教兴国战略、人才强国战略、创新驱动发展战略，完善国家创新体系，加快建设科技强国。"

根据世界知识产权组织发表的《2020 年全球创新指数报告》，中国名列第 14 名，被纳入创新型国家的行列。

何梁何利基金的成立是鼓励中国科技工作者自主研发和创新，特别是现在面对激烈竞争和国际保护主义的复杂政治环境，中国的科技研发更需要经得起考验，让中国在世界科技领域发挥更大的影响力。基金同人定会不断努力，配合国家的科研方针和方向，为奖励人才和促进中国科技发展发挥最大作用。

何梁何利基金捐款人

何善衡慈善基金会有限公司　　梁銶琚慈善基金会有限公司
何添基金有限公司　　　　　　伟伦基金有限公司

2021 年 6 月于香港

Preface

The COVID-19 pandemic significantly disrupted peoples' lives, commercial activity and economic development around the world in 2020. Given the tremendous challenges of last year, the donors of the Ho Leung Ho Lee Foundation wish to convey their heartfelt gratitude and appreciation to the members of the Board of Trustees, the Investment Committee and the Selection Board, as well as to all the Foundation's volunteers, for their tireless efforts to ensure the Foundation continued to operate smoothly and carry on with its important activities despite the testing external environment.

Last year was the first year of operation of the Foundation's Beijing Representative Office and it was pleased to report that the Selection meeting and Award Presentation Ceremony were successfully held despite the challenging conditions. The Foundation was deeply honoured to have Vice Premier Liu He of the State Council as its guest of honour at the ceremony, during which he presented the awards and delivered an important speech. Although the Foundation's Hong Kong representatives were unable to participate in the Selection meeting and the Award Presentation Ceremony in person due to the pandemic, the successful conclusion of these events highlights the commendable adaptability, resilience and capabilities of the members of the Board of Trustees and the Selection Board. The donors are delighted that the Foundation's activities are in such safe and competent hands.

Through the diligent efforts of the members of the Investment Committee, the financial position of the Foundation remains solid despite the tumultuous international financial markets in 2020. The donors sincerely thank the committee for ensuring that the Foundation continues to enjoy a level of financial good health that will support its long-term goals and operation. Although the worldwide situation with COVID-19 is still evolving, the donors are hopeful that, through large-scale vaccination programmes and the concerted efforts of all countries, the pandemic will soon be brought under effective control and economic activity and growth around the globe will get back on track.

At the Fifth Plenary Session of the 19th Central Committee of the Communist Party of China held in October 2020, it was stressed that "we should adhere to the core position of innovation in the overall situation of China's modernization drive, take self–reliance and self–improvement in science and technology as the strategic support for national development, face the forefront of world science and technology, the main economic battlefield, the major needs of the country, and the people's life and health, and thoroughly implement the strategy of rejuvenating the country through science and education, the strategy of strengthening the country through talents, the strategy of driving development with innovation, to improve the national system of innovation and speed up the establishment of a science and technology power".

China ranks 14th in the 'Global Innovation Index 2020', published by the World Intellectual Property Organization, and is also ranked as one of the world's most–innovative economy.

A founding principle of the Ho Leung Ho Lee Foundation is to encourage Chinese scientific and technological professionals to engage in independent and innovative research and development (R&D). As the international economic environment becomes more competitive and geo–political considerations become more complex, it is crucial that China continues to forge ahead with innovative R&D in all areas of science and technology. This will support robust long–term economic development and further reinforce the nation's standing as a major global player in driving innovation and advancing scientific and technological knowledge.

The Foundation will continue to strongly support national policy objectives and priority research by rewarding outstanding scientists and promoting the development of science and technology in China.

Donors of Ho Leung Ho Lee Foundation

S. H. Ho Foundation Limited   Leung Kau Kui Foundation Limited

Ho Tim Foundation Limited   Wei Lun Foundation Limited

June 2021, Hong Kong

何梁何利基金评选委员会 2020 年度工作报告

信托委员会主席、评选委员会主任　朱丽兰

（2020 年 11 月 3 日）

尊敬的刘鹤副总理，

尊敬的沈跃跃副委员长，

尊敬的万钢副主席，

各位领导，各位嘉宾，同志们，朋友们：

　　金秋时节，天高云淡。党的十九届五中全会胜利召开，我国"十三五"规划即将圆满收官，"十四五"规划将开启我国全面建设社会主义现代化强国的新征程。在两个百年目标的历史交会点上，在举国上下学习贯彻五中全会精神的热潮中，我们相聚北京钓鱼台国宾馆，隆重举行何梁何利基金 2020 年度颁奖大会，向 52 位杰出科技工作者授予何梁何利科学与技术奖励的崇高荣誉。这是我国科技界、教育界和社会各界的一大盛事。

　　中共中央政治局委员、国务院副总理刘鹤，全国人大常委会副委员长沈跃跃同志，全国政协副主席万钢同志，科技部党组书记、部长王志刚同志以及各部门领导亲临大会指导，给予我们莫大鼓舞。在此，我谨代表何梁何利基金，对党和国家领导同志的亲切关怀和悉心指导表示衷心感谢，对科技界、教育界和社会各界嘉宾和代表光临本次盛典表示热烈欢迎，对在香港通过线上视频参会的捐款人代表、信托委员和香港嘉宾表示热烈欢迎和衷心感谢！

　　下面，我代表基金评选委员会做工作报告。

一、关于 2019 年度基金信托委员会的有关决定

今年 5 月 27 日，受疫情影响，何梁何利基金在香港恒生银行

和恒生银行北京分行通过在线视频召开信托委员会全体会议，圆满完成了各项预定的议程。

会上，基金捐款人代表梁祥彪先生致辞，热情赞扬在信托委员会、评选委员会、投资委员会和全体工作人员的努力下，基金稳步发展，评选工作卓有成效，基金三大科技奖项权威性与公信力与日俱增。基金捐款人代表向各位评委、各位志愿者表示衷心感谢。

信托委员会会议在和谐、务实的氛围中审议并接受了基金投资委员会截至 2019 年 12 月 31 日和 2020 年 3 月 31 日的投资情况报告；审议并通过了基金评选委员会 2019 年度工作总结和 2020 年工作设想；审议评选委员会关于《何梁何利基金评选章程》的修订草案；决定继续聘请毕马威会计师事务所为基金稽核师，负责基金审计工作，并对毕马威事务所多年来义务承担基金财务审计工作致以诚挚谢意。

这里，我想做两点说明。

一是 2019 年面对全球金融市场复杂激烈动荡，基金投资委员会积极应对，年内投资回报 7.9%，基金市值取得 7.42 亿港元的较好成绩。进入 2020 年，随着新冠疫情在全球蔓延，世界经济严重受挫。受此影响，今年一季度基金回报下跌 7.02%，基金市值维持在 6.86 亿港元。但基金有足够底气和韧性争取回升空间。为此，信托委员会决定在贯彻自身过紧日子的前提下，今年仍然拨付奖金总额 1200 万港元，与去年持平。这笔资金来之不易，我们要感谢投资委员会面对复杂环境所做出的艰苦努力和出色贡献。

二是根据《中华人民共和国境外非政府组织管理法》的要求，何梁何利基金（香港）北京代表处已于 2019 年 11 月 20 日经北京市公安局批准，在京注册登记成立。代表处的业务主管单位为中华人民共和国科学技术部。为此，信托委员会通过决议，对《何梁何利基金评选章程》做适当修订，明确基金的法律地位，并对个别条款适当修正。我们深信，何梁何利基金将伴随全面依法治国的主旋律，沿着法制轨道为推进科学技术奖励事业迈出坚实步伐！

二、关于今年基金评选委员会评选工作

今年年初，评选委员会办公室向境内外提名人共发出提名推荐书 2300 多份。受疫情影响，截至 4 月 20 日，共收到提名推荐书 865 份，有效被提名人 826 人，其中"科学与技术成就奖"3 人、"科学与技术进步奖"474 人、"科学与技术创新奖"349 人，总数与去年大体持平。

今年 8 月 3 日至 5 日，何梁何利基金 2020 年度专业评审会在北京铁道大厦举行。来自全国的 120 多位高端专家应聘担任专业评委。经过初评产生何梁何利基金"科学与技术成就奖"候选人 3 名、"科学与技术进步奖"候选人 72 名、"科学与技术创新奖"候选人 34 名，一并提交本次何梁何利基金评选委员会全体会议终评。

今年 8 月 27 日至 28 日，评选委员会全体会议在北京友谊宾馆举行；应到委员 20 位，实到 19 位，其中 3 位海外评委受境外疫情影响，分别在香港和美国通过线上视频出席部分会议。会议经过两天紧张工作，本着公平、公正、公开的评选方针，坚持评选过程不受任何部门和个人干预、不为个别权威人士左右的原则，经过科学评议、优中选优，评选产生"科学与技术成就奖"2 名、"科学与技术进步奖"30 名、"科学与技术创新奖"20 名，2020 年度何梁何利基金评选工作画上圆满句号。

今年何梁何利基金最高奖项的得主是两位在不同领域毕生耕耘、贡献卓著，以其杰出科学技术成就和卓越科学家精神赢得评选委员会高度赞扬的中华民族的优秀儿女。

一位是共和国勋章获得者、我国呼吸疾病领域的领军科学家。他毕生致力于重大呼吸道传染病等防治研究，取得丰硕成果；他牵头建立的新发特发呼吸道传染病的"预防 – 监测 – 治疗 – 控制"链式周期管理体系居于国际领先水平；他率领团队进行长达 9 年的研究，在世界上率先提出慢阻肺早防早诊早治新策略这一具有里程碑意义的进展。在 2003 年抗击非典和 2020 年抗击新冠病毒两场战役中，他临危受命、奔赴一线，在疫情研判、科学决策、临床救治、

重症抢救等多个方面发挥重要作用，为祖国和人民立下了赫赫战功。

一位是国家荣誉称号获得者、敦煌研究院名誉院长。她扎根敦煌五十七载，潜心从事石窟考古研究，是我国文物保护、研究、弘扬、管理的科学探索者和实践者；她主编敦煌考古史上首部巨著——《莫高窟第266~275窟考古报告》，内容翔实，准确全面，堪称世界之最；她突破传统石窟考古方法，构建了多学科深度交叉融合的考古新模式；她启动数字敦煌工程，志在实现敦煌石窟文物数字化永久保存和永续利用，为保护和弘扬祖国文化遗产做出彪炳史册的贡献。

在习近平新时代中国特色社会主义思想指引下，我国科学技术事业步入历史跃升期。从823位被提名人中优中选优、脱颖而出的50位"科学与技术进步奖"和"科学与技术创新奖"的获奖人，科技成果丰硕、创新业绩喜人，人人都有一张十分靓丽的成绩单。他们是我国优秀科技人才、战略科技人才、领军科技人才、青年科技人才的杰出代表。总的来说，今年获奖科学家成果有以下几个特点。一是基础研究、应用基础研究原创性突出，从"0到1"的科学成就不断涌现。二是关键技术创新不断突破瓶颈约束、打破封锁，畅通全程产业链，为保障经济发展提供有力支撑。三是产业创新在产学研深度融合基础上提质提速，为新兴产业发展和传统产业改造升级赋能。四是区域创新催生边远、贫困和少数民族地区特色科技发展，加快区域经济转型升级和乡村振兴战略发展。五是医学药学、生命科学领域科技创新硕果累累，人民至上、生命至上，为人民生命安全不断带来福音。六是面向国家战略需求、抢占科技制高点成为创新驱动发展的重中之重，多项关键核心技术已经实现自主自控。七是获奖人结构合理，最大84岁，最小37岁，科学与技术进步奖获奖人平均58.7岁，科学与技术创新奖获奖人平均52岁。青年优秀人才脱颖而出，中青年成为获奖科学家主体。八是自主知识产权和总体创新能力出现质的跃升。今年获奖人在国际期刊发表论文10853篇，人均208.7篇；拥有发明专利1821项，人均35项，较2019年有大幅提高。不少获奖科学家整合知识产权、实施品牌战略、抢占国家标准或行业标准的高地。经过初步评估，今年获奖人的主要科技成果全部达到国际先进水平。其中，85.6%的成果已经在国际竞争中从"并跑"进入"领跑"方阵。

各位嘉宾，同志们，朋友们，奖励杰出科技人才是国家和全社会的神圣使命，是一项功在当代、泽被永远的崇高事业。1994年3月，香港爱国金融实业家何善衡、梁銶琚、何添、利国伟先生共同捐资创立了何梁何利基金。当时，香港还属于港英政府管辖，四位捐款人宣布：这个基金只用于奖励为祖国科技事业做出杰出贡献的中华人民共和国公民。他们的这段宣言，表达了香港有识之士爱国爱港、爱科学爱人才的拳拳之心。26年过去，四位基金创立者都已在九旬高龄离开了我们，我们深深地怀念他们。今天，四位捐款人的家属、子女、孙子女秉承爱国先驱的志向，一如既往地推进这项崇高的奖励事业，薪火传承、生生不息，续写老一辈的创举、善举和义举。在此，我谨向年轻一代捐款人代表表达由衷的敬意，致以亲切的问候。

同志们、朋友们，党的十九届五中全会提出坚持创新在我国现代化建设全局中的核心地位，把科技自立自强作为国家发展的战略支撑。获奖科学家和广大科技人员要遵循习近平总书记在科学家座谈会上的殷切期望，面向世界科技前沿、面向经济主战场、面向国家重大需求、面向人民生命健康，向科学技术的深度和广度进军。何梁何利基金作为国家科技奖励的一部分，也将以新的政治站位不忘初心、牢记使命，在总结经验基础上，进一步健全评审机制、提高评选质量，把何梁何利奖办得更具特色、更有影响，为建设社会主义现代化强国再立新功。

让我们站在新的历史起点上，以习近平新时代中国特色社会主义思想为指导，深入实施科教兴国战略、人才强国战略、创新驱动发展战略，加快我国从科技大国走向科技强国的历史性跨越，为实现"两个一百年"奋斗目标、实现中华民族伟大复兴的中国梦而努力奋斗！

谢谢大家！

2020 Work Report of the Selection Board of Ho Leung Ho Lee Foundation

Zhu Lilan, Chairperson of the Trust Board and Director of the Selection Board

(November 3, 2020)

Dear Vice Premier Liu He,

Dear Ms. Shen Yueyue, Vice Chairperson of the Standing Committee of the National People's Congress,

Dear Mr. Wan Gang, Vice Chairman of the Chinese People's Political Consultative Conference,

Dear leaders, guests, comrades and friends:

On this golden autumn day, the sky is high, and the clouds are light. The Fifth Plenary Session of the 19th CPC Central Committee was victoriously convened, the implementation of the 13th Five-year Plan draws to an end, and the formulation of the 14th Five-year Plan marks the start of a new journey of building China into a great socialist modern country in an all respects.

At this moment of historical convergence between the fulfillment of one centenary goal and the pursuit of another centenary goal, when people all over the country enthusiastically learn and implement the guiding principles of the Fifth Plenary Session of the 19th CPC Central Committee, we gather at Diaoyutai State Guesthouse in Beijing to hold the 2020 Awarding Ceremony of the Ho Leung Ho Lee (HLHL) Foundation. At this ceremony, the science and technology prizes of the HLHL Foundation, which represent a great honor, will be granted to 52 outstanding science and technology workers. The granting of these prizes is a grand event for the education circle, science and technology circle and all other walks of life.

Comrade Liu He, member of the Political Bureau of the CPC Central Committee and vice premier of the State Council, Comrade Shen Yueyue, vice chairperson of the Standing Committee of the National People's Congress, Comrade Wan Gang, vice chairman of the Chinese People's Political Consultative Conference, Comrade Wang

Zhigang, secretary of the Leading Party Members' Group of the Ministry of Science and Technology and minister of Science and Technology, and leaders of many other departments attend the meeting to give their guidance. Their arrival brings great joy and encouragement to us.

On behalf of all my colleagues at the HLHL Foundation, I would express my heartfelt thanks to the leaders of the CPC and the State for their care and guidance, and extend my warmest welcome to the distinguished guests from the education circle, science and technology circle and all other walks of life for their presence at this ceremony. I will also give my warmest welcome and sincere thanks to representatives of donors, members of the Trust Board and other distinguished guests from Hong Kong who are participating in this ceremony through online video!

Next, I will deliver the report on the work on behalf of the Selection Board of the HLHL Foundation.

I. About the Decisions of the Trust Board of the HLHL Foundation in 2019

On May 27, 2019, the Trust Board of the HLHL Foundation held the plenary meeting. Affected by the COVID-19 epidemic, the plenary meeting was held between Hang Seng Bank in Hong Kong and Beijing Branch of Hang Seng Bank through online video. All the scheduled agendas were smoothly completed.

At the meeting, Mr. Leung Cheung Biu, representative of donors, delivered a speech, in which he warmly praised the HLHL Foundation for its steady development under the concerted efforts of the Trust Board, the Selection Board and the Investment Board as well as all the working personnel, the effective work of selecting prize winners and the steadily increased authority and public credibility of the three major HLHL prizes. The representatives of donors expressed their heartfelt thanks to all judges and all volunteers.

In a harmonious and pragmatic atmosphere, the meeting of the Trust Board deliberated and approved the investment reports made by the Investment Board up to the following two dates: December 31, 2019 and March 31, 2020. It deliberated and approved the report on the work of the Selection Board for 2019 and the work plan of the Selection Board for 2020. It deliberated the draft revisions to the *Selection*

Regulation made by the Selection Board. It also decided to continue to engage KPMG LLP as the Fund Auditor to take charge of the auditing of the HLHL Foundation, and expressed sincere thanks to KPMG LLP for its free-of-charge auditing of the financial affairs of the HLHL Foundation over the years.

Here, I would like to give the following two explanations.

First, in 2019, by actively responding to a complex and volatile global financial market, the Investment Board delivered a satisfactory performance, with the rate of return reaching 7.9 percent, and the market value of the Foundation standing at 742 million HK dollars. Since the beginning of 2020, the world economy has suffered a severe setback with the global spread of COVID-19 epidemic. Affected by the economic downturn, the Foundation saw a drop of 7.02 percentage points in its rate of return, with its market value maintained at 686 million HK dollars in the first quarter of 2020. However, the HLHL Foundation has sufficient confidence and resilience in striving for a rebound.

Given such a situation, the Trust Board decided that, under the precondition of "living on a tight budget", it would still allocate a total sum of 12 million HK dollars as the prize money this year, which is equivalent to that of last year. It is hard to obtain this sum of money. We express our thanks to the Investment Board for its considerable efforts to deal with the complicated situation as well as its extraordinary contributions.

Second, in accordance with the *Law of the People's Republic of China on the Administration of Activities of Overseas Non-Governmental Organizations within the Territory of China*, the Beijing Office of the HLHL Foundation (Hong Kong) was established and registered in Beijing on November 20, 2019 with the approval of Beijing Municipal Public Security Bureau. The competent authority of the business of Beijing Office is the Ministry of Science and Technology of the People's Republic of China.

To adapt to this change, the Trust Board adopts a resolution of making appropriate amendment to the *Selection Regulation* to clearly define the legal position of the HLHL Foundation, and making appropriate amendments to individual clauses of the *Selection Regulation*. We are convinced that the HLHL Foundation will make solid steps in promoting the undertaking of scientific and technological rewarding under the background of comprehensively promoting law-based governance and in accordance with law.

II. The Work of Selecting the Winners of the Prizes of the HLHL Foundation in 2020

Early this year, the office of the Selection Board sent more than 2300 nomination forms to proposers at both home and abroad. Affected by the epidemic, the Board received 865 letters of recommendation by April 20, 2020. There were a total of 826 effective nominees, a number almost equivalent to that of last year, including 474 nominees for the "Prize for Scientific and Technological Progress", 349 nominees for the "Prize for Scientific and Technological Innovation", and three nominees for the "Prize for Scientific and Technological Achievements".

On August 3-5 this year, the special review meeting of the HLHL Foundation in 2020 was held at Beijing Railway Hotel. More than 120 high-end experts were engaged to serve as judges in different specialties. In the preliminary evaluation, the meeting selected three candidates for the "Prize for Scientific and Technological Achievements", 72 candidates for the "Prize for Scientific and Technological Progress" and 34 candidates for the "Prize for Scientific and Technological Innovation." The meeting submitted the list of all the above-mentioned candidates to the plenary meeting of the Selection Board of the HLHL Foundation for final evaluation.

On August 27-28 this year, the Selection Board of the HLHL Foundation held a plenary meeting at Beijing Friendship Hotel. Of the 20 members of the Selection Board who should have arrived at the meeting, 19 members turned up. Affected by the epidemic in the overseas regions, three overseas judges partially participated in the meeting through online video in Hong Kong and the U.S. respectively.

The meeting lasted for two days, with all members working on a tight schedule. The selection work pursued the policy of impartiality, fairness and openness, and adhered to the principles that it should be free from interference from any department or individual and should not fall under the control of any authoritative person. Based on scientific evaluation and the practice of selecting the best ones from among the excellent candidates, the Selection Board selected two winners of the "Prize for

Scientific and Technological Achievements", 30 winners of the "Prize for Scientific and Technological Progress", and 20 winners of the "Prize for Scientific and Technological Innovation", satisfactorily completing the work of selecting the prize winners in 2020.

The winners of the highest HLHL prize in 2020 are two eminent scientists who have devoted their entire life in different fields, and won high acclaims by the Selection Board with their outstanding achievements in science and technology as well as their lofty scientific spirit.

One winner is a leading respiratory disease expert in China and recipient of the Medal of the Republic. He devotes his whole life to the prevention and control of major respiratory diseases, and has achieved fruitful results in this regard. The chain cycle management system featuring "prevention–monitoring–treatment–control" for preventing and controlling new and idiopathic respiratory diseases, which is established under his leadership, holds a leading position in the world. Having studied chronic obstructive pulmonary disease (COPD) for nine years with a team under his leadership, he put forward the new strategy of treating the disease ahead of others in the world. Featuring early–prevention, early–diagnosis and early–treatment, the strategy marks a progress of milestone significance.

In the battle against SARS in 2003 and the battle against COVID–19 epidemic in 2020, he was respectively entrusted with formidable tasks at critical moments, and played an important role in many respects, such as studying and judging the epidemic situation, making scientific decisions, giving clinical treatment to patients, and rescuing severe patients. He has accomplished brilliant exploits for China and the Chinese people.

The other winner is the director of Dunhuang Research Academy and winner of a national honorary title. Having dedicated herself to the archaeological study on Dunhuang Grottoes for 57 years, she has explored and put into practice the scientific ways in protection, research, publicity and management of cultural relics in China. She was the chief compiler of *The Archaeological Report on Mogao Grottoes No.266–275*, which is the first monumental work of its kind in the archaeological history of Dunhuang. Boasting rich content and accurate and comprehensive account, the book is arguably a unique masterpiece in the world. She has made breakthroughs in the methodologies of conducting archaeological surveys by establishing a new archaeological model whereby various branches of learning are integrated across boundaries and at a deep level. She has pioneered the project of "Digital Dunhuang" by digitalizing cultural relics with the intention of permanent preservation and sustainable use of them. She has made historical contributions to preserving and publicizing the cultural heritages of China.

Under the guidance of Xi Jinping Thought on Socialism with Chinese Characteristics for a New Era, China's science and technology undertaking has entered a period of historical leap. A total of 50 winners of "Prize for Scientific and Technological Progress" and "Prize for Scientific and Technological Innovation" are selected from among 823 candidates. Having a series of noticeable accomplishments to his or her credit, each of these prize winners has scored fruitful scientific achievements and delivered gratifying performances in making innovations. They are the epitome of excellent scientific talents, strategic scientific talents, leading scientific talents and young scientific talents in China. To sum up, the achievements of the prize-winning scientists this year have the following characteristics.

First, outstanding original achievements have been scored in the fields of basic research and applied basic research, with scientific achievements "from zero to one" appearing one after another. Second, efforts have been made to constantly eliminate bottlenecks and constraints in the innovation of critical technologies, with the aim to lift blockades, to facilitate the formation of entire-process industrial chain, and to supply vigorous support for guaranteeing the economic development. Third, efforts have been made to improve the quality and increase the speed of industrial innovation based on deep integration of industry, university and research, thus empowering the development of emerging industries and transformation and upgrading of traditional industries. Fourth, regional innovations trigger the development of technologies with distinctive characteristics in border regions, poverty-stricken regions and the regions inhabited by ethnic minorities, and accelerate the transformation and upgrading of regional economy and the development of the strategy of rural vitalization. Fifth, impressive accomplishments have been acquired in the fields of medicine, pharmacology, and life science. Developed following the principles of "putting people in the first place" and "putting people's lives first", these achievements constantly bring benefits to protect people's lives and security. Sixth, the achievements meet national strategic needs and race to control commanding points in science and technology, becoming the top priorities in promoting the innovation-driven development. Several critical core technologies are already in the possession of and/or under the control of China. Seventh, the prize winners are characterized by a reasonable distribution of age. The oldest prize winner is 84 years old, and the youngest one is 37 years old. The average age of the winners of the "Prize for Scientific and Technological Progress" is 58.7 years, and the average age of the winners of the "Prize for Scientific and Technological Innovation" is 52 years. The young excellent talents have come to the fore. The prize winners are mainly composed of middle-aged and young scientists. Eighth, the prize winners have demonstrated qualitative improvement in terms of proprietary intellectual property rights and the overall capacity of making innovation. This year, the prize winners have published 10853 academic papers in international periodicals, or 208.7 papers for each person. They possess 1821 invention patents, or 35 invention patents for each person. Such numbers are markedly increased when compared with those of 2019.

Many prize-winning scientists attach importance to integrating intellectual property rights with their research results by implementing brand strategy and racing to control commanding points in formulating national standards or industrial standards.

According to preliminary evaluation, the major scientific achievements obtained by prize winners this year have all reached the world advanced level. A total of 85.6 percent of these achievements reflect the fact that the prize winners who used to "run along with" their international competitors gradually "run ahead of" their international competitors.

Guests, comrades and friends, rewarding excellent scientific talents represents both a sacred mission for the State and the society at large and a glorious undertaking that contributes to the present age and benefits the people of future generations.

In March 1994, four patriotic financial industrialists in Hong Kong, Mr. Ho Sin-Hang, Mr. Leung Kau-kui, Mr. Ho Tim and Mr. Lee Quo-Wei jointly donated money to establish the Ho Leung Ho Lee Foundation. Although Hong Kong was still under the jurisdiction of British Hong Kong government at that time, four donors announced that the HLHL Foundation would reward only the citizens of the People's Republic of China who make outstanding contributions to the scientific and technological development of the motherland. These words reveal true sentiments and sincerity of the men of insight in Hong Kong, and express their love for motherland, Hong Kong, science and talents.

We still cherish the memory of these four founders of the HLHL Foundation who all passed away at the age of over 90 during the past 26 years. Upholding the ideal of their patriotic fathers and grandfathers, the relatives, children and grand-children of these four donors promote this pioneering, benevolent and virtuous act as always by continuing the glorious undertaking. Here I would express my heartfelt thanks and give my kind regards to all the representatives of the donors of a younger generation.

Comrades and friends:

It was proposed at the Fifth Plenary Session of the 19th CPC Central Committee that innovation is put at the heart of China's modernization drive, and that self-reliance and self-improvement in science and technology are regarded as the strategic support for China's development. The prize-winning scientists and all other science and technology workers should follow the ardent expectations expressed by General Secretary Xi Jinping at the seminar with scientists by orienting their tasks to the following four aspects: targeting the global science frontiers, increasing scientific and technological support to serve economic development, striving to fulfill the significant needs of the country and benefit people's lives and health, and striving for achievements in science and technology at a still higher level and in still wider scope.

As part of China's scientific and technological rewarding system, the HLHL Foundation will adopt new political stance, and stay true to its original aspiration and founding mission. Based on summarizing its past experience, it will further improve the evaluation mechanism and the evaluation quality, so as to highlight the characteristics of and enhance the influences of its prizes, and make new contributions to building a great modern socialist country.

Standing at the new historical starting point, let's continue to implement the strategy of rejuvenating the country by relying on science and technology, the strategy to make China a talent-strong country, and the innovation-driven development strategy under the guidance of Xi Jinping Thought on Socialism with Chinese Characteristics for a New Era, accelerate the pace of turning China from a large country in science and technology into a science and technology power, and work still harder towards the Two Centenary Goals and fulfill the Chinese Dream of rejuvenating the Chinese nation!

Thank you!

目　录

刘鹤出席何梁何利基金 2020 年度颁奖大会

序………………………………………………… 何梁何利基金捐款人

何梁何利基金评选委员会 2020 年度工作报告 …………… 朱丽兰

何梁何利基金科学与技术成就奖获得者传略
　　钟南山 ……………………………………………………（ 3 ）
　　樊锦诗 ……………………………………………………（ 7 ）

何梁何利基金科学与技术进步奖获得者传略
　　数 学 力 学 奖 获 得 者　叶向东 ……………………（ 13 ）
　　物 理 学 奖 获 得 者　汪卫华 ……………………（ 17 ）
　　物 理 学 奖 获 得 者　颜学庆 ……………………（ 21 ）
　　化 学 奖 获 得 者　张锁江 ……………………（ 24 ）
　　化 学 奖 获 得 者　赵宇亮 ……………………（ 28 ）
　　气 象 学 奖 获 得 者　胡　非 ……………………（ 32 ）
　　地 球 科 学 奖 获 得 者　郭华东 ……………………（ 35 ）
　　生 命 科 学 奖 获 得 者　程和平 ……………………（ 39 ）
　　农 学 奖 获 得 者　陈　志 ……………………（ 42 ）
　　农 学 奖 获 得 者　范国强 ……………………（ 46 ）
　　农 学 奖 获 得 者　沈建忠 ……………………（ 50 ）
　　医 学 药 学 奖 获 得 者　季加孚 ……………………（ 54 ）
　　医 学 药 学 奖 获 得 者　卢光明 ……………………（ 58 ）
　　医 学 药 学 奖 获 得 者　沈　锋 ……………………（ 62 ）
　　医 学 药 学 奖 获 得 者　吴德沛 ……………………（ 66 ）

医学药学奖获得者　徐兵河 …………………………（69）

医学药学奖获得者　朱　兰 …………………………（73）

机械电力技术奖获得者　何湘宁 ……………………（76）

机械电力技术奖获得者　宋永华 ……………………（80）

机械电力技术奖获得者　王国庆 ……………………（84）

电子信息技术奖获得者　樊邦奎 ……………………（88）

电子信息技术奖获得者　刘泽金 ……………………（91）

电子信息技术奖获得者　吴　枫 ……………………（94）

电子信息技术奖获得者　杨德仁 ……………………（98）

冶金材料技术奖获得者　冯吉才 ……………………（101）

冶金材料技术奖获得者　朱　荣 ……………………（105）

资源能源技术奖获得者　刘清友 ……………………（109）

工程建设技术奖获得者　罗　琦 ……………………（113）

工程建设技术奖获得者　谭家华 ……………………（116）

工程建设技术奖获得者　周绪红 ……………………（119）

何梁何利基金科学与技术创新奖获得者传略

青年创新奖获得者　陈小前 …………………………（125）

青年创新奖获得者　常　超 …………………………（129）

青年创新奖获得者　鲁军勇 …………………………（132）

青年创新奖获得者　麦立强 …………………………（136）

青年创新奖获得者　张　澄 …………………………（140）

青年创新奖获得者　赵永生 …………………………（144）

区域创新奖获得者　何　黎 …………………………（147）

区域创新奖获得者　刘国道 …………………………（151）

区域创新奖获得者　王爱勤 …………………………（155）

区域创新奖获得者　张宗亮 …………………………（159）

产业创新奖获得者　程博闻 …………………………（163）

产业创新奖获得者　贾振华 …………………………（167）

产业创新奖获得者　李晋闽 …………………………（171）

产业创新奖获得者　凌　祥 ……………………………（175）

产业创新奖获得者　路建美 ……………………………（178）

产业创新奖获得者　王　琪 ……………………………（182）

产业创新奖获得者　魏世忠 ……………………………（186）

产业创新奖获得者　曾　毅 ……………………………（190）

产业创新奖获得者　赵元富 ……………………………（194）

产业创新奖获得者　朱衍波 ……………………………（197）

附　录

何梁何利基金评选章程 …………………………………（203）

关于何梁何利基金获奖科学家异议处理若干规定 ……（213）

关于何梁何利基金评选工作若干问题的说明 …………（218）

关于何梁何利基金（香港）北京代表处公告 …………（237）

何梁何利基金捐款人简历 ………………………………（239）

何善衡 …………………………………………………（239）

梁铢琚 …………………………………………………（239）

何　添 …………………………………………………（241）

利国伟 …………………………………………………（241）

何梁何利基金信托人简历 ………………………………（248）

朱丽兰 …………………………………………………（248）

孙　煜 …………………………………………………（249）

钟登华 …………………………………………………（249）

郑慧敏 …………………………………………………（250）

沈祖尧 …………………………………………………（251）

何梁何利基金评选委员会成员简历 ……………………（257）

CONTENTS

Liu He Attended the 2020 Award Ceremony of Ho Leung Ho Lee Foundation

Preface ·· Donors of Ho Leung Ho Lee Foundation

2020 Work Report of the Selection Board of Ho Leung Ho Lee Foundation
·· Zhu Lilan

PROFILES OF THE AWARDEES OF PRIZE FOR SCIENTIFIC AND
　TECHNOLOGICAL ACHIEVEMENTS OF HO LEUNG HO LEE FOUNDATION
　　Profile of Zhong Nanshan ··· （5）
　　Profile of Fan Jinshi ·· （10）

PROFILES OF THE AWARDEES OF PRIZE FOR SCIENTIFIC AND
　TECHNOLOGICAL PROGRESS OF HO LEUNG HO LEE FOUNDATION
　　Awardee of Mathematics and Mechanics Prize, Ye Xiangdong ············· （15）
　　Awardee of Physics Prize, Wang Weihua ························· （19）
　　Awardee of Physics Prize, Yan Xueqing ························· （22）
　　Awardee of Chemistry Prize, Zhang Suojiang ···················· （26）
　　Awardee of Chemistry Prize, Zhao Yuliang ······················ （30）
　　Awardee of Meteorology Prize, Hu Fei ························· （33）
　　Awardee of Earth Sciences Prize, Guo Huadong ·················· （37）
　　Awardee of Life Sciences Prize, Cheng Heping ·················· （40）
　　Awardee of Agronomy Prize, Chen Zhi ························· （44）
　　Awardee of Agronomy Prize, Fan Guoqiang ···················· （48）
　　Awardee of Agronomy Prize, Shen Jianzhong ···················· （52）
　　Awardee of Medical Sciences and Materia Medica Prize, Ji Jiafu ·········· （56）
　　Awardee of Medical Sciences and Materia Medica Prize, Lu Guangming ··· （60）

Awardee of Medical Sciences and Materia Medica Prize, Shen Feng ········ (64)

Awardee of Medical Sciences and Materia Medica Prize, Wu Depei ········· (67)

Awardee of Medical Sciences and Materia Medica Prize, Xu Binghe········· (70)

Awardee of Medical Sciences and Materia Medica Prize, Zhu Lan ············ (75)

Awardee of Machinery and Electric Technology Prize, He Xiangning········ (78)

Awardee of Machinery and Electric Technology Prize, Song Yonghua ······· (82)

Awardee of Machinery and Electric Technology Prize, Wang Guoqing······· (86)

Awardee of Electronics and Information Technology Prize, Fan Bangkui ···· (89)

Awardee of Electronics and Information Technology Prize, Liu Zejin ········ (93)

Awardee of Electronics and Information Technology Prize, Wu Feng ········ (96)

Awardee of Electronics and Information Technology Prize, Yang Deren ····· (99)

Awardee of Metallurgy and Materials Technology Prize, Feng Jicai ········· (103)

Awardee of Metallurgy and Materials Technology Prize, Zhu Rong··········· (107)

Awardee of Resources and Energies Technology Prize, Liu Qingyou ········ (111)

Awardee of Engineering and Construction Technology Prize, Luo Qi········ (114)

Awardee of Engineering and Construction Technology Prize, Tan Jiahua ··· (117)

Awardee of Engineering and Construction Technology Prize, Zhou Xuhong ···· (120)

PROFILES OF THE AWARDEES OF PRIZE FOR SCIENTIFIC AND
TECHNOLOGICAL INNOVATION OF HO LEUNG HO LEE FOUNDATION

Awardee of Youth Innovation Prize, Chen Xiaoqian ··························· (127)

Awardee of Youth Innovation Prize, Chang Chao ····························· (130)

Awardee of Youth Innovation Prize, Lu Junyong ····························· (134)

Awardee of Youth Innovation Prize, Mai Liqiang ····························· (138)

Awardee of Youth Innovation Prize, Zhang Cheng ···························· (142)

Awardee of Youth Innovation Prize, Zhao Yongsheng ························· (145)

Awardee of Region Innovation Prize, He Li································· (149)

Awardee of Region Innovation Prize, Liu Guodao···························· (153)

Awardee of Region Innovation Prize, Wang Aiqin ··························· (157)

Awardee of Region Innovation Prize, Zhang Zongliang····················· (161)

Awardee of Industrial Innovation Prize, Cheng Bowen ····················· (165)

Awardee of Industrial Innovation Prize, Jia Zhenhua ·················· (169)

Awardee of Industrial Innovation Prize, Li Jinmin ························ (173)

Awardee of Industrial Innovation Prize, Ling Xiang ····················· (176)

Awardee of Industrial Innovation Prize, Lu Jianmei ·················· (180)

Awardee of Industrial Innovation Prize, Wang Qi ······················· (184)

Awardee of Industrial Innovation Prize, Wei Shizhong ················ (188)

Awardee of Industrial Innovation Prize, Zeng Yi ······················· (191)

Awardee of Industrial Innovation Prize, Zhao Yuanfu ·················· (196)

Awardee of Industrial Innovation Prize, Zhu Yanbo ····················· (199)

APPENDICES
REGULATIONS OF HO LEUNG HO LEE FOUNDATION ON THE EVALUATION
AND EXAMINATION OF ITS PRIZES AND AWARDS ················ (207)

REGULATIONS ON HANDLING THE COMPLAINT LODGED AGAINST
THE PRIZE-WINNER WITH HO LEUNG HO LEE FOUNDATION ···· (215)

EXPLANATIONS ON SEVERAL ISSUES ON THE SELECTION WORK OF
HO LEUNG HO LEE FOUNDATION ································ (225)

PUBLIC ANNOUNCEMENT OF THE BEIJING REPRESENTATIVE
OFFICE OF THE HO LEUNG HO LEE FOUNDATION (HONG KONG)
·· (238)

BRIEF INTRODUCTION TO THE DONORS TO HO LEUNG HO LEE
FOUNDATION ·· (243)

Brief Biography of Dr. S. H. Ho ································ (243)

Brief Biography of Dr. Leung Kau-Kui ······················ (243)

Brief Biography of Dr. Ho Tim ································ (245)

Brief Biography of Dr. Lee Quo-Wei ························· (246)

BRIEF INTRODUCTION TO THE TRUSTEES OF HO LEUNG HO LEE
FOUNDATION ·· (252)

Brief Biography of Professor Zhu Lilan ······················ (252)

Brief Biography of Mr. Sun Yu ······························· (253)

Brief Biography of Mr. Zhong Denghua ······················ (254)

Brief Biography of Ms Louisa Cheang ·································· （254）

Brief Biography of Joseph Jao-Yiu Sung ····························· （255）

BRIEF INTRODUCTION TO THE MEMBERS OF THE SELECTION BOARD OF

HO LEUNG HO LEE FOUNDATION ·························· （270）

何梁何利基金科学与技术成就奖获得者传略

PROFILES OF THE AWARDEES OF PRIZE FOR
SCIENTIFIC AND TECHNOLOGICAL ACHIEVEMENTS OF
HO LEUNG HO LEE FOUNDATION

钟 南 山

钟南山，1936 年 10 月出生，福建厦门人。胸肺科医生，呼吸系统疾病防治领军人物。1960 年毕业于北京医学院（现北京大学医学部），1979—1981 年作为访问学者在英国爱丁堡大学及英国伦敦圣巴弗勒医学院学习，1971 年返回广州后就职于广州医学院（现广州医科大学）至今。1979—2012 年任广州呼吸疾病研究所（现广州呼吸健康研究院）所长，1987—1992 年任广州医学院第一附属医院院长，1992—1994 年任广州医学院党委书记，1992—2002 年任广州医学院院长，2005—2010 年任中华医学会会长，2007—2017 年任呼吸疾病国家重点实验室主任，现任广州国家实验室主任、国家呼吸系统疾病临床医学研究中心主任、国家呼吸医学中心荣誉主任。于 1996 年当选中国工程院院士。2020 年新冠肺炎疫情期间，钟南山担任国家卫健委高级别专家组组长、新冠疫情联防联控工作机制科研攻关专家组组长。"共和国勋章"获得者。

钟南山是我国新发突发重大呼吸道传染性疾病（如 SARS、H1N1、H5N6、H7N9、MERS、COVID-19）、慢性阻塞性肺疾病、支气管哮喘、慢性咳嗽等呼吸系统疾病防治的领军人物，致力于推动国家在重大呼吸系统传染病及慢性呼吸系统疾病早防早诊早治的发展和体系建设。先后主持国家"973""863""十五""十一五""十二五"科技攻关、国家自然科学基金重大项目、WHO/GOLD 委员会全球协作课题等重大课题十余项。在国际学术期刊发表 SCI 论文 230 余篇，其中包括 *New England Journal of Medicine*、*Nature Medicine*、*The Lancet*、*American Journal of Respiratory and Critical Care Medicine*、*Chest* 等呼吸疾病研究领域的国际权威刊物，总引用次数超过 12000 次；出版《呼吸病学》《全民健康十万个为什么》《内科学》（全国统编教材）等各类专著 20 余部；获得发明专利近 60 余项、实用新型专利 30 余项。先后获得国家科技进步奖二等奖、教育部科学技术进步奖一等奖、广东省科技进步奖一等奖等国家级、省部级科技奖励 20 余项；先后获得全国白求恩奖章（2004）、南粤功勋奖（2011）、吴阶平医学奖（2011）、中国工程院光华科技成就奖（2016）、"全国高校黄大年式教师团队"称号（2017）、改革先锋（我国公共卫生事件应急体系建设的重要推动者，2018）、最美奋斗者（2019）、全国创新争先团队奖（2020）、共和国勋章（2020）等荣誉及奖励。

钟南山在 2003 年抗击非典及 2020 年抗击新冠肺炎的战役中，作为我国公共卫生事件应急体系建设的重要推动者，一直奋斗在抗疫的第一线。

2003 年抗击非典，长期在一线临床参与非典治疗的钟南山认定元凶并非衣原体，而是一种新型病毒。被任命为广东省非典医疗救护专家指导小组组长的钟南山主持制定了《广东省非典型肺炎病例临床诊断标准》，成为治疗和预防非典型肺炎的重要文件，由广东省卫生厅印发给各市和各医疗单位。钟南山当时提出的"三早三合理"防治措施得到了时任国务院总理温家宝的高度认可，并成为我国 SARS 诊治指南的基础，使得广东省 SARS 病死率全球最低（3.8%）。在"三早三合理"基础上，钟南山首次提出构建重大呼吸道传染性疾病临床防治体系，该体系成为我国突发呼吸道传染病诊治指南的制定基础，提高了我国近十年的呼吸道传染病疫情治愈率，相关成果获国家科技进步奖 2 项。

2020 年抗击新冠，钟南山连夜奔赴抗疫一线、在火车上小憩的照片感动中国。在疫情形势研判、流行病学研究、临床救治、重症抢救、药物筛选、疫苗研发等多个方面，他领导团队成员迅速行动，取得临床救治及科研攻关的丰硕成果；领导专家组对疫情进行科学研判，倡导"早防护、早发现、早诊断、早隔离"，为政府实施社区联防联控提供了科学依据，并作为我国科学家代表在国际上发出"中国声音"、交流"中国经验"贡献了重要力量。2020 年 4 月，英国爱丁堡大学公布年度杰出校友，钟南山以超过 90% 的票数当选，校方称"钟南山的成就和他在中国应对新冠肺炎疫情的努力让我们产生共鸣"，并提到他在 2003 年中国抗击非典疫情期间的杰出贡献。

在六十余载的临床及科研工作中，钟南山十分关注慢性呼吸系统疾病的早防早诊早治。慢性阻塞性肺疾病（简称"慢阻肺"）是威胁人民健康的隐蔽杀手，国际上主流的诊疗指南基本上是关注有症状的患者，而轻视疾病早期无症状或症状轻微的患者（占全部患者90%以上）。钟南山率领团队进行了长达12年的研究，发现早期干预能使慢阻肺小气道病理形态部分逆转，并率先提出了慢阻肺早防早诊早治新策略，首创适合中国患者的简便价廉治疗方案，建立慢阻肺社区综合防控新模式，有效预防慢阻肺的发生及发展。钟南山是我国慢性呼吸系统疾病早期防治研究的开拓者，为提高我国慢性气道疾病防治水平做出重要贡献。慢阻肺发病与防治成果获国家科技进步奖二等奖。

钟南山在培养呼吸疾病临床及科研人才方面做出了重要贡献。他注重培养基础与临床、理论与实践相结合的人才，师从钟南山的学生在呼吸系统疾病的不同领域都撑起一片天，桃李满天下。此外，钟南山重视从本科教育开始培养学生。2010年广州医科大学开设"南山班"，钟南山亲任班主任，打造"从南山班到南山院士"的全链条培养机制。南山班提倡"全程导师制、重英语、强人文、强科研、早临床"。钟南山希望"班上的学生从一年级起就能亲身接触病人，不要只满足于做一个医生，而要努力成为一名出色的临床医学家"。在钟南山的带领下，一支优秀的教师队伍成长起来，呼吸学科教师团队荣获首批"全国高校黄大年式教师团队"称号，南山学院教师团队被评为"全国教育系统先进集体"。

在每一次公共卫生事件暴发之际，钟南山都勇担大局、毫无畏惧，化解卫生危机，他一心为民，全心全意从百姓的角度解决民生难题。"敢医敢言"是社会给予钟南山的评价，"顶天立地为人民"是钟南山对团队的要求，不惜一切代价保护人民群众的生命安全和身体健康正是钟南山及团队践行的宗旨。在临床救治、科学研究和教书育人的道路上，钟南山从不故步自封，继续奉献在国家和人民需要的医疗卫生健康事业上。他将党和人民给予的荣誉看作是一种责任，85岁高龄仍然奋斗在一线，为国家请战、为人民的健康请战！

Profile of Zhong Nanshan

Zhong Nanshan, born in October 1936, chest physician, the Academician of Chinese Academy of Engineering, Director of Guangzhou National Laboratory, Director of National Clinical Research Center for Respiratory Disease, has been appointed the head of Senior Expert Group of the National Health Commission and head of Interagency Mechanism Scientific Research Group during the COVID-19. He was the first man to announce in public that there is "human-to-human" transmission of COVID-19.

Professor Zhong is national leader in the prevention and treatment of major respiratory infectious diseases, chronic obstructive pulmonary disease, bronchial asthma and other respiratory diseases in China. He has published more than 540 international peer-peer papers (Total citations:

10,800, H-index 50), on world's top medical journals such as NEJM, Lancet and JAMA. He also published more than 400 papers in national journals sponsored by the Chinese Medical Association; and various monographs *Asthma: From Basic to Clinical, Internal Medicine Textbook, Respiratory Diseases* he had nearly 60 invention patents. His practical and scientific treatment experience contributed a lot to public health policy shaping of China &Global in every pandemic incident.

During the SARS outbreak in 2003, Prof. Zhong opposed the view that typical chlamydia was the cause of SARS. His expertise provided a scientific basis for treatment decision-making in time. Professor Zhong's team explored "three earlies and three rations" treatment protocol in a short time, namely, early diagnosis, early isolation, early treatment, rational use of corticosteroids, rational use of ventilators, and rational treatment of comorbidities). This protocol contributed to the 3.3% SARS mortality rate in Guangdong, which was the world's lowest SARS mortality rate.

Professor Zhong has been leading the development of a number of Chinese guidelines for the diagnosis and management of bronchial asthma, COPD, chronic cough, SARS, highly-pathogenic avian influenza and COVID-19. Since March 2020, Professor Zhong has attended more than thirty international webinar meetings on epidemic prevention and control, including the US, the UK, France, Germany, Italy, Spain, Canada, Japan, Korea, India, Iraq and Nepal. The meetings aimed to share the Chinese experience to help these countries to deal with COVID-19 epidemic. He has also called for greater attention to the spread of novel coronavirus in a number of countries, addressing the importance of implementing the "Four Earlies" principles: early protection, early detection, early diagnosis, and early isolation. In September 2020, he was nominated as a member of COVID-19 Independent Panel for Pandemic Preparedness and Response, WHO.

Professor Zhong, shouldering the responsibilities in the outbreak of three coronavirus events this century, has made great efforts in clinical diagnosis, medication, scientific research and governmental strategies. He proposes "One world, one fight" to gather all the resources and strength to fight against the epidemic.

樊 锦 诗

樊锦诗，女，1938年7月出生于北平。考古学家，敦煌研究院名誉院长，中央文史研究馆馆员，曾任第三任敦煌研究院院长（1998—2014年）。

1963年从北京大学毕业后，樊锦诗一直在敦煌从事石窟考古、保护、研究、弘扬与管理实践，在西北偏远的戈壁沙漠深处打造和培养出了一支在石窟寺领域具有国际领先水平的综合团队。通过不断探索与实践，创建了基于价值和系统论的世界遗产综合保护管理体系；突破传统石窟考古学方法和手段，创建了多学科深度交叉融合的石窟考古新模式；广泛开展国际合作，创立了我国石窟科学保护方法体系；提出了数字敦煌构想，研发了高保真、高精度石窟文物数字化成套关键技术，实现了敦煌石窟文物数字化永久保存和永续利用；首次在国内开展了遗产地游客承载量研究，建成了我国首个石窟高科技数字展示中心，创建了世界遗产展示利用新模式，为我国文化遗产保护事业做出了突出贡献。

一、构建了基于价值和系统论的敦煌石窟综合管理保护体系

自20世纪80年代，樊锦诗带领团队在全国率先开展了世界文化遗产的科学管理体系构建探索，通过基于系统论的莫高窟价值科学认知，主导制定了中国第一部世界文化遗产保护专项法规《甘肃敦煌莫高窟保护条例》，首次将文化遗产整体保护管理纳入政府法制治理体系；作为中方主要参编人员，参与编制了《中国文物古迹保护准则》，并依据该准则主持编制了《敦煌莫高窟保护总体规划》。经过近40年的创新驱动、战略引领，逐步构建了"以文物保护为基础、以学术研究为核心、以文化弘扬为目的"的世界遗产地"十位一体"综合发展模式，保障了有效保护与展示利用之间的动态平衡，成功实现了以敦煌文化为代表的中华优秀传统文化的全球推广，全面提升了敦煌石窟的国际影响力。2010年在巴西召开的世界遗产委员会第34届会议认为，敦煌研究院的科学综合保护管理体系为全球世界遗产地的管理树立了一个极具意义的典范形象，并将敦煌莫高窟的科学管理作为典型案例向各国世界遗产地分享。

二、创建了多学科深度交叉融合的石窟考古新模式

樊锦诗主持编写的多卷本记录性考古报告《敦煌石窟全集》第一卷《莫高窟第266～275窟考古报告》，采用三维激光扫描测绘技术、文物数字化、计算机绘图等方法，解决了石窟建筑结构极不规整、彩塑造型复杂情况下的信息采集与表征等难题，准确表达了洞窟结构、遗迹空间分布、壁画彩塑制作工艺和时代关系等，实现了石窟考古测绘的新突破；采用C-14测年和多种无损/微损分析技术，首次准确给出了壁画绘制年代，获取了传统考古方法无法揭示的大量微观信息，在石窟内容和艺术特点方面提出了新见解。在石窟考古方面，跨出社科领域、融合自然科学，构建了石窟考古的系统科学理论方法与技术体系。

《莫高窟第266～275窟考古报告》既是全面、科学、系统的档案资料，也是莫高窟永久保存、研究利用的基础数据，可为其他石窟考古报告的撰写提供范例。该成果得到国内外知名学者的认可，先后获甘肃省哲学社会科学优秀成果奖一等奖、中国社科领域研究最高奖"吴玉章人文社会科学奖优秀奖"、法兰西科学院第二届"汪德迈中国学（终身成就）奖"，被国学大师饶宗颐先生评价为"既真且确，精致绝伦，敦煌学又进一境，佩服之至"。

三、创立了敦煌石窟科学保护方法体系

受自然和人类活动的长期作用，历经千年且材质脆弱的敦煌莫高窟出现了多种病害，存在随时毁坏的风险。在极为艰苦的条件下，樊锦诗以问题为导向、以人才培养为核心，通过精心策划、统筹考虑，积极寻求与国际顶尖团队合作，创造性地提出了一套敦煌石窟保护的科学方法体系。

在风沙防治方面，由樊锦诗和阿根纽共同领导的国际合作团队深入开展了莫高窟崖顶风沙危害成因及运移规律研究，提出了防沙网和植物林带阻沙的防治措施。在此基础上，樊锦诗带领团队不断探索与创新，通过长期综合风沙防治试验研究，研发了集沙网阻沙、砾石压沙、化学固沙、生物治沙的成套防治技术，形成了以"固"为主、"阻、输"结合的综合风沙防护体系，使窟区积沙量减少85%，全面改善了莫高窟参观环境，大幅降低了风沙对石窟的危害。

在古代壁画保护方面，国际合作团队以莫高窟第85窟为例，深入开展石窟环境研究、病害机理阐释、石窟价值解读、保护材料研发，并在《中国文物古迹保护准则》的指导下探讨了古代壁画保护修复方法与科学保护程序。在此基础上，樊锦诗领导团队通过全国石窟壁画保护的大量工程实践，提出了不同壁画病害的科学防治方法与流程，首次在全国构架了古代壁画技术标准体系，形成的古代壁画成套技术被推广应用于全国16个省（自治区、直辖市）的200多项文物保护工程，并开始向阿富汗、尼泊尔、乌兹别克斯坦等"一带一路"沿线国家辐射，实现了中国壁画保护由"跟跑"到"领跑"的根本转变。

在古代壁画原位无损表征体系和监测预警构建方面，樊锦诗通过主持"973"课题，在国内率先开展了古代壁画原位无损分析技术装备研发及无损表征体系构建，通过多种无损技术协同作用对文物信息的全面揭示，改变了传统文物分析和研究模式，实现了文物研究手段的重大变革和创新；带领团队提出风险清单、研究风险阈值，并基于风险理论构建了我国文化遗产领域首个基于物联网技术的石窟监测系统，为实现文化遗产预防性保护打下了坚实的基础。

四、研发并构建了高保真、高精度石窟文物数字化成套技术

20世纪90年代，樊锦诗通过承担"863"计划"濒危珍贵文物的计算机存贮与再现系统研究"等课题，在我国率先开始了壁画数字化技术的研发与探索，以实现敦煌壁画和彩塑的永久保存和永续利用。通过20多年不断探索，形成了一整套集图像采集、数据加工、安全存储和有效管理为主要内容的壁画数字化关键技术与系列规范，建成了"数字敦煌资源库"，上线了以30个洞窟高清数据为主要内容的"数字敦煌"全球共享资源平台，实现了敦煌石窟资源的永久保存、敦煌文化的全球广泛传播。

五、创建了世界遗产展示利用新模式

樊锦诗通过精准预判全球旅游发展趋势，率先开展石窟游客承载量研究，完成了行业技术标准编制；向全国政协提出建设我国首个石窟数字展示中心的超前构想，主持拍摄文化遗产实景超高清球幕电影，实现窟内文物窟外沉浸式体验的展示目标；基于监测预警体系、石窟数字展示中心，构建了世界文化遗产"总量控制、线上预约、数字展示、实体参观"的旅游开放新模式，使莫高窟游客承载量增加一倍，参观体验度大幅提升，为世界文化遗产地的旅游开放提供了中国方案。新模式获"中国质量奖"，是全国文化领

域以及西部地区首个中国质量领域最高奖。

樊锦诗从北京大学毕业后，带着强烈的事业心和责任感来到敦煌，坚守大漠57年，先后承担国家及省部级研究课题10余项，主持国际合作10余项，出版专著13部，发表学术论文123篇，编制国家和行业技术标准3部，为敦煌文化遗产事业奉献了一生的心血和精力，为我国石窟考古事业做出了巨大的贡献。樊锦诗具有高尚的品格和家国情怀，她择一事、终一生，先后获全国杰出专业技术人才、全国先进工作者、双百人物、改革先锋、"文物保护杰出贡献者"国家荣誉称号等数十项国家级荣誉，被誉为"敦煌的女儿"，带领团队全面提升了敦煌学与石窟考古的国际影响力，得到了党和国家的高度评价和肯定。

Profile of Fan Jinshi

Fan Jinshi, female, born in Beijing City in July 1938, is Director Emeritus of the Dunhuang Academy, Researcher of China Central Institute for Culture and History and famous archaeologist now. She was the third director of Dunhuang Academy from 1998 to 2014, first Chairman of the National Research Center for Conservation of Ancient Wall Paintings and Earthen Sites, part-time Professor and Tutor for Ph.D candidates in Lanzhou University, Vice-Chairman of ICOMOS-China, and Vice-Chairman of Chinese Association of Dunhuang and Turfan Studies. She was also selected among the First Level of Gansu Provincial Leading Talents and enjoyed Special Allowances of the State Council.

Ever since she graduated from Beijing University in 1963, Fan Jinshi has been engaged in cave archaeology, conservation, research, promotion and management practice. In the remote northwest Gobi desert, she has built and fostered a comprehensive team of international leading level in the field of cave temple research and conservation. Through gradual exploration and practice, she has established a comprehensive conservation and management system based on value and system theory, set up a new cave archaeology model of multidisciplinary integration in depth by breaking through traditional cave archaeology methods, carried out extensive international cooperation, established a scientific conservation methodology for cave temples in China, put forward the Digital Dunhuang proposal and developed a set of key technologies for Hi-Fi and high-precision digitization of cave cultural relics, succeeding in perpetual conservation and sustainable utilization of digital Dunhuang cultural relics, conducted visitor-carrying capacity research for the first time in China, founded the Mogao Grottoes Visitor Center, the first high-tech digital display center for caves in China, and created a new model for the display and utilization of world heritage. All this has greatly contributed to the cause of national cultural heritage conservation.

何梁何利基金科学与技术
进步奖获得者传略

PROFILES OF THE AWARDEES OF PRIZE FOR
SCIENTIFIC AND TECHNOLOGICAL PROGRESS OF
HO LEUNG HO LEE FOUNDATION

数学力学奖获得者

叶 向 东

叶向东，1963 年 3 月出生于安徽省宁国市。1979—1985 年在中国科学技术大学数学系学习，分别获得学士、硕士学位。1986—1990 年在苏联莫斯科大学数学力学系学习，获得副博士学位。1991—1993 年在意大利国际理论物理中心从事博士后研究。1993 年回国至今在中国科学技术大学工作，现为中国科学技术大学数学科学学院教授、中国科学院院士。叶向东长期从事基础数学中拓扑动力系统、遍历理论以及它们在组合数论中应用的研究，在动力系统的结构及其应用、熵与复杂性理论等方面做出了系统的创造性工作。在国际高水平数学杂志上发表论文 90 多篇，是该领域有国际影响的学者。1996 年获得国家杰出青年科学基金；2000 年被聘为教育部长江学者特聘教授；2019 年当选中国科学院院士；曾获国家自然科学奖二等奖、陈省身数学奖和安徽省科学技术奖一等奖。叶向东一直从事本科生教学和研究生培养工作，已毕业博士研究生 18 名，曾获宝钢教育基金优秀教师奖、中国科学院优秀导师奖、全国优秀博士学位论文指导教师等荣誉。

一、动力系统结构与多重遍历理论

动力系统的一个中心课题是研究其结构。Furstenberg 在动力系统结构及其在组合数论中的应用等方面做出的奠基性工作是其获得沃尔夫奖和阿贝尔奖的主要成果之一，并引发了人们对多重遍历平均是否在模或逐点意义下收敛的深入研究。在研究中，Host 和美国科学院院士 Kra 等构建了涉及幂零李群的遍历系统结构定理与多重遍历平均间的联系，证明了模意义下的多重遍历定理。叶向东与合作者针对如何建立极小系统涉及幂零李群的结构定理及其与多重回复性、逐点多重遍历定理有何关联开展研究。

一方面，与邵松合作得到最大幂零因子产生的机制，从而建立了极小系统涉及幂零李群的结构定理；与黄文、邵松合作构建了多重回复性与涉及幂零李群的结构定理间的联系。Host-Kra-Maass 在论文中介绍幂零系统的概念时指出：叶向东与合作者的工作建立了这些概念和拓扑回复性之间"进一步的深刻联系"。

另一方面，证明了遍历 distal 系统逐点多重遍历定理。菲尔兹奖得主 Bourgain 于 1990 年建立了逐点二重遍历定理。对于多重情况，叶向东与合作者建立拓扑模型，将拓扑与遍历的方法相结合，对遍历 distal 系统证明了逐点多重遍历定理。后续研究者 Donoso 等在论文引言中称"最显著"的两项工作是 Bourgain 和叶向东与合作者的上述工作，并称拓扑模型的使用为"原创性的应用"。在法国 CIRM 举办的国际会议上，美国艺术与科学院外籍院士 Weiss 将叶向东与合作者的这一工作作为他报告的中心内容进行专门介绍。Host 和 Kra 在美国数学会出版的专著引言中，用"令人惊奇的"来描述拓扑结构定理可以用来证明某些系统的逐点多重遍历定理，并指出此方面研究"始于黄－邵－叶的工作"。

二、动力系统熵理论

熵是至今为止动力系统中最重要的不变量之一。熵是整体定义的，熵的局部化理论从系统的局部性质入手来刻画整体性质。叶向东与合作者对具有本质不同的正熵和零熵系统进行了系统研究。

1. 用局部化思想研究正熵系统

Kolmogorov 引入的测度 K－系统是遍历理论中一类重要的系统。叶向东与合作者提出了反映熵的局部性质的概念——测度熵串，由此解决了涉及熵串、拓扑 K－系统、正熵的等价刻画等一系列问题。美国学者 Kerr 和 Li 等评价测度熵串概念是 Z－系统测度熵和拓扑熵的局部性研究的一个"关键工具"。

2. 用局部化思想研究零熵系统

叶向东与合作者提出了序列熵对的概念，建立了极小零值系统的结构定理，解决了法国学者 Blanchard 等人的公开问题。引入了零熵系统新的不变量即极大熵，并证明其取值为离散的，同时推广了著名数学家 Alon 等人重要的组合引理，美国《数学评论》评述"这是一个重要的结果"。

三、动力系统复杂性

动力系统的一个重要课题是研究系统的复杂性以及不同复杂程度的系统之间的关系。不交性关注的是两个系统的相互独立性。叶向东和合作者在这些方面开展了系统研究。

1. 证明了 Devaney 混沌蕴含 Li-Yorke 混沌

在数学领域，人们十分关注不同混沌定义间的相互关系，特别是 1975 年由 Li-Yorke 首次在数学中引入的混沌、1986 年涉及初值敏感性的 Devaney 混沌以及正熵之间的关系。叶向东与黄文将拓扑动力系统一般理论引入混沌的研究中，证明了 Devaney 混沌蕴含 Li-Yorke 混沌。此结果引发了国内外学者的进一步研究，是混沌研究中重要的文献之一。Blanchard 等在证明正熵蕴含 Li-Yorke 混沌这一重要结果的论文中指出，他们的文章"受益"于叶向东与黄文的工作；美国学者 Akin 等基于叶向东与黄文的方法得到一个结果，并称其为"黄－叶等价性"。

2. 得到与所有极小系统不交的充分必要条件

类比于自然数的互素，Furstenberg 于 1967 年在动力系统中引入不交性的概念并提出问题：刻画与所有极小系统以及刻画与所有 distal 系统不交的系统。后者很快被解决，而前者 50 多年后仍未被完全解决。最近，叶向东与合作者完全解决了 Furstenberg 提出的上述问题。

此外，叶向东与合作者出版了专著《拓扑动力系统概论》。通过出版专著和组织国内、国际学术会议，叶向东为遍历理论和拓扑动力系统的现代理论在中国的普及和人才培养做出了贡献。

Awardee of Mathematics and Mechanics Prize, Ye Xiangdong

Ye Xiangdong, born in Ningguo City of Anhui Province in March 1963, is professor at the University of Science and Technology of China（USTC）. He studied at Moscow State University and obtained his Ph.D degree in 1991. Then he went to ICTP for the post-doc research. He returned to China in 1993 and work at USTC up till now.

The main research interesting of Ye is topological dynamics, ergodic theory and their applications. He has published more than 90 research papers, severs as editors of several mathematical journals and gave plenary or invited talks in many international conferences. Due to his contribution, he received the S. S. Chern prize and won the State Natural Science Award. Xiangdong Ye was elected as a member of Chinese Academy of Sciences in 2019. The following is a brief introduction to his achievements.

1. The structure theorems and multiple ergodic averages

Establishing the structure theorem for an ergodic system Furstenberg gave an elegant dynamical proof of Szemeredi's theorem. This structure theorem was refined by Host-Kra, and Ziegler. A natural question arises as whether we have a similar finer structure theorem in topological dynamics. Host-Kra-Maass showed that regionally proximal relation of order d is an equivalence one for minimal distal systems and conjectured that the distality assumption was superfluous. Shao-Ye worked out a new approach and finally confirmed the conjecture.

The norm convergence of multiple ergodic averages was confirmed around 2005. The problem on pointwise convergence of multiple ergodic averages is much harder, and is open till now. It should be mentioned that Bourgain in 1990 answered the question for 2 terms. Using a method which is a combination of topological and measure theoretical natures Huang-Shao-Ye made a breakthrough by establishing the pointwise convergence of multiple ergodic averages for an ergodic distal system.

2. Local entropy theory

Entropy is one of the most important isomorphic invariants in dynamics. The local entropy theory began with the seeking of the topological counterpart of the measurable Kolmogorov system. In 1992 Blanchard introduced the notion of entropy pair. Ye and his coauthors made essential contribution to the theory in a series papers. Noticing that the definition of entropy pairs for a measure can not be extended to n > 2 directly, Huang—Ye introduced the notion of entropy tuples for a measure which works for any natural numbers. Then the local variational principal connection topological and measurable entropy tuples is obtained. As a consequence, a new characterization of positive entropy was obtained.

3. Chaotic behaviors of dynamical systems

It was Poincare who realized that small perturbation may course big changes in the future. Nowadays, positive entropy, Li—Yorke's chaos, Devaney's chaos et al are popular definitions of chaos. So the natural question is to figure out the relationship among the definitions. In 2002 Huang—Ye made a breakthrough by showing that Devaney's chaos implies Li—Yorke's one. This is one of the most cited papers in the related fields.

物理学奖获得者

汪卫华

汪卫华，1963 年 7 月出生于安徽省宁国市。中国科学院物理研究所研究员，中国科学院极端条件物理重点实验室主任，广东松山湖材料实验室主任。2013 年当选美国物理学会会士，2016 年当选发展中国家科学院院士。汪卫华长期从事非晶物理和材料的基础研究，在非晶动力学、形变物理机制、非晶材料研发和应用等方面做出了系统工作。相关工作获 2019 年和 2010 年国家自然科学奖二等奖、2000 年国家发明二等奖、2009 年周培源物理奖、国家科技进步奖二等奖；所领导的研究组 2001 年被中国科学院空间科学与应用总体部授予"载人飞船工程神舟二号应用任务先进集体"荣誉称号，2002 年被中国载人航天工程办公室授予"载人飞船工程神舟三号应用任务重要贡献奖"。2017 年获国际亚稳材料领域的杰出科学家奖、国家创新争先奖等，2020 年获伊朗花剌子模国际科学奖。

一、非晶物质的形成和稳定机制是非晶物理领域的挑战性问题

在系统研究非晶物质的弹性及其随结构变化规律的基础上，提出非晶物质的形成、形变、弛豫都可用流动来描述，其流动的势垒由弹性模量决定，弹性模量是控制非晶形成和性能的关键参量。建立了非晶弹性模量（包括杨氏模量、切变模量、体弹模量、泊松比）与其液体性质、振动特性、稳定性、玻璃转变、力学性能、形成能力等的关联，同时发现非晶物质的弹性模量与其组元模量和成分满足线性关联关系。提出通过调控非晶弹性模量来研究非晶合金的形成机理，控制其力学性能稳定性和形成的弹性模量判据。弹性模量判据包括探索塑性非晶材料的泊松比判据、调控非晶材料强度的杨氏模量判据、非晶合金稳定性判据、调控非晶材料玻璃转变温度的模量判据，这些判据为研究非晶物质领域的重要科学问题、探索性能可控的非晶材料提供了新的方法和理论，在非晶材料研究中发挥重要作用。文章被广泛引用。根据模量判据，研制出 10 多种具有功能特性的稀土基非晶新材料，如具有硬磁性的非晶合金、具有大磁熵和高制冷效率的潜在非晶合金制冷材料、具有重费米子行为的非晶合金、有多重自旋玻璃效应的非晶合金，开辟了功能特性块体非晶合金研究新的方向。研制出多种兼有塑料的热塑性、稳定性和形成能力的金属塑料，这类非晶合金材料可像塑料一样在较低温度（如热水中）进行成型和形变，回到室温又恢复其优良的力学和导电性能。这类材料的发现为改造传统金属材料的加工工艺提供了新的思路，在众多领域有潜在应用价值，同时为研究过冷液体及非晶形成机理等科学问题提供了模型材料。这些新材料获美国发明专利，作为非晶制备的核心专利已转让给美国液态金属和苹果公司。*Nature Mater* 以"改变非晶研究面貌"为题报道该工作的意义。该工作入选 2005 年中国基础研究十大进展。国内外 50 多个研究组用该判据研制出多种非晶合金材料。最近，他们成功将材料基因组理念引入非晶材料研究，推动了新型非晶材料的高效开发和应用，推动了非晶软磁材料在国内的大规模应用。

二、非晶材料强度和形变的物理本质是尚未解决的前沿科学问题

非晶材料的形变、断裂等力学行为的机理完全不同于位错等结构缺陷主导的晶体材料，是材料科学中还没有解决的前沿科学问题。汪卫华通过对这些问题的系统研究发现，非晶材料中普遍存在的局域弛豫动力学现象，其激活能和非晶形变的基本单元的激活能相当，非晶的形变、屈服和玻璃转变有共同的结构起源，本质上都是外加能量造成的非晶和液态之间的转变。弛豫是非晶中局域形变的动力学反映，可表征非晶的形变单元。据此，他们提出了非晶材料形变的模型：即非晶的形变可用流变的物理图像加以描述，纳米尺寸的局域流变单元是非晶形变的承载单元，其激活能和弹性模量关联。该模型能解释非晶合金高强度和形变的物理起源，为认识非晶合金独特的力学性能提供了理论基础。德国哥廷根等国内外 30 多个研究组用该模型开展跟踪和拓展研究。*Progress Mater Science* 邀请汪卫华撰写了 170 页系统总结非晶合金流变模型的综述论文。美国著名非晶物理科学家 K. Ngai 将弹性模型工作作为一个章节收入他的非晶专著中。非晶变形机制的工作获 2009 年周培源物理奖。

三、脆性是非晶材料应用的最大难题

在对非晶物质形变机制深入研究的基础上，他们采用非平衡态统计力学方法证明非晶塑性和剪切带动力学状态的密切关系，并建立了量化的多重剪切带演化动力学模型；提出引入结构非均匀性能有效提高剪切带的密度并能控制其扩展，从而有效增强非晶合金塑性的设计方法。根据非均匀性的设计方法，发展出有大塑性形变能力和高韧性的非晶合金，并引领国内外 20 多个研究组发展出一系列新的塑性非晶合金。目前，非均匀性增加非晶塑性的机制已成为非晶材料领域的研究热点之一，非均匀设计方法被公认为是强化非晶合金材料的新途径。这些工作改变了脆性是非晶合金本征特性的传统观点，加深了人们对非晶合金形变、断裂机理的认识，对解决非晶合金形变问题和材料脆性应用难题做出重要贡献。*Science* 2008 年在 Perspective 专栏文章中将该工作列入非晶合金研究

最重要进展之一，被美国 *Discovery* 杂志列为 2007 年 100 项重要科技成果之一，还被评为 2007 年中国基础研究十大进展。由于其在解决非晶材料脆性应用难题、认识其形变机制方面的重要贡献，汪卫华于 2017 年被国际亚稳材料大会授予杰出科学家奖。

汪卫华培养了一批非晶物质科学领域的优秀人才，学生中有 5 人获得中国科学院优秀博士论文、2 人获全国百篇优秀博士论文。在国内外学术期刊发表专业论文 300 多篇，为重要学术期刊撰写综述论文 12 篇，在重要国际会议作邀请、大会报告 70 多次，获发明专利 25 项。

Awardee of Physics Prize, Wang Weihua

Wang Weihua was born in Ningguo City of Anhui Province in July 1963. WANG is a professor of Applied Physics in Institute of Physics in Chinese Academy of Sciences（CAS）. His research activities involved in structure, features, formation, mechanical and physical properties of amorphous glassy materials. Over the past decade, he has presented more than 70 invited presentation or plenary talk at various scientific international conferences, and delivered 50 invited lectures at many of the renowned research centres in China and abroad. And has published more than 300 papers in international journals including Science, Nature, PRL, Nature Mater. PRB, APL, and invited to published 12 review papers in the renowned journal such as Adv. Mater, Prog Mater Sci. and Mater Sci & Eng R. edited 2 books and 3 conference proceedings. He is currently the Director of Extreme Physical Conditions Laboratory of CAS, and Director of Songshan Lake Materials Laboratory, Dongguan, China. Prof. Wang had conducted research in Germany as an Alexander von Humboldt Fellow. He has also visited various world-renowned universities and research institutes as visiting professor. He is the Academician of CAS, and The World Academy of Science（TWAS）Fellow, and American Physical Society（APS）fellow.

How to describe structural disordered glasses is a challenge in physics. Wang Weihua is internationally known for his contribution to the understanding of dynamics, flow behaviours and properties of amorphous matter. He has made outstanding contributions to glassy physics through the systematic study of the elastic properties and relaxation dynamics in amorphous solids with disordered atomic structure and the exploration of metastable materials including amorphous alloys, glassy materials and related composites. He won international acclaim particularly through his basic studies on elastic properties, structure and mechanical and physical properties of metallic glasses. He finds the physical and mechanical properties, formation, features and plastic flow of metallic glasses are found to show clear correlation with their elastic moduli in glassy materials, and show compelling experimental evidence that the dynamic relaxation and the glass transition in metallic glasses are directly related through elastic moduli. He demonstrates that the elastic moduli as readily measurable physical parameters can be used for understanding and describing the most fundamental issues in glasses. The glass transition, relaxation, and atomic deformation under stress in metallic glasses can be treated as the flow phenomenon, and the flow is modelled as the change of their different configurations or activated hopping between inherent states in the potential energy landscape and controlled by activation energy barrier. Furthermore, he proposed an extended elastic model to describe the energy barriers of the flow both in glass systems. His work represents an important step forward and provides valuable insight into the fundamental understanding of the nature of glasses, and promises to be a fertile ground for future studies in glassy physics field.

He proposes some criteria based on the modulus of metallic glasses, and outline the guiding rules of its applications in tuning the various properties especially plasticity of metallic glasses. The contributions also involves in the metastable amorphous states made accessible by non-equilibrium solidification, includes the discovery of a series of new rare earth based bulk metallic glasses with unique physical properties, polymer-like cerium-based metallic glasses (So called metallic plastics). He applied the elastic moduli correlation to solve the problem of plasticity in brittle glassy materials contrasting from ductile crystalline metals and alloys. His work leads to the discovery of the role of nano-and and micro-level inhomogeneous on the nature and mechanical properties of glassy materials, and especially the development of a series of exceptional plastic metallic glassy materials. This importantly changes the conventional wisdom on the mechanical properties of the glassy materials, and would in turn permit more widespread, cost-effective application of these materials.

He is an internationally recognized scientist in glass physics and materials field. He has been a member of the International Advisory Committees of several related conferences. He has contributed to the growth of metallic glasses field in China by organizing some projects, national conferences.

物理学奖获得者

颜 学 庆

颜学庆，1977 年 7 月出生于湖南省永州市。2004 年毕业于北京大学物理学院，获理学博士学位。2008—2010 年获洪堡基金资助，在德国马普协会 MPQ 研究所进行合作研究。2010 年回国至今在北京大学物理学院重离子物理研究所工作，历任副教授、教授和博雅特聘教授。2017 年 8 月起任北京大学物理学院重离子物理研究所所长、核物理与核技术国家重点实验室副主任、北京大学应用物理与技术研究中心副主任、北京激光加速创新中心主任。2019 年 6 月起任北京大学物理学院副院长。担任世界超强激光科学中心委员、亚洲超强激光委员会委员、国家"十四五"科技部重大仪器专项指南规划委员会委员、中国核学会理事、中国粒子加速器学会常务理事、中国高能量密度物理专业委员会委员、中国物理学会秋季会议组委、中国物理学会核物理与加速器召集人和中国光学工程学会理事。

激光加速梯度比常规加速器高千倍以上，未来可能将加速器的尺寸缩小成千上万倍，将掀起一场新的科学技术革命。颜学庆长期从事离子加速器的理论和实验研究，系列研究推动了怀柔国家科学中心交叉研究平台——北京激光加速创新中心的设立，也推动了教育部和北京市"十四五"大科学设施——激光驱动多束流设备的立项，为怀柔国家创新中心的建设做出了贡献。他在 PRL/PRAB/APL 等国际权威刊物上发表论文 100 多篇，获得授权专利 20 项（完成专利商业许可 6 项）。在 2010 年获得国家自然科学杰出青年基金资助，2019 年获国家自然科学基金委创新群体资助。为科技部重大仪器专项（2012—2017）和科技部重点研发专项（2019—2030）首席科学家，曾入选中国核物理学会胡济民教育科学奖（2007 年）、德国洪堡学者（2008 年）、科技部创新人才（2015 年）、中组部万人计划创新人才（2016 年）、北京卓越青年科学家（2018 年）、美国加州大学（埃尔文分校）"Rostocker 杰出讲师"（2019 年）、2019 年世界加速器大会 Hogil Kim 奖。

提出和证实稳相光压加速方法，解决了激光驱动离子加速能量低、能散大的关键物理问题。在国际上首次提出了半经典的激光纳米靶离子加速理论模型，依照该模型开展的合作实验在几十微米的距离内将碳离子加速到 500 MeV，打破了当时激光加速的离子能量纪录。

基于新型加速方法和纳米靶材，建成了世界上首台超小型激光加速器辐照装置，开展了 3～10MeV 能量可调的高流强、短脉冲质子束传输测试，稳定地获得了 1% 能散 / 1～10pC 电量的质子束，首次实现了激光驱动离子加速到激光离子加速器的跨越。激光离子加速器目前已经成功用于磁约束等离子体内部二维磁场诊断和激光纳米靶氢硼聚变实验研究。

首次发现和证实"临界密度等离子体透镜"操控强激光新机制，证实碳纳米管泡沫靶作为均匀近临界密度等离子体，在相对论光强下可发挥聚焦透镜的作用，极大提升激光光强，陡化脉冲前沿。在这种纳米泡沫后再加上一层超薄纳米靶，可以有效增强光压加速过程，将离子能量提高数倍。近期，通过实验进一步观察到 580MeV 碳离子和 1.1GeV 金离子，打破了激光驱动离子的能量纪录。

Awardee of Physics Prize, Yan Xueqing

Yan Xueqing was born in Yongzhou City of Hunan Province in July 1977. In 2004, he graduated from school of physics, Peking University with a doctor of Science degree. From 2008 to 2010, he was funded by Humboldt Foundation to conduct cooperative research in MPQ Institute of German Max Planck. Since returning to China in 2010, he has worked in the Institute of Heavy Ion Physics, School of physics, Peking University. Since August 2017, he has been the director of Institute of Heavy Ion Physics, School of physics, Peking University, deputy director of State Key Laboratory of nuclear physics and nuclear technology, deputy director of Center of Applied Physics and Technology of Peking University, and director of Beijing laser acceleration innovation center. He is deputy Dean of School of physics, Peking University from June 2019. He has served as a member of the world super intense laser science center (IZEST), member of the Asian super intense laser Committee.

The laser acceleration gradient is more than 1000 times higher than that of conventional accelerators. Yan Xueqing proposed and confirmed the method of stable phase acceleration for ion acceleration driven by laser. He successfully built the first laser ion accelerator irradiation device, and stably obtained 1–10MeV proton beam with 1% energy spread, which is a leap from laser acceleration to laser ion accelerator. In 2010, he was funded by the National Natural Science Foundation for Distinguished Young Scholars (2010), and in 2019, he was funded by the National Natural Science Foundation of China for innovative groups. He is the chief scientist of the major instrument project (2012–2017) of the Ministry of science and technology and the key research and development project of the Ministry of science and Technology（2019–2030）. He was selected as Humboldt scholar of Germany（2008）, innovative talents of Ministry of science and Technology（2015）, innovative talents of ten thousand talents program of Organization Department of China（2016）, outstanding young scientist of Beijing（2018）and "Rostocker outstanding lecturer"（2019）of University of California（Irvine）. For his contribution to the theoretical and experimental research of laser accelerators, he won the Hogil Kim award at the 2019 world Accelerator Conference.

化学奖获得者

张 锁 江

张锁江，1964年11月出生于河南省林州市。中国科学院过程工程研究所研究员、博士生导师，中国科学院"百人计划"，国家杰出青年科学基金获得者，"万人计划"百千万工程领军人才，英国皇家化学会会士，中国科学院院士。1994年于浙江大学获博士学位，之后进入北京化工大学做博士后，1995年获日本文部省奖学金赴日本大学与小岛和夫教授合作开展研究，1997年受聘于日本三菱化学公司，2001年到中国科学院过程工程所工作。2008年起先后任过程工程所常务副所长、所长，并担任离子液体清洁过程北京市重点实验室主任、中国化工学会离子液体专业委员会主任、中国科学院大学化工学院院长、中国科学院绿色过程制造创新研究院筹备组组长等。兼任 *Green Energy Environ*、*Green Chem Eng* 和《过程工程学报》主编及 *Ind Eng Chem Res* 和 *Green Chem* 等国际期刊编委。

张锁江始终将离子液体基础研究与工业应用紧密结合，着力构建绿色化工过程变革性的技术体系，在离子液体构效关系、工程放大和工业应用三方面取得了一系列具有重要影响的原创性成果。

一、首次提出了离子液体 Z 键新概念，阐明了 Z 键的科学本质，建立了离子液体功能设计的新方法

离子液体在众多反应和分离过程中展现出优异特性，但是，离子液体具有特殊氢键、结构复杂、种类繁多，其高效筛选和功能化设计面临巨大挑战。张锁江采用理论模拟和实验表征相结合的策略，发现了离子液体中氢键与静电耦合的"共价键"内禀特性，提出了 Z 键、离子簇和准液体新概念，突破静电起决定性作用的传统认识，揭示了离子液体 Z 键的科学本质；历时十八年收集评价 4280 余种离子液体的物化性质数据（共计 18 万余条），建立了离子液体"结构 – 性能"网络数据库；提出了"离子片"划分新方法，发展了考虑 Z 键的分子力场模型，形成了多尺度耦合的离子液体性质预测方法，实现了离子液体开发从"经验尝试"到"精准设计"的跨越。

二、率先阐明了离子液体对反应和传递性能的影响机制，获得了反应器的工程放大规律，为离子液体绿色工程应用奠定了科学基础

离子液体中存在 Z 键作用和离子簇结构，其反应和传递规律明显区别于常规介质且缺乏原位研究手段，导致工程放大十分困难。张锁江结合先进的实验表征和跨尺度理论模拟技术，揭示了离子簇结构的形成机理，获得了 Z 键 / 离子微环境定向调控反应和传递过程的规律；研制了首套离子液体传递 – 反应耦合三维原位研究装置，提出了离子液体中气泡的生成、聚并等特殊运动形式，发展了曳力系数新模型，获得了离子床反应器的工程放大规律；提出了基于"绿色度"的多目标优化方法，并自主研发了新一代大型撤热列管反应器、超薄膜蒸发器等工业装置，成功用于实际工业过程。相关成果形成了离子液体多尺度调控的科学创见和工程放大基础，产生了重要的国际影响。

三、突破了离子液体规模制备、工艺创新和系统集成的难题，实现了多项绿色技术的工业应用

面向化工绿色化的重大需求，张锁江开发了基于离子液体的多项绿色成套技术，建立了离子液体规模制备、甲基丙烯酸甲酯 / 甲基烯丙醇、碳酸二甲酯 / 乙二醇、氨回收、电解液、青蒿素分离等工业装置 10 余套，取得显著的社会经济和环境效益。

1. 离子液体规模制备及电解液开发

开发了多功能反应器和通用性强的新流程，突破了分离纯化、质量不稳定等难题，建立了首套 200 吨 / 年离子液体制备装置；开发了基于离子液体的新型锂电池电解液，建立了 5000 吨 / 年成套装置并实现了工业生产。上述成果均通过了中国科学院鉴定，产品被国内外 100 余家单位使用。

2. 基于离子液体氢键强化原理的绿色工艺开发

针对重要化工产品乙二醇工艺污染重、能耗高等问题，研发了羟基、质子酸等功能化离子液体，突破了反应 – 分离耦合难题，开发了离子液体协同催化羰基化绿色新技术，完成了 3.3 万吨 / 年 CO_2 催化转化联产 DMC/EG 工业装置建设并实现稳定运行，正在建立 10 万吨 / 年的工业装置，该工艺被中国石化联合会鉴定为"世界首创，国际领先，是绿色工程与绿色化学应用的成功范例"，引领了离子液体绿色技术的产业化进程。

3. 替代有害原料 / 介质的绿色工艺开发

MMA、MAO 分别是有机玻璃单体和水泥减水剂封端剂，我国均采用氢氰酸 / 氯醇法生产，毒性大、污染重。张锁江研发了双功能离子液体等催化剂，建立了异丁烯法 2 和 10 万吨 / 年 MMA/MAO 成套装置，实现了工业生产，产值超亿元，通过了中国石化联合会鉴定；拓展形成了合成气法千吨级 MMA 成套技术，建成了国内首套千吨级工业试验装置并实现稳定运行，通过了中国石化联合会鉴定，被列为环境友好工艺推广。

张锁江通过多年的坚持创新，形成了从基础研究到工业应用的鲜明特色和优势，在国内外产生了重要影响。迄今在 *Nature Commun*、JACS、*Angew Chem*、*Chem Rev*、*Chem Soc Rev*、*AIChE J* 等重要学术刊物上发表 SCI 论文 500 余篇，总引 18000 余次，连续 6 年入选 Elsevier 高被引学者；组织并撰写专著 10 部；获授权专利 120 余件。创办国际期刊 *Green Energy Environ* 和 *Green Chem Eng*，任世界资源论坛（WRF）理事会成员，创办亚太离子液体与绿色过程（APCIL）国际会议，多次任美国 AIChE 年会专题 / 分会主席以及香山科学会议执行主席；组建离子液体专业委员会、"一带一路"绿色技术卓越中心及国际绿色技术联盟，带领研究所进入中科院创新研究院序列；两次担任"973"首席科学家，建立离子液体北京市重点实验室，获批基金委创新群体及重大项目；作为第一完成人，获国家自然科学奖二等奖、北京市技术发明奖、侯德榜化工科技成就奖、中国科学院科技促进发展奖等 10 余项奖励，是世界离子液体与绿色化工领域的领军人物。

Awardee of Chemistry Prize, Zhang Suojiang

Zhang Suojiang was born in Linzhou City of Henan Province in November 1964. He received his Ph.D degree from Zhejiang University in 1994, and then moved to Beijing University of Chemical Technology as postdoctoral fellow. In 1995, he won the scholarship of Japanese Ministry of Education and went to Japan to conduct collaborative research in Nihon University. In 1997, he was employed by Mitsubishi Chemical Corporation. In 2001, he joined the Institute of Process Engineering（IPE）, Chinese Academy of Sciences（CAS）as full professor via the "Hundred Talents" program. Since 2008, he served as the Director General of IPE, Dean of College of Chemical Engineering, UCAS, Director of the Beijing Key Laboratory of Ionic liquid Cleaning Process, Editor-in-Chief of *Green Energy Environ*, *Green Chem Eng* and *CJPE*, Fellow of RSC and Member of CAS.

Zhang Suojiang is a worldwide leading scientist in the field of ionic liquids（ILs）and green chemical engineering. He proposed the new concept of Z-bond for the first time, established the structure-property relationship and functional design method of ILs system, and revealed the scientific nature of the microscopic interactions of ILs. He elucidated the coupling mechanism of reaction-transport in ILs systems for the first time, which laid the scientific foundation for reactor amplification. More than 10 industrial applications based on ILs with independent intellectual property rights have been successful implemented, including 1）the large-scale preparation of ILs and the electrolyte based on ILs, 2）green processes development based on Z-bond strengthening principle of ILs, such as 33, 000 tons/year CO_2 catalytic conversion to DMC/EG industrial plant, 3）green processes have been developed to replace toxic raw materials/media, for example 20, 000-ton/year MMA/MAO industrial plant using isobutylene method.

On the whole, Prof. Zhang has been working tirelessly in the field of green chemical engineering in order to promote the basic research and applications of green media ILs. Up to now, He has published more than 500 peer reviewed papers, as well as 10 monographs and 11 chapters. And over 18000 citations with a citation H-index of 65 has been achieved. He issued more than 120 invention patents including 13 PCT/U.S./Japan patents. He won several awards, such as CAS Science and Technology Promotion and Development Prize (2017), Hou Debang Chemical Science & Technology Achievement Award (2014), Second-class Award of National Natural Science of China (2010), etc. In addition, he also actively promotes international and domestic academic exchanges. The ionic liquid Professional Committee and the International Green Technology Alliance have been founded under his promotion, which provide an efficient platform for the international academic and technical communications.

化学奖获得者

赵 宇 亮

赵宇亮，1963 年 2 月出生于四川省南充市。国家纳米科学中心研究员，中国科学院院士，发展中国家科学院院士，国家基金委创新群体学术带头人，国家杰出青年科学基金获得者。1985 年获四川大学化学系学士学位，后就职于中国核动力研究院，从事核燃料燃耗质谱分析方法研究。1989 年赴日本原子力研究所进修，随后在东京都立大学理学部获硕士、博士学位。先后在日本原子力研究所和日本理化学研究所工作，从事原子核裂变碎片质量分析以及 113 号超重元素合成研究。他在国外的研究工作中发现了"原子核最大变形度的不变性"规律，提出了原子核裂变释放能量的新公式；用实验结果首次证明了原子核裂变过程存在两条不同路径，揭示了裂变碎片质量分布和裂变核的变形度之间的相关性；此外，他和同事在国际上首次成功合成、分离出了一系列内包核燃料的碳纳米材料；与日本同事一起发现 113 号（Nh）新元素，成为亚洲科学家发现的载入元素周期表的第一个新元素，结束了亚洲国家对元素周期表无贡献的历史。

2001 年回国从核科学领域转入纳米科学领域，致力于纳米生物效应分析（纳米生物安全性）以及肿瘤纳米药物研究。带领团队创建了世界上第一个"纳米生物效应与安全性"实验室，也是我国第一个以纳米材料健康效应与生物安全性为研究方向的重点实验室，并成为该领域最具国际影响力的实验室之一，取得了一系列原创性研究成果。

一、建立定量分析方法，揭示纳米材料安全性的科学规律及其化学机制

解决体内纳米颗粒定量方法学难题，突破了体内纳米材料定量检测的瓶颈，建立原位定量检测方法，被国际学术界广泛使用。澄清了学术界关于碳纳米管生物毒性来源的长期争论，建立的碳纳米管中金属定量分析方法被 ISO/IEC 采用颁布为国际标准，被全球193 个国家认可和采用。

揭示了无机纳米材料和碳纳米材料的关键生物学 / 毒理学性质及其重要化学机制。率

先揭示了体内纳米材料安全性的"纳米尺寸－效应"关系、"纳米结构－效应"关系、"纳米表面－效应"关系等，为建立新领域知识体系提供了定量的科学依据。早期研究成果被国际上认为是该领域的"第一篇高被引论文"。

二、首次实现智能纳米机器人在活体内工作

发现多羟基化金属富勒烯纳米颗粒可以"监禁肿瘤"。经过十五年攻关，成功筛选出 $Gd@C_{82}(OH)_{22}$ 并在动物体内实现"监禁肿瘤"，阻止肿瘤转移和耐药性。巧妙借助肿瘤缺氧微环境，诱导富勒醇碳笼表面羟基质子化与去质子化转换，在体内实现高效抑制肿瘤干细胞复制。2009 年入选"中科院建院 60 周年基础研究成果"。被美国纳米药物主编评价"为肿瘤治疗提供新策略""有可能导致肿瘤治疗策略的变革"。

实现纳米机器人在活体（小鼠和猪）血管内稳定工作并完成肿瘤病灶定点药物输运。与同事一起设计构建具有机器人特性的可控 DNA 纳米结构，实现了纳米机器人在活体内定点输运药物的突破。被 *Nature Biotech*、*Nature Review Cancer* 等近百家国际媒体作为亮点报道，被美国 *Scientist* 杂志评为 2018 年世界"技术进步"，被 *Cell Review* 评价为"landmark 里程碑"，被两院院士评为 2018 年度"中国科学十人进展"。

三、在国际上率先建立纳米毒理学知识体系，推动了这个新领域的起步、发展与形成

于 2005 年领衔 11 个国家的学者编著了该领域的世界上第一部专著 *Nanotoxicology*，2007 年在美国出版，四次重印再版，被多所大学选为教材。2006—2016 年组织全国 16 所高校和研究所的学者按纳米材料分类编著出版了 15 部《纳米安全性》系列中文著作，为纳米科学这个新兴分支学科及其安全应用知识体系的建立和普及做出了开拓性贡献。2011 年，在中国毒理学会发起创建纳米毒理学专业委员会，2015 年发起创建了中国药学会纳米药物专业委员会，为新兴前沿学科在我国的形成和发展做出了重要贡献。

四、把纳米颗粒健康效应研究所积累的技术和知识应用到 PM2.5 雾霾颗粒健康效应研究，为国家制定检测、防护、控制标准等提供了科技支持

2015 年，针对北京以及京津冀地区雾霾污染严重影响居民健康的重大社会问题，牵头组建了雾霾健康效应与防护北京市重点实验室，探索北京以及京津冀地区雾霾细／超细颗粒的剂量－效应关系，建立雾霾细／超细颗粒健康效应评价和相关过滤、防护效果检测的实验方法及质量控制标准，为北京市大气颗粒物健康效应研究提供可靠的参考数据，为制定雾霾防护与控制提供科学参考。实验室在 2018 年评估中获得优秀。

五、第一时间奔赴新冠肺炎抗疫科技攻关第一线

2020 年春节，新冠肺炎疫情在武汉暴发。赵宇亮立即组建一支研发团队开展新型冠状病毒核酸高效检测试剂盒的研发。为了完成生产和注册工作，研发人员分别赶往广州、

深圳和武汉。赵宇亮在 2 月疫情最严重的时刻奔赴广州黄埔参加抗疫科技攻关，一直到 5 月初才回到北京。新冠检测试剂盒于 2 月 10 日经药监局应急审批绿色通道，获得中国食品药品检定研究院产品的注册检验，完成 300 多人临床检测，获得商务部出口许可；在黄埔实验室研发的手持式新冠抗体金标测定仪，首次将检测结果与人员定位等大数据分析相结合；研发新冠抗体纳米磁珠诊断仪以及每小时可以检测 280 人的全自动高通量新冠抗体检测仪等，多款产品获得欧盟 CE 认证书。

Awardee of Chemistry Prize, Zhao Yuliang

Zhao Yuliang was born in Nanchong City of Sichuan Province in February 1963. He is professor of Chemistry, Chinese Academy of Sciences, the Director-General, National Center for Nanosciences and Technology, China. He graduated from Sichuan University in 1985, and received Ph.D at Tokyo Metropolitan University (Japan) in 1999. He moved to Chinese Academy of Sciences from RIKEN/Japan in 2001.

He proposed the toxicology study of engineered nanomaterials in 2001, and is a pioneer with innovative ideas for initiating the study on nanosafety issues. His work focuses on biological effects/activities of nanomaterials with an emphasis on the establishment of reliable and valid analysis methods for discovering the biological effects of nanomaterials/nanomedicines in vivo, understanding of the chemical mechanisms of nanosafety and safe application of nanomaterials. These have led to an ISO standard analytical method being adapted by ISO/IEC 193 member countries, the establish nanosafety assessment framework for occupational exposure of nanomaterials, the discovery of a new-concept nanomedicine for cancer therapeutics, etc.

Before 2001, he and colleagues in Japan discovered the Element 113 (Nh) which is first new element that has been discovered in Asia and filled in the Element Periodic Table.

He published $\sim$ 500 peer-review scientific papers, with citation by >47,000 times (H-index 113); edited and published 15 books (3 books in English and 12 in Chinese), with his earliest efforts on systematizing the knowledge for nanosafety in category of nanomaterials, and made significant contribution to building the knowledge framework for nanosafety issue.

He delivered >370 plenary and invited lectures at conferences, universities/institutes worldwide. He was invited to serve as a nanosafety expert/advisor by UNEP (United Nations, 2006), OECD (Nanosafety Team, 2006), Finland (2010), France (2009), Canada (2007), etc.

CAS Outstanding Science and Technology Achievement Prize (2019), The elected Member of TWAS (2018), National Prize for Natural Sciences (2018), the Academician of CAS (2017), TWAS Prize in Chemistry (2016), National Prize for Natural Sciences (2012), China Award for Outstanding Contribution on Toxicology (2015), the 60 Years Achievement of Chinese Academy of Sciences (2009); Beijing Award for Leading Talent in Science & Technology (2014), etc. Chinese Academy of Sciences–Bayer Young Scientist Award (2006), Beijing Award for Science and Technology (2008), the National Natural Science Fund for Distinguished Young Scholars (2005), etc.

气象学奖获得者

胡 非

胡非，1962年出生于湖南省常德市。中国科学院大气物理所研究员，中国科学院大学教授、博士生导师。1983年毕业于国防科技大学应用力学系，1994年获中国科学院大气所博士学位。曾任中国科学院可持续发展战略研究组成员，中国科学院大气物理所学术委员会副主任、大气边界层物理和大气化学国家重点实验室主任、北京市气象局特聘专家。现任中国工业与应用数学学会理事兼气候与环境数学专业委员会主任、中国气象学会城市气象专业委员会副主任、全国专业标准化技术委员会委员、北京2022冬奥会气象中心专家指导委员会专家以及第九届IAMAS中国国家委员会委员等。胡非主要从事大气边界层湍流基础理论及其在大气环境和风能利用等领域的应用研究，主持过一系列重大的基础研究和应用研究项目，目前是国家重点研发计划项目"陆地边界层大气污染垂直探测技术"的首席科学家。

一、主持建成城市边界层高塔综合探测系统，提出湍流新理论

胡非主持了北京325米气象塔综合探测系统的改进设计、建设和长期稳定运行，该塔目前是国际上唯一在超大城市全天候运行的环境气象观测塔，为国内外大量综合科学实验和城市规划、气象预报与环境保护做出重要贡献；塔上关键仪器和数据采集系统均为自主研制，采样频率可达国际最高100赫兹的新型超声风速仪UTA-2，打破了外国垄断和技术封锁。主持完成了我国第一部气象高塔观测资料集；在国家自然科学基金项目、科技支撑计划项目和重点研发计划项目等支持下，主持、设计和实施了白洋淀非均匀下垫面边界层综合立体观测、京津冀地区三圈大气环流（海陆风、山谷风和城市热岛环流）观测以及包括超大型系留气艇、飞机和激光雷达走航在内的大气边界层理化垂直结构协同观测等大型科学实验。在边界层和湍流结构的基础研究方面，他在国际上提出"物质边界层高度"新概念和不同于传统Richardson级串的湍流"同步级串"新理论，导出的

温度场湍流高阶结构函数公式显著优于经典 Kolmogorov 理论公式；揭示出湍流相干结构在边界层阵风和起沙扬尘中的重要机制，在沙尘暴预报中起到了重要作用。

二、最早主持研制我国城市空气污染数值预报模式系统

最早主持我国首个城市空气污染预报模式系统的研究（中国科学院"九五"重大项目和"知识创新工程"重要方向项目），被当时的国家环保总局和中国气象局联合发文作为首选模式推荐到全国 47 个重点城市应用，该模式系统及其研发团队为中国科学院大气物理所后来发展更先进的、在全国各地得到广泛应用的多尺度空气污染预报模式打下了基础。提出了大气污染预报动力和统计联合降尺度方法以及混沌动力学和机器学习融合预报方法，实用且在数学上有一定创新；最早将曾庆存院士提出的"自然控制论"理论应用于实际的大气污染溯源和优化控制。他是我国境内最大日遗化武埋藏点（哈尔巴岭）销毁工程中大气扩散的观测系统设计、建设以及观测和扩散模拟的主要实施者，为销毁日遗化武做出了重要贡献。

三、主持完成全国风能资源详查和评价，发展边界层风能气象学

胡非是发改委和财政部联合立项的我国最大规模"风能资源详查"项目的副总师兼数值模拟专项总师。该项目在全国各地新建了 400 多座专用测风塔，设计了多重降尺度和耦合精细模拟方案，完成了我国全部国土范围一公里格距的高分辨率风能资源详查和分布图谱，成为我国风能资源开发利用的重要决策依据。他率先提出了"边界层风能气象学"的概念，发展了大气边界层湍流脉动风随机分形模拟和风速斜坡（爬坡）结构模拟等理论方法和技术，可为风电预报提供理论支撑和关键参数；主持研发的包含多种先进动力和统计降尺度以及后处理方案的"大型风电场短期数值预报模式系统"也得到实际应用。

胡非发表研究论文 180 多篇，独立和参与撰写专著 4 部，培养硕士、博士与博士后50 多人，其中包括我国大气科学领域的第一个国外博士后。1995 年获中国科学院"百人计划"资助，1996 年获"赵九章优秀中青年科技工作奖"，2005 年获中国人民解放军科技进步奖二等奖、2011 年获"中国科学院杰出科技成就奖"（主要完成者）。由他主持完成的《中国科学院北京气象塔观测资料集》获 1997 年科技部颁发的《国家科技成果证书》（第一完成人）。

Awardee of Meteorology Prize, Hu Fei

Hu Fei, born in Changde City of Hunan Province in 1962, is a researcher in the Institute of Atmospheric Physics（IAP），Chinese Academy of Sciences（CAS）. He is mainly engaged in the study of atmospheric boundary layer physics, atmospheric turbulence theory and atmospheric environment. He was one of the eight members of the "Sustainable Development Strategy Research Group" of CAS. He once served as the deputy director of the academic committee of IAP, the director of the State Key Laboratory of atmospheric boundary layer physics and Atmospheric Chemistry (LAPC), and the special invited expert of Beijing Meteorological Bureau. At present, he is the director of the climate and environmental mathematics Committee of the Chinese society of industry and Applied Mathematics (CSIAM), the deputy director of the urban meteorology Committee of the Chinese meteorological society. He has presided over the development of China's first generation of numerical prediction model system of urban air pollution, the fourth "National Wind Energy Resources Investigation and Evaluation" project.The project has built more than 400 dedicated wind measuring towers all over the country, designed multiple down-scaling and coupling fine simulation schemes, and completed the detailed survey and distribution map of high-resolution wind energy resources with a grid distance of one kilometer in China, which has become an important decision-making basis for the development and utilization of wind energy resources in China. At present, he is the chief scientist of the National Key Research and Development Plan project. He has made important achievements in the study of turbulence. For example, he proposed a new similarity synchronous cascade model, which is different from the traditional Richardson cascade, and then derived a new formula of higher-order structure function of intermittent turbulence temperature field, which is superior to the classical Kolmogorov turbulence theory formula. He also found that the height of the atmospheric boundary layer determined by the detection of water vapor and pollutants is different from that determined by the wind speed and temperature, and then proposed a new concept of "material boundary layer height", which is an innovation of the theory of the atmospheric boundary layer. He has published more than 180 research papers in both Chinese and English, independently and participated in the writing of 4 monographs, supervised more than 50 graduate students, and won the "Zhao Jiuzhang excellent young and middle-aged scientific and technological work award" (first-class prize), "Outstanding scientific and technological achievements award of Chinese Academy of Sciences" and other awards.

地球科学奖获得者

郭 华 东

郭华东，1950年10月出生于江苏省丰县。中国科学院院士，俄罗斯科学院外籍院士，芬兰科学与人文院外籍院士，发展中国家科学院院士，国际欧亚科学院院士。曾任中国科学院遥感应用研究所副所长和所长、中国科学院对地观测与数字地球科学中心主任、中国科学院遥感与数字地球研究所所长。任国家遥感应用工程技术中心首任主任、中国科学院遥感信息重点实验室首任主任、中国科学院数字地球重点实验室首任主任。现任中国科学院空天信息创新研究院研究员、学术委员会主任。发表SCI论文210多篇，出版著作19部，他引4000余次。获国家科技进步奖二等奖2项、三等奖2项，省部级自然科学一等奖2项、科技进步奖5项，俄罗斯地理学会170周年Przewalski奖，亚洲遥感协会金奖，俄罗斯宇航联合会齐奥尔科夫斯基奖章，其带领的"对地观测大数据应对气候变化"团队获联合国全球脉动奖项。

郭华东从事空间地球信息科学研究，在遥感信息机理、雷达对地观测、数字地球科学等方面取得系列成果。

一、系统揭示雷达电磁波与典型地物目标作用机理

自20世纪70年代后期，系统开展成像雷达与地物相互作用的机理研究。建立了无植被沙丘雷达散射几何模型，揭示了熔岩对电磁波的去极化现象及其机理，证实了长波段雷达对干沙的穿透性，发现了干沙覆盖下的古河湖和古长城。论证的我国第一颗雷达卫星参数被立项采用，我国雷达卫星总体单位评价其研究"为我国第一代合成孔径雷达卫星波段的选择提供了科学依据，并为该卫星的立项做出了重要贡献"。入选航天飞机雷达地形测图（SRTM）计划首批42位首席科学家团队，被聘为航天飞机成像雷达SIR-C/X-SAR计划全球52位首席科学家之一，受邀为航天飞机雷达国际科学工作组成员，被亚洲遥感学会推选为亚洲水稻雷达卫星技术委员会主席。国际上称其"在中国和国际雷达

遥感研究与应用领域起到了引领作用"。英文著作被列为国际雷达遥感教科书，成果被用于 NASA 航天飞机雷达论证书和加拿大雷达卫星 2 号技术报告及雷达卫星手册。被聘为加拿大国家遥感中心"全球雷达遥感计划"成员，被选为 7 个大型国际雷达遥感计划的项目首席专家之一。提出"月基对地观测"概念并获国家科技计划支持，专著《全球变化科学卫星》和《月基对地观测》在国内外影响广泛。

二、建成多平台多波段对地观测信息处理技术与应用系统

提出挖掘"波段、极化、振幅、相位"电磁波"资源"学术思路，推动发展星载雷达系统，组织完成先进机载对地观测系统建设。主编"空间信息获取与处理系列专著"，对推动该领域发展起到重要作用。国家验收委员会评价由其任专家组组长的"863"计划 308 主题成果"开拓了我国对地观测系统技术发展的新局面，为国家经济建设、国家安全做出了重大贡献"。担任 CAS Earth 卫星首席科学家，致力推出我国新型地球科学卫星。

建立了金矿资源探测、气候变化应对、世界遗产保护、地震灾害监测四大应用系统和神舟飞船陆地应用系统。在新疆发现 18 处成矿靶区并提交黄金储量 18 吨和远景储量 70 吨；"对地观测大数据应对气候变化"获联合国全球脉动奖项；主持建成 UNESCO 国际自然与文化遗产空间技术中心，UNESCO 对中心一期运行成果评估为"取得了杰出成就"。担任中国科学院"汶川地震灾害遥感监测与灾情评估"工作组组长，主持汶川、玉树、庐山三次重大地震灾害遥感监测，建立了重大地震灾情全天时全天候和主被动遥感观测体系。"汶川地震灾害遥感"被评为 2008 年度国内十大科技新闻，玉树地震遥感监测工作组被中共中央、国务院、中央军委授予"全国抗震救灾英雄集体"称号，芦山地震遥感数据被国务院会议采用。促成灾害风险综合研究计划（IRDR/IPO）落户我国，国际科联称这是"亚洲地区首次承办的国科联系统大型科学研究计划"。

三、建设数字地球科学平台和地球大数据科学工程

主持完成数字地球原型系统建设，UNEP 专家组评价"该数字地球原型系统代表了其在全球数字地球领域中的领导作用，为国际科学与工程领域特别是空间信息技术与应用领域做出了具有里程碑意义的贡献"；主持建成数字地球科学平台，国际专家组评价"数字地球科学平台提供了地球科学数据综合分析功能，使中国成为数字地球领域科技创新的领导者之一"。主编出版由 18 个国家的 100 余位科学家历时 4 年共同撰写的《数字地球手册》国际专著，发行 8 个月来，全球下载量逾 60 万次；创刊主编的《国际数字地球学报》影响因子达 3.985。创建的国际数字地球学会已成为该领域最重要的国际学术组织，先后成为国际科学理事会成员、全球地球观测组织成员。

提出科学大数据概念并开展系统研究，核心内容被列入国务院《促进大数据发展行动纲要》；主持的中国科学院战略先导专项"地球大数据科学工程"被列入联合国可持续发展技术促进在线平台；主持撰写的《地球大数据支撑可持续发展报告》2019 年度和

2020 年度报告作为中国政府正式文件在 74 届、75 届联大和联合国 SDG 峰会发布，外交部评价"彰显我国发展合作引领地位，引起国际社会热烈反响"。

发起数字丝路国际科学计划（DBAR）并任主席，参加者来自 58 个国家、国际组织和国际计划，建立了 8 个国际卓越中心，成立了 9 个国际工作组，在国际上影响广泛。受邀在 *Nature* 上发表文章《构建数字丝路》，多篇 *Nature* 论文予以呼应。美国国家战略智库新美国安全中心分析指出"中国科学院开展的数字丝路工作正扩大中国空间信息领域的影响力"。

Awardee of Earth Sciences Prize, Guo Huadong

Guo Huadong was born in Feng County of Jiangsu Province in October 1950. He is a member of the Chinese Academy of Sciences, a Foreign Member of the Russian Academy of Sciences, a Foreign Member of the Finnish Society of Sciences and Letters, and a Fellow of The World Academy of Sciences for the advancement of science in developing countries (TWAS). He presently serves as Honorary President of the International Society for Digital Earth (ISDE), Member of the UN 10-Member Group to support the Technology Facilitation Mechanism for SDGs, Director of the International Center on Space Technologies for Natural and Cultural Heritage under the Auspices of UNESCO, Chair of the Digital Belt and Road Program (DBAR), and Editor-in-Chief of the *International Journal of Digital Earth*, *Big Earth Data*, and *China Scientific Data*. He served as President of the Committee on Data for Science and Technology (CODATA), President of ISDE, and Chairman of the International Committee of Remote Sensing of Environment. He specializes in remote sensing, radar for Earth observation, and Digital Earth science. He has published more than 500 papers and 19 books, and is the awardee of 17 domestic and international prizes.

1. Research on the imaging mechanism of synthetic aperture radar

He established a radar scattering geometric model for non-vegetated sand dunes, theoretically proving SAR's ability to penetrate dry sand. Based on this he discovered segments of the Great Wall of the Ming and Sui dynasties in desert areas buried by the sand. He developed radar polarimetric theory and researched the de-polarization phenomena of volcanic lava and multi-polarization response phenomena of plants. He has been a Principle Investigator in eight major international radar remote sensing programs, including SIR-C/X-SAR, Radarsat, Envisat, SRTM, and ALOS programs, and was elected Chair of the Technical Committee of RiceSAT for the Asian Association on Remote Sensing. He proposed the concept of Moon-based Earth observation. His publication "Scientific Satellite and Moon-based Earth Observation for Global Change" has garnered great attention.

2. Multi-platform and multi-band earth observation information processing and applications

He has modeled the relation between curve structures and ore deposits, and developed a three–step model combining remote sensing, geochemistry, and geoengineering. He delineated 18 highly–mineralized prospecting targets for gold, copper and tin, which eventually led to the discovery of gold deposits. He proposed the idea of using space technologies for research on mechanisms and methodologies related to environmental variables sensitive to global change, and he led a project that was named by the United Nations Global Pulse as one of the "Projects to Watch" in the Big Data Climate Challenge of 2014.

He established an all–weather, day and night remote sensing monitoring system for the Wenchuan, Yushu, and Lushan earthquakes in 2008, 2010, and 2013, which greatly facilitated rescue operations and made significant contributions to disaster relief. His team was collectively recognized as a "National Hero in Earthquake Relief Work" by the Central Government of China. Based on these achievements, ICSU selected his institute to host the Integrated Research on Disaster Risk IPO, "the first time an international office of this type has been hosted in Asia". He explored the use of space technologies to monitor world heritage sites, and through his experience and endeavors in this field he co–initiated and ultimately established the UNESCO Centre on Space Technologies for Cultural and Natural Heritage in 2009, appointed as the Founding Director by UNESCO.

3. Digital earth science and big earth data science

He led a research team to build the first Digital Earth Prototype System in China. He is the main founder of ISDE. He founded, as Editor–in–Chief, the *International Journal of Digital Earth*, which has an impact factor of 3.985. He published the book "Manual of Digital Earth", written by more than 100 authors from 18 countries over four years as a forward–looking examination of the positive development of Digital Earth.

He promoted the concept of scientific big data, and he is the Chief Scientist of the Big Earth Data Science Engineering Program (CASEarth). CASEarth was selected as a partner for the UN TFM online platform. His team's report titled "Big Earth Data in Support of the Sustainable Development Goals" was selected as the Chinese government's official document released in the 74th Session of the UN General Assembly. He initiated DBAR, which established eight International Centers of Excellence. His paper titled "Steps to the digital Silk Road" was published in *Nature*.

生命科学奖获得者

程 和 平

程和平，1962年12月出生于安徽省桐城市。中国科学院院士，北京大学分子医学研究所教授，北京大学分子医学南京转化研究院院长，国家"十二五"重大科技设施多模态跨尺度生物医学成像中心首席科学家。1980—1987年就读于北京大学力学系，获学士和生物工程专业硕士学位；1984—1987年辅修生物学系生理学专业，获第二学士学位；1987—1989年任教于北京大学无线电电子学系；1995获美国马里兰大学医学院生理学博士学位。2004年获聘美国NIH老年研究所终身资深研究员。迄今发表论文170余篇，被引用17000余次，其中10多篇刊于 *Science*、*Nature* 和 *Cell*。

一、细胞钙信号研究

发现钙火花，由此创立一个新的研究领域——钙火花学。其原始论文于1993年发表于 *Science*，曾被誉为100多年来十篇最杰出的心肌研究论文之一。成果被写入国内外多种生理学和医学教科书。

二、线粒体活性氧研究

发现线粒体超氧炫，又称线粒体炫，受到国际同行广泛关注。

三、高端科研仪器创制

主持国家重大科研仪器设备研制专项"超高时空分辨微型化双光子在体显微成像系统"项目，研制国际首创的2.2克微型化可佩戴式双光子荧光显微镜。成果获评"2017年中国科学十大进展"，与微型化单光子成像一起获评 *Nature Methods* "2018年度方法"。曾获2016年度国际心脏学会研究成就奖、首届全国创新争先奖等。

与同人创建北京大学分子医学研究所、北京大学分子医学南京转化研究院，实现产学研一条龙布局。2016 年创办了北京超维景生物科技有限公司，研发高端生物医学成像装备。2014 年参与规划筹建国家生物医学成像大设施，目前作为首席科学家领衔建设怀柔多模态跨尺度生物医学成像设施。

依托前期科研成果，程和平团队打造了"南京脑观象台"（Nanjing Brain Observatory，NBO），汇集北京大学团队的 2.2 克微型化双光子显微镜、超分辨显微镜、光片荧光显微镜等，同时研发新一代脑成像装备和脑成像大数据集成技术，构建从突触、神经元集群到神经环路、再到全脑水平的全景式脑功能成像体系，为实现"分析脑、理解脑、模仿脑"的目标打造超级工具，开启脑科学研究的新范式并启迪类脑人工智能研究。

Awardee of Life Sciences Prize, Cheng Heping

Cheng Heping, born in Tongcheng City of Anhui Province in December 1962, is a Member of the Chinese Academy of Sciences.

Heping's scientific motivation is to decipher physiological principles underlying cellular functions and signaling. During his Ph.D study, he discovered "calcium sparks" — elementary events of excitation–contraction coupling in heart cells. Individual sparks arise when tiny packets of Ca^{2+} are released from the sarcoplasmic reticulum through clusters of ryanodine receptors. The summation of thousands of discrete sparks results in an intracellular Ca^{2+} transient that activates the cell to contract. In a flurry of discoveries made with many collaborators, he demonstrated that Ca^{2+} sparks in blood vessels negatively regulate vascular tone; subsurface Ca^{2+} sparks in dorsal root ganglion sensory neurons trigger vesicle secretion; and spark–like events from TRPM7 and IP_3 receptors, called "calcium flickers", steer cell migration in fibroblasts. These findings have revolutionized our view of cellular Ca^{2+} regulation and signaling, its hierarchical organization, dynamism, and design principles to achieve, all at once, signaling versatility, specificity, and efficiency.

Through two–decades of vigorous innovation, he and collaborators have uncovered a molecular trilogy at cardiac dyads, the smallest units of cardiac excitation–contraction coupling–Ca^{2+} sparklets arise from the opening of single L–type Ca^{2+} channels and trigger Ca^{2+} sparks *via* the Ca^{2+}–induced Ca^{2+} release mechanism; at the same time, Ca^{2+} blinks, the reciprocal Ca^{2+} signal in the sarcoplasmic reticulum, develop and reveal a surprisingly large local Ca^{2+} depletion that helps to terminate the ongoing spark. More recently, by re–engineering a new generation of genetically–coded Ca^{2+} indicators and by devising a nanodomain–targeting strategy, he has further characterized Ca^{2+} nanosparks in the dyadic clefts. This trilogy is deranged in the failing heart, where ryanodine receptor clusters are orphaned from their L–type Ca^{2+} channels, such that Ca^{2+} sparks often occur in diastole, contributing to cardiac arrhythmogenesis. In the course of this work, he has also gained a reputation for his quantitative and analytical style. He has developed mathematical models of Ca^{2+} sparks and blinks, and devised the first automated spark detection algorithm for the research community.

While investigating the mitochondrial Ca^{2+} response to sparks, he and collaborators made the serendipitous discovery of mitochondrial "flashes", which reflect bursts of superoxide production entangled with many other signals at the single-organelle level. Attracted to the beauty and complexity of the flash, in recent years he has dedicated himself to this new research direction. Emerging evidence indicates that, much more complex than sparks, the flash constitutes another type of elemental and ubiquitous signaling event that participates in vital physiological processes from metabolism to cell-fate regulation, and from stress responses to aging. To further this quest into flash biology, he is currently leading an effort to develop a miniaturized two-photon microscope with superior resolution and sensitivity that would make it possible to image mitochondrial flashes as well as Ca^{2+} signals in live animals under natural conditions.

Currently, he is heading a team to build up the Nanjing Brain Observatory (NBO) which provides the capability of mesoscale imaging of brain activities at high throughput. With the generous support of Nanjing Jiangbei New Area government, the NBO is now equipped with more than ten setups of mTPMs of different types, alongside ultrasensitive structured illumination microscope and Volumetric Imaging with Synchronized on-the-fly-scan and Readout (VISoR). A dozen or so early-bird projects are ongoing through collaborations with experts in cortical working memory, sleep, autism, depression, neural pharmacology, and neuronal regeneration. As such, NBO will not only serve the hub to accelerate the idea-to-discovery process for individual scientists, but also establish the core competence for the launch of China and international brain science initiatives, for instance, valuable mesoscale brain functional atlas for the entire community.

农学奖获得者

陈　　志

　　陈志，1955年3月出生于吉林省东丰县。工学博士，研究员。1982—2010年在中国农业机械化科学研究院工作，先后担任所长、副院长、院长。1989年、1992—1993年先后在奥地利 Wintersteiger AG 公司、意大利米兰大学从事合作研究。2010—2016年在中国机械工业集团有限公司担任总工程师兼中国机械工业集团有限公司中央研究院院长，并先后担任中国农业机械学会理事长、土壤植物机器系统技术国家重点实验室主任、亚洲农业工程学会副主席、国际农业与生物系统工程学会主席，同时吉林大学、中国农业大学、江苏大学等担任兼职教授、博士生导师。

　　陈志长期从事农业装备技术研究，在玉米果穗收获、籽粒收获及全株收获等方面做出了一系列开创性研究工作，创建出符合中国玉米特殊农艺需求的三大机收技术装备体系，实现了中国玉米不分行摘穗收获、高含水率玉米低损籽粒收获及全株玉米全价值收获。

一、首创玉米不分行果穗收获技术与装备

　　针对我国玉米种植农艺复杂的国情，提出了先摘穗－剥皮、再离田－脱粒的中国特色分段式收获技术路线，发明了偏心弧形指仿生不分行摘穗割台和轴－径双向变量加载仿生剥皮装置，被国际农业与生物系统工程学会前主席 Tadeusz 教授评价为国际首创。

　　提出仿生摘穗原理，发明了相邻机械收获单元交叉优化布局机构，创制了偏心弧形指仿生不分行摘穗割台，首次实现了无须对行定位、无须电液辅助校准、全行距（40～90cm）精准节能摘穗，果穗漏摘率由6.3%降至0.77%。研制的不分行玉米果穗收获机成为我国玉米跨区机收经典机型。

　　首创轴－径双向变量加载仿生剥皮技术和双向异步包裹式仿生剥皮装置，解决了单向固定间隙下剥皮啃伤大、苞叶粘附残留多的难题，苞叶剥净率由85%增至95.5%，已成为摘穗玉米收获机的标配技术。

二、发明高含水率玉米仿生柔性脱粒技术

揭示了玉米籽粒机械损伤机理，发现籽粒法向加载易发应力集中的规律，提出果穗切向加载、籽粒－芯轴低应力弯曲断裂分离的新型脱粒加载方式，变冲击脱粒为揉搓脱粒，脱粒载荷有效利用率提高30%。运用界面力学和仿生学理论，仿黄牛舌部乳突结构发明了"脱粒单元＋凹板筛"的表面构型，设计的"仿生脱粒单元－果穗－仿生凹板筛"双重脱粒界面仿生结构实现了以果穗为柔性物料流、籽粒为刚性加载体的刚柔耦合脱粒，籽粒损伤率由13.6%降至1.2%，解决了高含水率玉米籽粒直收损伤率高的世界性难题。该技术已在7家行业骨干企业转化应用，产品累计销售1072台。

三、研制成功玉米作物全价值利用系列多功能收获技术装备

针对玉米作物全株多元化利用的现实需要，围绕青饲玉米和玉米秸秆、芯轴等分类收获，创新研制了4个系列装备，为玉米作物全价值利用提供了装备支撑。

1. 玉米青饲收获技术装备

采用圆盘刀低位切割、拨禾圆筒高位夹持和物料卧式喂入的技术原理，构建了圆盘刀悬浮固定、切割－拨禾差速作业技术体系，成功研制出首套立式塔型圆盘割台，成为国内青饲料收获标配装置。研制的低耗滚筒切碎装置具有复合挤压式破节裂皮及交错排列式椭圆曲线刃口等特性，攻克了青饲玉米的混合物料喂入与切碎、籽粒破碎等关键技术，实现了切割与输送、切碎和抛送一体化。研制的青饲收获机主要技术指标达到国际同类产品先进水平，是国产青饲收获机的主力机型。

2. 果穗－茎秆兼收技术装备

针对中国独有的摘穗收获工艺，提出了垂直方向拉伸摘穗、水平方向切割秸秆的工作原理，发明了一种摘穗与茎秆切割同步、物料双通道分类输送的双层结构割台，研制成功的果穗－茎秆兼收玉米收获机实现了一次进地、果穗－秸秆同机同步分类收获，果穗、秸秆收获质量高，土壤压实小，成为农业农村部主推机型，在全国12个省市推广应用。

3. 籽粒－芯轴兼收技术装备

发明了变间隙轴流脱粒技术，研制成功"圆柱脱粒滚筒＋锥形凹板筛"玉米籽粒直脱、籽粒－芯轴兼收工艺和装置，实现了玉米脱粒载荷随物料厚度递减的自适应调节，研制的世界首台玉米籽粒与芯轴同步联合收获机在辽宁、吉林、黑龙江及内蒙古4省区推广应用。

4. 玉米秸秆打捆收获技术装备

针对玉米秸秆粗壮、节硬和皮韧等机械特性，攻克了无土捡拾、压劈调质、大截面预压均匀布料、二次压缩成型与密度反馈控制、打结机构多动作相位耦合等关键技术，保证了打捆密度均匀一致，解决了大截面捆型（900毫米×1200毫米）的成型规整和多

工序同步协调难题。研制的 3 种方捆打捆机成捆率 98.4%，捆型密度 100～200 千克/立方米可调，总损失率达 6.8%，生产率达 25 捆/小时（大方捆）、120 捆/小时（小方捆），主要技术指标达到国际同类产品先进水平，占国内玉米秸秆打捆机 60% 的市场份额。

陈志获授权国家发明专利 16 件，发表学术论文 96 篇（其中 SCI/EI 收录论文 33 篇），出版著作 13 部，在我国玉米机械化收获领域的研究成果在全国玉米主产区、近百家企业推广应用，累计产销 10.27 万台，实现产值 112.23 亿元。作为第一完成人主持的"东北玉米全价值仿生收获技术及装备"获 2019 年国家技术发明奖二等奖，"玉米籽实与秸秆收获关键技术装备"获 2011 年国家科学技术进步奖二等奖，发明的"玉米果穗剥皮装置及具有该装置的玉米果穗剥皮机"获得中国专利优秀奖，并获得全国首届杰出工程师奖、全国创新争先奖、中国农业机械化发展 60 周年杰出人物等荣誉称号。

此外，陈志率先实施农业装备技术创新工程，为农机行业科技创新、学科建设和人才培养做出了积极贡献。主持建立了国家首个农机创新型企业，提出并创建了以土壤植物机器系统技术国家重点实验室为技术核心层、以农业机械国家工程技术研究中心为技术转化层、以农业机械中小企业创新服务平台为技术辐射层和以农业装备产业技术创新战略联盟为纽带的"四位一体"农机装备技术创新的新机制，促进了行业科技资源聚集、关键共性技术的研发和转化应用，2010 年获国家科技进步奖二等奖。

陈志积极推进学科建设和发展，培养博士生 14 名、硕士生 23 名；主编出版了《中国农业机械化工程》等学术著作；作为执行主编，推动《农业机械学报》成为我国农机领域唯一的 EI 全文收录期刊，并入选国家高质量科技期刊；由他主编的《农业机械设计手册》是我国现代农业装备领域的首部手册，在高校、企业、科研单位等累计应用 3 万余册，成为农业机械工程领域的必备工具书。

Awardee of Agronomy Prize, Chen Zhi

Chen Zhi was born in Dongfeng County of Jilin Province in March 1955. He graduated from China Agricultural University with a doctorate degree in engineering. In 1989, 1992–1993, he engaged in cooperative research in Wintersteiger AG in Australia and the University of Milan in Italy. From 1996 to 2010, he served as the president of the Chinese Academy of Agricultural Mechanization Sciences. 2010–2016, he served as the chief engineer of the China National Machinery Industry Corporation. He successively served as the chairman of the Chinese Society of Agricultural Machinery, the director of the State Key Laboratory of Soil–plant Machinery System Technology, the vice president of the Asian Association for Agricultural Engineering (AAAE), and the president of International Commission of Agricultural and Biosystems Engineering (CIGR). He is the adjunct professors of Jilin University, China Agricultural University, Jiangsu University, etc.

Chen Zhi has made a series of pioneering research work in corn ear harvesting, corn grain harvesting and whole plant harvesting. He created the first corn unbranched ear harvesting technology and equipment, invented the high water content corn bionic flexible threshing technology, and successfully developed a series of multifunctional harvesting technology equipment of the full value of crops utilizes. These research results have been promoted and applied in the main corn producing areas and nearly 100 enterprises across the country. The cumulative production and sales of 102700 units have achieved an output value of 11.223 billion yuan. All the achievements made by Chen Zhi has effectively promoted the mechanization of corn harvesting in China and freed farmers from heavy labor. Chen Zhi has won the second prize of the National Technology Invention Award in 2019 and the second prize of the National Science and Technology Progress Award in 2011, authorized 16 national invention patents, published 96 academic papers (33 papers were indexed by SCI/EI), published 13 books, and trained 14 doctoral students and 23 master students. He also has won the first National Outstanding Engineer Award, National Innovation Award, and Outstanding Person of the 60th Anniversary of China's Agricultural Mechanization Development. Chen Zhi has made active contributions to promote the scientific and technological innovation, discipline construction, talent training and international exchange of the agricultural machinery industry.

农学奖获得者

范 国 强

范国强，1964年6月出生于河南省禹州市。1984年、1986年和1991年先后获得河南农业大学、东北林业大学和中国科学院植物研究所农学学士、农学硕士和理学博士学位，1991—1994在中山大学做博士后。现为河南农业大学教授、博士生导师，新世纪"百千万人才工程"国家级人选。获得国家有突出贡献中青年专家、全国优秀科技工作者、全国模范教师、河南省科学技术杰出贡献奖等荣誉称号。

范国强从事泡桐研究，在泡桐新品种培育、丛枝病发生机理与防治及泡桐生物学方面做出了一系列开创性的研究工作。

一、泡桐新品种培育研究

首次利用现代生物技术手段创制泡桐新种质，为泡桐新品种培育开辟了新途径。

1. 建立四倍体泡桐种质创制体系，创建国内外首个四倍体泡桐种质资源库

以白花泡桐和豫杂一号泡桐等6个种、2个品种二倍体泡桐为材料，利用秋水仙素化学诱变筛选出了不同四倍体泡桐诱导最佳方法，获得四倍体泡桐幼苗群体，建立了简便、高效和实用的四倍体泡桐种质创制体系；创建四倍体泡桐种质资源库，为林木多倍体育种提供技术支撑。

2. 首次发现DNA甲基化变化是四倍体泡桐呈现优良特性的主要原因之一

四倍体白花泡桐基因组大小为1017 Mb，杂合率为0.9%左右，重复序列比例达到50%，SNP、SV和Short InDel较二倍体分别增加了35.2%、69.4%和54.3%。不同二倍体泡桐染色体加倍前后的DNA遗传背景发生了变化。四倍体泡桐总DNA甲基化水平均高于其二倍体，DNA甲基化模式随甲基化水平变化而变化。

3. 鉴定出与四倍体泡桐优良特性密切相关的基因，为加快泡桐分子聚合育种奠定基础

四倍体泡桐叶片中参与光合作用的捕光复合体II叶绿体结合蛋白、叶绿素还原酶

以及与抗逆相关的转录因子、过氧化氢酶和多酚氧化酶等基因表达水平较二倍体高，miRNA172的靶基因在四倍体泡桐中表达水平低，四倍体泡桐中染色质重塑复合体SWI/SNF相关亚基表达水平较二倍体低。

4. 创建一套四倍体泡桐苗木繁育和丰产栽培技术体系，推动了泡桐产业的快速发展

分别通过不同四倍体泡桐适生区苗木繁育和栽培技术研究，建立了一套苗木繁育和丰产栽培技术体系，加快了泡桐栽培的科学化和标准化进程。

二、泡桐丛枝病发生机理及防治研究

揭示泡桐丛枝植原体与泡桐互作的致病机制，建立了高效的丛枝病防治技术体系，引领国内外植原体病害研究新方向。

1. 绘制世界上第一张泡桐丛枝植原体基因组完成图，创建了泡桐丛枝植原体病害发生模拟系统

发现泡桐丛枝植原体基因组由一条大小为891641bp的染色体和两个分别为4485bp和3837bp的质粒组成；鉴定并验证PaWB20为泡桐丛枝植原体的致病效应子；基于植原体数量与幼苗形态变化的有效关联，建立了泡桐丛枝植原体病害发生模拟系统。突破了制约丛枝植原体－泡桐互作研究瓶颈，为解决泡桐丛枝植原体致病机制这一世界性难题提供了关键技术手段。

2. 阐明致病效应子抑制泡桐先天免疫的分子机制

完成了泡桐健康苗和丛枝病苗DNA甲基化图谱。经适宜浓度DNA甲基剂、抗生素处理，泡桐丛枝病病苗均可恢复健康状态，基因组甲基化水平上升、甲基化模式发生变化。在此基础上发现PaWB20与泡桐细胞膜蛋白结合进入细胞内，使泛素化的pauSPL3/6与DSK2/RAD23结合后被26S蛋白酶体降解，从而抑制细胞内生长素合成，植株呈现丛枝症状，为阐明其致病机制奠定了理论基础。

3. 揭示丛枝植原体引起泡桐染色质3D构象及其功能变化的机制，创建了泡桐丛枝植原体致病模型

首次完成泡桐3D基因组图谱绘制，发现丛枝植原体导致泡桐染色质3D构象发生变化。利用现代组学分析方法，发现miRNA、LncRNA、CircRNA、Rubisco、POR、CTR1磷酸化与丛枝病发生特异相关。利用鉴定出泡桐丛枝病发生关键的lncRNA、miRNA和circRNA构建了其ceRNA网络，验证丛枝病发生关键miRNA156-pauSPL3/6。基于病原与寄主互作研究建立了丛枝植原体致病模型。

4. 突破抗病品种培育和药物研发关键技术，创建了泡桐丛枝植原体病害综合防控体系

基于泡桐丛枝植原体致病机制，利用现代生物技术培育出抗病泡桐新品种、研发出抗泡桐丛枝植原体药物；制定泡桐丛枝病防治技术标准，建立了抗病良种培育、药物防治和营林技术等关键技术集成创新的综合防控体系，实现了防控技术的标准化和产业化。

三、泡桐生物学研究

创新性地开展泡桐生物学基础研究，奠定了我国泡桐研究在国际上的领先地位。

1. 绘制出世界第一张泡桐基因组精细图谱，为国内外木本植物遗传解析提供了重要遗传信息

确定白花泡桐原始种基因组大小为 547.9 Mb，建立了包括 20 个完整连锁群白花泡桐基因组精细图谱。组装序列的 contig N50 长度为 66.8K、scaffold N50 长度为 900.7K，平均 GC 含量为 33.2%。白花泡桐共有 31105 个基因和 39119 个转录本，基因平均长度为 4.7Kb；重复序列占白花泡桐基因组的 49.1%，长末端重复序列占总基因组的 41%；基因组中有 1329 个 tRNA 基因、2776 个 rRNA 基因、249 个 miRNA 和 277 个 snRNA 基因。发现白花泡桐在 2 千万年前和 1.4 亿年前发生了 2 次全基因组复制事件。

2. 阐明泡桐属不同种的遗传进化关系，为确定泡桐起源及保存泡桐核心种质提供了理论支撑

以重测序 SNP 数据为基础，发现泡桐属 9 个种间均存在单核苷酸多态性、短片段插入和缺失及基因组结构变异。检测到 SNP 位点数量在 2.8 ～ 4.6M，兰考泡桐和鄂川泡桐中 90% 以上为杂合型；Short InDel 数量在 0.7 ～ 1.3M，主要分布在非基因区，数量最多的是川泡桐。结构变异数量在 5.4 万～ 9.8 万，大部分发生在基因区，最多的两个种是兰考泡桐和南方泡桐。9 种泡桐可以分成 3 组，一组为毛泡桐、台湾泡桐和川泡桐，其中川泡桐和台湾泡桐亲缘关系最近；一组为白花泡桐、南方泡桐、楸叶泡桐、鄂川泡桐和兰考泡桐，其中南方泡桐和白花泡桐亲缘关系较近、鄂川泡桐和兰考泡桐亲缘关系较近；山明泡桐单独列为一组，说明该种与其他 8 种泡桐的亲缘关系最远。

Awardee of Agronomy Prize, Fan Guoqiang

Fan Guoqiang was born in Yuzhou City of Henan Province in June 1964. Now, he is a professor and doctor supervisor of Henan Agricultural University, Professor Fan is engaged in researching of Paulownias, and has made a series of pioneering research work in new Paulownia variety cultivation, the occurrence mechanism and prevention of Paulownia witches' broom disease, and the biology of Paulownias.

1. Research on the cultivation of new Paulownia varieties

A new germplasms of Paulownia was first created using modern biotechnology, which opened up a new way for the cultivation of new Paulownia varieties.

The germplasm creation system of tetraploid Paulownia was created and the first tetraploid

Paulownia germplasm resource bank at home and abroad was established. Using six species and two varieties of diploid Paulownia, including *Paulownia fortunei* and *Paulownia 'Yuza1'* as materials, the best induction methods of different tetraploid Paulownia were screened using colchicine chemical mutagenesis, and the tetraploid Paulownia seedling population was obtained. A simple, efficient and practical tetraploid Paulownia germplasm creation system was established. The tetraploid Paulownia germplasm resource bank was established, which would provide technical support for tree polyploidy breeding. It was found out for the first time that changes of DNA methylation was one of the main reasons for the excellent characteristics of tetraploid Paulownia. The genes closely related to the fine characteristics of tetraploid Paulownia were identified, which laid a foundation for accelerating molecular polymerization breeding of Paulownia. A set of technology system for seedling breeding and high-yield cultivation of tetraploid Paulownia has been established, which promoted the rapid development of Paulownia industry.

2. Research on the occurrence mechanism and prevention of Paulownia witches' broom disease

The pathogenic mechanism of the interaction between Paulownia witches' broom phytoplasma and Paulownia was revealed, and an effective technology system for prevention and treament of witches' broom disease was established, which led a new research direction of phytoplasma disease at home and abroad. The world's first complete genome map of the Paulownia witches' broom phytoplasma was drawn, and a simulation system of Paulownia witches' broom disease occurrence was established. The molecular mechanism of pathogenic effectors inhibiting Paulownia innate immunity was clarified. The mechanism of the changes on 3D conformation and function of Paulownia chromatin caused by phytoplasma was revealed, and the pathogenic model of Paulownia witches' broom was established. It has broken out the key technologies of disease-resistant varieties breeding and drug research and development, and established a comprehensive prevention and treatment system of Paulownia witches' broom disease.

3. Research on the biology of Paulownia

The basic research on Paulownia biology has been carried out innovatively, which laid the leading position of Paulownia research in the world. The first complete genome map of Paulownia was drawn, which provides important genetic information for genetic analysis of woody plants at home and abroad. The genetic evolutionary relationship of different species of Paulownia was clarified, which provided theoretical support for determining the origin and preserving core collection of Paulownia.

农学奖获得者

沈 建 忠

沈建忠，1963年3月出生于浙江省桐乡市。1980—1985年就读于北京农业大学（现中国农业大学）兽医学专业，获农学学士学位；1985—1988年就读于北京农业大学基础兽医学专业，获农学硕士学位；1994—1997年就读于中国农业大学理学院农药学专业，获理学博士学位。1988年至今在中国农业大学动物医学院工作，现任动物医学院院长、国家兽药安全评价中心主任、国家兽药残留基准实验室主任、动物源食品安全检测技术北京市重点实验室主任。兼任教育部高等学校动物医学类专业教学指导委员会主任委员、国务院学位委员会第八届学科评议组成员、国家动物健康与食品安全创新联盟理事长、中国毒理学会副理事长、中国检验检测学会副理事长、中国奶业协会副会长、中国饲料工业协会副会长、联合国粮农组织／世界卫生组织食品添加剂联合专家委员会专家等。中国工程院院士，教育部长江学者特聘教授，国家杰出青年科学基金获得者，国家百千万工程领军人才。

主要从事动物源性食品药物残留检测技术、动物源病原微生物耐药性形成与控制等领域的研究工作。

一、兽药及有害化合物残留快速检测技术研究

肉蛋奶中的药物及有害化合物残留是世界性问题，针对20世纪90年代我国在兽药及有害化合物残留检测领域缺少快速检测产品、检测灵敏度不够、检测产品稳定性差等关键问题，沈建忠带领团队取得了一系列创新性成果。一是发展了兽药及有害化合物抗体制备的理论与技术。他率先提出了以目标导向为核心的小分子半抗原设计，创新了半抗原设计理论，抗体成功率提高50%以上。在抗体制备技术上，从传统的小分子化合物多抗、单抗技术发展到重组抗体技术，大幅提高了抗体性能，系统建立了兽药等小分子化合物抗体制备的技术体系，成功构建了一个涵盖主要兽药、霉菌毒素、非法添加物、

库容量超过 500 种的抗体资源库，满足了企业和政府机构日常检测的需要，为应对食品安全突发事件提供了储备。二是利用组合抗体、多点设计模式、定向标记等技术发展了包括酶联吸附、侧流层析、荧光偏振、化学发光等残留快速免疫分析技术，达到国际先进水平。三是突破残留快速检测产品核心试剂配方和工艺技术瓶颈，解决了长期以来我国快速检测产品灵敏度低和稳定性差的难题。在此基础上，研发出兽药、非法添加物、霉菌毒素等残留快速检测产品 80 余种，其中获农业部产品备案批准文号 22 种、获国家重点新产品 2 个和北京市自主创新产品 22 个。产品具有灵敏度高、检测速度快、操作简便等特点，已在全国 31 个省市的 1000 余家检测机构及伊利、雨润、三元等 1500 余家食品生产加工企业残留监测中广泛应用，用于快速检测肉蛋奶及饲料中抗菌药物、三聚氰胺、黄曲霉毒素和瘦肉精等残留，有效保障了食品安全，产生了巨大的经济社会效益。以上成果打破了国外技术和产品垄断，迫使进口产品在中国的市场份额从 2002 年的 90% 以上降至 20% 左右，价格成本大幅下降，带动了残留检测试剂产业的快速发展。上述产品和标准为提升我国兽药残留检测试剂产业的技术水平和完善动物源性食品兽药残留监控技术体系做出了重要贡献。

二、动物源细菌耐药性的形成与控制

抗菌药物广泛使用引起的动物源细菌耐药性问题已成为影响养殖业健康发展和公共卫生安全的重大威胁。针对我国动物源细菌耐药性本底不清的状况，沈建忠带领团队历时十余年，在细菌耐药性领域构建了涵盖 26 个省市含近 70 万条数据的动物源细菌耐药性数据库，探明了畜禽主要病原菌耐药性的变化趋势，揭示了多种细菌耐药性的产生与传播机理。一是在食品动物、零售肉类和人群中发现并确证了可转移的多黏菌素耐药基因 mcr-1，从分子水平上揭示了临床抗感染的"最后一道防线"药物多黏菌素耐药性快速发展的成因；进一步研究阐明了动物源性食品的消费和水产养殖生产及消费对 mcr-1 及其携带菌在人群中的定植和传播起关键作用，而入院前使用抗生素和靠近养殖场居住是导致患者定植和感染 mcr-1 携带菌的关键因素。上述研究明确了养殖业使用多黏菌素对人类健康的潜在风险，引起全球学术界、新闻媒体和各国政府部门的高度关注与重视，推动世界卫生组织、欧洲药品管理局等国际组织和多个国家及时调整对多黏菌素使用风险的管理政策，为我国出台兽用抗菌药规范使用和减量化行动的管理政策提供了关键性的科学依据和理论支持。二是率先发现了四环素修饰酶 Tet（X）变异体 Tet（X3/X4）介导大肠杆菌和鲍曼不动杆菌对替加环素产生高水平耐药的新机制，并揭示了其在动物、食品和临床中的流行情况。三是首次从动物源链球菌、大肠杆菌等细菌中发现 cfr 基因以及从肠球菌等细菌中发现 optrA 基因，携带该两类基因的耐药细菌可对临床治疗革兰氏阳性菌感染的"最后一道防线"药物恶唑烷酮类抗生素耐药。以上发现表明临床治疗多重耐药菌严重感染的"最后一道防线"被全面突破的风险急剧上升，为防控重要耐药菌/耐药基因沿动物性食品生产链或环境的传播扩散提供了理论依据。

基于上述研究成果，沈建忠已带领团队获国家技术发明奖二等奖、国家科学技术进步奖二等奖、北京市自然科学奖一等奖、中华农业科技奖科学研究成果奖一等奖、北京市科学技术奖一等奖等荣誉；他本人还获得中华农业英才奖、首都劳动奖章、全国创新争先奖状、全国优秀科技工作者等荣誉称号。在 *The Lancet Infectious Diseases*、*Nature Microbiology*、*Analytical Chemistry*、*Biosensors & Bioelectronics*、*Food Chemistry* 等国际顶尖期刊发表论文 259 篇，单篇最高引用 2587 次；获国家发明专利授权 75 项，主持制定 56 项国家和行业标准，主编著作和教材 8 部。

Awardee of Agronomy Prize, Shen Jianzhong

Shen Jianzhong was born in Tongxiang City of Zhejiang Province in March 1963. As a member of the Chinese Academy of Engineering, he is Dean of the College of Veterinary Medicine（CVM）in China Agriculture University（CAU）, Director of National Reference Center for Veterinary Drug Safety Evaluation, Director of National Reference Center for Veterinary Drug Residue Analysis, Chairman of China Animal Health and Food Safety Alliance, Vice Chair of Chinese Society of Toxicology.

Shen has made significant contribution to two major areas. First, the research team has developed key theory and detection techniques of veterinary drug residues and other biochemical hazardous factors, by establishing a reservoir including over 500 antibodies for recognizing major veterinary drugs, fungi toxins, and other illegal additives; over 80 fast detection kits have been successfully developed and widely adopted by government and private sectors, which delivered enormous social and economic value. Second, in the last two decades, the research team has accumulated extensive knowledge of emergence and transmission antibiotic resistance through one health approach, by discovering several novel antibiotic resistance genes highly critical to public health, such *mcr* and *tetX*, and identifying the potential transmission route of antibiotic resistance genes in the food supply chain, which provide important scientific evidence for controlling the spread of antibiotic resistance and issuing key regulation and polices.

In the last decade, more than 30 research grants have been awarded from Ministry of Science and Technology, etc. more than 200 highly impact research articles have been published in the peer-reviewed journals with over 3000 citations, including The Lancet Infectious Diseases, Nature Microbiology, Analytical Chemistry, Biosensors & Bioelectronics, Food Chemistry, and more than 70 patents has been granted. Due to the outstanding achievements, he has received the First Prize of Beijing Natural Science Award in 2019, Capital Labor Medal in 2016, the Second Prize of National Technology Invention Award in 2015, the First Prize of National Agriculture Science and Technology Award in 2013, National Agricultural Scientific Research Talent in 2012, the Second

Prize for National Scientific and Technological Progress in 2006 and the First Prize of Beijing Science and Technology Award in 2005. Over 100 graduate students have graduated from this research group.

Shen has been an active committee member of multiple national organization and science community including: Joint FAO/WHO Expert Committee on Food Additives, Veterinary Food Hygiene Society of Chinese Society of Animal Husbandry and Veterinary Medicine, National Committee of Experts on Veterinary Drug Residues, China Feed Industry Association, National Technical Committee for Standardization of Feed Industry, National Committee for the Review of Food Safety Standards, etc.

医学药学奖获得者

季 加 孚

季加孚，1959年12月出生于内蒙古自治区呼和浩特市。1990年获北京医科大学医学硕士学位，2015年获英国卡迪夫大学博士学位。1990年至今在北京大学肿瘤医院工作，历任胃肠肿瘤外科主治医师、副主任医师、主任医师、副教授、教授。1999—2000年在美国斯坦福大学进行肿瘤学合作研究。2011年7月至今任北京大学肿瘤医院院长、大外科主任、恶性肿瘤转化研究北京市重点实验室主任。2012年12月起担任恶性肿瘤发病机制及转化研究教育部重点实验室主任、北京大学肿瘤研究中心主任。先后担任国际胃癌学会主席，亚洲外科学会常务委员，中国抗癌协会副理事长，中国医疗保健国际交流促进会副会长，中华医学会常务理事、外科学分会秘书长兼常务委员，中国医师协会外科医师分会肿瘤外科医师委员会主任委员，*Chinese Journal of Cancer Research* 主编。以第一完成人获国家科技进步奖二等奖1项、中国抗癌协会科技奖一等奖1项、中华医学科技奖一等奖1项、教育部科学技术进步奖一等奖1项，并获吴阶平－保罗·杨森医学药学奖、英国文化教育协会职业成就奖及中菲亚洲国际和平奖。国家卫生健康委有突出贡献专家，北京学者，美国外科学会会士，英国皇家外科学院院士，约翰斯·霍普金斯大学医学院兼职教授。

季加孚从事胃癌外科工作36年，针对胃癌诊治关键点攻坚克难，创新性提出以关键血管为解剖标志、以血管外膜为平面的模块化手术规范，彻底破解胃癌手术难掌握、难推广及死亡率高的世界难题；以综合治疗模式和微创技术为核心，以多中心临床研究为手段，使中国胃癌微创手术比例上升了45%，患者3年无病生存率提升22%，成功突破疗效瓶颈；创建全球规模最大的胃癌样本库，并通过高通量组学研究先后在胃癌细胞侵袭转移机制、胃癌预后突变特征、新辅助化疗反应相关分子分型的多组学表征方面取得重要研究成果，为阐明胃癌个体化治疗的分子机制奠定了关键的理论基础。研究成果带领中国胃癌治疗跻身国际一流行列。

一、突破手术技术难题，创建模块化手术规范，实现胃癌手术全球共识

1. 创建模块化手术规范，在全国范围成功推广

率先提出"以关键血管为解剖标志、以血管外膜为平面"的核心理念，定义胃癌 D2 手术的 12 个标准模块，形成了完整网膜囊切除、保脾第 10 组淋巴结清扫和间置空肠代胃重建等系列关键技术，创建"胃癌 D2 手术规范"。2008 年开始在全国巡讲，培训医师逾万人次，经 31 个省级行政区、85 家主要中心验证，目前国内 D2 手术死亡率已降至 0.24%。与美国国家癌症中心合作，主持编写国内首部胃癌临床指南，将 D2 手术作为我国胃癌手术标准，中国数据首次成为全球分期系统的重要组成部分。

2. 推广中国经验，解决全球手术标准化难题

针对高死亡率带来的全球手术标准化难题，作为国际胃癌学会主席，带领国际专家团在意大利、日本、印度等国进行培训及手术演示，主办第 12 届国际胃癌大会，向 48 个国家介绍中国经验，为制定 D2 手术国际共识起到了关键作用。韩国胃癌学会主席 Han-Kwang Yang 评价："季加孚的模块化手术推动了 D2 手术在全球的应用"。目前，欧洲胃癌临床研究已将 D2 手术列为标准术式并进入临床实践。鉴于其在推进胃癌全球手术共识等方面的突出贡献，季加孚于 2017 年被英国皇家外科学院授予院士称号。

二、以围手术期治疗模式和腹腔镜技术为核心，突破手术瓶颈，使中国胃癌治疗水平居国际领先地位

1. 创新围手术期治疗模式，显著改善患者生存

创建围手术期治疗模式，并作为中国区负责人完成亚洲首个胃癌国际研究 CLASSIC，结果发表于 Lancet（2012）及 *Lancet Oncology*（2014），确立 CapOX 为围手术期治疗首选方案，改变了临床实践。中国患者 3 年无病生存率从 56% 提升至 78%，是迄今降低复发风险最多的临床研究，成果入选中国科技期刊优秀论文。为精准识别治疗获益人群，首次应用人工智能手段构建双标影像组学模型，判断隐匿性转移的准确率达 92%，成果发表于欧洲肿瘤学会官方期刊 *Annals of Oncology*。仅 2014 年以来主持领导的中国胃肠肿瘤外科联盟使 13.4 万名患者直接受益于新型治疗模式，改善了胃癌诊疗现状。研究成果获国家科技进步奖二等奖。

2. 创新开展腹腔镜研究，降低 D2 手术创伤

率先完成全球首个腹腔镜 D2 手术Ⅲ期研究 CLASS-01，形成腹腔镜下神经显露与功能保留、腹腔镜淋巴结特异显色及精细解剖等技术，首次证明腹腔镜可实现与开腹 D2 手术相同的切除效果，同时加速术后恢复。这是全球发表于医学四大期刊的首篇胃癌微创外科论著，标志胃癌微创理念得到学界广泛认同。术前化疗后腹腔镜手术研究成果被全球最大临床决策支持系统 UpToDate 引用，成为该领域唯一参考循证医学证据。主持成立大中华腹腔镜胃癌研究与发展委员会及能量外科学院，主持制定腹腔镜胃癌手术指南 1

部，3年来全国腹腔镜手术比例上升了45%。

三、创建全球最大的胃癌样本库，率先开展胃癌组学研究，阐明个体化治疗重要分子机制

1. 最早建立胃癌样本库及管理规范，支撑国内外重大研究

率先于1996年建立国内首个胃癌样本资源库，储存样本21.6万例，随访20年以上，为世界规模最大。编写国内该领域最早的两部著作并确立质量管理规范。支撑国内外重大研究104项，获邀参加国际肿瘤基因组计划。在"十二五"项目支撑下，创建全国多中心恶性肿瘤临床样本资源库，通过共享平台提供重要的样本资源基础。

2. 率先开展胃癌组学研究，识别胃癌复发转移及疗效相关的重要标志物

率先进行胃癌高通量组学研究，识别关键标志物，纠正了国际上对RF1等3个细胞系的错误认知，为人类胃癌细胞系研究提供了重要的数据基础。揭示导致CCND1、ERBB2等癌基因拷贝数增加的基因组结构变异，为胃癌发生发展和药物靶点识别提供了新的证据支持。

针对标志物开展系列研究：①侵袭转移：首次报道C8orf76等分子影响胃癌细胞侵袭转移的机制；②免疫治疗：证实瘤内浸润淋巴细胞与PD-L1表达显著影响胃癌预后；③疗效预测：首次揭示DAP-3缺失导致化疗耐药并影响预后的机制。

3. 揭示胃癌发生细胞起源的关键科学问题

创建CRISPR-Avidin-Biotin ssDNA系统，其Knock-in效率较国际现行方法提高了40倍，突破了胃癌起源和干细胞分化轨迹跟踪等问题的技术瓶颈。阐明胃食管结合部和远端胃双发癌基因特征的差异及克隆独立起源。

Awardee of Medical Sciences and Materia Medica Prize, Ji Jiafu

Ji Jiafu was born in Hohhot City of Inner Mongolia Autonomous Region in December 1959. Since he graduated from Beijing Medical University in 1990, he has served in Peking University Cancer Hospital as an outstanding leader of China's top cancer hospital and nearly all academic associations of medicine, leading all recent technological and theoretical innovations in the treatment and research of gastric cancer in China.

China accounts for 44.1% of gastric cancer patients in the world. As an academic surgeon and educator, Jiafu Ji has been promoting the path-breaking standardized surgery training programs throughout the country, which has revolutionized the surgical practice of gastric cancer in China and has benefited more than 12000 surgeons, leading to a significant increase in the radical resection rate by 25% (67% to 92%), and a decrease in perioperative mortality to 0.24% in

China. He led the first phase Ⅲ trial in the world in the last decade, which confirmed the surgical and oncological safety of laparoscopic gastrectomy in locally advanced cases, resulting in an increase by 45% in the proportion of minimally invasive surgery for gastric cancer in China. As an oncologist, Jiafu Ji promotes the application of multi-disciplinary treatment of gastric cancer and has pioneered neo-adjuvant chemotherapy therapy for gastric cancer in China, which led to a significant increase in 3-year disease-free survival rate by 22% (56% to 78%). As a cancer scientist, he has also established the largest gastric cancer biobank in the world with 216 thousand samples, the first Chinese national clinical database covering 134 thousand gastrointestinal cancer patients, and profiled the Chinese gastric cancer genome. Through high-throughput omics research, his team has successively achieved multi-omics characterization of gastric cancer, identifying critical markers related to gastric cancer recurrence, metastasis and treatment efficacy. His team also created the "CRISPR-Avidin-Biotin ssDNA" system, which has a knock-in efficiency 40 times higher than the current methods, breaking through the technical bottleneck of gastric cancer origin and stem cell differentiation research. These efforts enable elucidation of the molecular mechanism of individualized treatment of gastric cancer.

Focusing on the above-mentioned critical points of gastric cancer aetiology, diagnosis and treatment, his seminal efforts have led to a dramatic 20% increase in gastric cancer survival in China, as well as better accessibility and improvement of health care and research. He was rewarded as the Scholars of Beijing and received the China National Science and Technology Progress Award. In 2017, Jiafu Ji was elected as the president of the International Gastric cancer Association and had been promoting the collaborations between east and west. Jiafu Ji has demonstrated his passion, commitment, and dedication to fighting against gastric cancer with domestic and international peers and colleagues.

医学药学奖获得者

卢 光 明

卢光明，1957年6月出生于湖南省涟源市。东部战区总医院医学影像中心主任、主任医师；南京大学医学院临床综合教研室主任、教授。从事医学影像诊断37年，学术造诣深厚。专注心脑血管病、肿瘤、神经系统疾病等重大疾病诊疗中的关键问题，开拓探索医－生－工结合交叉学科研究模式、创新转化影像诊断技术体系，搭建影像转化前沿研究平台，培养影像创新科技人才；整体提出疾病防治关口前移理念并推广影像实践，取得了突出的科技成就。

一、创立心脑血管疾病防控关口前移的关键影像技术，整体提高我国心脑血管病诊疗水平

心脑血管病是危及人民健康的常见重大疾病。针对心脑血管病快速、无/微创、精准诊断的临床需求，研发应用以双能量CT为主的系列心血管病防治关口前移的创新关键技术，评价其临床安全性、有效性及适应证，建立了心脑血管病CT规范检查的技术和应用体系。创新研发并转化应用系列双能量CT新技术，尤其是肺栓塞的双能量CT技术实现了CT从解剖到功能评估的跨越，提高了外周肺栓塞的检出率（由67%提高至89%）。创建了全身双超低CTA成像技术体系，如使冠状动脉CTA辐射剂量从15.4mSv降至最低0.1mSv，对比剂用量低至30mL，且有高的诊断准确性（93%），为心血管病防控关口前移提供最佳技术保证。研发的双能量CT等系列新技术实现自动化颅骨去除，配合靶血管重组技术，可大幅度提高微小病变检出率（如将颅内小动脉瘤的检出率提高了30%）。依据血流动力学原理研发了双能量CT肺肾依序成像新技术，一次检查同时满足显示肺动脉和肾静脉，优化检查流程，降低对比剂用量（仅为60mL），将肺栓塞和肾静脉血栓危重症的检出率提高到33%和22%，为临床预防抗凝治疗、改善预后提供了科学依据。相关工作发表于本专业国际顶级期刊 *Radiology* 等，被列为北美放射学年会百年庆典纪念文章肺

栓塞双能量 CT 技术主要进展，被写入国际体部 CT 和磁共振协会双能量 CT 白皮书、美国卒中协会蛛网膜下腔出血诊治指南等。主编专著《双能量 CT 应用指南》《全身 CT 血管成像诊断学》，指导并引领中国双能量 CT 及 CT 血管成像的应用。牵头制定了《心血管 CT 辐射剂量优化中国专家共识》《CT 辐射剂量诊断参考水平专家共识》，对规范我国 CT 安全使用起到推动和引领作用。相关成果获国家科技进步奖二等奖和中华医学科技奖一等奖。

二、创立肿瘤微环境分子影像新技术，提出肿瘤影像分子分型新理念，显著提高肿瘤患者诊断准确率

肿瘤微环境与肿瘤之间交互关系复杂，是影响肿瘤精准诊疗的重要因素。提出肿瘤影像分子分型新理念，应用分子影像技术对肿瘤细胞及微环境标志物进行多元精准、实时动态、在体无创观察，并在影像指导下对肿瘤进行精准治疗：研发了基于二氧化硅和金纳米材料的多种分子影像探针，提出"优先刻蚀"的合成新策略，并据此创制了具有垂直介孔和中空柔性结构的分子探针，将药物分子的加载效率提高了 62 倍，肿瘤细胞质富集效率提高了 26 倍；基于上述分子影像探针，创建了肿瘤双重靶向技术，可逆肿瘤微环境 1 个 pH 以内的微小酸度差异，将肿瘤靶向显示能力提高 5 倍；创建了高分辨光声成像技术，在治疗后第 3 天可显示肿瘤新生血管细微变化，提前预测疗效；创建了影像指导下的诊疗一体化技术，使光治疗的有效率从 52% 提高到 98%，将保乳术后肿瘤局部复发率降低了 87%；将 ^{18}F– 阿尔法肽Ⅱ探针向乳腺癌临床患者转化，使诊断敏感性显著提高到 97.6%、阴性预测值提高到 85.7%、阳性预测值提高到 89.1%。相关工作提高了肿瘤精准诊疗水平，显著推动了肿瘤分子影像技术的进步。工作发表于 *Adv Mater*、*J Am Chem Soc*、*J Nucl Med* 等材料学、化学以及影像学权威期刊，被 *Sci Transl Med* 选为研究亮点并配发述评，认为"为肿瘤辅助光热治疗送来了曙光"，入选 ESI 前 1% 高被引论文。相关成果获得江苏省科学技术奖一等奖、华夏医学进步奖一等奖等奖项，作为第一主编编写我国第一部《分子影像学》全国高等学校研究生规划教材。

三、揭示多种脑功能疾病的影像特征，为早期精准诊疗提供重要依据和新手段

针对传统常规结构影像不能显示异常的脑功能性病变，开发了以血氧水平依赖为主的多模态功能 MRI 新技术，创建了用于脑功能异常诊断的生物影像指标。通过长达 25 年的研究，解决了癫痫灶活动 MRI 定位检测的临床关键问题，对病灶隐匿癫痫的分类诊断准确性达到 83.9%；构建癫痫网络影像模型，促进国际抗癫痫联盟癫痫症状新分类癫痫网络理论基础的形成；率先揭示额叶 – 边缘系统脑区功能连接的减低可作为多种应激障碍脑改变的共性影像生物学表征，为创伤应激心理损伤的诊断和鉴别诊断提供了客观稳定的脑影像学信息，诊断敏感性和特异性分别达到 85.2% 和 82.5%。采用全脑功能连接等静息态功能 MRI 新算法揭示皮层（前扣带回）– 基底节 – 丘脑环路损害是肝性脑病认知功能损害的核心，阐明了肝性脑病患者认知功能障碍的神经病理机制。验证了肝性脑病早期诊断的脑功能和血流生物影像指标，如发现动脉自旋标记灌注 MRI 上右侧壳核和前扣带回血流量阈值为 50.6 和 $73mL*min^{-1}*100g^{-1}$ 诊断轻微肝性脑病的敏感性为 93.8% 和 87.5%。相关工作发表于 *Brain*、*Radiology*、*Hum Brain Mapp* 等期刊。组织制定了《磁共振成像安全管理中国专家共识》。相关成果获教育部科技进步奖一等奖 2 项。

Awardee of Medical Sciences and Materia Medica Prize, Lu Guangming

Lu Guangming was born in Lianyuan City of Hunan Province in June 1957. He is currently the director and chief physician of the Medical Imaging Center of the General Hospital of the Eastern Theater Command, and concurrently the director, professor, and doctoral supervisor of the Clinical Teaching and Research Section of Medical School of Nanjing University.

Guangming Lu specializes in the field of medical imaging diagnosis, and has attained prominent achievements in academia. Specializing in major diseases that affect human health—especially cardio cerebral vascular diseases, tumors, and nervous system diseases—he has introduced and developed many advanced medical imaging technologies that improve the accuracy of early diagnoses, as well as advancing prevention and treatment for these diseases.

1. Established key imaging technology for the prevention and control of cardio-cerebrovascular diseases and improved the diagnosis and management level of cardio-cerebrovascular diseases in China

Cardio-cerebrovascular diseases are common and major diseases, undermining the health of the aging demographic group in the population. In response to the clinical needs of rapid, non-/minimally invasive, and accurate diagnosis of cardio- cerebrovascular diseases, he has developed and applied a series of dual-energy CT based innovative key technologies for the prevention and treatment of cardiovascular diseases, evaluated its clinical safety, effectiveness and indications, established the standardized CT technology and application system for cardio-cerebrovascular diseases. He developed and applied of a series of novel dual-energy CT technologies, especially for dual-energy CT technology for pulmonary embolism detection, fulfilling functional evaluation of pulmonary embolism, and improved the detection rate of peripheral pulmonary embolism (67% vs 89%). He has developed whole body double ultra-low CTA technology system, reduced coronary CTA radiation dose from 15.4mSv to a minimum of 0.1mSv and reduced contrast agent volume as low as 30ml, maintained high diagnostic accuracy (93%). He also developed a series of new technologies such as automated skull removal dual-energy CT and target vessel reformation improving the detection of small lesions (for example, the detection rate of intracranial aneurysms increased by 30%). He developed a new combined dual-energy CT pulmonary angiography and renal CT venography based on the hemodynamics principle, which can satisfactorily display pulmonary artery and renal veins with just one scan, optimizing the workflow and reducing contrast medium volume (only 60 mL), improving the detection rates of pulmonary embolism and renal vein thrombosis to 33% and 22%, respectively. His related work was published in the top international journals, such as *Radiology* and so on, and was cited by the 100th Annual meeting commemorative article of the Radiological Society of North America, by dual-energy CT white paper endowed by International Body CT and Magnetic Resonance Association, and American Stroke Association guidelines for diagnosis and treatment of subarachnoid hemorrhage. As an Editor-in-chief, he published the books of "Dual Energy CT Application Guide" and "Whole Body CT Angiography Diagnostics", guiding and leading the application of dual energy CT and CT angiography in China. He also published as corresponding author "Expert Consensus on Optimizing Cardiovascular CT Radiation Dose in China" and "Expert Consensus on Diagnostic Reference Level of CT Radiation Dose", promoting the standardization for safe CT use in China. He has won the second prize of National Science and Technology Progress Award and the first prize of Chinese Medical Science and Technology Award.

2. Established new molecular imaging technologies for tumor microenvironment, significantly improved the diagnostic accuracy of tumor

3. Revealed the imaging characteristics of a variety of brain diseases, providing important neuroimaging basis for their early diagnosis and proper treatment

医学药学奖获得者

沈　锋

沈锋，1962 年 3 月出生于江苏省苏州市。1992 年毕业于第二军医大学肝胆外科学专业，获医学博士学位。1992—1994 年在哈佛大学麻省总医院进行博士后研究。1994 年至今在第二军医大学（海军军医大学）东方肝胆外科医院工作，2005—2006 年担任东方肝胆外科医院医教部主任，2007—2015 年担任东方肝胆外科医院副院长。曾担任国际肝胆胰协会理事、亚太肝脏外科发展委员会主席团副主席、亚太肝胆胰协会理事兼秘书长等学术职位。现任中华医学会肝脏外科学组副组长、中国抗癌协会肝癌专业委员会副主委和全军肝胆外科专业委员会主委，是我国外科学传世之作《黄家驷外科学》第 8 版副主编、《肝癌》主编。

原发性肝癌主要包括肝细胞癌（简称肝癌）和肝内胆管癌（ICC），是我国高发的重大恶性疾病。沈锋从事该病外科治疗 35 年，专注于个体化外科治疗的探索，并独创性地建立了基于临床病理预后预测的个体化外科治疗体系。

一、肝内胆管癌的"中国列线图"分期标准

ICC 恶性程度极高，除外科切除，缺乏有效治疗，不能切除者生存时间仅 3～8 个月，近年来发病率在全球范围内快速上升。

1. 建立国际首个 ICC 个体化分期标准

肿瘤分期是选择治疗的基础。既往国际上根据肿瘤 – 淋巴结 – 转移（TNM）分期方法提出 5 种 ICC 分期。沈锋验证后发现这些分期缺乏个体化预测功能，通过对 449 例患者 10 年随访数据分析和预测技术探索，建立了首个预测个体术后生存概率的列线图分期，发表在肿瘤学权威刊物 *J Clin Oncol*，被国际本领域称为"中国列线图"。

美国肝胆胰协会主席 Jarnagin 教授牵头验证了各种分期，评价中国列线图准确性"最好""良好适用于西方患者"；欧洲学者证实中国列线图的优越性；日本肝癌研究组

（LCSGJ）评价其"精确设计""优于日本全国分期"。国际 12 个中心联合在东西方患者中验证所有分期，报道中国列线图是"唯一"能准确预测预后的分期标准。该病 TNM 分期奠基者 Pawlik 教授评价列线图具有个体化治疗价值；采纳沈锋的学术观点，新一版 TNM 系统做出重要修改，相关技术被推广应用至 23 种其他疾病。

2. 率先提出病因指导 ICC 个体化治疗的观点

胆结石和乙型肝炎是 ICC 最常见病因。沈锋发现结石相关 ICC 的侵袭转移能力远高于乙肝相关 ICC，提出病因指导 ICC 个体化治疗的观点。针对病因，提出用宽切缘切除胆结石 ICC，抗病毒抑制乙肝相关 ICC 的复发，显著提高了疗效。基于他的发现，国际 15 个中心联合验证并证实病因对 ICC 个体化治疗的独特价值。

3. 系统创新 ICC 外科治疗技术

沈锋团队完成 42 项 ICC 临床研究，在国际上首次用病理学证据证实淋巴结切除具有根治性；用列线图预测建立个体化放射介入抗复发方案，使 5 年复发率降低 5.5%；建立预后评分标准筛选适合再切除的复发后 ICC，使再切除后 3 年生存率达到 35.3%。

沈锋团队施行国际最大量 ICC 手术（3200 例），理论和技术创新使 5 年生存率达到 35.2%，被国际本领域研究大量引用，代表目前该病外科治疗水平；10 年生存率达到 8.4%，是国际上该病患者生存超过 10 年的唯一报道。发表该病临床 SCI 论著 71 篇；纳入 4 个国际指南。沈锋的工作推动国际 ICC 个体化外科治疗的起步和进步，为确立我国该病治疗的国际领先地位发挥了重要作用。

二、肝癌的"预测生存、预测微血管侵犯"治疗选择策略

精准选择肝癌治疗是本领域的重大学术问题。鉴于肝癌缺乏分子分型指导个体化决策、病情复杂多样，沈锋独创性地基于临床病理大数据建立了针对 7 种不同病情的个体化预后预测关键技术，借此实现的决策方法如下。

1. 用"预测生存"个体化筛选适合肝切除的患者

肝切除是肝癌最常用治疗方法。对于临床常见的多发性肝癌，国际上基于传统肿瘤分期建立的 12 种肝切除选择标准（包括国际巴塞罗那标准）备受争议。沈锋创用此类肝癌的不同发生机制筛选患者（肝内转移所致者疗效差，多中心发生者疗效好），并发现了术前区别两种机制的影像学特征，借此建立生存预测评分（NDR）。以 NDR 选择患者，使术后 5 年生存率达到 44.7%，显著优于欧美和日韩的报道，获得国际同行的验证和高度肯定。

2. 用"预测微血管侵犯（MVI）"个体化选择治疗方法

肝癌有肝切除、消融、肝移植等多种治疗，如何选择是国际焦点问题。近年来，用预测 MVI（肝癌转移的病理标志）进行治疗选择成为国内外关注的全新策略。沈锋在国际上最早提出预测 MVI 可用于选择治疗，通过临床病理大数据建立国际首个 MVI 个体化预测模型，为选择治疗提供关键性工具。同时证实了 MVI 预测的实用价值。系列研究发

表在外科首位刊物——美国医学会会刊·外科学（*JAMA Surg*）等。*JAMA Surg* 以"术前评估迈出新的一步"为标题发表述评，评价他"对挑战性问题做出令人感兴趣的贡献"。

三、肝癌的基于风险预测的复发防治新方法

肝癌术后 5 年复发率超过 70%，是本领域的重大疑难问题。

1. 基于"复发风险预测和靶抗原表达"进行肝癌复发预防

沈锋通过进一步甄别术后复发转移的高危因素，建立风险预测评分，并证实介入治疗等使高风险者的复发率降低 17.5%；组织多中心随机对照试验，建立国际首个肝切除术后靶向放射免疫抗复发技术（使用针对 HAb18G/CD147 抗原的 ^{131}I- 美妥昔单抗），使抗原阳性者的早期复发率降低 35.9%。*Lancet Gastroenterol Hepatol* 评价其工作是将肝癌标志物与靶向治疗相结合的重要和独特的研究。

2. 基于高强度证据提出肝癌复发治疗选择标准

再切除和消融是肝癌复发后的最常用治疗，但国际大量研究对如何选择分歧较大。沈锋开展国际唯一一项随机对照研究，发现再切除对复发肝癌 >3 cm、甲胎蛋白 >200 ng/mL 者的疗效显著优于消融，首次为治疗决策提供高等级证据；结合大量技术改进，使复发患者的 5 年生存率达到 68.4%，优于国际报道。

综合应用抗复发新技术，使 5 年总体复发率下降了 21.2%，相关工作得到诸多国际学术组织、权威刊物和学者的高度肯定，部分成果纳入国际肝癌协会《肝癌诊治专家共识》等 5 个国际指南。

Awardee of Medical Sciences and Materia Medica Prize, Shen Feng

Shen Feng was born in Suzhou City of Jiangsu Province in March 1962. He received his medical degree（1992）from Second Military Medical University. He spent two years at the Massachusetts General Hospital as a surgical pathology research fellow（1992–1994）. Feng currently is the chief surgeon and professor of the Third Affiliated Hospital（the Eastern Hepatobiliary Surgery Hospital）of Naval Medical University. He also serves as the Vice Director of the Liver Surgery Group of Chinese Medical Association, the Vice Director of the Liver Cancer Committee of Chinese Anti-Cancer Association, and the Chairman of the Military Hepatobiliary Surgery Association. Feng's international contributions have been recognized through his appointments to Member at Large of the International Hepato-Pancreato-Biliary Association（IHPBA）and Secretary of the Asian-Pacific Hepato-Pancreato-Biliary Association（A-PHPBA）.

Feng has been engaged in the surgical treatment of primary liver cancer（PLC）for 35 years.

He has creatively established an individualized treatment system based on prognostic prediction using clinicopathological data. His academic effort effectively promotes the treatment of PLC. For the treatment of intrahepatic cholangiocarcinoma (ICC), one of highly aggressive tumors in PLC, Dr. Feng established the first prognostic nomogram to facilitate individualized surgical treatment for ICC, which was designated "Chinese nomogram" by international colleagues. With this accurate tool and his other achievements in the surgical technique, Dr. Feng achieved leading long-term surgical prognosis of ICC. For the treatment of hepatocellular carcinoma (HCC), Dr. Feng proposed a new concept of "predicting survival probability, and predicting microvascular invasion" to assist precise selection of candidate for different therapeutic modalities and effectively making treatment decision. Based on the results of a serial important and original studies, Dr. Feng carried out relapse prevention for HCC according to recurrence-risk prediction and target antigen expression. Based on high-level evidence from the only randomized clinical trial in the world, he put forward the reasonable selection between surgical resection and ablation for recurrent HCC.

Feng and his colleagues have carried out nearly 10000 hepatobiliary operations and he is also dedicated to spreading new theories and technologies in the hepatobiliary surgery, which resulting in his outstanding contributions in China. Dr. Feng is a hepatobiliary surgeon with high academic standing.

医学药学奖获得者

吴 德 沛

吴德沛，1958年10月出生于江苏省徐州市。主任医师、教授、博士生导师。1982年获苏州医学院学士学位并留校任职，长期从事临床医疗、教学和科研工作。1988年和1998年先后获苏州医学院内科学（血液病学）硕士和博士学位。1992—1994年在法国南特大学中心医院担任访问学者，研修造血干细胞临床移植技术。回国后，受聘苏州大学附属第一医院主任医师、教授、血液科主任。先后担任江苏省血液研究所副所长、苏州大学造血干细胞移植研究所所长、国家血液系统疾病临床医学研究中心常务副主任。现任中华医学会血液学分会主任委员、中国医师协会血液科医师分会副会长、中华医学会内科学分会常务委员、欧洲血液与骨髓移植协会（EBMT）全球委员会委员、*Journal of Hematology & Oncology* 副主编、*Chinese Medical Journal* 编委、《中华血液学杂志》副总编。

吴德沛从业近40年，致力于血液系统疾病的基础和临床研究，带领团队成员在血液恶性肿瘤和出凝血异常的精准诊疗、造血干细胞移植体系的优化等方面做出了系列开创性研究工作，成功主持完成了江苏省首例非血缘台湾供髓造血干细胞移植，为医学发展和患者健康带来了深远的积极影响。基于此，苏州大学附属第一医院血液学科获批成为国家血液系统疾病临床医学研究中心。

带领项目组在国内率先建立高效遗传学诊断平台，培养了全国80%的遗传学诊断专业人员。发现两类白血病遗传学新亚型，被纳入 WHO 诊断标准；建立了5株白血病细胞系，成为国际白血病研究的通用工具；阐明了急性红白血病、变异型急性早幼粒细胞白血病等发病关键分子机制，显著提升了中国白血病研究的国际影响力；阐明了骨髓增生异常综合征（MDS）遗传学亚型演化机制，创建分子遗传学检测技术并应用于临床。牵头国家"十一五"科技支撑计划，制订了首个中国人群 MDS 去甲基化药物（地西他滨）推荐治疗方案，改写药物说明书；主持编写了中国首部 MDS 诊治指南，提高了规范化诊疗水平。

带领项目组建立血液系统疾病出凝血异常精准诊断技术体系，创建移植相关出凝血异常、免疫性血小板减少、血栓性血小板减少性紫癜等诊疗新方案，5 株苏州单抗成为国际标准试剂。主持编写了 2 部中国诊疗共识，成果写入国内外 12 部指南。相关成果获得2019 年国家科技进步奖二等奖。

创建了单倍型供体与第三方脐血共移植的双重移植体系、干扰素活化的供体淋巴细胞输注治疗移植后复发新疗法和移植后并发症综合防治技术体系。带领科室年移植量达700 余例，累积移植量超 5000 例，规模位于全球前五、全国第二，总生存率较欧洲血液与骨髓移植学会同类患者提高了 11%，获圣安东尼 –EBMT 骨髓移植成就奖。

此外，吴德沛在 CAR-T 细胞治疗技术的创新与优化、骨髓衰竭性疾病的诊治优化等方面也做出了创新工作，由其带领的移植团队配型技术获美国权威学会 ASHI 认证，成为中国大陆唯一获此资质的机构。

吴德沛以通讯作者 / 第一作者身份发表 SCI 收录论文 163 篇，其中包括 *JAMA Oncol*、*Blood*、*Leukemia* 等血液 / 肿瘤领域内顶级期刊论文 13 篇以及骨髓移植最高期刊 BMT、BBMT 论文 28 篇。主编首部血液内科住院医生规培教材，主编专著 10 部，参编《内科学》统编教材 6 部。牵头制定国内指南 / 共识 5 部。获国家发明专利 3 项。培养博士研究生 47 名、硕士研究生 64 名，其中血液领域学科带头人 8 名。以第一完成人获国家科技进步奖二等奖 2 项，以第四完成人获国家科技进步奖二等奖 1 项；以第一完成人获教育部高等学校科学研究优秀成果奖一等奖 1 项、二等奖 1 项，江苏省科学技术奖一等奖 1 项，中华医学科技奖二等奖 1 项；获第十八届吴阶平 – 保罗·杨森医学药学个人奖和圣安东尼 –EBMT 个人成就奖。荣获全国劳动模范和先进工作者、中国好医生、全国优秀科技工作者、江苏省先进工作者、最美基层共产党员、国之名医卓越建树专家（人民网）等称号。

Awardee of Medical Sciences and Materia Medica Prize, Wu Depei

Wu Depei was born in Xuzhou City of Jiangsu Province in October 1958. He is chief physician, professor of medicine and tutor of medical doctor. He obtained Master Degree and Doctor Degree of internal medicine at Suzhou Medical College in 1988 and 1998, respectively. From 1992 to 1994, he visited Central Hospital of Nantes University for learning clinical technologies of hematopoietic stem cell transplantation（HSCT）. Over past 40 years, he is dedicated to the scientific and clinical researches focusing on hematological malignancies and HSCT. Currently, as a State-Council Allowance Obtained Expert, he is the director of the hematological department of the First Affiliated Hospital of Soochow University, deputy director of National Clinical Research Center for Hematologic Diseases, and director of Institute of Blood and Marrow Transplantation of Soochow University. In addition, he is also a member of the national committee of CPPCC, the president of Chinese Society of Hematology, vice chairman of Chinese Hematologist Association, standing member of Chinese Society of Internal Medicine, and member of Global Committee of EBMT. So far, as first author or corresponding author, he has published 163 articles on SCI journals including top journals in the field such as *JAMA Oncology*, *Blood*, *Leukemia*, etc. He is the chief editor of 10 academic books, including the first edition of textbook for residents' standardized training. He also participates in the formation of 6 editions of state-compiled textbook. Totally, 111 of his students have gained the master or doctor degree. He has acquired the National Prize for Progress in Science and Technology (second level) for twice as the first contributor, and once as the forth contributor. Other achievements include the 18th Wu Jieping–Paul Janssen Award, Saint–Antoine–EBMT Achievement, National Advanced Worker and Best Doctor in China, etc.

医学药学奖获得者

徐 兵 河

徐兵河，1958年2月出生于湖北省大冶市。1999年获中国协和医科大学医学博士学位。1991—1993年赴美国迈阿密大学医学院做研究工作，1993年回国至今在中国医学科学院肿瘤医院工作，任内科主任医师，先后担任内科副主任和主任。目前担任国家抗肿瘤药物临床研究中心主任，国家肿瘤质控中心乳腺癌专家委员会主任委员，国家癌症中心乳腺癌筛查与早诊早治专家委员会主任委员，国家抗肿瘤药物临床监测专家委员会主任委员，国家"重大新药创制"重大专项论证专家委员会成员，St. Gallen早期乳腺癌治疗国际专家共识指南团成员、晚期乳腺癌治疗国际专家共识指南团成员、欧洲肿瘤内科学会（ESMO）和欧洲肿瘤学院（ESCO）核心成员，北京协和医学院长聘教授。

带领团队30多年来专注乳腺癌领域前沿理论及技术研究，在乳腺癌的筛查早诊、个体化治疗和肿瘤耐药等方面做出了一系列的开创性研究工作。

一、乳腺癌的早期诊断

创建适合我国国情及女性乳房特征、以风险评估为基础的超声结合X线的乳腺癌个体化筛查新方法，发现可显著影响乳腺癌患病风险并可提高筛查效率的易感标记物，开辟了乳腺癌筛查早诊新方向；研究成果应用于248万女性，将I期诊断率从19%提高到筛查队列的66%，为我国乳腺癌早期诊断做出突出贡献。

二、乳腺癌的个体化治疗研究

自20世纪90年代末开始个体化治疗研究，主持我国第一个乳腺癌个体化治疗国家科技攻关项目，在治疗新策略、新模式和新技术等关键领域取得重大突破。建立了血清HER2蛋白的测定方法，率先开展单核苷酸多态与化疗敏感性研究。创建以分子分型为突破的个体化治疗新策略：国际上首创HER2阳性乳腺癌跨线治疗新模式；通过前瞻性随机分组临床研究，发现铂类药物治疗三阴性乳腺癌疗效显著；发现 CYP2D6 基因变异与管腔型乳腺癌内分泌药物治疗效果相关，创建了该基因指导下的内分泌治疗新技术，将患者 5 年生存率从 67.9% 显著提升到 90.9%。

三、乳腺癌的多药耐药研究

20 世纪 80 年代末，在国内首先提出乳腺癌多药耐药（MDR）概念并开展系列研究，发现 DNA 烷化剂耐药与谷胱甘肽（GSH）/ 谷胱甘肽转移酶（GST）相关，成为 90 年代初这一领域发表论文最多的中国研究者；发现 PAM 信号传导通路异常与 HER2 阳性乳腺癌耐药相关，为精准指导个体化治疗提供了新方法；创建克服 MDR 的新策略及新方案，开创了我国抗肿瘤创新药吡咯替尼基于 II 期临床研究结果快速审批上市的先河。

上述原创性成果发表于 *Lancet Oncology*、*Journal of Clinical Oncology*、*Annals of Oncology*、*Cancer Research* 等著名期刊，多次入选国内外乳腺癌年度重要进展，改变了乳腺癌诊疗临床实践，推动我国乳腺癌诊疗水平快速发展并跃居国际先进行列。

主持制订我国共识、规范和指南 18 部，系列成果被国内外指南采纳。获国家发明专利 8 项，出版专著 14 部。以第一完成人获国家科技进步奖二等奖 1 项、省部级奖励 14 项（其中一等奖 5 项），获第二届全国创新争先奖状。

Awardee of Medical Sciences and Materia Medica Prize, Xu Binghe

Xu Binghe was born in Daye City of Hubei Province in February 1958. He received his medical doctor's degree from Peking Union Medical College in 1999. From 1991 to 1993, he worked as a postdoctoral researcher at the University of Miami School of Medicine. Since returning to China in 1993, he has been working in cancer Hospital, Chinese Academy of Medical Sciences. He has been the chief physician for 22 years and has successively served as deputy director and director of Department of Medical Oncology. He is currently the director of the National Clinical Research Center for Anti-cancer Drugs, the Breast Cancer Expert Committee of the National Cancer Quality control Center, the National Cancer Center Breast Cancer Screening and Early Diagnosis Expert Committee the National Anti-cancer Drug Clinical Monitoring Expert Committee and the member of the National Expert Committee for the Demonstration of Major Projects of "Major New Drug Innovation and Production". He is also the panel member of the St. Gallen International Consensus on the Primary Therapy of Early Breast Cancer and ESO-ESMO as well as the faculty member of ESMO (European School of Medical Oncology) and ESCO (College of the European School of Oncology). He is a professor of Peking Union Medical College.

He has been leading the team to focus on the frontier theory and technology research in the field of breast cancer for more than 30 years, and has made a series of pioneering research work in the aspects of early detection, individualized treatment and drug resistant to breast cancer.

1. The early diagnosis of breast cancer

He created a new method of individual screening for breast cancer combining ultrasound and X-ray, which is based on risk assessment and is suitable for China's national conditions and female breast characteristics. He found susceptible markers that can significantly affect the risk of breast cancer and may improve the screening efficiency. The research results were applied to 2.48 million women, increasing the stage I diagnosis rate from 19% to 66% of the screening cohort, making an outstanding contribution to the early diagnosis of breast cancer in China.

2. Individualized treatment of breast cancer

Since the late 1990s, he has been conducting the first national scientific and technological research project on individualized treatment of breast cancer in China, and has made great breakthroughs in the key fields of new treatment strategies and technologies. He established a assay for serum HER2 protein and was the first to conduct single nucleotide polymorphism and chemotherapeutic sensitivity studies in China. He created a new strategy for individualized treatment that broke through with molecular typing: he proposed retreatment of anti-HER2 targeted therapy for advanced HER2-positive breast cancer; he was the first to find significant efficacy of platinum-based drugs in the treatment of triple negative breast cancer in a prospective randomized trial; he found that the variation of was related to the efficacy of endocrine drugs in Chinese breast cancer patients, and proposed and implemented individualized endocrine therapy for breast cancer based on the gene polymorphsim of CYP2D6, which significantly increased the 5-year survival rate of patients from 67.9% to 90.9%.

3. Multidrug resistance in breast cancer

In the late 1980s, he first put forward the concept of multi-drug resistance (MDR) in breast cancer in China and carried out a series of studies. He found that DNA alkylating agent resistance was related to glutathione transferase system, and became the Chinese researcher who published the most papers in this field in the early 1990s. He found that abnormalities in PAM signaling pathways were associated with HER2-positive breast cancer resistance, providing a new approach for precise individualized treatment. He created new strategies and regimens to overcome MDR. His works contributed to the rapid approval of pyrotinib, a new targeted drug, based on a phase II clinical trial in China.

The above original research results have been published in top international journals such as Lancet Oncology, Journal of Clinical Oncology, Annals of Oncology, Cancer Research, etc. They have been selected as important annual advances in breast Cancer both at home and abroad for several times, which have changed the clinical practice of breast Cancer treatment and promoted the rapid development of the diagnosis and treatment of breast Cancer in China.

He has won the second prize of National Science and Technology Progress award, 14 provincial and ministerial awards (including 5 first prizes) and the second National Award for Innovation. He presided over the formulation of 18 consensus, norms and guidelines on the diagnosis and treatment of breast cancer in China. A series of results have been cited by domestic and foreign guidelines. He has obtained 8 national invention patents and published 14 books.

医学药学奖获得者

朱　兰

朱兰，女，1964年3月出生于江苏省常熟市。1989年于北京协和医院妇产科工作至今。1997—1999年作为访问学者，先后在香港中文大学威尔斯亲王医院妇科分子生物学实验室和澳大利亚新南威尔士大学妇科及妇科泌尿中心研究交流。2004—2020年担任北京协和医院普通妇科中心主任，2020年8月起任北京协和医院妇产科主任。现任中华医学会妇产科分会候任主任委员，中华医学会妇产科分会妇科盆底学组组长，中国医师协会妇产科分会常委兼总干事，中国预防医学会盆底疾病防治专委会主任委员，中华全国妇女联合会第十二届常务委员，国家自然科学基金二审评审专家。兼任《中国计划生育与妇产科》主编、《中华妇产科杂志》副主编、*International Urogynecology Journal* 编委。

朱兰从事妇产科尤其是女性盆底学和女性生殖道畸形方面的临床及基础研究，从疾病的发病机制入手，探索新的治疗术式和规范制定。

一、自主创新适合我国国情的系列盆底重建技术新体系

创建适合国情和国人盆骨特点的具有自主知识产权的系列盆底重建术，向全国推广应用，突破国际垄断。研制出可重复使用、具有自主知识产权的系列盆底缝合器，创建了适合国人盆骨特点的"协和式盆底重建术""坐骨棘筋膜固定术"等系列经济实用的盆底重建术，比以往传统术式治愈率提高30%。提出盆底重建手术优化策略，显著降低了手术并发症，写入国际指南。牵头制定中国盆底功能障碍性疾病临床诊治规范及指南和临床路径，建立全国盆底重建手术并发症数据库。作为国际妇科泌尿协会学术委员会的唯一中国代表，参与国际指南的修订工作，推动与国际接轨的规范化诊疗技术。首次把生物3D打印技术应用于盆底重建，研发出具有自主知识产权的、适合中国人生理特点的盆底修复及重建产品，实现临床转化零突破，国产化产品已应用临床。

二、主持完成国家层面五万人群的尿／粪失禁、脱垂、性功能障碍的流行病学调查，为政府决策提供科学数据

首次完成中国成年女性尿失禁及下尿路症状、盆腔器官脱垂、女性性功能障碍的全国流行病学和国内最大样本量的成年女性粪失禁的流行病学调查，阐明了发病的主因和危险因素。严谨、科学、大样本流调为政府制定盆底疾病早诊早治决策提供了科学数据。研究结果被妇产科专科权威杂志登载，单篇引用次数已达 200 余次。

三、从组织形态、神经病理及女性激素水平等方面揭示盆底疾病发病机制

系统揭示了组织形态、神经病理与女性盆底疾病的病因、发病机制间的关联性。发现了盆底疾病的支持组织（结构）异常组织形态学特征，首次阐明了雌激素受体与 SUI 发生的关系，发现了雌激素补充疗法治疗 SUI 不佳的原因；盆底组织神经肽及其受体的研究解释了并非所有 POP 患者均发生 SUI 的临床疑惑。研究结果两次被国际妇产科杂志评为最佳研究奖。

四、建立中国盆底康复防治三级模式

在前期流行病学及基础研究的基础上，与中华预防医学会共同牵头开展全国层面的"中国女性盆底功能障碍防治项目"，以电生理技术为主要诊断和干预手段，探索、建立并推广中国盆底康复筛查中心、诊治中心、技术指导中心三级综合防治模式，成立中华预防医学会盆底疾病防治专委会。举办"中国妇女盆底功能障碍防治项目技术培训班"50多期，培训 2 万多名医护人员，5000 多人获中华预防医学会"中国妇女盆底功能障碍防治研讨班"结业证书。全国开展盆底康复筛查及治疗稳步增长，项目开展单位达 2160 家，盆底筛查惠及人群达 1000 万人，真正做到"关口前移治未病"，为早诊早治盆底疾病开辟了良好局面。获得 2017 年中华预防医学会科技进步奖一等奖。

五、创建系列女性生殖道畸形矫正术式

传承协和疑难罕见病诊治优势，经过 30 余年临床实践取得了国际领先成果。国际上首创具有自主知识产权的生物补片法人工阴道成形术，在国内数百家医院推广应用，得到国际同行认可；创建系列生殖道畸形矫正新术式，显著改善患者生理功能。提出保护生育功能的生殖道畸形诊疗新策略，效果显著。阴道斜隔切除术取代了传统开腹患侧子宫切除术，达到了患者术后 85% 妊娠的理想疗效。同时，建立了逾千例国际最大的中国多中心女性下生殖道畸形临床及生物标本数据库。

以第一作者或通讯作者发表论文 400 余篇，其中 SCI 论文 150 余篇，单篇最高他引231 次；获专利 8 项；出版专著 14 部，包括应 Springer 邀请主编国际第一部生殖道畸形英文专著；获得国家科技进步奖二等奖 2 项。以第一完成人获中华预防医学会科学技术

奖一等奖、华夏医学科技奖一等奖、北京市科技进步奖二等奖、全国第九届青年科技奖和中国第二届女医师五洲女子科技奖等。

Awardee of Medical Sciences and Materia Medica Prize, Zhu Lan

Zhu Lan, female, was born in Changshu City of Jiangsu Province in March 1964. She has been working at Peking Union Medical College Hospital（PUMCH）for 31 years and is the supervisor of MD and Ph.D candidates. Professor Zhu was the director of general gynecology center，department of Obstetrics and Gynecology，PUMCH from 2004 to 2020. She was elected as the director of the department of Obstetrics and Gynecology，PUMCH in August，2020. She is now the president designate of Chinese Society of Obstetrics and Gynecology，Chinese Medical Association；standing committee member and general secretary of society of Obstetrics and Gynecology，Chinese Medical Doctor Association；President of society of Pelvic Floor Disease Prevention，Chinese Preventive Medicine Association and president of the Urogynecology & Reconstructive Pelvic Surgery Society，Chinese Medical Association.

As the principle investigator，she has completed multi state-class and ministry-class projects. At present，she is in charge of several projects funded by Natural Science Foundation of China and National Industry Foundation. As the first author or corresponding author，she has published more than 140 SCI indexed papers and hundreds of papers on national key professional journals. She is the owner of 12 medical patents and she is the chief editor and translator of many academic publications.

In 2019，she won the first prize of Chinese scientific and technological progress award as the first accomplisher. In 2016，she was awarded the national "March 8th Red-Banner Holder" by All-China Women's Federation. In 2013，she won the first prize of Scientific and technological progress award granted by National Ministry of Education. In 2010，she won the first prize of Beijing municipal scientific and technological progress award by Beijing Government. In 2007，she won the first prize of scientific and technological progress award by National Ministry of Education.

机械电力技术奖获得者

何 湘 宁

何湘宁，1961 年 5 月出生于湖南省长沙市。1982 年和 1985 年分别获南京航空学院（现南京航空航天大学）学士和硕士学位，1989 年获浙江大学博士学位。1985—1986 年在航空工业总公司 608 研究所任助理工程师。1991 年获英国皇家学会皇家奖学金，赴英国 Heriot-Watt University 从事博士后研究。1994 年回国，在浙江大学电机系任教。1999—2002 年作为访问教授分别在美国 University of California at Irvine、澳大利亚 Monash University 从事合作研究。何湘宁是国务院学位委员会第八届学科评议组成员（电气工程），国家自然科学基金委员会工程与材料科学部第九、第十、第十三、第十四届专家评审组成员。1997 年以来，担任过浙江大学学位委员会委员、电工学科学位委员会主任、电力电子技术研究所所长、应用电子学系主任、电气工程学院副院长等。现为浙江大学电力电子技术国家专业实验室主任。英国电气工程师学会会士，美国电气与电子工程师学会会士。

何湘宁长期从事电力电子领域的科学技术和工程应用研究，在电力电子变换拓扑理论和调控方法上取得了系统的创造性学术成就。原创性成果不仅在国际同行中享有极高学术声誉，确立了我国电力变换拓扑与控制相关研究的国际引领地位，而且被国内外著名机构、工业界大量引用和广泛应用，取得了显著的社会和经济效益。发表 SCI/EI 论文 156/392 篇，论著总他引 17306 次，其中 Web of Science 他引 5821 次、中国知网他引 7290 次；授权国家发明专利 63 件。曾获 2016 年国家自然科学奖二等奖、2013 年国家技术发明奖二等奖、47 届瑞士日内瓦国际发明展览会金奖和省部级科技成果一等奖 5 项。

一、高增益电力变换的多自由度调控机制和电路拓扑构造理论

电力电子变换技术改变电能形态，以实现源／网／荷端交直流形式多样化，既支撑常规交流电网向新一代交直流混联电网的转变，又极大提升荷端电能使用效率，已成为新能源、高速牵引、智能电网、国防装备中电能系统的基础与核心。然而，源（如光伏、储能等）和网/荷端的电压落差巨大，使得电力变换低效，装备极端条件运行。电压的高增益适配和高效率转换是长期困扰该学科的科学难题。

何湘宁率先从调控自由度的视角探索电压增益极限与适配这一学科前沿问题，创建新增调控自由度、电磁应力和电压增益的相互作用模型，发现多自由度协同运行机制。提出的多自由度调控结构把升压倍数从不到10倍大幅拓展到40多倍（甚至更高），电压转换灵活适配，消除极端运行条件，实现了从单自由度调节到多自由度调控的根本转变。进一步提出电压增益拓展单元概念，不仅涵盖已有的高增益变换结构，而且还可推演出系列新型拓扑族，从而创建了高增益变换拓扑的普适构造理论，成为国内外高增益电路拓扑形成准则。该成果揭示了高增益电力变换多自由度调控和拓扑构造的基本规律，确立了高增益变换理论和方法研究的国际引领地位，解决了国防型号装备与工业电源系统实现高功率密度/高效率变换的关键科学问题。成果获国家自然科学奖二等奖，这也是电力电子学科首个国家自然科学奖。

二、基本单元串－并协同的多电平变换原理、控制方法和容错策略

随着电网、高铁、储能等能源动力产业的迅猛发展，其核心电力变换装备容量已达百/千兆瓦等级。但长期以来，已有拓扑和控制无法解决大容量装备性能提升难题。何湘宁坚持基础研究与工程应用结合，在多电平拓扑理论、控制策略和容错技术上取得显著成果。

提出了多电平结构基本单元的概念和基本单元串－并（并－串）协同的多电平电路拓扑统一构造原理，已成为多电平通用拓扑研究的两大方法之一，可涵盖目前高压传动领域应用最广的级联型拓扑以及柔性直流输电工程中应用最多的模块化多电平拓扑。提出控制自由度融合的多电平调制方法，导出系列全新PWM脉冲，谐波含量可减少80%以上。出版首部含多电平变换器故障容错和冗余设计方法的专著。该成果被麻省理工学院、帝国理工等世界名校及GE、ABB等跨国公司的专家学者大量引用和应用。理论方法和技术发明应用支撑了系列大容量电力传动系统升级换代，性能水平迈入世界一流，产品应用于众多国家重点工程，满足了国家对高端装备的重大需求。获国家技术发明奖二等奖。

三、电力电子变换原理和工程应用的多学科交叉研究

等离子体放电特种电源是环境保护、生物医疗、材料处理等工程领域的核心装备。特种电源高频调控是电力电子、等离子体物理及相关工程学科交叉研究的突出难题，需要普适意义的新原理和方法。何湘宁提出宽频域多参数配置的高频特种电源测试方法，为多参数解耦控制提供了科学依据。提出脉冲密度/宽度协同的负荷顺应性技术，实现了非线性强时变负荷下大范围线性调功和稳定放电。提出的高频电力变换网－荷主动匹配与参数综合调控方法实现了等离子体特种电源设计从经验主导型向理论指导型转变。研

制我国首套超大功率高频高压等离子体电晕处理机电源系统。开发系列表面处理特种电源装备，产品广泛应用于军工、环保、医疗等国家安全和民生的重大领域。

自电力电子技术诞生以来，人们对它的理解和研究仅停留在电能变换和功率调控的层面。何湘宁和研究团队发现了电力电子变换的信息本征属性，从本质上揭示了电能变换与信息调制过程的一致性。在此基础上，提出了基于电力电子变换的功率调控与数据交互深度融合的调制方法，无须附加通信硬件和相关软件，即可实现能量与信息的同步调制与协同传输，大大扩展和提升了电力电子变换器的综合性能。此科学发现发表在 *Nature Communications*，为电力电子与通信技术学科的交叉研究奠定了理论基础。

Awardee of Machinery and Electric Technology Prize, He Xiangning

He Xiangning was born in Changsha City of Hunan Province in May 1961. He received the B.Sc. and M.Sc. degrees from Nanjing University of Aeronautical and Astronautical, Nanjing, China, in 1982 and 1985 respectively, and the Ph.D degree from Zhejiang University, Hangzhou, China, in 1989.

From 1985 to 1986, he was an Assistant Engineer at the 608 Institute of Aeronautical Industrial General Company, Zhuzhou, China. From 1989 to 1991, he was a Lecturer at Zhejiang University. In 1991, he obtained the Royal Fellowship from the Royal Society of U.K., and conducted research in the Department of Computing and Electrical Engineering, Heriot-Watt University, Edinburgh, U.K., as a Post-Doctoral Research Fellow for two years. In 1994, he joined Zhejiang University as an Associate Professor. Since 1996, he has been a Full Professor in the College of Electrical Engineering, Zhejiang University. He was the Director of the Power Electronics Research Institute, the Head of the Department of Applied Electronics, Vice Dean of the College of Electrical Engineering and he is currently the Director of the National Specialty Laboratory for Power Electronics, Zhejiang University. Dr. He worked as a visiting/guest professor for cooperation research in U.S.A. in 1999 and in Australia in 2002.

He is the PI of 12 international joint projects with universities and companies in U.S.A., U.K., Japan, Netherlands and so on. He is the PI for more than 50 national, provincial and industrial research and development projects. His achievements in power electronics modeling and simulation, as well as active and passive lossless soft-switching of power converters are highly recognized by international and national experts in power electronics community. His achievements in multi-level converters topologies and PWM control, regulation methods and circuits formation of high step-up power conversion, and distributed structure and control of power electronics system are widely cited and applied worldwide. His achievements applied to the organic material processing, environmental protection and renewable electricity generation, which are the cross-disciplinary subjects, have made great contribution to the nation. He has published more than 500 papers indexed by SCI and/or EI, and held more than 60 patents. His research and development work has won the State Natural Science Award, State Technology Invention Award, Golden Prize of Geneva International Invention Exhibition, and five provincial and ministerial Scientific and Technological Progress awards.

机械电力技术奖获得者

宋永华

宋永华，1964 年 1 月出生于四川省巴中市。1984 年获成都科技大学（现四川大学）电气工程学士学位；1989 年获中国电力科学研究院博士学位。1989—1991 年任清华大学电机系博士后研究员。1991—1996 年先后就职于英国布里斯托大学、巴斯大学、利物浦约翰摩尔斯大学；1997—2006 年任英国布鲁奈尔大学教授、副校长（2004—2006 年）；2007—2008 年任英国利物浦大学教授、副校长、西交利物浦大学执行校长；2009—2012 年先后任清华大学电机系教授、清华大学校长助理，国家海外高层次人才引进工作专项办公室主任；2012—2017 年任浙江大学常务副校长、教授，浙江大学国际联合学院创院院长；2018 年至今任澳门大学校长、智慧城市物联网国家重点实验室主任、讲座教授。英国皇家工程院院士，欧洲科学院院士（外籍），国际欧亚科学院院士，国际电气电子工程师学会会士，英国工科技术学会会士，中国电机工程学会首批会士，中国电工技术学会副理事长，第九和第十届中国电机工程学会副理事长，中国教育发展战略学会副会长，澳门特区政府科技委员会顾问，澳门科学技术协进会名誉会长，澳门中华教育会副会长。曾荣获英国布鲁奈尔大学科学博士学位、巴斯大学荣誉工程博士学位和爱丁堡大学荣誉理学博士学位。

宋永华长期从事电力系统清洁安全高效运行领域的重大科学与技术问题的理论研究和实际应用工作。在英国工作期间，针对电力系统高效与安全运行紧密耦合的复杂数学优化问题，建立兼顾经济指标与技术约束的安全分析模型，成为国际通用的电力系统分析软件 PSAT 的基础模型；为所有类型的 FACTS 装置建立了统一的潮流稳态模型，可用于任意结构的 FACTS 装置以及大规模实际系统的分析与优化，出版了灵活交流输电领域的世界上第一部英文专著；率先开展现代优化理论的应用研究，攻克了一系列大规模、含复杂约束与多时段耦合的电力系统优化难题。其成果获评"在先进计算技术应用于重组后电力系统运行控制方面取得国际认可的领先成果，不仅提出新的概念和方法，而且将他的理念付诸实际应用"。

2009 年回国后，宋永华重点聚焦于电力系统需求侧灵活资源参与调控的理论和关键技术。围绕随机性新能源电力的大规模消纳这一世界性难题，在我国发电侧调节资源已较为充分利用的情况下，提出了挖掘需求侧负荷调控潜力参与新能源电力系统运行的新理论，探索出了一条"荷随源动"实现新能源高效就近消纳、保障电网安全经济运行的新技术路线。围绕这一国家重大能源战略需求，宋永华带领团队取得了一系列重大创新性成果并获得大规模成功应用。

一、集中式冶炼负荷深度平滑调控技术

揭示了电解铝负荷内阻突变随生产边界变化的统计规律，通过对突变的前馈抑制，化解了内阻非线性对调控稳定性的影响，解决了电解负荷无法深度调控的难题。提出了冶炼负荷调频的深度平滑控制技术，研发了面向百千安级直流电流的专用电磁耦合调节系统，在国际上首次实现了 GW 级单体电解铝负荷参与风电接入比例超过 30% 的孤立电网调频，应用于"863"示范项目，保障了该孤立电网风电的全额消纳。提出了抑制负荷功率冲击与无功电压补偿的联合控制技术，保障了系统电压质量与稳定性水平，防止了因炼钢负荷功率冲击造成低压导致的新能源连锁脱网事故。

二、海量分散式负荷稳定调峰的聚合控制技术

针对负荷调节潜力难以量化问题，构建了与发电机全维度等效的空调负荷时 / 频域统一模型，量化了负荷可调容量、速度、持续时间等动态特性，实现负荷调控技术与现有电网调度控制体系的联结。为突破用户舒适度对空调调节功率的限制，研制了柔性调控终端，面向空调负荷、电动汽车负荷等分散式负荷，发明了多时间尺度协调控制技术，实现了用户侧的秒级无感调控，负荷调控覆盖高舒适度要求的商业用户。针对负荷群调节难以持续问题，提出了分散负荷的分层汇聚方法，发明了负荷群时序优化调控技术，有效抑制了集群负荷功率反弹，首次实现了空调集群持续 1～3 小时稳定调峰。推广到分布式光伏装机占全国 1/5 的浙江电网，完成了 4.2GW 负荷调控资源系统集成，规模达峰荷 5.98%，保证了电网安全运行，实现 9.3GW 浙江分布式光伏全额就地消纳。

三、适应源荷多重不确定性的电网运行风险控制技术

提出了考虑多重不确定性的可调负荷多状态可靠性模型，构建了多约束电网的运行风险调控系统，实现了负荷集群对高比例新能源电力系统功率失衡的闭环响应，实现光伏高渗透区域户均年停电时间由 2.6 小时降至 16 分钟。提出基于负荷集群端对端通信的有功 - 无功协同电压预测控制技术，实现馈线末端的电压平滑支撑，有效降低了光伏高渗透电网电压越限风险，应用区域中 / 低压母线电压越限次数下降 65.4%。发明了基于就地量测快速响应并回溯修正的负荷协同控制技术，克服了通讯时延和个体差异导致负荷

参与集中调频的功率振荡，调频速度和一致性同时满足了大规模分散负荷集群秒级精准响应电网调频的需求，为大规模新能源馈入创造安全受电空间。成功应用至浙江、上海等 11 个省市，输出应用至吉隆坡、迪拜等地的海外工程，产生重大经济社会效益。

宋永华自 2002 年起担任澳门特区政府科技委员会顾问，为澳门科技发展建言献策，推动澳门在回归后建立科技发展基金、成立科学馆、支持大学科研等布局。2018 年担任澳门大学校长后，领衔组建并获批我国第一个智慧城市物联网领域的国家重点实验室。担任澳门科学技术协会荣誉会长和澳门中华教育会副会长，团结和凝聚爱国爱澳科技力量。

Awardee of Machinery and Electric Technology Prize, Song Yonghua

Song Yonghua was born in Bazhong City of Sichuan Province in January 1964. From 2018 onwards, Song has been serving as the rector, director of State Key Laboratory of Internet of Things for Smart City and chair professor at the University of Macau. Yonghua Song has long been engaged in research and practical application in the field of security and efficient operation of power systems.

Firstly, developing the centralized smelting load control technology. His work revealed the statistical law of the change of internal resistance of electrolytic aluminum load with production boundary. Through the feedforward suppression, the influence of the nonlinear internal resistance on the control stability was resolved, and the issue that the electrolytic load could not be deeply controlled was solved. He proposed the deep smoothing control technology for smelting load frequency modulation, and developed a dedicated electromagnetic coupling regulation system for hundreds of kiloamps of DC current, and realized for the first time in the world, the isolated power grid with GW-level single electrolytic aluminum load participating in the isolated system with over 30% wind power integration. His methodology was applied to the 863 demonstration project which ensured the full consumption of wind power of the isolated grid. The joint control technology of suppressing load power shock and reactive voltage compensation was proposed to ensure the system voltage quality and stability level, and prevented any new energy chain disconnection accident caused by low voltage due to steelmaking load power shock.

Secondly, developing an aggregation control technology of massive distributed Temperature Control Loads (TCLs) for peak load shaving. Aiming at the difficulty of quantifying the regulation potential of TCLs, a unified generalized model in time/frequency domain was constructed overall equivalent to the generator, and the dynamic characteristics of load regulation, including capacity, speed, and duration were characterized. In this way, the load regulation can be integrated with the existing power dispatch system. In order to break through the limitation of user comfort on TCL regulation, a flexible control terminal was invented. For TCLs and electric vehicles, a multi time scale coordinated control framework was developed, realizing friendly control of users in seconds and extending load regulation to commercial users with high comfort requirements. In order to sustain the duration of load aggregator regulation, a hierarchical clustering method for distributed loads is proposed, and the time sequences of load aggregators are optimized, which effectively suppress cluster rebound of load power and realize stable regulation of TCL aggregators for 1−3 hours for the first time across the world. The innovative technology was applied in Zhejiang Power Grid, which accounted for 1/5 of the installed distributed photovoltaics(PVs)in China. Up to 4.2GW load regulation resources were integrated, with a scale of 5.98% of the province peak load. This work ensures the secure operation of the Zhejiang power grid with completely local consumption of 9.3GW distributed PVs.

The third is power grid operation risk controlling in terms of multiple uncertainties of power supply and demand. A multi−state reliability model for flexible loads was established, and a multi−constrained grid operation risk dispatch system was developed, which realized the closed−loop response of load clusters to the power imbalance in a system with high−proportion renewable energy. This system reduced the annual interruption duration from 2.6 hours to 16 minutes in PV highly penetrated areas. An active−reactive coordinated voltage model predictive control (MPC) based on peer−to−peer communication of load aggregators was proposed to realize the smoothly voltage support at the end of feeders, and the number of voltage over−limit incidents in the application area was decreased by 65.4%. A load control technique based on on−site quick response and recurrent correction was proposed, which eliminated the power oscillation in load centralized control caused by communication delay and individual differences. The response speed and consistency met the system requirements of primary frequency regulation concurrently and a safe power receiving space for large−scale infeed renewable energy was created. The innovative technologies were applied to 11 provincial power grids in China, and has been exported for use in overseas projects in Kuala Lumpur, Dubai and other places, generating significant economic and social benefits.

机械电力技术奖获得者

王 国 庆

　　王国庆，1966 年 4 月出生于河北省承德市。1988 年获清华大学机械工程系学士学位，同年分配到中国运载火箭技术研究院所属的首都航天机械公司从事航天工艺研究与应用工作。1997 年到美国俄勒冈科技研究学院做访问学者，1998 年获材料科学与工程硕士学位并回到首都航天机械公司。2005 年起在中国运载火箭技术研究院工作，2010 年在清华大学机械工程系获博士学位。2019 年起任中国航天科技集团有限公司首席信息官。现为中国航天科技集团有限公司首席工艺专家、装备发展部先进制造技术专业组副组长、国防焊接自动化技术研究应用中心理事长，国际宇航科学院通信院士，清华大学兼职教授，英国帝国理工学院兼职教授，中国航天先进制造技术与装备发展论坛发起人和第一届会议执行主席及第二届会议主席，全国搅拌摩擦焊接与加工学术会议两位发起人之一和第一届及第二届会议共同主席。曾任首都航天机械公司副总经理 / 总工程师、中国运载火箭技术研究院副院长 / 总工艺师、中国航天科技集团公司工艺专家组组长、中国宇航学会飞行器制造工艺委员会主任委员。

　　王国庆长期从事航天大型复杂金属构件连接与装配集成方法、技术及其特殊工艺装备研究。在新一代航天装备超薄壁螺旋曲面结构、大型薄壁柔性结构、厚壁复杂结构等高性能加工、高精度装配及高品质连接方法与技术等方面做出了一系列创新性研究与应用工作。获国家科技进步奖特等奖 1 项、二等奖 2 项，第二十届中国专利金奖，2017 年英国焊接研究所布鲁克奖。

一、创建航天特大／大型箭体结构新一代制造关键技术体系

1. 针对长征五号火箭特大型柔性结构制造、装配与连接特殊难题，提出总体制造工艺路线，突破核心制造技术，实现火箭特大型主体结构的高精度制造，为成功研制长征五号火箭做出突出贡献

ø5m 箭体结构制造是长征五号火箭研制中的重大瓶颈，首次采用新型铝合金，面临特大型构件形／性协同制造、精准装配及焊接接头强度损失控制等重大难题。提出铝合金"大尺度构件形性精确制造，部段精准装配与高品质连接"技术路线，主持攻克 ø5m 异形截面框环及变幅宽长瓜瓣的精确成形与加工关键技术，匹配设计成形与热处理过程，解决大尺度结构残余应力释放及回弹变形等难题，实现特大型构件形／性协同精确制造；发明中厚板高强铝合金"无坡口"高品质弧焊新方法，突破空间结构大角度爬坡等关键技术，解决中厚板新型铝合金焊接难题，接头强度相对传统熔焊接头提高了 18%；提出大尺度弱刚性筒段精准装配尺寸控制方法，基于筒段弹性变形调控相邻筒段周长和形状一致性，解决大尺度筒段无塑性损伤精准装配难题；发明并主持研制国内首台套超大超长贮箱铣／装／焊复合新装备，攻克超长贮箱多点刚柔协调支撑等关键技术，解决贮箱自重和刚性不足导致的变形等难题，实现了超长贮箱精准装配和高质量焊接。

上述成果在我国首次创建了 ø5m 箭体结构制造工艺及装备技术体系，解决了我国新一代大型火箭研制的重大关键难题。

2. 发明大型复杂薄壁结构精确高效制造新方法和成套新装备，突破箭体结构批产制造瓶颈，实现了箭体结构核心关键制造技术升级换代

从"十五"开始，我国航天发射任务平均每五年增长一倍，以数量保质量的传统生产方式无法满足发射需求，成为完成北斗导航等国家任务的重大瓶颈。围绕上述瓶颈，提出火箭铝合金构件"精确、高效、绿色"的批量化制造思路，在国内率先突破航天高强铝合金大型复杂薄壁构件搅拌摩擦焊接制造工艺、质量控制等工程应用关键技术，发明针对变曲率空间薄壁结构的恒压力搅拌摩擦焊接方法，主持突破铝合金大型复杂薄壁构件封闭环缝无匙孔搅拌摩擦焊等关键技术，解决转速与压入量等多变量精确匹配及弱结合特有缺陷控制难题；发明贮箱环缝搅拌摩擦焊接系统，主持研制了大型复杂薄壁构件搅拌摩擦焊接成套装备；主导编制国内首套搅拌摩擦焊航天行业标准，解决工程应用重大基础问题，构建了航天大型铝合金构件搅拌摩擦焊接工艺－质量－装备－标准技术体系，ø3.35m 贮箱焊接一次合格率近 100%，承载内压能力提高 30%，使我国成为继美国之后第二个实现贮箱搅拌摩擦焊接技术应用并成功飞行的国家。自动钻铆是火箭批产的重要途径，难点在于筒形壳段钻铆多工艺集成及专用装备研制。发明火箭薄壁筒形壳段自动钻铆方法，研制出钻铆专用数控装备，解决了钻孔、送钉、压铆等多工艺集成难题，钻铆效率提高 3 倍，一次合格率近 100%。

上述成果建立了 ø3.35m 箭体结构核心关键工艺与装备新体系，已应用于火箭批产，

颠覆了以数量保质量的传统生产方式，探月中心评价该成果"大幅提高了我国运载火箭质量可靠性和研制生产效率"。

以上部分成果获 2018 年国家科技进步奖二等奖。

二、提出超薄壁空间曲面管束精密成形装配与高品质连接新方法

作为氢氧火箭发动机产生及传递推力的核心部件，螺旋管束式喷管是由数百根超薄壁变截面管空间螺旋密排焊接成形的轻质钟形结构，其内型面轮廓尺寸精度直接影响发动机效率，制造难点在于喷管成形装配、多管束间焊道跟踪及高品质拼焊。提出螺旋管束式喷管延伸段装配方法，突破"内撑外压分段收紧"复杂应力状态管束成形装配关键技术，实现数百根管束截面无畸变精密成形装配，保证了管束间间隙为零；提出"羊角型"特殊接头结构特征识别方法，建立基于三条纹结构光视觉传感的多特征点识别及曲率预测的图像处理技术，突破具有大曲率变化特征的空间螺旋焊道自动跟踪技术瓶颈；发明"羊角型"截面薄壁管束自填充精密焊接技术，主持研制出具有参数反馈控制功能的自动化焊接装备，实现喷管高品质拼焊精密制造，保证了喷管内型面轮廓尺寸精度及性能。

上述成果支撑氢氧火箭发动机喷管减重显著，提高了发动机综合性能，在低温火箭研制中发挥重要作用，火箭发动机专家评价该成果"是液氢液氧发动机制造技术的重大创新"。上述成果获 2012 年国家科技进步奖二等奖。

Awardee of Machinery and Electric Technology Prize, Wang Guoqing

Wang Guoqing was born in Chengde City of Hebei Province in April 1966. He graduated from the Department of Mechanical Engineering of Tsinghua University in 1988 and was assigned to Capital Aerospace Machinery Company（CAMC）of China Academy of Launch vehicle Technology（CALT）to work on research and application of aerospace technologies. In June of 1997, he was sent by the Chinese government as a visiting scholar to Oregon Graduate Institute of Science and Technology, U.S. He returned CAMC in June of 1998 with a master degree of Material Science and Engineering. He earned a doctorate degree of Material Science and Engineering from Tsinghua University in 2010. Since 2005, he had been working for CALT until he was assigned as chief information officer of China Aerospace Science Corporation（CASC）in December of 2019. Currently he is chief manufacturing technology expert of CASC, deputy director of advanced manufacturing group of China's Equipment Development Department, chairman of Research and Application Center of Defense Welding Automation Technology, corresponding member of the International Academy of Astronautics (IAA), visiting professor of Tsinghua University and Imperial College London, UK., founder of China Advanced Aerospace Manufacturing and Equipment Development Forum and the executive chairman of the 1st Forum and the chairman of the 2nd, one of two founders of National Academic Conference on Friction Stir Welding and Processing and the co-chairman of the 1st and 2nd Conference. He has served as vice general manager and general engineer of CAMC, vice president and chief manufacturing technology officer of CALT, leader of manufacturing technology expert team of CASC and chairman of Committee of Spacecraft Manufacturing Technology of Chinese Society of Astronautics.

Wang Guoqing has been engaged in research on integration theory, technology and dedicated equipment for joining and assembly of large-scale complex metal aerospace structures. He has conducted a series of innovative studies and made a significant accomplishment in engineering application of high-performance processing, high-precision assembly and high-quality joining technology of spiral ultra-thin wall structure, large-scale flexible thin wall structure and complex thick wall structure. He won a special prize (rank 56 /100) and two second prizes (rank 1 at both) of National Scientific and Technological Progress Award , a Gold Award of the 20th WIPO-CNIPA Award for Chinese Outstanding Patented Invention and a Brooker Award of The Welding Institute, TWI, UK, 2017.

电子信息技术奖获得者

樊 邦 奎

樊邦奎，1958年出生于北京市。1980—1992年在张家口通信学院基础教研室任教员/讲师。1989—1997年在北京理工大学信号与信息处理专业攻读硕士、博士。1992年至今在北京市信息技术研究所工作，历任六室副主任、主任/高级工程师，副所长、所长、高级工程师。其间，1999—2000年在美国密苏里大学信号处理研究方向做高级访问学者。1995年当选中国工程院院士。

樊邦奎是我国无人机系统技术领域带头人，近三十年来在科研一线承担无人机技术总体、系统研制和关键技术攻关工作，并开展国家无人机产业发展战略研究，先后完成十多项国家、部委重大工程科研项目，构建了无人机系统体系，攻克了无人机数据链、光电侦察高精度目标定位和合成孔径雷达高质量成像等多项关键技术，推动建立了无人机市场的技术生态。获国家科技进步奖特等奖项、一等奖1项、二等奖4项，省部级科技进步奖一等奖7项；荣立一、二等功各1次；获授权发明专利18项，出版专著5部，发表论文15篇；带领团队获集体一等功。

设计并实现大中小型无人机系统体系，创建了无人机体系架构、技术体制和系统装备三维、十六要素体系模型。提出了行业级无人机四种型谱飞行平台、三种数据链、两类载荷以及地面控制站系列化系统架构，构建了标准功能、接口模型，能够快速集成、迭代为满足多部门需求的系列产品。设计了涵盖5个频段，视距和超视相结合、中继卫星与通信卫星相配合、机动站与固定站相组合的无人机数据链体系结构，主编7项国家标准，统一了行业级无人机测控链路技术体制。主编、主译《国外无人机大全》《无人机手册》等专著，为国内无人机技术发展、科学普及做出了重要贡献。

攻克无人机载合成孔径雷达运动补偿技术，提出了多源、多维度数据联合估计与天线平台控制技术途径，解决波束指向稳定问题，实现雷达回波幅度平稳。利用数据域补偿低阶航迹误差与图像域补偿高阶航迹误差及域间迭代的技术策略，解决雷达回波相位补偿问题。采用上述技术，在无人机姿态大范围波动情况下实现了高分辨率清晰成像，达到了国际先进水平。

提出并实现光电目标实时定位新方法，针对共线定位精度低和空间交会视场中心点定位的不足，提出了目标共线定位与多点交会的差分定位技术。利用外测量和卫星导航两种定位的优势，提出了伪码测距、干涉仪测向定位与卫星定位组合定位方法。目标定位精度与美军全球鹰无人机水平相当。

Awardee of Electronics and Information Technology Prize, Fan Bangkui

Fan Bangkui was born in Beijing City in 1958. He is a Chinese academic leader in the field of Unmanned Aerial Vehicle (UAV). Over recent 30 years, he has been rooted in the front line of academic research and advanced technology development, taking responsibility for UAV system design, development, and implementation with cutting edge technologies. He has also directed the development strategy of the national UAV industry, and completed more than 10 major engineering and research projects funded by Nation and Ministries, which related to the establishment of the architecture of UAV systems, UAV Datalink technologies, high-precision target localization for photoelectric reconnaissance, and high-quality synthetic aperture radar (SAR) image, etc. He also promoted the development of the tech ecosystem of the UAV market worldwide. He has won a Grand Award, a First Award and 4 Second Awards of National Science and Technology Progress Award, and 7 provincial-level science and technology progress awards in China. He was granted 18 invention patents, published 5 monographs and 15 papers.

He has designed and implemented the UAV system architecture in different size, created a three-dimensional (i.e., UAV architecture, technique and equipment) model. He has proposed an industrial-strength serialize system framework, including four types of Flight Platforms, three types of Datalinks, two types of Loads and Ground Control Station, furtherly constructed a series of products with well recognized standard functions and interfaces, which can swiftly be integrated and iterated to meet different customer needs. In addition, he has sucessfully designed the datalink architecture for UAVs, covering five frequency bands, combining light-of-sight with over-the-horizon, while relaying satellites with communication satellites, and mobile stations with fixed stations. He has edited seven national standards and unified the technique structure of Telemetry & Control Link for UAVs in industrial-class. He has edited or translated monographs such as *The Encyclopedia of Foreign UAVs, The Handbook of UAVs*, etc., made a significant contribution to the development and scientific popularization of UAV technology in China.

He has conquered motion compensation technique of unmanned aircraft system contained SAR, proposed the approach using multi-source and multi-dimensional data estimation and antenna platform control mode to solve beam directivity stability, furtherly guarantee the stable amplitude of radar echo. He has also solved the problem of radar echo phase compensation by the strategies of compensating low–order track error by data domain, compensating high–order track error in image domain and inter–domain iteration. Using the above strategy, high–resolution and clear imaging is collected under the condition of large–scale fluctuation of UAV attitude, which has reached the international advanced level.

He has proposed and realized a new method for real–time positioning of photoelectric targets. Aiming at the shortcomings of the center point positioning of the field of view in space rendezvous and the low accuracy of collinear positioning, he investigated target collinear positioning and differential positioning for multi–point rendezvous. In addition, he utilized the advantages of external measurement and satellite navigation, a combined positioning method of pseudo–code ranging, interferometer direction finding/positioning by interferometer and satellite positioning was proposed, which has reached the international advanced level.

电子信息技术奖获得者

刘泽金

刘泽金，1963 年 10 月出生于山东省无棣县。1983 年毕业于山东大学，1997 年获国防科学技术大学博士学位。历任国防科学技术大学应用物理系助教、讲师、副教授，应用物理系某研究室副主任、主任，理学院某研究所教授、副所长、所长，理学院副院长，光电科学与工程学院副院长、院长，国防科学技术大学科研部部长，国防科技大学副校长。现为中央军委科学技术委员会常任委员，中国光学学会副理事长。作为主要完成人获国家科技进步奖一等奖 2 项、二等奖 1 项，2005 年获中国科协"求是"杰出青年实用工程奖，2012 年被授予全国优秀科技工作者称号，2009 年荣立一等功 1 次。2017 年当选中国工程院院士。

刘泽金长期从事高能激光系统和技术研究，是我国高能激光工程领域的学术带头人之一，为我国高能激光发展做出了系统性、开拓性的贡献。

一、提出一套高能激光系统工程设计方法，领衔研制多个高能激光系统

高能激光系统研制涉及多个学科，是一项复杂的系统工程。历史上多个研发项目因技术可行性和系统应用未充分验证，工程集成后达不到预期效果而下马。以应用需求和预期效果为导向，明确技术体系和工程设计方案至关重要。

刘泽金自 1986 年起一直从事高能激光系统和技术研究，作为技术负责人全程主持过多个高能激光系统研究与设计。在某项高能激光系统研究中，他结合应用需求背景，在高能激光光源、激光与物质相互作用、激光大气传输和目标特性研究的基础上提出高能激光系统应用模型，按照应用环节推演功率密度阈值、蒙气差修正、提前量设置、激光光源功率和光束质量等技术要求，设计激光效应试验，验证了技术可行性和模型正确性，自主设计了技术体系，为系统研制提供了依据。在高能激光系统工程研制中，针对工程优化设计理论缺乏、没有完备的分系统技术指标体系可参考等现实难题，他提出高能激光系统技术参数优化匹配理论，结合当时的技术基础制订了完备的分系统技术指标。

着眼解决高能激光系统各单元遇到的科学技术问题，刘泽金带领团队优化设计系统参数，提升系统综合性能，开展高能激光系统综合设计、系统集成、系统性能测试、综合验证试验、技术路线论证及应用概念等研究，设计了系列验证和评估试验方案，有效降低了高能激光系统研制和试验风险。他带领团队在激光与物质相互作用的效应机理、高能激光光源、激光系统高效热管理、激光大气传输特性分析、目标跟踪等方面开展了深入研究，攻克了多项关键技术。

在刘泽金的主持下，团队研制出多个高能激光系统，研究成果获国家科技进步奖一等奖2项、二等奖1项。

二、提出大功率光纤激光相干合成的新途径，推动光纤激光相干合成研究迈向新台阶

光纤激光具有转换效率高、光束质量好、结构紧凑等诸多优点，但受限于热效应、非线性效应等因素的影响，单束光纤激光的输出功率有限，对多束激光进行光束合成是实现更高功率输出的必由之路。构建模块化的光纤激光阵列，并对阵列光束进行相干合成，是实现高功率和高光束质量激光的理想解决方案之一。

刘泽金带领团队围绕光纤激光相干合成的核心科学技术问题，对其物理机制、理论模型、实现方法、传输效能与光束质量评价等问题开展了深入研究，率先将随机并行梯度下降（SPGD）算法引入光纤激光相位控制，在国际上首次实现了基于SPGD算法光纤激光放大器相干合成；基于优化式自适应算法的光纤激光锁相技术，实现了有一定谱线宽度激光的相干合成，改变了相干合成只能用单频激光的传统认识，提出多种子源光纤激光放大器概念（可有效抑制非线性效应，从而实现大功率输出），于2010年在国际上首次突破千瓦级光纤激光相干合成；提出窄线宽光纤激光非线性效应抑制和功率提升的有效方案，于2016年研制成功1.9千瓦线偏振窄线宽光纤激光放大器，实现了5千瓦级4路光纤激光相干偏振合成（为该方案当时国际最高值）；提出相干合成光束质量的评价准则，解决了传统光束质量因子不能很好描述相干合成光束质量的难题。

刘泽金团队取得的研究成果得到国内外同行的广泛认可，报道多波长相干合成实验的论文被选为光学领域国际著名期刊 *Optics Letters* 网络版封面文章，刘泽金本人受法国学者邀请参与编写专著 *Coherent laser beam combining*。2016年出版专著《高平均功率光纤激光相干合成》，2016年撰写光纤激光合成光束质量评价国家标准。刘泽金带领的研究团队通过理论和实验分析，提出并验证了光纤激光相干合成向大功率、大阵元数目扩展的可行性，促进了我国在光纤激光相干合成领域的理论和技术发展，推动光纤激光相干合成研究迈上新台阶。

相关成果获湖南省自然科学奖一等奖1项，2009年、2011年两度入选"中国光学重要成果"。

三、开展高光束质量大功率单纤光纤激光器研究，实现我国光纤激光领域的重大突破

高光束质量大功率光纤激光器在工业加工和国防领域等都有重要应用，然而单纤光纤激光器的功率提升面临众多技术难题，需在高功率光纤器件制作、热致模式不稳定效应抑制、受激拉曼散射效应抑制等方面开展深入研究。

刘泽金带领团队从分析光纤激光产生和非线性效应物理机制入手，建立了含自发辐射项的低净增益光纤激光器理论模型，提出了同带泵浦用光纤激光器中增益光纤掺杂浓度、长度、截面及光栅反射率等系统参数的设计优化准则，突破了自发辐射和寄生振荡抑制关键技术，解决了石英基掺镱光纤 1018 纳米波段因净增益小难以实现大功率输出的难题；发现了时域不稳定性引发受激拉曼效应的机理，提出了万瓦级功率放大过程中非线性效应抑制方法，设计了万瓦级光纤激光优化方案，大幅提升了受激拉曼散射效应的产生阈值；建立了热致模式不稳定理论模型，提出了光纤激光振荡器和放大器中热致模式不稳定效应的抑制方案；发明了大功率弱拉锥低损耗泵浦/信号合束器、双包层光纤与玻璃锥棒熔接方法、光纤器件综合冷却方法，研制出高性能光纤合束器和光纤端帽，有效降低了泵浦合束器中的信号插入损耗，为大功率单纤光纤激光器的实现提供了器件支撑。

刘泽金带领研究团队在光纤激光器非线性效应抑制、高功率光纤器件研制等方面取得多项重大突破，于 2016 年成功研制同带泵浦高光束质量万瓦级光纤激光器，标志着我国成为国际上第二个掌握该类型光纤激光技术的国家，相关成果获中国光学工程学会技术发明奖一等奖 1 项。

Awardee of Electronics and Information Technology Prize, Liu Zejin

Liu Zejin was born in Wudi County of Shandong Province in October 1963. He graduated from the Shandong University with a bachelor's degree in 1983, and attained his Ph.D degree from National University of Defense Technology in 1997. In National University of Defense Technology, he successively held the posts of assistant, assistant professor, associate professor, professor and vice-president of the university. He is currently a member of the Science and Technology Committee of the Central Military Committee, PLA. He is also a part-time professor and tutor for Doctor degree in NUDT. He was elected as academician of the Chinese Academy of Engineering in 2017.

Liu Zejin has devoted himself to the high energy laser system and laser technology research. He is one of the leading scientists in high energy laser engineering in China. He has made great contributions to the development of high energy lasers.

电子信息技术奖获得者

吴 枫

吴枫，1969 年 7 月出生于湖北省天门市。网络流媒体专家。1992 年获西安电子科技大学工学学士学位，1996 年和 1999 年分别获哈尔滨工业大学工学硕士和博士学位。博士毕业后加入微软亚洲研究院，历任副研究员、研究员和首席研究员。2014 年加入中国科学技术大学，现任中国科学技术大学信息与智能学部部长、类脑智能技术及应用国家工程实验室主任。

吴枫长期从事网络流媒体的基础理论和关键技术研究，先后牵头承担了国家基金委杰青项目、国家基金委创新群体项目和科技部重点专项等，建立了网络流媒体的非均匀率失真理论，攻克了网络流媒体的高效压缩和精准适配技术难题，在国际标准竞争中实现了从无到有、从弱到强的突破，在手机、高清摄像机等规模化应用的成果推动了我国在该领域的跨越式发展，获 2015 年国家自然科学奖二等奖和 2019 年国家技术发明奖二等奖。在人才培养方面，牵头探索中科大－微软本科生校企联合培养模式，在全国范围内产生了较大影响，获 2019 年安徽省教学成果特等奖。IEEE Fellow，视频领域顶级期刊 IEEE TCSVT 主编，IEEE 数据压缩标准委员会主席，在网络流媒体领域具有重要国际影响力。

网络流媒体是通过互联网把大规模的媒体内容实时流畅地传输给海量用户，其面临的巨大挑战是互联网缺少服务质量保障、网络状态复杂多变。吴枫从 1997 年便开展了网络流媒体的原理、技术、标准化和工程应用研究，推动了我国网络流媒体的工程应用和产业发展。发表英文学术专著 1 部、学术论文 300 余篇，授权中、美发明专利 106 项。

一、网络流媒体的非均匀率失真理论

香农的率失真理论是网络流媒体的基础，刻画了码率压缩和造成的失真之间的关系，指导了高效压缩和精准适配的技术发展。但是该理论建立在数据电报传输的基础上，没有针对多媒体广泛存在的非均匀特性及其网络传输的特性，这是网络流媒体发展首先需要解决的理论难题。

针对多媒体时空关联的各向异性，发现了用局部方向计算构建任意方向变换的计算关系，建立了任意方向变换新体系，解决了任意时空关联的多媒体信号在变换域紧致表达的难题；针对多媒体视觉感知的差异性，揭示了结构和纹理在视觉感知上的重要性与信息熵大小的反向规律，发现了结构编码与纹理合成的融合计算机理，显著提升了视觉感知测度下的率失真性能；针对多媒体传输的网络化特性，发现了利用网络节点存在的相似结构和纹理作为条件互信息的编码机理，建立了基于条件互信息的多媒体率失真理论，在网络流媒体领域发展和完善了香农的率失真理论。

非均匀计算理论与方法获 2015 年国家自然科学奖二等奖。

二、网络流媒体的高效压缩

视频是网络流媒体最主要的数据，其高效压缩是节省网络带宽的有效手段。随着分辨率的不断提升，视频时空关联的非均匀特性越来越精细、越来越复杂，传统视频压缩方法采用简单的平移运动模型，无法精准刻画前景的复杂变化以及背景的局部遮挡，成为长期制约高清视频压缩效率提升的瓶颈。

针对视频前景的复杂变化，发现了投影运动模型在时空关联表达的参数约束关系，建立了参数归约化的仿射运动模型，实现了旋转、缩放等非线性时空关联的率失真优化表达，在国际标准中首次突破了沿用近四十年的平移运动模型；针对视频背景的局部遮挡，建立了从视频时空信息到三维场景的反演模型，发明了局部区域动态更新的背景重建方法，提出率失真优化的局部区域码率分配技术，在视频会议、实时监控等高清网络流媒体应用中实现了压缩效率的倍升。

视频压缩技术的标准化是在网络流媒体中大规模应用的前提，吴枫和团队的 56 项技术提案被国际国内标准采纳，其中时空关联再同步技术被 MPEG-4 采纳，成为我国首个进入视频压缩国际标准的技术；23 项技术提案被 H.265 采纳，国内单位排名第一，首次在重要视频压缩国际标准中与发达国家形成了相互制衡之势；作为 IEEE 1857 标准工作组执行主席，把国内视频压缩标准制定为 IEEE 国际标准，为国际推广奠定了基础。

视频编解码芯片是网络流媒体应用终端的核心，研制的 H.265 编解码器被高端智能手机芯片采用，芯片发货量已超过 1 亿片，推动智能手机成为网络流媒体的重要终端；研制的 H.264 和 H.265 专利技术被海思监控芯片采用，支撑海康威视研制了一系列高清摄像机，解决了我国网络流媒体产业发展缺"芯"的难题。

高清视频编码关键技术获 2019 年国家技术发明奖二等奖。

三、网络流媒体的精准适配

互联网是一个有线、无线并存的复杂网络，用户带宽共享和终端移动造成了实际传输带宽受限、波动剧烈。传统压缩方法生成的视频数据紧密耦合，无法在传输过程中精细调整码率，并且码率调整也造成了率失真性能显著降低，精准适配是网络流媒体亟待解决的工程技术难题。

针对压缩数据的优化解耦，建立了耦合数据丢失造成的重建误差传递和累积模型，发明了率失真优化的压缩数据分层预测耦合方法，提出了渐进精细可伸缩压缩方法；针对压缩数据的传输适配，建立了适应网络状态的分层数据多路径传输适配模型，实现了网络带宽波动的实时精准适配，联合研制了计算、存储和传输一体化的智能路由器；针对传输错误的渐进恢复，提出了数据丢失造成的重建误差渐进消除技术，在网络带宽升高下实现了传输错误的渐进恢复。

吴枫在网络流媒体的各个发展阶段都做出了重要贡献，由他牵头研制的 H.264 实时编码器作为当时国际最先进的 Windows 7 流媒体组件，编码器安装量达到 4.5 亿次，推动了网络流媒体的大规模应用；研制的全球第一套基于 LTE 承载的 H.265 流媒体系统，推动了移动网络流媒体的发展；网络适配技术应用小卫星组网传输，验证了高动态、高间歇网络环境下的数据传输，为天地一体的流媒体应用奠定了技术基础。相关技术也被广泛应用于快手的短视频、海信的安防系统、讯飞的远程医疗辅助诊断系统。

Awardee of Electronics and Information Technology Prize, Wu Feng

Wu Feng was born in Tianmen City of Hubei Province in July 1969. He received the B.S. degree in electronic engineering from Xidian University in 1992, and received the M.S. and Ph.D degrees from Harbin Institute of Technology in 1996 and 1999, respectively. He joined Microsoft Research Asia (MSRA) in 1999, working as associate researcher, researcher, and then principle researcher. He joined the University of Science and Technology of China (USTC) in 2014, where he is currently the chair of the Division of Information and Intelligence.

He has long been engaged in researching the theory and key technologies of media streaming. He led a number of important projects, including the project of the National Science Foundation of China for Distinguished Young Scholars, the project of the Science Fund for Creative Research Groups of the National Natural Science Foundation of China, and the project of the National Key Research and Development Program of China.

He established the non-uniform rate-distortion theory for multimedia, which develops Shannon's rate-distortion theory considering the non-uniform characteristics of multimedia and the transmission characteristics. Guided by the non-uniform rate-distortion theory, he solved several key technical problems of efficient compression and adaptive transmission for media streaming. 56 technical proposals made by him and his team have been adopted into international or domestic video coding standards. His contributions made our nation achieve important breakthrough in the competition of international video coding standards. He also made important contributions in each development stage of media streaming including the wired Internet stage and the mobile Internet stage. His developed technologies are widely used in Kwai's short video service, Hisense's video surveillance systems, and iFlytek's remote auxiliary medical diagnosis systems.

He received the Second-Class Prize of National Natural Science Award (ranked first) in 2015, and the Second-Class Prize of National Technological Invention Award (ranked first) in 2019. For education, he first explored the university-enterprise joint teaching approach between USTC and MSRA, which had a great impact nationwide, and received the Special-Class Teaching Achievement Award of Anhui Province (ranked first) in 2019. He has gained international reputation in the field of media streaming, and he is elected Fellow of IEEE, the editor-in-chief of IEEE TCSVT, which is a top-tier journal in the video processing area, and the chair of IEEE DCSC.

电子信息技术奖获得者

杨 德 仁

杨德仁，1964年4月出生于江苏省扬州市。1985年本科毕业于浙江大学材料系，1991年在浙江大学材料系（硅材料国家重点实验室）获半导体材料工学博士学位，1993年在浙江大学博士后流动站出站。1997年被浙江大学特批为教授，1998年被批准为博士生导师。其间，分别在日本东北大学、德国 FREIBERG 工业大学、瑞典 LUND 大学工作和进行访问研究。1998—2020年任浙江大学硅材料国家重点实验室副主任、主任。

现任浙江大学工学部主任、半导体材料研究所所长、硅材料国家重点实验室学术委员会主任、浙大宁波理工学院院长，国家自然科学基金委创新研究群体、科技部重点领域创新团队、教育部长江学者创新团队和浙江省重点科技创新团队负责人。兼任国家重大科技专项（02）总体专家组成员，中国可再生能源学会常务理事、光伏专业委员会副主任。中国科学院院士。

杨德仁长期从事半导体硅材料的研究，涉及超大规模集成电路用硅单晶材料、太阳能光伏硅材料、硅基光电子材料和纳米半导体材料。面向国家对集成电路（IC）等半导体器件的重大需求，针对制约 IC 器件可靠性、成品率的硅材料关键科学技术问题，在硅晶体的缺陷调控、晶体制备等方面取得了具有重要国际学术影响的系统性、创造性成就。

一、微氮直拉硅单晶的氮关缺陷性能、控制和应用

针对国际上现代 IC 用直拉硅单晶中纳米级缺陷控制的核心难题，提出掺氮控制缺陷的创新思路，系统揭示了氮关缺陷的物理性质，解决了其在 IC 应用的关键科学问题，实现了成果转化及规模生产，引起国际上广泛关注、跟进和应用，促进其成为国际 IC 用硅单晶主流品种之一。

二、微量掺锗硅单晶的生长、缺陷控制和应用

针对国际上 IC 器件用重掺硅单晶外延层产生失配位错的关键难题，提出微量掺锗减少晶格畸变的创新思路和技术，成功抑制了重掺硅外延层的失配位错，系统解决了其晶体生长、缺陷控制及在 IC 应用的基础科学问题，实现了我国特色硅单晶的成果转化及规模生产，引起国际关注和跟进。

三、纳米硅管等纳米半导体材料的制备

针对国际上未来 IC 器件对纳米硅材料的重大挑战，在纳米硅（点、线、管）领域取得系列创新成果；突破了纳米硅管制备的瓶颈，在国际上首先成功制备出纳米硅管，开创了纳米硅管制备和应用的基础研究，引起国际广泛关注和跟进，为其在未来 IC 上应用奠定了基础。

杨德仁在硅晶体的晶体生长、缺陷工程的基础研究上取得重大成果，研究成果不仅产生一定的国际影响，而且在生产实际中产生重大经济效益。以第一获奖人获得国家自然科学奖二等奖 2 项，国家技术发明奖二等奖 1 项，浙江省科学技术奖一等奖 4 项，省部级科学技术二等奖、三等奖及其他科技奖项 6 项；以第二获奖人获得省部级科技奖一等奖 1 项、二等奖 2 项。在 *Nature* 子刊等国际学术刊物发表 SCI 检索论文 840 多篇，SCI 论文他引 16100 多次；获得 160 多项国家授权发明专利（含美国发明专利 1 项）；主编、参著英文著作 6 本，编著中文著作 4 本，参著（编）中文著作 6 本，主编国际会议论文集 6 本。在国际会议上报告研究成果 100 多篇次，其中国际会议邀请报告 60 多次；担任 20 次国际会议（分会）主席以及 60 多个国际学术会议的顾问（学术/程序）委员会委员，并担任 *Superlattices and Microdefects* 主编及 *Silicon*、*Physica Status Solidi* 等国际学术杂志编委。

Awardee of Electronics and Information Technology Prize, Yang Deren

Yang Deren was born in Yangzhou City of Jiangsu Province in April 1964. He is an academician of Chinese Academy of Science, and the president of NingboTech University. He is the dean of Faculty of Engineering, and the Cheung Kong Professor at State Key Laboratory of Silicon Materials（School of Materials）at Zhejiang University in China. He received his bachelor in 1985 and his Ph.D degree in 1991 from Zhejiang University, and then has worked there. In 1990's, he worked in Japan in 1993, Germany in 1995 and Sweden in 1999 as a visiting researcher. In 1997, he was promoted to be a full professor by Zhejiang University, and then promoted to be the Cheung

Kong Professor in 2000 by the Ministry of Education of China. He received the National Science Fund for Distinguished Young Scholars in China in 2002, won the Award of National Nature Science in 2005 and 2013 as well as the Award of National Technical Invention in 2019, and the Award of Chinese Young Science and Technology in 2006. He was elected to be an academician of Chinese Academy of Science in 2017.

He is vice director of China Photovoltaic Association, member of Expert Team of Chinese Keystone Special Projects, member of Board of Chinese Renewable Energy Association, member of Board of Chinese Crystal Association, member of SEMI China PV Committee, and chief scientist of a National key project for basic research of China.

He has engaged in the research of silicon materials used for microelectronic devices, solar cells, opto-electric and nano-devices. He systematically investigated nitrogen-doped Czochralski silicon used for ultra larger scale integrity circuits, and revealed that nitrogen-doping can suppress COP defects, increase mechanical strength, and improve the ability of internal gettering by enhancing oxygen precipitation, and enhance nitrogen-doped Cz silicon to be widely used in ULSI industry in all over the world. He invented germanium-doped crystal silicon, and systematically investigated its technology of growth, behavior and defects. Moreover, he applied this technology and material in ULSI and photovoltaic industry. He also reported the fabrication of silicon nano-tubes and selenium nono-tubes for the first time in the world, and systematically investigated the fabrication and behavior of silicon nano-dots, nano-wires and nanotubes as well as their devices.

In the past 30 years, he has authored 17 books as an author or co-authors including 6 books in English, such as Handbook of Photovoltaic Silicon published by Springer, and edited 6 proceedings of international conferences. He has published over 840 SCI cited research papers in international peer reviewed journals, such as Natural Comm., AM, Nano Lett. JACS, APL, PRB and et al, with the total number of over 16100 citations by SCI cited papers published by other groups. His *h* index is 64. He also holds 159 Chinese patents. In the past, he chaired or co-chaired 21 international conferences/symposia and was appointed as the member of international committee of more than 60 international conferences. He also presented more than 60 invited talks in international conferences. He is the editor-in-chief of Superlattices and Microstructures, and also the editor of 4 international journals, such as Physica Status Solidi, Silicon et al.

冶金材料技术奖获得者

冯 吉 才

  冯吉才，1958年10月出生于山东省东平县。1983年、1992年在哈尔滨工业大学焊接工艺及设备专业分获工学学士及工学硕士学位，1996年获日本大阪大学工学研究科生产加工（焊接）专业工学博士学位。1998—1999年，任日本大阪大学接合科学研究所特聘研究员。1997年至今任哈尔滨工业大学先进焊接与连接国家重点实验室教授。2009—2015年，任哈尔滨工业大学威海校区校长，2016年至今任哈尔滨工业大学先进焊接与连接国家重点实验室主任，2018年至今任中国焊接学会理事长。曾任国务院学位委员会第六届评议组材料科学与工程组成员、教育部第六届科技委材料学部委员、国家自然科学基金委第十届及第十一届工程与材料学部专家评审组成员、《材料科学与工艺》期刊主编、中南大学粉末冶金国家重点实验室第四届学术委员会委员和清华大学先进成形制造教育部重点实验室第一届学术委员会委员。

  主要从事异种材料焊接冶金研究，针对异质金属和陶瓷/金属两类典型的性能特异材料体系，系统研究了电子束焊接、钎焊、扩散焊与水下焊接过程的本质特征，在增强界面润湿、组织与性能调控、接头应力缓和方面取得了重要科研成果，理论及技术创新突出，实际应用效果显著。担任宇航员失重训练水槽及大型空间环境模拟器（均为亚洲最大）的焊接制造总师，解决了大型容器的焊接变形等关键技术。厚板窄间隙焊接及冶金控制技术应用于深潜器钛合金载人球壳焊接制造，替代了进口。所带领的团队为我国航空航天、海洋工程及核电等领域重要部件的研制创新提供了关键理论与技术支撑，获得国家自然科学奖二等奖1项及国家技术发明奖二等奖1项。

一、发明了异质金属的熔钎焊新方法（低熔点金属熔化、钎焊高熔点金属）

  发现了低熔点液膜减小异质金属熔钎焊润湿阻力的界面活化现象，提出了利用表面液膜改善润湿的新思路。低熔点金属涂层在电弧热作用下发生熔化形成表面液膜，并与钎料发生预合金化，改善了润湿平衡条件，利用镀锌层促进了铝钎料在钢基体表面的润湿和铺展，阐明了合金元素对界面反应产物的影响机制，发现合金元素对铝/钢界面化合物的抑制效应；建立了电源动态特性曲线及能量密度方程，发现了熔钎焊过程的非均质扩散现象，确定了铝/钢、镁/钢熔钎焊金属间化合物层的相组成，阐明了接头的断裂特性，形成了热输入－冶金联合抑制界面脆性化合物的焊接冶金调控方法。铜－钢电子束自熔钎焊技术解决了航天发动机喷管的焊接瓶颈问题，长征五号、六号、七号运载火箭的大部分发动机喷管采用该技术制造，使我国成为世界上第三个掌握该焊接技术的国家。

二、发明了陶瓷（或复合材料）与金属的复合反应扩散连接新方法

揭示了陶瓷/金属界面原位自生反应钎焊机理，阐明了取向生长陶瓷晶须界面强化与应力缓解机制，研制出能产生多级共晶反应的耐高温钎料，获得了18种重要反应相生长的动力学参数，突破了陶瓷与金属界面反应层成长的预测和调控难题。提出了界面微结构设计应力重构缓解陶瓷/金属接头应力的新思路，形成了非平直界面以及界面载荷传递的应力调控理论，揭示了基于界面组织及微结构设计的应力调控机制。发展了原位自生反应钎焊陶瓷/金属的方法，揭示了陶瓷晶须在焊缝内固相和液相条件下的生长机制和动力学过程，实现了陶瓷晶须在界面及接头处形貌及分布的有效调控，揭示了陶瓷与金属接头热膨胀、模量以及硬度等性能的梯度过渡分布规律，阐明了有序陶瓷晶须在陶瓷与金属接头界面的强化、载荷传递及应力缓解机制。氧化铝陶瓷和铝合金焊接用于核检测仪器的制造，氧化铝陶瓷和不锈钢的复合反应扩散连接技术分别用于核电贯穿件的国产化及某型号潜液泵的制造，扩展技术还用于汽车电动机碳－铜换向器的批量生产。

三、提出了异质金属扩散焊接的质量调控思路

发明了复合阻隔层抑制异质金属扩散焊界面脆性化合物的方法，揭示了全固溶阻隔层的设计准则，基于待焊接体系的冶金相容性与焊接性，建立了从原子半径和原子电负性出发的阻隔层选择原则，从源头上阻断了界面化合物的生成。提出了低温固相扩散焊调控界面化合物的思路，发现了等离子体活化、氢致活化和反应活化低温扩散焊调控界面化合物的特性与机制，阐明了异质金属接头的低温固相焊接机理。自主研制了等离子体活化扩散焊一体化设备，并实现了非晶合金、单晶合金及金属间化合物的低温扩散焊。提出了纳米多层膜自蔓延反应活化扩散焊接异质金属的新思路，阐明了自蔓延反应中间层设计准则，揭示了界面反应与焊接机理，依靠中间层反应放热辅助界面连接，基于反应产物设计提高接头的高温服役性能，达到低温焊接、高温使用的目的。基于扩散焊技术基础理论成果，解决了常规扩散焊过程中焊合率和扩散层厚度相互矛盾的难题，为我国高超风洞设计提供理论及技术支撑，也成功实现了航天推进系统钛管路与不锈钢组件的可靠焊接；界面优化控制理论与技术成功解决了汽车发动机油冷器等产品的焊接质量控制问题。

四、阐明了水下焊接冶金机理、传质传热机理、电弧特性、焊接过程与水环境交互作用机理等基础理论

建立了冶金行为－传质过程－熔池动态－焊接缺陷－微观组织－力学性能的内在联系；开发了新型水下焊接切割设备、工艺和材料，填补了我国水下200米湿法焊接技术、水下湿法药芯焊丝、水下半自动焊接设备等技术空白；提出并构建了基于X射线高速成像技术的水下焊接实时监测方法及系统，突破了水下焊接物理过程表征技术瓶颈，获取了清晰的水下湿法焊接熔滴过渡过程以及熔池内部特征，率先明确了水下湿法焊接熔滴过渡类型，为新型水下焊接技术的开发奠定了基础；针对核电水下修复技术要求，开发了水下焊接机器人及其作业技术以及水下激光焊接／增材修复技术及装备。研究成果为"渤海湾碧海行动"提供了技术支撑，解决了沉船打捞扳正桩头水下焊接等关键技术问题，取得了良好的社会经济效益。

Awardee of Metallurgy and Materials Technology Prize, Feng Jicai

Feng Jicai was born in Dongping County of Shandong Province in October 1958. He achieved his Bachelor and Master degree in welding process and equipment from Harbin Institute of Technology in 1983 and 1986. He obtained his Ph.D from Joining and Welding Research Institute Osaka University in 1996. He joined the State Key Laboratory of Advanced Welding and Joining, Harbin Institute of Technology as a professor since 1997 and became the director of the State Key Laboratory of Advanced Welding and Joining in 2015. He has also been appointed as the president of the Chinese Welding Society since 2018.

Feng, Jicai's research focuses on the welding metallurgy of dissimilar materials, including joining of dissimilar metals and joining of ceramic with metal. He systematically investigated the nature of electron beam welding, brazing, diffusion bonding and underwater welding and obtained scientific achievements in enhancing interfacial wetting, controlling the microstructure and the properties of the joints and moderating the residual stress in the joint. His contribution includes developing the welding brazing method for dissimilar metal joining (fusion welding for the low-melting-point metal and brazing for high-melting-point metal), introducing the novel composite reaction diffusion bonding method for ceramics (composite materials) / metal joining, developing the approach to control the diffusion bonding quality of dissimilar metals, and revealing the mechanism for underwater welding metallurgy and heat and mass transfer, demonstrating the arc characteristics and illustrating the interaction mechanism between the welding process and the water environment.

He was the chief welding engineer of the largest Asian buoyancy tank for cosmonaut weightlessness training and large space environment simulator and he overcome the deformation problem in large vessel welding. The developed narrow gap welding metallurgy controlling technics have been applied to the welding of the titanium submersible, which has replaced the imported products. The developed special welding has offered essential support for developing and manufacturing the key components in aerospace, ocean engineering and nuclear power industries of our country.

冶金材料技术奖获得者

朱　荣

朱荣，1962年12月出生于江西省萍乡市。1983年毕业于江西冶金学院（现江西理工大学）炼钢专业。1983年8月—1990年8月工作于江西钢厂（现新余钢铁公司），历任电炉车间炉前工、炉长、技术员、主任。1990—1996年在北京科技大学钢铁冶金专业攻读硕士及博士学位；1996年毕业留校工作至今，历任讲师、副教授、教授/博士生导师。目前担任中国金属学会专家委员会委员、电冶金分会主任委员、特殊钢分会副主任委员，高端金属特种熔炼与制备北京市重点实验室主任，流体与材料相互作用教育部重点实验室主任。承担并完成了多项国家重点研发项目，获国家科技进步奖二等奖3项、省部级一等奖6项，出版专著5部，授权发明专利100余项，发表论文200余篇。获首届全国创新争先奖状、全国优秀科技工作者、中国产学研合作创新奖、北京市师德先锋，入选首批"全国高校黄大年式教师团队"。

朱荣30余年来立足炼钢领域的工程需求，逐步形成了以炼钢流程喷射冶金为特色的学术思想和理论体系。带领组建了国际一流的炼钢流程喷射冶金研究团队，主持建成了世界领先的高温冶金－热态射流试验平台，开辟了喷射冶金在电弧炉炼钢应用的全新领域，是电弧炉炼钢基础理论、应用技术的变革与创新，为我国电弧炉炼钢技术及装备进步做出了卓越贡献。2004年起，针对温室气体排放和钢铁生产节能环保的严峻局面，创造性发现了CO_2在炼钢生产过程中的应用价值，开创了CO_2在炼钢生产中资源化应用的新时代，取得了卓有成效的进展，将对世界钢铁工业产生重要影响。

一、电弧炉炼钢工艺技术变革及创新

结合电弧炉炼钢特点，提出了多介质喷射冶金方法以及高速射流带动冶金反应器中物质和热量快速传输的技术思路，从理论和工程应用上解决了射流在炉内衰减快的世界难题，并完成工艺及装备的自主和集成创新，实现了高效洁净和绿色低耗。撰写的《现代电弧炉炼钢用氧技术》《电弧炉炼钢技术及装备》等多部论著促进了中国电弧炉炼钢技术进步。

1. 电弧炉炼钢高效冶炼技术

首次提出并形成新一代电弧炉炼钢技术——电弧炉炼钢复合吹炼技术，即以集束射流供氧、同步长寿底吹等强化搅拌技术为核心，实现电弧炉炼钢高效吹炼的技术集成，在具有世界先进水平的电炉钢生产线成功应用，引领了电弧炉炼钢喷射冶金技术的发展。发明的炼钢用集束射流系列喷吹技术采用射流外包裹高温燃烧气体形成"伴随流"的方法，获得不易衰减的高速气体射流（原射流长度的 2 倍），实现高强度化学能输入；同步底吹搅拌技术是国际上唯一实现底吹寿命与炉龄同步（1000 炉）的"中国制造"技术。

电弧炉炼钢复合吹炼技术作为钢铁行业"十二五"重点推广项目，至 2018 年已在国内外百余座电弧炉应用，覆盖 40% 以上的电炉钢产能，取得冶炼时间缩短 30%、氧气利用率提高 40%、钢铁料消耗减少 5% 的冶金效果。

将炼钢集束射流技术跨领域应用于航天材料抗氧化烧蚀检测。搭建了高温环境材料抗氧化烧蚀实验平台，完成了国家重大科学仪器设备开发专项"集束射流气动热－力耦合环境模拟试验舱"课题，实现了高端材料的快速低成本筛选。

2. 电弧炉炼钢钢液洁净技术

提出冶炼过程"气泡－粉剂－熔渣－金属液"低碳多相体系钢液深度净化理论，颠覆了传统的渣－钢界面反应净化钢液方式，实现了钢液洁净冶炼。

采用气－固喷吹冶炼新技术，向熔池内直接利用 O_2 喷射 CaO 等粉剂，依靠气体裹挟熔态渣粒直接快速深脱磷；探明了金属熔池 CO_2-Ar 多元介质气泡高效吸附脱氮机理，研发了多元介质混合喷吹脱氮工艺及装备，突破了电弧炉炼钢高端特钢氮含量控制瓶颈；独创的出钢过程连续喷粉脱氧技术利用微粒碳瞬态生成 CO 气泡，实现无铝硅快速脱氧，解决了炼钢流程高效脱氧去夹杂难题。

钢液洁净化技术实现了全废钢电弧炉冶炼终点磷快速脱至 0.004%、终点氮由 0.0060% 以上稳定降至 0.0045%、喷粉脱氧达 $150 \times 10^{-6} \sim 200 \times 10^{-6}$，钢中初始沉淀脱氧产物减少 30%。该技术应用到国家支撑课题"三峡大型水轮机组转轮铸件洁净钢冶炼技术"，解决了三峡电站转轮铸件长期进口的困局；合作研发的高洁净冶炼高钒高耐磨合金技术满足了我国对高端金属耐磨材料的重大需求。

3. 电弧炉炼钢绿色化

研究了电弧炉冶炼与余热回收协调生产的方法，提出并建立了"供电－供氧－脱碳－余热"能量平衡及"供电－供氧－预热－二噁英治理"绿色循环的双工况智能匹配和协同运行体系，实现了余热回收 20kgce/t、二噁英排放 <0.1ng-TEQ/Nm^3 的国际先进水平。完成了国家支撑项目绿色节能环保炼钢电弧炉关键技术及装备研发课题。

朱荣在电弧炉炼钢领域的学术思想及工程实践推动了中国电弧炉炼钢学科的发展和行业科技进步，是中国现代电弧炉炼钢技术的主要开创者。

二、开创炼钢流程 CO_2 资源化应用新途径

1. 将温室气体 CO_2 作为资源应用于炼钢过程降尘

揭示了炼钢烟尘的产生机理和变化规律，将炼钢烟尘治理完全依靠后处理转变为前抑制，颠覆了炼钢烟尘的传统治理方式，是炼钢过程温室气体利用和固体废弃物治理的重要变革。

2. 基于 CO_2 的洁净化炼钢技术

探明了 CO_2 用于炼钢脱磷的热力学机理及动力学规律，改变了炼钢脱磷的控温方式，突破了长期困扰炼钢高效深脱磷的技术瓶颈；揭示了 CO_2 气泡在钢液中的上升规律及 CO_2-O_2 混合喷吹的 C-O 平衡关系，研发了 CO_2 深脱氮及脱氧方法，实现了低磷、低氮高品质钢的规模化生产。

2018 年，中国金属学会评价委员会一致认为该技术发明创新性突出，成果达到国际领先水平。周国治院士、东京大学月桥文孝教授一致认为该技术思想是对冶金物理化学的重要补充及完善。该技术成果被列为钢铁行业"十二五"重点推广项目，并于 2018 年获评《世界金属导报》世界钢铁工业十大技术要闻。

Awardee of Metallurgy and Materials Technology Prize, Zhu Rong

Zhu Rong was born in Pingxiang City of Jiangxi Province in December 1962. From September 1990 to March 1996, he studied for master's degree and doctor's degree in iron and steel metallurgy at Beijing University of science and technology He graduated in 1996 and has been working in school since then. He has been a lecturer, associate professor, Professor / doctoral supervisor.

For more than 30 years, Professor Zhu Rong has gradually formed an academic thought and theoretical system based on the steel-making process and spray metallurgy based on the engineering needs of the steel-making field. He has led the establishment of a world-class research team on spray metallurgy of steel-making process, presided over the construction of the world's leading high-temperature metallurgy hot jet test platform, opened up a new field of application of spray metallurgy in EAF steelmaking, which is the transformation and innovation of basic theory and application technology of EAF steelmaking, and has made outstanding contributions to the progress of EAF steelmaking technology and equipment in China. Since 2004, in view of the severe situation of greenhouse gas emission and energy conservation and environmental protection in steel production, the application value of CO_2 in steel-making production has been creatively discovered, and a new era of resource application of CO_2 in steel-making production has been created, and fruitful progress has been made, which will have an important impact on the world steel industry.

EAF steelmaking is one of the main steelmaking methods in the world, and is the core link of scrap recycling. Energy consumption and carbon emission are only 1 / 3 of the long process of BF-BOF steelmaking. Therefore, the development of EAF steelmaking is an important path to realize the recycling and green transformation and upgrading of iron and steel industry. However, although the emergence and development of EAF steelmaking has gone through a hundred years, due to the limitation of traditional steelmaking methods and means, it is difficult to improve the material and energy transfer speed in the smelting process, and the technical shortcomings such as long smelting cycle, low energy utilization rate, unstable quality and serious dioxin pollution can not be broken through for a long time. These key problems are particularly prominent in China.

Based on the characteristics of EAF steelmaking, Zhu Rong put forward the technical idea of multi-media jet metallurgy, in which high-speed jet drives the rapid transfer of material and heat in metallurgical reactor, solves the world problem of rapid attenuation of jet in furnace from theory and engineering application, and completes the independent and integrated innovation of process and equipment, realizing high efficiency, clean, green and low consumption. He has written many works, such as oxygen technology for modern EAF steelmaking and EAF steelmaking technology and equipment, which has promoted the progress of EAF steelmaking technology in China.

CO_2 emission has become the focus of global attention. It is urgent for steel industry to seek new technologies to reduce or utilize CO_2. In 2004, Zhu Rong put forward the academic idea of CO_2 resource utilization in steel-making process, systematically studied the physical and chemical nature of CO_2 at steel-making temperature, and found that CO_2 has the characteristics of controlling the temperature of steel-making fire spot zone and can inhibit the generation of smoke and dust; meanwhile, he also found that CO_2 can strengthen the molten pool mixing and reduce the content of phosphorus, nitrogen and oxygen in molten steel. The theoretical system of carbon dioxide steelmaking is an innovation and supplement to the traditional steelmaking theory.

资源能源技术奖获得者

刘 清 友

刘清友，1965 年 10 月出生于重庆市开县。1997 年获西南石油大学石油机械专业博士学位。1997—1999 年在重庆大学机械传动国家重点实验室从事博士后研究工作。1986 年在西南石油大学任教，先后担任教研室主任、钻头实验室主任、机械系副主任、机电工程学院常务副院长、研究生部主任。2010—2014 年任西南石油大学副校长，2014—2018 年任西华大学校长，2018 年 12 月起任成都理工大学校长。现为钻头实验室学术委员会主任、油气藏地质及开发工程国家重点实验室学术带头人、四川省机械工程学会副理事长、四川省石油工程学会副理事长。

刘清友是我国石油钻采装备领域的知名专家，长期围绕深层 / 超深层、深水 / 超深水及页岩气开采对石油钻头及装备的特殊需求和重大难题开展研究，为推动我国石油钻头及装备进入世界先进行列做出了重大贡献。

一、发明钻头多因素动态设计新方法和个性化钻头设计制造技术，研制的系列产品在国内外推广应用

"钻头不到，油气不冒"。统计表明：钻头费用仅占钻井成本的 3% ～ 5%，但它对钻井成本的影响高达 30% ～ 70%，钻头一直是国内外油气开发研究的热点问题。20 世纪，我国钻头技术完全依靠国外。80 年代初，我国先后从美国全套引进牙轮钻头和金刚石（PDC）钻头生产线，但不转让设计分析等核心技术。掌握钻头设计分析与研发技术是实现钻头国产化必须攻克的重大难题。

深井地层压力和温度高，岩石性质复杂，钻柱振动剧烈。此前，国内外钻头大多采用给定钻压和均质岩石假设条件下的单因素静强度设计，没有考虑钻柱三维振动、井底岩性随机变化及钻井参数等影响，难以解决深井 / 超深井牙轮钻头钻速慢、寿命短及金刚石钻头地层适应性差等世界性难题。

在前人研究基础上，刘清友主持研制出能模拟深井/超深井岩石可钻性和破岩机理等多套专用实验装置；在相关实验基础上，创建了不同钻头结构与不同岩石相互作用的钻柱系统动力学模型，揭示了钻柱振动、岩石性质、井眼轨迹和钻井参数等对钻头性能的影响规律，由此发明了钻头多因素动态设计新方法，实现钻头设计从单因素到多因素、从静态到动态的突破，不仅实现了钻头设计国产化，而且达到国际先进水平。该方法在我国80%以上的牙轮钻头设计中应用并转让到美国，研制出多个系列高转速长寿命牙轮钻头，成果在企业转化累计生产10万余只。

基于原有批量化钻头设计和制造技术不能满足难钻地层和页岩气水平井等特殊需求，迫切需要针对不同地层和不同钻井条件研制个性化钻头，以满足我国复杂难钻条件钻井提速对高性能钻头的需求。此前，钻头个性化设计制造技术被少数国家垄断，部分产品甚至对我国禁售。刘清友带领团队历经10余年自主研究，形成具有完全自主知识产权的个性化钻头设计、分析、研发、制造及产业化技术体系，研制出牙轮钻头、PDC钻头及复合钻头三大类10余个系列个性化钻头，累计生产20余万只，在我国90%的深井难钻地层钻井提速中应用，多次创造亚洲超深井的钻井纪录，并出口到美国、加拿大、俄罗斯等30余个国家，其中小井眼高速钻头占美国25%的市场，产值100余亿元。

以上成果获2009年国家科技进步奖二等奖1项。

二、发明深水/超深水管柱动力学分析方法，研制出世界首套海洋环境与钻井工况耦合作用的深水管柱力学模拟实验系统，为"海洋石油981"等深水平台的钻井安全提供技术支撑

深水管柱的优化配置及安全控制是制约我国深水/超深水油气高效开发的重大难题。据统计，深水管柱系统失效导致的深水钻井事故约占60%、井控失效约占20%。此前，国内外深水管柱的研究仅限于海流引起隔水管、生产立管等涡激振动、疲劳破坏和单因素拖曳实验，与实际工况差异太大，不能完全满足我国南海等恶劣海况对钻完井安全的迫切要求。

刘清友在多年开展钻柱系统动力学研究的基础上，创建了海洋环境与钻井工况耦合作用下的深水管柱系统动力学模型及分析方法，发明能模拟深水管柱实际工况的力学实验系统，通过理论和实验研究揭示了深水管柱动力学特性和失效机理，发现"三分之一效应"（隔水管在剪切流作用下距海面1/3处变形及应力最大）和"上下边界效应"（隔水管上下两端张力与钻井液密度及排量成正比）；同时，在国内外率先开展钻完井双层管柱力学特性和磨损机理研究，主编全球首部《深水浮式平台－钻完井管柱－防喷器系统安全设计与操作手册》。该成果在"海洋石油981"和Jasper等深水平台成功应用，为国内外深水钻井管柱安全提供了技术支撑。

以上成果作为四个创新点中的第二个创新点，获得2014年国家科技进步奖特等奖。

三、攻克振动控制、泵头体寿命及轻量化设计等核心技术，为我国研制出世界首台超高压大功率 3000 型压裂泵及其在页岩气开发中应用做出了重大贡献

我国页岩气埋藏深、地应力高，大多在山区，高效开发我国页岩气资源需要超高压大功率（最高压力 140MPa、单机功率 ≥ 2500hp）的压裂装备支撑。此前国内外压裂装备（最高压力 <105MPa、单机功率 ≤ 2250hp）不能满足需要，研制超高压大功率压裂装备是解决我国页岩气高效开发的重大难题。

为此，刘清友带领团队创建了超高压大功率压裂泵系统动力学模型，自主研制了泵头体冲蚀磨损实验装置；在理论和实验研究基础上提出基于抗疲劳裂纹扩展的泵头体材料调控方法，使超高压泵头体平均寿命达到 600 小时的世界最高水平；提出基于缸数、冲程、冲次、连杆负荷、传动结构的"五因素"轻量化设计技术，实现超高压大功率车载压裂泵的轻量化设计，最大功率质量比达 0.28kW/kg 的世界领先水平，为我国成功研制出世界首台 3000 型压裂装备并在涪陵页岩气规模化开采中广泛应用提供了重要支撑，实现了我国压裂装备从引进到进入世界先进水平的跨越。

以上成果获 2015 年国家科技进步奖二等奖。

刘清友先后获国家科技进步奖特等奖 1 项、二等奖 2 项，省部级一等奖 6 项；获首届全国创新争先奖状、国家首批"万人计划"领军人才、长江学者特聘教授和全国优秀科技工作者等荣誉；获授权发明专利 39 件（国际专利 6 件）；发表论文 170 篇，他引 2251 次，出版专著、教材专著 6 部；培养博士后 12 名、博士研究生 30 余名，形成了一支高水平研究团队。

Awardee of Resources and Energies Technology Prize, Liu Qingyou

Liu Qingyou was born in Kaixian of Chongqing City in October 1965. He served as President of Chengdu University of Technology from December 2018. He is as also as the director of the Academic Committee of Bit Laboratory, the academic leader of the State Key Laboratory of Oil and Gas Reservoir Geology and Exploitation, vice president of Sichuan Mechanical Engineering Society and vice president of Sichuan Petroleum Engineering Society.

Liu is a well-known expert on drilling and production equipment technology in China, and has long been conducting research on the special needs and major problems of deep/ultra-deep, deepwater/ultra-deepwater and shale gas production for bit and equipment more than 30 years, and makes a significant contribution to promoting China's bits and equipment to enter the world's advanced ranks.

Firstly, Liu invented a new multi factors dynamic design method of bit and personalized design and manufacturing technology of bit, and developed a series of products applied at home and abroad. It was suggested by statistical analysis that the cost of bit only accounts for 3% ~ 5% of the drilling cost, but its impact on the drilling cost is as high as 30% ~ 70%. The bit has always been a hot issue in oil and gas development research at home and abroad. In the last century, China's bit technology completely relied on foreign countries. In the early 1980s, China successfully imported a complete production line of roller bit and PDC bit from the United States, but did not transfer core technologies such as design analysis. The design and manufacturing technology of bit was a major problem that must be overcome to realize bit localization.

Deep/ultra−deep wells have high formation pressure and temperature, complex rock properties, and intense drill string vibration. Previously, the single factor static strength design method was adopted in most domestic and foreign countries during bit design under the assumption of a given WOB and homogeneous rock without considering the influence of drill string three−dimensional vibration, accidental changes in bottom hole lithology and drilling parameters, so it was difficult to solve the world−wide problems of low penetration rate, the short service life of cone bit and low formation adaptability of PDC bit in deep/ultra−deep well.

Secondly, Liu invented the dynamic analysis method of deep water/ultra−deep water string, developed the world's first deep water string mechanical simulation experimental system taking the coupling effect between the marine environment and drilling condition into account, providing technical support for drilling safety of deepwater platform such as "Offshore Oil 981".

Thirdly, Liu overcome the core technologies of vibration control, pump head life and lightweight design, and made great contributions to the development of the world's first ultra−high pressure and high−power type 3000 fracturing pump and its application in shale gas development.

工程建设技术奖获得者

罗 琦

罗琦，1967年出生于四川省富顺县。1991年起在中国核动力研究设计院设计所工作；2009—2020年任中国核动力研究设计院院长；2020年3月至今任中核集团副总工程师、中国原子能科学研究院党委书记。2019年当选中国工程院院士。

罗琦是我国核动力反应堆设计研发领军人，历任多型国家重大工程副总师、总师。获国家科技进步奖一等奖1项、二等奖1项，省部级一等奖6项，个人一、二等功各1次。获国家高新工程突出贡献个人奖、国防科技工业杰出人才奖，入选国家百千万人才工程。

一、主持完成新一代核动力研发平台研制，解决研发方法和手段，实现研发水平跨代提升

新一代核动力研发平台是全新的技术跨越。罗琦发明平台研制工艺技术，攻克复杂堆芯设计技术等难题，创建我国核动力数字化设计研发体系和先进试验研究平台，解决新一代核动力设计研发的方法和手段，整体水平国际先进，堆芯设计技术等国际领先。成功应用于新型军用核动力、现役主战核潜艇、自主三代核电"华龙一号"、二代加核电批量研发，产生重大效益。获国家科技进步奖一等奖1项。

二、发明反应堆主工艺技术，主持攻克反应堆堆芯故障及改进技术

反应堆系统是研制的关键。罗琦发明冗余多驱动反应堆技术，解决原方案任务完成可靠度不足的难题，实现工程应用；针对堆芯故障导致批量建造停滞的严重问题，主持攻克"堆芯更换、故障分析、改进和验证"技术，实现堆芯可靠性提高一个量级，彻底解决批量建造停滞问题。

三、主持完成新一代动力试验堆工程研制；主持完成某大功率长寿期水面核动力反应堆技术攻关，实现技术重大跨越

主持完成新一代陆上试验堆工程建设，实现潜艇核动力技术水平跨代提升；某大功率长寿期水面核动力反应堆是全新一代技术，罗琦发明多环路长燃耗反应堆技术，完成样机研制和试验验证，技术水平总体国际先进、部分国际领先，所攻克的技术被国家采纳并批准工程应用。

Awardee of Engineering and Construction Technology Prize, Luo Qi

Luo Qi was born in Fushun County of Sichuan Province in 1967. He began working at the design institute of Nuclear Power Institute of China in 1991. From January 2009 to March 2020, he served as the president of Nuclear Power Institute of China. Since March 2020, he has been the deputy general engineer of China National Nuclear Corporation, and secretary of the Party Committee of China Institute of Atomic Energy. He was elected an academician of the Chinese Academy of Engineering in 2019. Luo Qi is China's leading scientist in designing and developing nuclear power reactors, having been the deputy general engineer and general engineer of several national major projects.

He was in charge of and completed the development of the new generation nuclear power research and development platform. Under his leadership, cross-generational improvements have been achieved in the research and development methodologies and means, which have been put into successful use and generated significant beneficial results. The new generation nuclear power research and development platform represents an entirely new leap in technology. The platform developed under the charge of Luo Qi has been successfully applied in the development of new-type military nuclear power, main battle nuclear-powered submarine in commission, Hualong One technology (a domestically developed third-generation reactor), and the research of second-generation plus reactor in batches. It has generated significant benefits.

Luo Qi has invented the main technologies of nuclear reactor, was in charge of fixing the breakdown in the reactor core and improving technology, and resolved the difficulty of the stagnation in development and research in batches. To address the severe problem that the breakdown in the sector core leads to the stagnation of manufacturing in batches, he took charge of the development of the technologies of "replacing the reactor core, analyzing the breakdown, making improvement and conducting test." With the application of these technologies, the reliability of the reactor core has been improved by 10 times, and the problem of stagnation in the manufacturing in batches has been fundamentally solved.

Luo Qi was in charge of and completed the development of the new–generation nuclear power test reactor. He was in charge of and completed the technological innovation of XX high–powered longevity period water surface nuclear power reactor. The innovation has realized significant leap in technology, and has been applied in engineering projects with the approval of the state. He invented the multiple–loop long burn–up reactor technology, and completed the development and experimental testing of the prototype employing the technology. The technology of the prototype on the whole occupies an advanced position in the world, and partially holds an international leading position. It has been adopted by the state and applied in engineering projects with the approval of the state.

工程建设技术奖获得者

谭 家 华

谭家华，1946 年 4 月出生于湖北省宜昌市。上海交通大学船舶海洋与建筑工程学院教授。

在长江口航道整治和洋山深水港建设工程中，谭家华带领团队与施工单位一起进行了软体排的施工工艺及砂袋的力学性质研究，完成了十余艘软体排铺放与砂袋抛放船及相关设备的设计。该产品经专家组鉴定达到世界先进水平。获 2000 年上海市科学技术进步奖二等奖。

在长江口导堤的建设中，谭家华带领团队通过长期理论和试验研究，解决了抛石整平作业瓶颈，研制出了自升式大桩靴抛石整平平台——航工平 1 号，取得了很好的社会经济效益并通过专家组鉴定。鉴定委员会一致认为，"航工平 1 号"项目具有较高的学术成果，有独创性，达到了国际先进水平。获 2007 年上海市科学技术奖三等奖。

大型绞吸挖泥船是远海岛礁建设、近海围海造地及港口航道建设的重大装备，20 世纪初国内无设计、无制造、无配套，核心技术受制于人。谭家华带领团队与兄弟单位合作对其关键技术开展研究，攻克大型绞吸挖泥船海底岩土挖掘、钢桩台车定位、疏浚输送与装备总装集成等"卡脖子"难题。2004 年建成"航绞 2001"，打破了完全依赖进口的局面；2006 年建成"天狮"号，标志我国绞吸挖泥船的设计制造达到国际同等水平；2010 年建成"天鲸"号，标志我国绞吸挖泥船的研制迈入世界先进行列；2015 年研制"新海旭"，作业能力属世界领先水平。迄今为止，谭家华所在团队设计的大型绞吸挖泥船已有 60 余艘，形成 12 亿方岩土的年疏浚产能，与进口相比，平均研制周期缩短 35%、平均建造成本降低 44%，使我国成为疏浚强国。这些绞吸挖泥船承担远海岛礁建设、"一带一路"国内外港口建设等重大工程 211 项，在维护国家安全和推进国家战略中发挥了无可替代的关键作用，实现了大型绞吸挖泥船从"被封锁"到"限制出口"的历史性跨越发展，为我国领土 / 领海权益维护和重大基础设施建设提供了大国重器。经专家组鉴定，达到国际领先水平。获 2018 年中国机械工业科学技术特等奖、2019 年国家科技进步奖特等奖。

谭家华的工作和贡献得到国内外专家和同行的充分肯定，为地区和行业经济建设做出了重要贡献。

Awardee of Engineering and Construction Technology Prize, Tan Jiahua

Tan Jiahua, born in Yichang City of Hubei Province in April 1946, graduated from Ship Engineering Department of Shanghai Jiaotong University in 1969 and has been teaching since graduation.From 1993 to 1994, he worked as a visiting scholar at Yokohama National University in Japan. He is the team leader of Marine Design & Research Institute in Shanghai Jiaotong University and is State-Council Special Allowance obtained expert.

Professor Tan is one of the experts firstly start developing of offshore engineering and special equipments. Pioneer, initiator and organizer of independently development of large cutter suction dredger. He made breakthrough in crucial technologies with major entities. His achievements have been making great contribution towards technique upgrading, port construction for The Road And Belt, and island building.

1. Development of new ship

In view of the low efficiency problem of transport, Professor Tan and his team carried out researches to improve the propulsion efficiency of inland tugboats in Hangzhou, Zhejiang Province. They also developed new ship type of river-sea direct coal transport, carried out research on shallow draught and super shallow draught transport ship type. The new ship type experienced a long period of development and application, and increased the tonnage of Qiantang River sea transport ship from 300 tons to 1500 tons.

2. Geotextile laying equipment

Professor Tan and his team, as well as construction enterprises and shipyards, developed special geotextile laying equipment for construction of soft row. Professor Tan's work has solved the difficult problem by indigenous method at low price and simplified technique, identified by the expert group as world's leading technology.

3. Rubble leveling platform

Professor Tan led the team to carry out theoretical and experimental research on the basic law of the self-lifting rubble leveling equipment, successfully designed and constructed the self-lifting rubble leveling equipment: "Hang Gong Ping 1".

4. Large cutter suction dredger

Professor Tan leads the team of Marine Design & Research Institute of Shanghai Jiaotong University and starts independent research and development and industrialization of large suction dredging equipment at sea for nearly 20 years. Professor Tan and his team engaged in the core technology of large cutter suction dredger, as well as 18 enterprise of construction, shipbuilding and facility. They solved the problems of high strength rock and reef excavation, positioning of pile trolley in harsh environment, long distance transportation of dredged materials and integrated design. So far, Tan Jiahua team has designed 59 large cutter suction dredger, which played an irreplaceable role in the maintenance of national territorial sea security and promote the national strategy.

As a result of the outstanding contribution of scientific research, since 1992 he has won more than 10 awards of different levels, including Special Class Prize of the National Science and Technology Progress Award, provincial and ministerial level prize. In 2019, he won the "Xin Yixin Naval Architecture and Ocean Engineering Lifetime Achievement Award". Due to outstanding achievements in teaching and graduate training, he has won the title of Shanghai excellent educator and Shanghai Talent Award.

工程建设技术奖获得者

周绪红

　　周绪红，1956年9月出生于湖南省南县。工学博士，重庆大学教授，著名土木工程专家。中国工程院院士，日本工程院外籍院士，英国结构工程师学会会士和英国皇家特许结构工程师。1982年、1986年和1992年相继获得湖南大学土木系工学学士、硕士和博士学位。1999—2002年任湖南大学副校长；2002—2018年先后担任长安大学校长、兰州大学校长和重庆大学校长。2014年创建重庆大学钢结构工程研究中心（2017年此中心认定为重庆市协同创新中心）并担任主任至今；2018年创建国家钢结构工程研究中心西南分中心并担任主任。兼任中国钢结构协会名誉会长，中国金属结构协会荣誉会长，国家钢结构工程技术研究中心技术委员会主任，中国土木工程学会常务理事，中国力学学会常务理事，桥梁工程结构动力学国家重点实验室学术委员会主任委员，国家海上风力发电工程技术研究中心学术委员会委员，中国住建部建筑结构标准化技术委员会副主任委员，中国住建部建筑金属应用技术专家委员会委员，中国教育部科学技术委员会国际学部主任，国家自然科学基金委工程材料学部专家咨询委员会委员，中国工程院主席团成员，重庆市科技创新专家咨询委员会委员，联合国工业发展组织国际太阳能技术促进转让中心高级专家等专业学会或政府咨询机构的重要职务；并兼任10余本国内外学术期刊的主编、编委或顾问。

　　周绪红长期从事土木工程专业的教学与科研工作，在钢结构和钢－混凝土混合结构体系研发、理论研究和工程应用方面做出了突出贡献。

一、创新发展了冷弯薄壁型钢结构体系，推动了冷弯薄壁型钢结构从低层向多层发展

　　首次提出采用振动梁函数求解薄板大挠度方程组的半能量法，完善了板件、板组稳定及其屈曲后承载力计算理论；提出了开口薄壁构件的弯扭屈曲和畸变屈曲计算理论与设计方法，以及组合墙体和组合楼盖的计算理论与设计方法；研发了我国第一栋多层冷弯型钢住宅。

二、创新发展了钢 – 混凝土混合结构体系，推动了超高层建筑的发展

提出了钢管约束混凝土结构体系，建立了这种新结构体系及其构件、节点的分析理论与设计方法；创新发展了交错桁架结构体系，首次进行了大比例结构的试验研究，建立了系统的分析理论和设计计算方法，研发了我国第一栋交错桁架结构房屋；提出了装配式钢管混凝土异形柱框架 – 剪力墙体系，创新发展了支撑巨型框架 – 核心筒体系，完善了抗震设计方法，提出了竖向变形差异计算与控制方法。

三、发明了单向预应力双向配筋混凝土叠合楼板，推动了房屋建筑的装配化与绿色化发展

提出了板的极限承载力设计理论和方法；建立了人 – 楼板耦合的荷载模型和计算分析方法，提出了楼板的舒适度控制方法。这种楼板在工程中大量应用，大大减少甚至免除了模板和支撑。

四、首次提出桥梁结构钢 – 混结合段构造和钢锚板组合索塔锚固体系，建立了分析理论与方法，为复杂关键部位的设计提供了依据

上述成果在世界第三高楼深圳平安金融中心（高 592.5m）、沈阳宝能环球金融中心（高 568m）等高层大跨建筑结构、桥梁结构、海洋结构、地下结构中广泛应用，成果被10 余部国家或行业技术标准采纳，并编制成多层冷弯薄壁型钢结构、钢管约束混凝土结构、交错桁架结构、叠合楼板专门技术标准，取得了显著的技术经济效益和社会效益，推动了土木工程行业的科技进步。

周绪红先后获得国家科技进步奖一等奖 1 项、二等奖 3 项，省部级科技进步奖一等奖 11 项，国家教学成果奖二等奖 2 项；获得第二届全国创新争先奖状、重庆市科技突出贡献奖、陕西省突出贡献专家称号、甘肃省领军人才称号、中国钢结构协会组合结构杰出贡献奖、钢结构行业突出贡献专家和中国钢结构三十年领军人物称号。授权知识产权108 项；主编和参编国家与行业标准 10 部，出版专著 3 部、教材 9 部，在国内外有影响力的期刊发表论文 490 余篇。

Awardee of Engineering and Construction Technology Prize, Zhou Xuhong

Zhou Xuhong was born in Nan County of Hunan Province in September 1956. He is a famous civil engineering expert and the Professor of Chongqing University now. In 1992, he earned his

Ph.D at Hunan University, China. He was vice President of Hunan University from 1999 to 2002, and then successively served as President of Chang'an University, Lanzhou University and Chongqing University from 2002 to 2018. Based on his outstanding scientific and technological achievements, he was elected Academician of Chinese Academy of Engineering (CAE) in 2011, and Foreign Associate of Engineering Academy of Japan (EAJ) in 2019, and Fellow of the Institution of Structural Engineers and Royal Chartered Structural Engineer of UK in 2016.

Professor Zhou has been engaged in teaching and researching of civil engineering specialty for a long time. He has made outstanding contributions in the research and development of novel systems in steel structure and steel-concrete hybrid structure, and their structural analysis theory and engineering application. He innovatively developed the cold-formed thin-walled steel structure system, which promoted the development of this structure from low level to multi-level. The first multi-storey cold-formed steel residential building in China is developed by him. He innovatively developed the steel-concrete hybrid structure system, which promoted the development of super high-rise buildings. He put forward the steel tube confined concrete structure system, and innovatively developed the staggered truss structure system and the mega frame-core tube system with brace. He also invented a kind of laminated concrete floor slab prestressed in one direction and reinforced in two directions, which promotes the assembly and greenization development of housing construction. In addition, as the main leader of four famous universities, he has made outstanding contributions to the reform and development of higher education in China.

He has successively won 1 first prize and 3 second prizes of the State Scientific and Technological Progress Award issued by China State Council, and 11 first prizes of Provincial and Ministerial Scientific and Technological Progress Award, and 2 second prizes of National Teaching Achievement Award (Higher Education), and holds 108 authorized intellectual property rights. He has edited or participated in the compilation of 10 national or industrial technical specifications and published 3 academic monographs, 9 university textbooks and more than 490 academic papers in influential journals.

He has also won many industry and government honors successively, such as National Innovation Award, the title of the leading figure of China's steel construction for thirty years, award for outstanding contribution to science and technology of Chongqing municipality , and expert with outstanding contribution of Shaanxi province, and leading talent in Gansu province, etc.

何梁何利基金科学与技术创新奖获得者传略

PROFILES OF THE AWARDEES OF PRIZE FOR SCIENTIFIC AND TECHNOLOGICAL INNOVATION OF HO LEUNG HO LEE FOUNDATION

青年创新奖获得者

陈 小 前

陈小前，1975 年 9 月出生于湖南省双峰县。1991 年考入国防科技大学航天技术系，2001 年获航空宇航科学与技术博士学位并留校任教，历任国防科技大学航天与材料工程学院空间技术研究所教研室副主任、副所长、学院训练部部长等，2015 年担任航天科学与工程学院院长。2017 年调入军事科学院，组建国防科技创新研究院并担任首任院长。2017 年当选国际宇航科学院通信院士，同年获得国家自然科学基金杰出青年基金和国防科技卓越青年基金资助。先后担任国家"863"高技术某主题专家组副组长，国际宇航联合会委员，国家高分重大专项专家，中国仪器仪表学会空间仪器分会副理事长等。研究成果先后获得国家技术发明奖二等奖 1 项、国家科技进步奖二等奖 1 项以及省部级一等奖 4 项，获第二届全国创新争先奖章、"求是"杰出青年实用工程奖、中国青年科技奖；入选国家高层次人才特殊支持计划、军队科技领军人才培养对象、国家百千万人才工程等。

陈小前主要从事飞行器设计研究工作，在飞行器先进设计方法、新概念微纳卫星技术与航天器在轨服务技术等方面做出了一系列开创性的研究工作。

一、飞行器先进设计方法

针对飞行器总体设计面临的学科领域多、学科间耦合关系复杂等难题，自 1998 年攻读博士学位起，在国内率先开展飞行器 MDO 理论的系统研究。针对飞行器总体的建模复杂性、计算复杂性、组织复杂性等技术挑战，通过二十多年的持续研究，突破了面向 MDO 的系统建模方法、近似方法、系统灵敏度分析技术、设计空间搜索策略、优化过程、集成设计环境等一系列关键技术，建立了较为完整的 MDO 理论体系，出版了国内首部 MDO 专著《飞行器多学科设计优化理论与应用研究》。近年来，针对飞行器总体设计方案对稳健性和可靠性的迫切需求，进一步将研究重点聚焦于如何处理飞行器设计中的不确定性问题，突破了不确定性分析、不确定性优化以及 UMDO 优化过程等关键技术，研究成果形成了国内首部 UMDO 专著《飞行器不确定性多学科设计优化理论与应用》。先后发表相关论文 150 余篇，他引 2000 余次，在国内外产生了较大影响。基于上述理论研究成果开发的设计平台在多个航空航天工业部门推广应用，并成为多家单位飞行器数字化设计平台的核心组成部分，与航天工业部门联合成立了飞行器多学科设计优化研究中心，较好地推动了我国飞行器总体设计水平的快速提升。研究成果获 2017 年湖南省自然科学奖一等奖，并获得国家杰出青年基金资助。

二、新概念微纳卫星技术

针对我国微纳卫星发展所急需解决的卫星设计、管理、应用等技术挑战，自 2005 年起开展微纳卫星关键技术研究，提出了卫星高功能密度设计方法，发明了多种海空目标识别载荷，先后主持研制完成 10 颗微纳卫星，探索形成了以"先进设计、灵活管理、高效应用"为特点的微纳卫星系统研发之路，处于国内领先、国际先进水平。其中，"天拓一号"采用世界首创的高功能密度单板纳星体系结构，突破了高功能密度设计与集成、一体化通信协议与可配置软件核、星载舰船信号识别与处理等技术；2012 年发射成功，作为国内首颗 AIS 卫星拥有 21 家长期用户，在亚丁湾护航、神舟飞船应急搜救等任务中发挥重要作用，获 2015 年国家技术发明奖二等奖等。"天拓三号"为国际首个六星异构微纳卫星集群，包括 1 颗主卫星、1 颗国内首个手机卫星和 4 颗国际最小飞卫星，突破了异构多星匹配设计与共位发射、集群自主组网和协同控制、分布式载荷设计与综合应用等技术；2015 年发射成功，完成国际上首次空间自组织网络在轨试验，实现了大范围船舶 / 飞机识别，国内长期用户 23 家，在国际民航空管标准制定、北极航道分析等任务中发挥重要作用，获 2019 年国家科技进步奖二等奖。

三、航天器在轨服务技术

航天器在轨服务是未来航天技术发展的必然趋势，以此为背景，陈小前自 2006 年带领团队在国内率先系统开展在轨服务技术研究工作，并完成了国内首部《航天器在轨服务技术》专著。在此基础上，根据国际发展趋势和国内迫切需求，将研究重点确立为航天器在轨加注技术。在国家"863"计划支持下，作为项目负责人组织全国优势单位组成攻关团队，以在轨加注要求的"可靠对接、高效密封、稳定传输、精确检测"为目标，突破了基于结构变形的空间软对接技术、微重力流体内角流动管理技术、推进剂量高精度动态测量等一系列关键技术，完成了包括卫星软捕获与高效密封全功能服务单元、可重复填充板式表面张力贮箱、超声波流量检测系统等在内的航天器自主在轨加注系统试验样机研制，建成了国内规模最大、功能最完整的地面综合试验系统。2011 年，相关成果参加了国家科技部"十一五"成果展并得到党和国家领导人的高度评价。在上述研究基础上，担任总师设计了"天源一号"在轨加注飞行试验系统，2016 年搭载长征七号入轨并圆满完成全部试验，使我国成为第二个掌握卫星在轨加注主要关键技术的国家。总结撰写了国内首部卫星在轨加注技术学术专著，并获国家科学技术学术专著出版基金资助。研究成果获 2017 年军队科技进步奖一等奖，并获首届国防科技卓越青年基金资助。

陈小前重视人才培养工作，已培养博士研究生 25 名、硕士研究生 35 名。所指导的研究生获全国优秀博士学位论文 1 篇、省部级优秀学位论文 12 篇，2 名博士研究生获教育部学术新人奖，1 名博士生获得第 66 届国际宇航联合大会学生论文竞赛中国赛区第一名、全球总决赛第三名。其本人连续多年被评为优秀研究生导师。

Awardee of Youth Innovation Prize, Chen Xiaoqian

Chen Xiaoqian was born in Shuangfeng County of Hunan Province in September 1975. In 2017, he was transferred to Academy of Military Sciences to establish National Innovation Institute of Defense Technology and was assigned to be the first dean of this new institute. In 2017, he was elected as the corresponding academician of the International Academy of Astronautics (IAA).

Chen Xiaoqian is engaged in the research of aircraft design, and has made a series of pioneering research work in the aspects of advanced design method of aircraft, new concept micro/nano satellite technology and spacecraft on orbit service technology.

1. Advanced design method of aircraft

In view of the problems of multiple disciplines as well as their complicated relationship in the overall design of aircraft, he has carried out the pioneering and systematic research on aircraft MDO theory in China since 1998 when he was pursuing his Ph.D degree. Aiming at the technical challenges such as modeling complexity, computational complexity, and organizational complexity of aircraft, a series of key technologies such as system modeling method, approximation method, system sensitivity analysis technology, design space search strategy, optimization process and integrated design environment for MDO have been broken through by their continuous research for more than twenty years, and a relatively systematic MDO theory framework has been established, the first MDO monograph in China "Aircraft Multidisciplinary Design Optimization Theory and Application Research" was published. In recent years, in view of the urgent demand for robustness and reliability in the overall design of aircraft, he focuses on how to deal with the uncertainty in aircraft design, and breaks through the key technologies of uncertainty analysis, uncertainty optimization and UMDO optimization process. The first UMDO monograph in China "Theory and Application of Multidisciplinary Design Optimization for Aircraft Uncertainty" was published by summarizing these research achievements.

2. New concept micro/nano satellite technology

In view of the technical challenges of satellite design, management and application, which are urgently required to be solved in the development of micro/nano satellites in China, he has taken the pioneering research on the key technologies since 2005. He has proposed the design method of satellite high function density, and has invented a variety of sea-sky target recognition payloads. He has taken charge of the design and manufacture of 10 micro/nano satellites, and has explored a product development road of micro/nano satellite system characterized by "Advanced design, Flexible management and Efficient application".

3. Spacecraft on orbit service technology

Spacecraft on orbit service is an inevitable trend in the future development of space technology. Based on this background, he and his team have carried out the pioneering research work of "On Orbit Service Technology" in China since 2006, and published the first monograph of "Spacecraft On Orbit Service Technology" in China. On this basis, he keeps the focus on the spacecraft on orbit refueling technology considering the international development trend and domestic urgent demands.

青年创新奖获得者

常　超

　　常超，1983年出生于山西省太原市。清华大学学士（2002级）、博士（2006级），美国斯坦福大学博士后（2011—2013年）。现任军事科学研究院国防科技创新研究院前沿交叉技术中心副主任、研究员、博士生导师，西安交通大学兼职教授、国防科技创新特区主题首席科学家、创新工作站首席专家。获国家自然科学二等奖、部级科技进步奖一等奖2项；IEEE NPSS Early Achievement Award 年度全球唯一获奖人、首位获奖中国学者；获陈嘉庚青年科学奖、亚太等离子体物理青年学者奖、中国青年科技奖特别奖、中国科学探索奖。国家万人计划领军、国防卓越青年基金、国家自然基金优秀青年基金获得者。IEEE 国际会议 APCOPTS 大会主席、2020 ICOPS 组委会主席、全国等离子体大会组委会主席。*IEEE Trans. Micro. Theo. Tech.* 副主编、*IEEE Trans. Plasma Sci.* 高级编辑。中国生物物理学会太赫兹生物物理分会主任。空间微波国家级重点实验室 & 教育部太赫兹重点实验室学术委员会委员。以第一／通讯作者发表 SCI 论文60篇，以第一发明人获授权发明专利20项。

　　常超主要从事高功率微波、太赫兹生物物理研究，在高功率微波击穿机理及抑制方法方面做出创新性研究工作。

一、在国际上提出了突破高功率微波系统功率容量瓶颈的原理和方法

　　高功率微波（HPM）可以光速攻击飞机和导弹的电子信息系统，是未来信息化战争的"杀手锏"武器、保卫国家安全的颠覆性技术。击穿是限制 HPM 系统功率、作用距离的核心瓶颈和国际性难题。常超在国际上建立了高功率微波击穿理论模型，诊断了介质／真空、介质／大气界面等离子体纳秒时空演化规律，提出了周期性表面和谐振磁场两种抑制电子倍增、提高 HPM 击穿阈值的新原理和新方法，实验证实提高十亿瓦级微波系统功率达4倍。上述成果获国家自然科学奖二等奖、部级科技进步奖一等奖。

二、提出基于激光驻波波荡器的高增益自由电子激光（FEL）的新方法

相比传统光源，基于激光驻波波荡器的高增益自由电子激光（FEL）的新方法显著提高了 FEL 的亮度和光子数，提出并研制世界上首台微波波荡器并产生高次相干辐射。

三、提出 THz 在有髓神经中继接力传输模型

Science 提出 125 个世界级科学问题，第二个是意识的生物学基础。人及动物能对外界刺激快速反应，表明体内存在高速信息通路。而迄今探测的脑电和神经电都是低频 100Hz 以下。Hodgkin 和 Huxley 因发现离子跨膜产生神经电传导获诺贝尔奖，但是 Hodgkin 为解释有髓神经电传导引入同轴电报方程，其成立的金属边界条件在生物液体环境不存在。常超提出 THz 在有髓神经中继接力传输模型：信息以髓鞘为等效"介质光纤"高速传输；信息在朗飞结处被放大。实验证实，髓鞘在特定频段有高折射率、约束电磁能量。提出神经表面有序水分子传递太赫兹信息原理，为解释人类意识基础、太赫兹调控脑功能、增强学习能力做出贡献。

四、发现太赫兹调控离子通道相变提高离子流速的机理，研究了 THz 电磁刺激调控神经水通道蛋白的渗透能力在正常渗透相与超级渗透相之间的转变

一维受限水加载膜通道，施加特定频率的 THz 电磁刺激：1.39-THz 电磁刺激远离体相水对电磁波吸收频域，该电磁刺激的能量被受限水强烈吸收。水通道蛋白渗透能力的相变具有 THz 频率依赖性。

去甲肾上腺素（NE）作为中枢神经抑制性递质，由交感节后神经元和脑内肾上腺素能神经末梢合成和分泌。研究了 NE 分子构象相关的振动特性和分子间相互作用的 THz 指纹谱，用于分子探测和识别的生物标记。相关研究发表在英国皇家化学会刊。

Awardee of Youth Innovation Prize, Chang Chao

Chang Chao was born in Taiyuan City of Shanxi Province in 1983. He got Bachelor and Ph.D of Tsinghua University, Postdoctorial in Stanford University. Deputy Dean and Researcher of Advanced Research Center.

The principle and methods of suppressing HPM window multipactor by periodic surface profiles were proposed, improving the microwave radiation power capacity by 4 times. Achieving China State Science Award and first price of China Ministerial Scientific Award.

High power microwave (HPM) as one important frontier community has the character of transient giga-watt peak power and pulse width of tens of nanoseconds. HPM system only works in vacuum status, and dielectric window works for isolating inner vacuum and outer air as well as high efficient radiation. When HPM transmitted to window, the intense electromagnetic field triggers secondary multipactor and breakdown, microwave is absorbed, reflected and cut-off, seriously limiting the power capacity of system and becoming the bottleneck of HPM technology development and international challenge. The mechanisms of HPM window breakdown at vacuum and air side were discovered. Models of secondary electron multipactor, space charge field, plasma discharge were established, diagnosing the nanosecond temporal and spatial evolution of plasma at dielectric/vacuum and dielectric/air interface.

The existed theory for HPM window breakdown is based on ideal vacuum of secondary multipactor, neglecting the absorbed gases at vacuum/dielectric interface and induced desorption during multipactor forming local high pressure. The project group systematically studied the HPM window breakdown mechanisms, and established HPM multipactor and plasma models, and published in main journals of plasma community, including: 1. Multipactor dynamics models of collision and ionization and multipactor in desorbed gases (Phys. Plasma 15, 093508, 2008); 2. Space charge field model for combined multipactor and plasma (Phys. Plasmas16, 053506, 2009), 3. HPM plasma discharge global model (Phys. Plasmas16, 033505, 2009); 4. Accumulation of electrons and heat in repetitive HPM pulses (Phys. Plasmas17, 053301, 2010).

The temporal and spatial evolution of plasma at dielectric/vacuum interface in single nanosecond and GW HPM pulse is diagnosed, discovering thin layer near vacuum/dielectric interface and brightness enhancing after main HPM pulse. Bright light emission in gas desorption layer is discovered in PIC simulation, and the averaged electron energy is sufficiently high to excite atoms and to keep ionization n_e, leading to brighter emission, published in *Appl. Phys.*

The temporal and spatial evolution of plasma at dielectric/air interface in single nanosecond pulse is diagnosed, discovering teeth-profile plasma spatial distribution similar to E-field profile, but more brighter near dielectric/air interface and becoming thin layer of light emission after microwave pulse. In PIC simulation, space charge sheath exists near dielectric surface, improving the local electron energy and density, thus, breakdown and light emission is stronger near dielectric surface compared with free space, published in *Phys. Rev. E.*

Multipactor dynamics on two dimensional rectangular and triangular, three dimensional wavy surface, were studied, obtaining the influence and principle of characteristic dimension and slope, microwave mode, frequency, and field on multipactor suppression, and demonstrating improving the microwave radiation power capacity by 4 times.

青年创新奖获得者

鲁军勇

鲁军勇，1978 年 6 月出生于湖北省鄂州市。2010 年毕业于海军工程大学电气工程学院，获工学博士学位。2013 年任海军工程大学电力电子技术研究所研究员，2018 年任海军工程大学军用电气科学与技术研究所教授。科技部重点领域创新团队"电磁能武器技术"团队负责人，中国电工技术学会电磁发射专委会副主任委员，舰船综合电力技术国防科技重点实验室学术委员会副主任委员，军委科技委某国防科技专业专家组专家，军委装备发展部海军某技术专业组专家。鲁军勇是两型国家重点型号的总设计师、副总设计师，"973"项目首席，国家杰出青年科学基金、首届国防卓越青年基金获得者，入选国家"万人计划"领军人才、国家百千万人才工程、军队科技领军人才培养对象。研究成果获国家科技进步奖特等奖 1 项、创新团队奖 1 项，军队科技进步奖一等奖 5 项，以第一发明人授权发明专利 42 项。获军队杰出专业技术人才奖、求是杰出青年实用工程奖、中国发明创业奖等，立个人一等功 1 次、二等功 2 次和三等功 1 次。

鲁军勇长期从事电磁发射技术研究，在电磁发射直线电机技术、电磁轨道发射技术等领域取得一批重大原创性成果。

一、分段供电高速脉冲直线电动机技术

电磁发射系统是利用电磁力将载荷在短距离内加速到高速的新型高效能发射系统，在运行速度、转化效率、可控性和全寿期成本等方面具有传统方式无可比拟的优势，是继机械能、化学能以来的又一次能量运用革命，在军民领域均有重大的战略意义。

作为某重大项目副总设计师和直线电机主任设计师，历经多年艰苦攻关，系统解决了超大功率脉冲直线电机在极端使用环境下的设计、分析、制造和试验难题：①提出了环形无槽绕组脉冲直线电机技术，相对传统直线电机，推力密度大幅提升，电机整体高度大幅降低，有效解决了该类电机适装性难题；②建立了考虑大电流饱和效应、多定子耦合效应、电磁参数频变等多因素耦合的长初级直线电机高阶非线性数学模型,解决了电磁发射直线电机电磁特性精确建模难题;③揭示了长初级直线电动机动态和静态纵向边端效应的影响机理,发现了分段供电直线电机阻抗不平衡规律,构建了长初级直线电机强边端效应数学模型;④发明了一种长初级串联分段供电的网络结构,建立了串联分段供电暂态模型,大幅降低了电磁力波动,解决了长行程直线电机分段接力加速难题。研制成功的电磁发射系统样机具有完全自主知识产权,达到了当今国际领先水平。综合上述成果,发表论文52篇,授权专利19项。

二、电磁轨道发射理论与技术

电磁轨道发射系统利用电磁能将载荷发射至几千米每秒的超高速,瞬时功率高达数万兆瓦,是一个挑战极限的强脉冲电磁系统。国内外诸多学者在此领域进行了几十年的研究,但始终未能实现工程化应用。

作为某重大项目总设计师,鲁军勇带领团队经过数年的潜心研究,系统解决了脉冲能量存储、转换、变换等一系列技术难题:①提出脉冲混合储能技术,大幅降低了电网瞬时功率需求,突破了混合储能系统能量转移算法、轮序模型、能量调控与保护策略等一系列难题;②揭示了高速滑动电接触分界面枢轨熔蚀机理,建立了多物理场强耦合模型,解决了循环电磁热力多场耦合冲击、熔化磨损等复杂环境下高速带电金属烧蚀难题;③精确建立了发射装置热损耗时空分布模型,提出了连续脉冲模式下的热量管理方法,实现了系统的快速高效冷却;④基于场路耦合分析方法,建立了全系统精确仿真模型,提出了一种多目标自适应暂态控制策略,可有效对不同发射载荷所需的储能能量进行实时自适应调节。综合上述成果,发表论文36篇,授权专利18项,出版学术专著1部。因贡献卓著,于2017年荣立个人一等功。

三、电磁发射系统极限安全使用理论

电磁发射系统因功率超大、时间极短和重复频率要求高,系统所用材料、器件在短时重复非周期暂态工况下存在极限安全边界,现有的周期稳态或准稳态的设计分析理论已无法满足要求。

作为"973"项目首席,鲁军勇带领团队系统解决了电磁发射包含的储能元件、开关器件、金属材料在极限工况下的失效机理问题:①建立了多变量耦合作用下电磁发射系统的极限安全使用预测模型,提出了性能评估方法和等效测试方法,解决了系统极限安全使用的设计难题;②揭示了脉冲电容器电压在保持阶段的下降机理,提出了脉冲电容器能量密度和寿命协同提升设计方法,开发了高比能长寿命电容器样机;③揭示了晶闸管在连续浪涌模式下的失效机理,建立了脉冲晶闸管瞬态热仿真模型和极限使用寿命预测模型,研制出大容量脉冲晶闸管样机;④建立了特种金属材料在循环非周期暂态下的极限使用响应模型,揭示了特种金属材料在循环脉冲使用极端工况下的劣化规律,开发出高强高导高延伸率金属材料。上述成果发表论文 36 篇，授权专利 15 项，带动了我国一系列新材料、新器件的开发和产业化，产生了显著的社会经济效益。

综合以上三个方面的基础研究，鲁军勇系统突破了电磁发射理论与技术难题，推动了电磁能装备研制模式由实验主导向理论指导转变，拓展了传统电气工程的学科领域，促进了多学科交叉融合。共发表论文 124 篇、培养博士生 14 名，主讲电磁发射技术、直线电机技术等 4 门硕士生和博士生课程，为我国电磁发射技术的基础研究、技术应用和人才培养做出了突出贡献。

Awardee of Youth Innovation Prize, Lu Junyong

Lu Junyong was born in Ezhou City of Hubei Province in June 1978. In 2010, He graduated from the Naval University of Engineering（NUE）and achieved the Ph.D degree. In 2013 he was appointed as researcher of the Power Electronic Technology Research Institute of the NUE. In 2018, he became a Professor with the Institute of Military Electrical Science and Technology of the NUE.

Lu has long been engaged in the research on electromagnetic launch（EML）technology, and achieved a number of significant original accomplishments in the fields of EML linear motor technology and electromagnetic（EM）rail launch technology.

1. Technology of high speed pulse linear motor for piecewise power supply

As deputy chief designer of a major national project and chief designer of linear motors, Prof. Lu has experienced arduous research for many years and successfully solved difficult problems of the design, analysis, manufacture and test of ultra-high power pulse linear motors in the conditions of extreme use.（1）He created technology of the ring-shaped slotless winding pulse linear motor. Compared with the traditional linear motor, this motor increases its thrust density and decreases its overall height significantly, thereby solving the problem of its adaptation effectively.（2）The establishment high-order nonlinear mathematical model of the long primary linear motor according to the large-current saturation effect, multi-stator coupling effect, and frequency variation of EM parameters helps solve the problem of the accurate modeling of the EM characteristics of the EML linear motor.（3）By revealing the mechanism affecting the dynamic and static longitudinal side effect of the long primary linear motor, it is found that the impedance of the piecewise-power-supply linear motor is unbalanced. So a mathematical model of the strong end effect of the long primary linear motor is established.（4）The invention of a network structure of long primary serial piecewise power supply and the establishment of a transient model of series piecewise power supply have greatly reduced fluctuation in EM force during the relay acceleration and solved the problem of sectional relay acceleration of the long–stroke linear motor.

2. Theory and technology of EM rail launch

As chief designer of a certain major national project, he has led the team to work at it for many years and at last, systematically solved a series of technical problems, such as pulse energy storage, conversion and transformation, which include: (1) Proposing the pulse hybrid energy-storage technology, which can sharply reduce the demand for instantaneous power, and solving a series of problems, such as energy transfer algorithm, rotation sequence model, energy regulation and protection strategy. (2) Revealing the mechanism of erosion of the armature and rail sliding at high–speed on the electrical contact interface, and establishing a strong–coupled multi–physics model to deal with the problems of high–speed metal electrical ablation under the complex conditions such as cyclic EM thermal coupled multi–physics load impact and melting–wear. (3) Establishing an accurate spatial–temporal distribution model of the launcher heat loss, and proposing the heat management method used in a continuous pulse mode, to make the system cool rapidly and efficiently. (4) Establishing a whole system accurate simulation model based on the field–circuit coupling analysis method, and presenting a multi–objective adaptive transient control strategy, which can be used for effective, real–time and adaptive adjustment of the stored energy needed for different launch loads.

3. Ultimate safety theory for electromagnetic launch system

As a chief of 973 program, he has leaded his team to make breakthroughs in the failure mechanisms of energy storage components, switching devices and metal materials in the EML system operating under the ultimate condition. The breakthroughs include: (1) Establishing prediction model for the ultimate safe use of EML system and proposing the methods of performance evaluation and equivalent test of the system, which can solve the design problems for its ultimate safe use. (2) Explaining the mechanism of voltage drop of the pulse capacitor in the maintenance stage, proposing a design method of improving energy density and pulse capacitor life, and developing a hige–energy density and long–life capacitor prototype. (3) Revealing the failure mechanism of the thyristor in the mode of continuous surge, establishing the model of simulating the transient heat and predicting the ultimate use life of the pulse thyristor, and developing a large–capacitor pulse thyristor prototype. (4) Establishing a response model of special metal materials under circular aperiodic transient conditions for ultimate safe use, explaining the degradation law of the special metal materials used in a cyclic pulse state under extreme conditions, and developing high–strength, high–conductivity and high–extension metallic materials.

青年创新奖获得者

麦立强

麦立强，1975 年 12 月出生于河南省周口市。武汉理工大学材料学科首席教授，材料科学与工程学院院长。2004 年获武汉理工大学材料学博士学位，随后在武汉理工大学工作。2006 年起在佐治亚理工学院（2006—2007 年）、哈佛大学（2008—2011 年）、加州大学伯克利分校（2017 年）作为博士后、高级研究学者开展合作研究。2014 年获国家杰出青年科学基金资助；2016 年入选长江学者特聘教授、"万人计划"科技创新领军人才，获中国青年科技奖、光华工程科技奖，任国家重点研发计划纳米重点专项专家组成员；2018 年获国际电化学能源大会卓越研究奖；2019 年入选英国皇家化学会会士和科睿唯安全球高被引科学家，获国家自然科学二等奖。

麦立强从事纳米能源材料与器件研究，发现纳米线具有各向异性、快速的轴向电子输运和径向离子扩散以及可沿轴向集成金属接触电极的特征，在纳米储能器件的组装、原位表征、材料电导率与结构稳定性协同提升等方面具有独特优势，并以纳米线储能材料与器件为主要核心，做出了一系列创新性和系统性的研究工作。

一、创建单根纳米线器件原位表征材料电化学过程的普适新模型

结合纳米线兼具各向异性和可沿轴向集成金属接触电极的优势，率先将微纳器件工艺与纳米线电化学储能器件高度集成，构筑了国际上第一个单根纳米线电化学储能器件，搭建了皮安级高精度的电学/电化学/光谱学测试系统，将电极材料–集流体界面、电极材料–电解质界面从混合界面中抽离出来，克服了复杂界面相互干扰、常规测试系统电学/电化学信号弱、收集信号难以解析等难题。通过对单根纳米线的原位表征，建立了单根纳米线的结构、电输运、电极充放电状态与容量衰减之间的直接联系，发现充放电过程中离子脱嵌导致材料结构劣化，造成纳米线电极材料与集流体之间由欧姆接触转变为肖特基接触，同时使材料电导率下降，揭示了容量衰减的本征机制。该电化学表征模型具有普适性，推动了电化学表征科学与技术的发展。成果被国际著名纳米科学家、美国莱斯大学阿加延教授等评价为"强有力的诊断工具""为检测纳米尺度的反应机理提供了深刻见解"，并被自然出版集团《亚洲材料》进行专题报道。麦立强受 Nature 邀请撰写专题评述论文《实时监测电池退化》，引起广泛关注与好评。

二、发现纳米线分级协同效应

针对材料结构劣化导致容量衰减的科学问题，麦立强从构筑材料复杂微观结构着手，进行了提升结构稳定性的研究，发现将不同尺寸的纳米材料单元组装成复杂分级结构，可在提高比表面积的同时有效抑制自团聚。提出了梯度静电纺丝法，打破不同材料晶体生长取向不同的限制，实现了 20 余种分级结构纳米线的可控制备；提出"自组装－取向搭接"普适性制备方法，丰富了储能用新型分级异质结构的制备科学。分级结构的构筑大幅提升了储能器件的能量密度和循环稳定性，其中梯度静电纺丝法制备的纳米线材料在 9500 次超长循环后容量保持率仍高达 80%，远优于同类材料（2000 次循环后容量保持率不足 80%）。成果被美国 IBM 公司、美国通用汽车公司和德国博世公司研发实验室等引用和关注，并被业内专家评价为"重大进展""具有超常提升的电化学性能"和"巨大的应用潜力"。

三、发现电子／离子双连续效应

针对材料电导率下降导致容量衰减的科学问题，麦立强从调控电极材料电子／离子双连续输运入手，进行了材料电化学性能的调控。提出电子／离子双连续通道的新概念，推导出半中空双连续结构提升电子／离子输运的理论公式，揭示出科学内涵，并发明了同轴半中空纳米线材料的制备技术。为了从本征属性实现电子／离子的双连续输运，他进一步提出了预嵌入优化策略，建立了离子预嵌入提升电输运性能的理论体系，发现离子预嵌入引入杂质能级可改善材料能带结构、提升电导率；提出溶剂分子预嵌入策略，通过屏蔽效应和自润滑效应实现快速的离子传输动力学。该研究指导制备的电子／离子双连续传导纳米线材料电导率提升 27 倍，构筑的储能器件在保持高能量密度的同时功率密度提高 6 倍，从理论上解决了难以同时保持高能量密度和高功率密度的国际难题并得到验证。其中，提出的预锂化思想和策略引起诺贝尔化学奖得主威廷汉姆和德国戴姆勒股份公司等广泛关注、引用和肯定。

上述研究成果被 40 余部权威工具书和材料学专著收录，在国际上受到 38 位院士在内的 48 个国家／地区 950 余个科研机构的学者正面评价和重点引用，获得 100 余项中国发明专利授权。麦立强受邀在《自然》《化学评论》《先进材料》等著名期刊撰写系列综述论文，受邀出版中文专著《纳米线储能材料与器件》。基于储能器件能量密度、功率密度和循环寿命协同提升，他进一步突破产业化关键技术，成立了新能源领域的科技公司，与东风汽车等著名企业进行产学研合作与成果转化，推动了我国纳米能源材料与器件领域的发展。

Awardee of Youth Innovation Prize, Mai Liqiang

Mai Liqiang was born in Zhoukou City of Henan Province in December 1975. He is the chair professor of materials science and the dean of School of Materials Science and Engineering, Wuhan University of Technology (WUT). Liqiang Mai has been engaged in research on nano-energy materials and devices.

I. An original universal model for in situ characterization of the electrochemical processes in the materials using a single nanowire device was established

Combining the advantages of anisotropy of nanowires and the ability to integrate metal contact electrodes along the axial direction, Liqiang Mai integrated the micro-nano device with nanowire electrochemical energy storage devices for the first time, and he designed and assembled the first single nanowire electrochemical energy storage device in the world, and established the picoampere-level high-precision electrical/electrochemical/spectroscopic test system, which overcomes the problems of weak electrical/electrochemical signals and difficult analysis of the collected signals in conventional test systems. Through the *in situ* characterization of single nanowire, the direct connection between the structure, electrical transport, electrode charging and discharging state and capacity fading of single nanowire was established. It was found that the ion insertion/deinsertion during discharging and charging process led to the deterioration of the material structure and the change from Ohmic contact to Schottky contact between the nanowire electrode material and collector, and then the decrease of the conductivity of the material. Therefore, the intrinsic mechanism of capacity fading was revealed. The electrochemical characterization model is universal and promotes the development of electrochemical characterization science and technology.

II. Discovery of hierarchical-synergistic effect in nanowire

To address the scientific problem of capacity degradation due to structural deterioration of materials, Liqiang Mai has been working on improving the structural stability of the materials from the point of the complex microstructure. Liqiang Mai found that by assembling nanomaterial units of different sizes into complex hierarchical structures can effectively inhibit self-agglomeration while increasing the specific surface area. He proposed the gradient electrospinning method to break the restriction of different crystal growth orientation of different materials, and realized the controlled preparation of more than 20 kinds of hierarchical-structure nanowires; meanwhile, he proposed the universal preparation method of "Self-assembly-Oriented attachment", which enriches the preparation science of new hierarchical heterogeneous structures for energy storage. The construction of the hierarchical structure greatly improved the energy density and cycling stability of energy storage devices, in which the capacity retention of the nanowire cathode material prepared by gradient electrospinning method was as high as 80% after 9500 cycles, which was much better than the performance of similar materials (whose capacity retention was less than 80% after 2000 cycles).

III. Discovery of electron/ion bi-continuous effect

To address the scientific problem of capacity fading due to the decrease in material conductivity, Liqiang Mai regulated the bi-continuous electronic/ionic transport of electrode materials to control the electrochemical properties of the materials. Liqiang Mai put forward the new concept of electron/ion bi-continuous channel, deduced the theoretical formula of electron/ion transport in the half-hollow bi-continuous structure, revealed the scientific connotation, and enriched the preparation science of coaxial half-hollow nanowire materials. In order to realize the bi-continuous electrons/ions transport from the intrinsic properties, Liqiang Mai further proposed the optimization strategy of pre-intercalation, established the theoretical system of improving the electrical transport performance of ions pre-intercalation. It was found that the introduction of the impurity level in the pre-intercalation of ions improved the energy band structure of materials and improved the electrical conductivity. On the other hand, the solvent molecule pre-intercalation strategy is proposed to realize fast ion transfer kinetics through shielding effect and self-lubricating effect. The electric conductivity of the electron/ion bi-continuous conduction nanowire material prepared under the guidance of this study is improved by 27 times, and the power density is increased by 6 times while high energy density is maintained. Therefore, the international difficulty of achieving high energy density and high power density at the same time is solved theoretically and verified. The thought and strategy of pre-lithiation has attracted the attention, citation and affirmation of Nobel Prize winner Whittingham and Daimler ag, etc. Until today, CATL, BYD and other well-known companies and enterprises in the field of new energy widely use the pre-lithiation technology.

青年创新奖获得者

张　澄

张澄，1980年3月出生于山东省济南市。2004—2009年经山东大学医学院/美国贝勒医学院联合培养获医学博士学位，2010—2011年在美国俄克拉荷马大学医学院进行博士后研究。2011年回国至今在山东大学齐鲁医院工作，任心内科教授、主任医师、博士生导师，教育部和国家卫健委重点实验室副主任，长期从事动脉粥样硬化性心血管疾病（ASCVD）发生机制和干预策略的基础和临床研究，取得了一系列重要进展。承担国家"863"重大课题、国家杰出青年基金等国家和省部级课题10余项；在 *Nat Med*、*Cell Metab*、*Nat Commun*、*J Am Coll Cardiol*、*Nat Rev Cardiol*、PNAS 等国际著名杂志发表SCI收录论文130余篇；作为第一完成人获得国家自然科学奖二等奖、中国青年科技奖、教育部自然科学奖一等奖、山东省自然科学奖二等奖。美国心脏病学院 Fellow（FACC），欧洲心脏病学会会士，教育部长江学者特聘教授，国家"万人计划"科技领军人才，国家首批"万人计划"青年拔尖人才，教育部新世纪优秀人才以及山东省"泰山学者"特聘教授。

一、发现炎症导致胶原代谢紊乱和斑块不稳定的新机制

1. 首次揭示 TNFα 介导细胞外基质合成减少的信号转导通路

已知炎症导致的斑块胶原降解增多是斑块破裂的重要因素，但炎症因子是否抑制斑块胶原合成尚不明了。张澄首次报告肿瘤坏死因子（TNF-α）抑制胶原合成酶限速酶（P4Hα1）的时效和量效关系，发现 TNF-α 反应元件位于 P4Hα1 启动子 −32bp 至 +18bp 的区域上，NonO 蛋白作为转录因子结合于 P4Hα1 启动子 TNF-α 反应元件上，通过 ASK1-MKK4-JNK1-NonO 通路调节 P4Hα1 的表达，从而发现 NonO 蛋白新的生物学功能。该研究应邀在 2006 年美国心脏协会年会上作大会报告，并发表于 *Arteriosc Thromb Vasc Biol*，该杂志配发编辑部评论指出"该研究发现了一个 JNK 通路抑制细胞外基质合

成的新机制，这是一个具有治疗意义的重大发现。"近年来，课题组进一步证明在 ApoE$^{-/-}$ 小鼠中，敲低 NonO 基因可通过抑制炎症和胶原降解而增强 AS 易损斑块的稳定性和降低腹主动脉瘤的发生率和严重性。

2. 首次发现 Ang II 通过上调 AMPK-AP2-MMP2 通路导致血管胶原降解和腹主动脉瘤

腹主动脉瘤（AAA）是 AS 的特殊类型，在 ApoE$^{-/-}$ 小鼠研究中发现基因敲除 AMPKα2 后抑制了尼古丁和 Ang II 所导致的 AAA。尼古丁和 Ang II 可通过激活 AMPK、活化 MMP2 的基因转录，最终导致血管壁胶原的降解和 AAA 的发生。研究结果发表在 *Nat Med* 后，被多家媒体报道和转载，该杂志发表编辑部评论指出"该研究打破了多年来吸烟与 AAA 机制关系研究的僵局，提出了二者之间关系的新见解。作者建立了吸烟与 AAA 发展之间重要的分子联系，鉴于此病目前尚无有效疗法，本研究为 AAA 患者提供了可能的治疗新策略。"

二、揭示 Treg 细胞和他汀调控 AS 炎症反应的新机制

1. 首次发现过继转移 Treg 可减少斑块破裂率和腹主动脉瘤发生率

发现在 ApoE$^{-/-}$ 小鼠中过继输注外源性 Treg 可剂量依赖性地抑制斑块炎症、改善胶原代谢并减少斑块破裂率；在 AAA 小鼠模型中，过继输注外源性 Treg 可显著降低 AAA 的发生率和严重性并揭示了其分子机制，这为 ASCVD 的治疗提供了新的靶点。两位美国科学院院士在 *Nat Immunol* 引用此文并指出"在人和鼠的非淋巴组织中，如 AS 斑块等，已证实存在特殊的 Treg 细胞群"。

2. 发现他汀抗炎的新机制

在 ApoE$^{-/-}$ 小鼠的研究中发现他汀治疗可显著增加小鼠斑块中 Treg 数量以及 TGF-β 和 IL-10 的表达，并可调节抗炎细胞（Tregs 和 Th2 细胞）与促炎细胞（Th17 和 Th1 细胞）之间的平衡，增加冠心病患者血清 Treg 数量和功能，揭示了他汀抗炎治疗新机制。*J Clin Invest* 发表综述对本研究给予高度评价，"他汀对于 Tregs 的作用有助于解释此药明确证实的多效性抗炎作用，值得进一步研究。利用药物增加 Tregs 数量对于易损斑块的治疗可能是一个切实可行的目标。"鉴于该研究成果，*Nat Rev Cardiol* 主编邀请张澄就 Treg 的心血管保护作用进行系统综述，该文入选 ESI 前 1% 高被引论文。

三、建立 ACE2-Ang-（1-7）的 ASCVD 治疗新轴线

1. 首次发现 ACE2 过表达可抑制早期 AS 病变和稳定晚期 AS 斑块

在新西兰兔中的研究发现 ACE2 过表达可抑制 AS 的早期病变，其分子机制是 ACE2 下调了血管壁细胞的 Ang II、ACE 和 AT1 受体的表达，上调了 Ang-（1-7）的表达。该研究发表于 PNAS，被评选为 2011 年中国百篇最具影响的国际学术论文。对于晚期 AS 斑块，ACE2 过表达可显著减少斑块内巨噬细胞和脂质含量，增加斑块内平滑肌细胞和胶原纤维的含量，从而显著降低斑块易损指数。这是国际上第一篇关于 ACE2 干预 AS 的实验

研究，被多个国际著名杂志广泛引用。

2. 首次证明 Ang-（1-7）可剂量依赖性地减轻斑块早期病变和稳定斑块晚期病变

研究发现 ACE2 降解 Ang II 所产生的小分子多肽 Ang-（1-7）可通过抑制 ERK/P38 和 JAK/STAT 通路并增强 SM22α 和 AT2 受体的表达，剂量依赖性地抑制 ApoE$^{-/-}$ 小鼠的早期 AS 病变。此外，Ang-（1-7）通过抑制促炎因子的表达和 MMPs 的活性，增强了 AS 斑块的稳定性。

3. 首次证明 ACE2 过表达和 Ang-（1-7）可改善糖尿病心肌病的左室重构和功能

在糖尿病性心肌病（DCM）大鼠模型中的研究发现，ACE2 过表达可显著逆转左室重构，改善左室的收缩与舒张功能，其作用优于血管紧张素 II 受体拮抗剂——氯沙坦，这一疗效的主要分子机制是 ACE2 抑制了成纤维细胞与心肌细胞调控胶原和 TGF-β 合成的交互对话。本研究发表于 *J Am Coll Cardiol* 后，该刊副主编、心力衰竭国际权威亲自撰写了编辑部评论，对研究给予了高度评价"这项研究表明，对于预防或者治疗心血管疾病尤其是涉及 RAS 系统激活的疾病，升高心肌内 ACE2 的活性可能是一个有益的策略。"张澄还发现 Ang-（1-7）可剂量依赖性地改善糖尿病心肌病的左室重构和功能，且与培哚普利有协同作用。

4. 发现 Ang 1-7 可减轻糖尿病性肾病的肾脏损伤

在糖尿病性肾病大鼠模型中的研究发现，Ang 1-7 可显著减轻糖尿病性肾病大鼠的肾脏纤维化和氧化应激损伤、改善肾功能，优于临床应用的缬沙坦。该文发表于 *Kid Int* 并入选国际 F1000 Prime，推荐专家指出"该研究第一次证实了 Ang（1-7）对于 STZ 诱发的糖尿病性肾病的有益作用。本研究的一个重要发现是，对于糖尿病性肾病的治疗，大剂量 Ang（1-7）较缬沙坦更有效。这提示，对于糖尿病性肾病的治疗，Ang（1-7）可能是比血管紧张素受体阻滞剂更强大的武器"。基于上述成果，张澄提出了心血管疾病中 ACE2-Ang1-7 治疗新轴线的概念，并应 *Nat Rev Cardiol* 主编的邀请对此概念进行系统综述。

5. 提出新冠病毒导致心肺损伤的关键机制

2020 年，张澄在抗击新型冠状病毒感染疫情的工作中，针对国内外关于新冠感染背景下 ACE2 是敌是友的学术争论，较早地提出了 ACE2 耗竭是新冠病毒导致心肺损伤的关键机制，并在新冠感染合并高血压患者的临床对照研究中证明了应用 RAS 抑制剂可显著降低住院期死亡率。

Awardee of Youth Innovation Prize, Zhang Cheng

Zhang Cheng was born in Jinan City of Shandong Province in March 1980. He received doctor's degree after joint training by Shandong University School of Medicine and Baylor College of Medicine, USA from 2004 to 2009. He conducted his postdoctoral study at the University of Oklahoma, USA from 2010 to 2011. Since he returned to China in 2011, he has worked at Qilu Hospital of Shandong University as a Professor of Medicine, chief physician, doctoral supervisor and a deputy director of the Key laboratory of Ministry of Education and National Health Commission. Dr. Cheng Zhang has long engaged in basic and clinical studies of the mechanisms and intervention strategies of atherosclerotic cardiovascular disease (ASCVD) . He has undertaken more than 10 national and provincial research projects, such as the National 863 Project and the National Outstanding Youth Fund. He first revealed the molecular mechanism of abdominal aortic aneurysm caused by smoking, discovered beneficial effects and molecular mechanisms of angiotensin converting enzyme 2 (ACE2) and angiotensin 1-7 (Ang 1-7) on ASCVD, put forward the concept of a novel ACE2-Ang1-7 axis for the treatment of ASCVD, proposed ACE2 depletion as a key mechanism of novel coronavirus-induced cardiac and pulmonary injury, proved the effectiveness of RAS inhibitors in lowering patient mortality in a controlled clinical study of novel coronavirus infection combined with hypertension, and found protective effects of regulatory T cells on animal models and clinical patients with ASCVD. Dr. Cheng Zhang published over 130 SCI-indexed papers in international renowned journals such as *Nat Med, Cell Metab, Nat Commun, J Am Coll Cardiol, Nat Rev Cardiol* and *PNAS*, and as the first accomplisher, won the second prize of National Natural Science Award China youth science, the first prize of Natural Science Award of Chinese Ministry of Education, the second prize of Natural Science Award of Shandong province, national excellent doctoral dissertation award, and China's most influential international academic paper award. He was awarded China May 4th Youth Medal and Shandong May 4th Youth Medal. He was elected Fellow of American College of Cardiology (FACC), Fellow of European Society of Cardiology Fellow (FESC), Yangtze Scholar of Chinese Ministry of Education, National Science and Technology Leading Talent of "Ten Thousand Plan", National Top Youth Talent of "Ten Thousand Plan", Outstanding Talent of the New Century of Chinese Ministry of Education, and Distinguished Professor of "Taishan Scholars" of Shandong Province.

青年创新奖获得者

赵 永 生

赵永生，1979 年 3 月出生于山东省沂源县。2006 年获中国科学院化学研究所理学博士学位，先后在美国加州大学洛杉矶分校及西北大学从事博士后研究。2009 年 10 月入选中国科学院化学研究所百人计划，任研究员、课题组长；2011 年获国家杰出青年科学基金支持；2015 年入选英国皇家化学会会士；2018 年入选万人计划领军人才。目前任中国科学院大学教授、中国科学院光化学重点实验室副主任，兼任中国化学会光化学专业委员会、纳米化学专业委员会、青年化学工作者委员会、中国材料研究学会纳米材料与器件专业委员会理事。

赵永生在国际上率先开展了有机纳米光子学材料与器件这一前沿研究方向，是该领域的代表人物之一。以新型可穿戴器件和下一代显示技术的关键需求为导向，利用化学思想发展了新型光子学功能材料。同时以有机材料的光子学特异性为突破口，揭示分子在凝聚态下的激发态动力学过程，发展了传统的光化学理论。

报道了国际上第一个有机纳米激光器，阐明了有机材料全新的粒子数翻转机理与光化学过程；发现了有机材料中的 Frenkel 激子可以与光子强耦合形成一种半光半物质的新的量子态——激子极化激元（EP），利用这种兼具激子和光子属性的准粒子，通过外场手段操纵激子的行为，解决了光功能材料中光子行为不能操纵的难题；首次在室温下实现了有机微纳体系激子的玻色 – 爱因斯坦凝聚，并在凝聚态下得到了与传统气液固态显著不同的激发态过程。相关工作被 *Nature* 进行专题评述，部分成果入选中国科学院《科学发展报告》中国科学家代表性成果，部分成果入选美国化学会评选的光化学领域年度重要前沿进展。作为代表性成果获 2014 年国家自然科学奖二等奖。

针对下一代显示技术的关键需求，发展了有机柔性光子器件可控加工新技术，突破了有机材料集成化面临的关键瓶颈，可控构筑了大面积集成光子回路及全色主动发光有机激光显示面板，相关研究已经列入北京综合性国家研究中心交叉研究平台重点建设项目，将为怀柔科学城建设做出贡献。部分工作被 *Nature Index* 选作中国科学家在化学交叉领域取得的突出贡献的代表性工作，部分成果入选英国皇家化学会评选的物理化学年度重要进展，部分成果作为代表性工作获 2016 年中国科学院杰出科技成就奖。

发展了具有自主知识产权的纳米光子学表征新技术，已完成技术转化并获得国际质量管理体系认证，在多家高校、研究所及企业推广，极大提升了我国在纳米光电子领域的整体创新能力和国际竞争力，相关技术获 2013 年中国分析测试协会科学技术奖一等奖。

赵永生的研究工作得到了国内外同行和学术团体的广泛认可。在国内获得了十余项有重要影响的学术奖励，除上述的奖项外，还获得中国青年科技奖、中国科学院青年科学家奖、中国化学会青年化学奖以及中国化学会最重要的学术奖项之一——赢创化学创新奖。在国际方面，赵永生于 2015 年获得英国皇家化学会的旗舰学术期刊设立的 ChemComm 未来科学家奖，这是这一奖项设立十几年来首次授予亚洲地区的青年科学家；2013 年荣获亚洲大洋洲光化学协会青年科学家奖，2014 年获中美化学教授协会杰出教授奖。赵永生目前担任多个高水平学术期刊的编委，包括 *Science China Chemistry*、*Research*、*Advanced Optical Materials*、*Scientific Reports* 等。曾应邀作为主编，组织二十几位国际同行撰写学术著作 *Organic Nanophotonics: Fundamentals and Applications*；作为客座主编，组织国际同行为期刊 *Advanced Optical Materials* 出版本领域的学术专辑。

赵永生在高水平的化学、材料及综合性学术期刊发表论文 170 余篇；应邀为 *Acc. Chem. Res.*、*Chem. Soc. Rev.* 等期刊撰写综述文章 10 余篇，文章引用 7500 余次；申请发明专利 25 项，包括 3 项国际专利，授权 10 项；在国际学术会议做大会报告、特邀报告、邀请报告共 60 余次。培养了一批有机光电子领域的优秀青年人才，独立工作 10 年以来，培养博士毕业生 25 名，其中 1 人获中国科学院院长特别奖、4 人获中国科学院院长优秀奖、3 人获中国科学院宝洁优秀研究生奖、多人次获博士研究生国家奖学金。毕业博士生及团队成员中，1 人获基金委优秀青年基金、1 人获北京市杰出青年基金、1 人入选中组部青年千人计划、13 人在国内高校和科研院所担任教授或副教授。

Awardee of Youth Innovation Prize, Zhao Yongsheng

Zhao Yongsheng was born in Yiyuan County of Shandong Province in March 1979. He has led the research of organic nanophotonic materials and devices in the world. Guided by the requirements of wearable devices and next-generation display technologies, his group has developed novel organic photonic materials. On this basis, they investigated the excited state dynamics at condensed state through the special photonic behaviors of organic molecular materials, which has contributed to further improve the theory of photochemistry and photophysics.

His group reported the first organic nanolaser, and demonstrated the unique advantages of organic materials in the field of photonics. They achieved organic microlasers with multiple RGB emission wavelength, and for the first time, Bose-Einstein Condensation of Frenkel excitons was realized at room temperature within nanoscale regime, which reveals totally different excited state processes from the traditional gas, liquid and solid states.

His group has further developed techniques for the scalable processing of large-area organic integrated photonic circuits, and constructed full-color organic laser display panels. In response to the research requirement in this field, they also developed distinctive instruments for the measurements of various time-resolved and spatial-resolved spectroscopy at nanoscale, which has been industrialized and promoted in many universities, research institutes, and enterprises.

For his remarkable contributions in organic nanophotonic materials and devices, Prof. Zhao has been awarded the National Science Foundation for Distinguished Youth Scholar in 2011. Now he has published over 170 peer-reviewed papers that collectively have been cited over 7000 times. Most of them are in high-profile journals on chemistry and materials science. He has filed 25 patents, contributed 3 book chapters, and delivered more than 60 plenary and invited talks in international academic conferences. He has been much honored to win a number of highly competitive academic prizes in China. For example, National Natural Science Award of China, Outstanding Science and Technology Achievement Prize of the Chinese Academy of Sciences, China Youth Science and Technology Award, the Chinese Chemical Society-Evonik Chemical Innovation Award, etc.

Prof. Zhao's achievement has also been recognized outside China. He was selected as the Fellow of Royal Society of Chemistry (FRSC), and recognized by the ChemComm Emerging Investigator Lectureship in 2015. This is the first time for this prestigious prize to be awarded to a young scientist in Asia area. He has also won the Asian and Oceanian Photochemistry Association Prize for Young Scientist, and the Chinese-American Chemistry Professors Association Distinguished Faculty Award. He has been invited to serve on the editorial boards for premier journals, as well as council members in several prestigious scientific societies. He has also shown strong leadership and service to the scientific community. Notably, he has edited a Springer book in 2015 named "Organic Nanophotonics: Fundamentals and Applications", also as the guest editor, he has organized a special issue on "Nano/Microscale Lasers" in Adv. Opt. Mater. in 2019.

区域创新奖获得者

何　黎

　　何黎，女，彝族，1962年8月出生于云南省昆明市。我国著名皮肤病学专家。1985年毕业于昆明医学院临床医学专业，2006年获云南大学遗传学博士学位。1986年至今在昆明医科大学第一附属医院皮肤科从事临床、教学、科研工作，其间于1993—1995年赴泰国朱拉隆功大学皮肤科做访问学者。2017年4月至今任昆明医科大学第一附属医院云南省皮肤病医院执行院长。

　　现任亚太皮肤屏障研究会副主席，中华医学会皮肤性病分会副主任委员，教育部创新团队带头人，国家临床重点专科负责人，全国痤疮研究中心首席专家，全国光医学及皮肤屏障研究中心负责人，云南省科技领军人才。先后获全国教书育人十大楷模、国之名医、全国优秀科技工作者、国家卫生计生突出贡献中青年专家、全国劳动模范荣誉称号；获云南省科技进步奖特等奖、一等奖、创新团队一等奖及发明专利一等奖，获国家发明专利授权13项，牵头制定行业团体标准6项、指南及专家共识10项（含功效性护肤品临床应用指南4项），主编专著及教材7部。

　　我国光损伤性皮肤病患者约3亿人，主要包括炎症和肿瘤两类。炎症性光损伤性皮肤病包括紫外线直接引起的慢性光化性皮炎和间接加重的痤疮、敏感性皮肤、黄褐斑等，肿瘤性光损伤性皮肤病包括日光性角化病、皮肤鳞状细胞癌等。云南地区紫外线照射强烈，光损伤性皮肤病尤为高发。何黎历经36年，直面光损伤性皮肤病易复发、难治愈这一世界难题，带领团队持续攻关，立足云南病源及植物资源优势，在致病机制、临床诊疗技术及产品研发等方面取得了一系列领先的创新成果，社会经济效益显著。

一、揭示光损伤性皮肤病致病新机制，为有效防治奠定了理论基础

　　从全国31个省份系统收集了痤疮、慢性光化性皮炎、敏感性皮肤、黄褐斑、皮肤癌等12种皮肤病样本4.6万份，建成涵盖临床信息、血样、皮损组织的国际首个病源样本

资源库，并采用数字化、智能化全方位管理。利用光损伤性皮肤病样本资源库，科学论证了皮肤屏障受损是该类疾病发生的共性特征，提出修复皮肤屏障是防治光损伤性皮肤病基础的新观点。

率先在国际上发现 5 个致病关键机制：①易感基因 *DDB2* 和 *SELL* 调控雄激素代谢及痤疮丙酸杆菌相关炎症反应，诱发重型痤疮；② CLND-5 表达降低致表皮通透屏障功能受损，引起敏感性皮肤；③ TNFAIP3 表达降低调控 NF-κB 释放炎症因子，引起慢性光化性皮炎；④ VEGF/endothelin-1 表达增加、TLR-2/TLR 上调释放炎症因子、皮肤屏障受损激活 P53/POMC/ TRP1 信号通路促进紫外线诱导色素增加，解锁了除色素代谢障碍外的血管因素、炎症反应、皮肤屏障受损均参与黄褐斑发生；⑤ DNA-PKc/SIN1 是皮肤癌发生的关键蛋白，紫外线通过 PI3K/Akt、TGFβ1/Smads 信号通路交互作用促进日光性角化病向鳞癌转化。研究成果发表在 *Nature Communications*、*Journal of Investigative Dermatology* 等高质量学术期刊。

二、参与创制我国功效性护肤品知名品牌"薇诺娜"，牵头制定行业标准及临床应用指南，推动大健康产业发展

依据机制研究提供靶标，从云南特色植物中发现青刺果、滇重楼、马齿苋、滇山茶等活性提取物分别具有修复皮肤屏障、抗痤疮丙酸杆菌、抗炎、抑制色素合成的功能。借助教育部创新团队平台，与云南贝泰妮生物科技集团创制出我国首个具有自主知识产权的功效性护肤品"薇诺娜"。产品通过国际权威机构法国贝桑松大学临床验证，其效果等同国外同类知名产品。"薇诺娜"产品已成长为云南生物医药大健康产业的一张名片。

率先在国内提出功效性护肤品的功效性和安全性必须得到实验及临床验证。根据国务院最新化妆品管理规定，化妆品的功效宣称必须有科学依据。何黎牵头组织专家制定了我国功效性护肤品原料质量、活性成分功效评价、产品安全及临床评价全方位的团体标准，正式颁布了《祛痘类功效性护肤品安全/功效评价标准》《祛痘类功效性护肤品产品质量评价标准》《祛痘类功效性护肤品临床评价标准》《舒敏类功效性护肤品安全/功效评价标准》《舒敏类功效性护肤品产品质量评价标准》《舒敏类功效性护肤品临床评价标准》6 个功效性护肤品团体标准；牵头制定了《抗粉刺类护肤品在痤疮中的应用指南》《功效性护肤品在慢性光化性皮炎防治中的应用指南》《舒敏保湿类护肤品在敏感性皮肤病中的应用指南》《功效性护肤品在儿童特应性皮炎中的应用指南》4 个临床应用指南，为临床医生合理应用功效性护肤品提供了指导，推动了我国功效性护肤品产业健康发展。

三、创新光损伤性皮肤病精准诊疗技术，潜心服务广大患者

1. 首创 4 个诊疗新技术

①黄褐斑：基于发病机制研究成果，首次采用无创皮肤检测等技术，创新性地将黄褐斑分为两期（活动期和稳定期）、两型（单纯色素型、色素合并血管型）。提出活动期

以药物联合功效性护肤品进行治疗，稳定期依据分型采用果酸、光电治疗。②敏感性皮肤：率先采用乳酸刺痛试验及辣椒素试验将敏感性皮肤分为两型，乳酸刺痛试验阳性诊断为伴刺痛瘙痒型敏感性皮肤，辣椒素试验阳性诊断为伴烧灼红斑型敏感性皮肤，有利于敏感性皮肤的精准治疗。③痤疮：依据痤疮分型分级进行优化治疗，轻型（Ⅰ级、Ⅱ级）采用功效性护肤品配合化学换肤，重型（Ⅲ级、Ⅳ级）采用药物联合功效性护肤品、光动力并提出应对痤疮慢性病进行全程管理。④慢性光化性皮炎：创新采用药物配合功效性护肤品序贯治疗，有效率由 50% 提高至 85.2%。以上诊疗新技术在全国得到广泛应用，已列入《中国黄褐斑治疗专家共识》《中国敏感性皮肤诊治专家共识》《中国痤疮治疗指南》，相关文章发表于 *International Journal of Cosmetic Science* 等。

2. 开辟皮肤病疑难患者诊断新思路

云南毗邻东南亚，微生物种类丰富，是皮肤疑难病高发地区。15 年来，何黎带领团队共收集 1120 例皮肤疑难病例，创新地采用病例讨论形式，总结出疑难皮肤病临床诊断新思路，出版《皮肤科疑难病例精粹》一、二、三辑，启发了国内同行对疑难皮肤病正确的诊断思路，提高了我国皮肤医师的临床诊断水平。

四、培养立足云南、服务边疆人才，创建特色优势学科

36 年来，何黎以"临床为导向，人才培养、搭建团队为契机，发展学科为目的"，与美国、法国、泰国等大学及中国科学院昆明植物研究所、云南贝泰妮生物科技集团联合培养了一批复合型人才，包括云岭学者、医学领军人才、中青年学术技术带头人 15 人、博士生、硕士生、东南亚学生 258 人。团队入选教育部创新团队。

Awardee of Region Innovation Prize, He Li

He Li, female, was born in Kunming City of Yunnan Province in August 1962. She is the famous dermatologist in China, Vice President of Asia Pacific Skin Barrier Association, Vice President of Chinese Society of Dermatology, executive Director of Yunnan Dermatology Hospital of the First Affiliated Hospital of Kunming Medical University. She has published 242 papers in journals, obtained 13 national invention patents, make 10 guidelines and consensus, 6 industry standards, 7 books and textbooks, won 1 special prize for Scientific and technological progress of Yunnan Province and 2 first prizes.

1. Revealed the new mechanism of photo dermatitisis, which laid the theoretical foundation for effective prevention and treatment

Established the largest biobank of 46000 photodermatitis samples. Demonstrated the impaired skin barrier function is the common risk for photodermatitis.

Revealed 5 pathogenesis of photodermatitis: ①SELL and DDB2 are susceptibility genes for severe acne, which involved in androgen metabolism and inflammation processes stimulated by Pacne. ② The expression of CLDN5 was decreased in sensitive skin which plays a vital role in the epidermal barrier function. ③ TNFIP3 down-regulation promotes UVB-induced inflammation via activation of the NF-κB pathway in chronic actinic dermatitis. ④ Besides the disorder of pigment metabolism, inflammatory reaction and disrupture of epidermal permeability barrier are involved in the occurrence of melasma via VEGF/endothelin-1, TLR-2/4 and P53/POMC/TRP1 signal pathway. ⑤ DNA-PKc/SIN1 play important role in squamous cell carcinoma, UV promotes the transformation of actinic keratosis to SCC through PI3K / Akt and TGFβ1 / Smads signaling pathways.

2. Participated in the creation of the famous Chinese efficacy skincare brand "Winona", led the formulation of industry standards and clinical guidelines

Through a partnership with Yunnan Beitaini Biotechnology Company, they set up Winona-the first efficacy skin care product with independent intellectual property right of China.In addition, 6 industry standards and 4 clinical guidelines for efficacy skin care products were formulated, which promoted the development of efficacy skin care industry in China.

3. Innovatived precise diagnosis and treatment technology for photodamage skin diseases

Four new stage classification and sequential treatment were established for melasma, sensitive skin, acne, chronic actinic dermatitis.By summarizing the diagnosis and treatment of 1120 difficult cases, three volumes of "Summary of Difficult Cases in Dermatology" were published.

4. Cultivated talents in Yunnan, served frontier areas, and created characteristic disciplines

In the past 36 years, she has jointly cultivated a number of comprehensive talents with other universities . Among them there are leading medical talents, young and middle-aged academic and technological leaders, and doctoral, master students.

区域创新奖获得者

刘 国 道

刘国道，1963年6月出生于云南省腾冲市。2006年毕业于华南热带农业大学（现海南大学）农学系，获农学博士学位。1985年至今在中国热带农业科学院工作，先后任农牧研究所所长、热带作物品种资源研究所所长，2010年7月起任中国热带农业科学院副院长。南京农业大学、海南大学、湖南农业大学等高校研究生导师。先后兼任联合国粮农组织热带农业平台执行委员会委员与观察员，国际橡胶研究与发展委员会理事，中国热带作物学会理事长，海南省植物学会理事长，全国牧草品种审定委员会副主任，全国热带作物品种审定委员会副主任，中国草学会第七届、第八届副理事长和第九届常务理事。

刘国道从事草学领域研究，在热带牧草资源收集、鉴定、评价与创新利用方面进行了一系列开创性研究工作。

一、热带牧草资源

经过30多年的努力，累计收集热带牧草种质资源14100多份，建立了农业农村部热带牧草种质资源圃和国家牧草种质资源保存中期（备份）库以及标本馆。命名并在国际上公开发表中国（海南）特有新物种5个、海南新记录属1个、新记录种55个。

二、热带牧草遗传育种

以第一或者主要完成人育成并通过国审牧草品种29个，获得新品种保护权2个。其中，热研4号王草年亩（1亩≈667平方米）产鲜草1.5万—2.5万千克，为我国南方最重要的刈割型禾草，已成为我国南方舍饲养殖的主要牧草，入选中国农业发展十年成就展；柱花草为华南地区最重要的热带豆科牧草，谓之"北有苜蓿，南有柱花草"，已成为南方草牧业的当家品种。新品种累计推广面积3800多万亩，经济、生态与社会效益显著。

三、牧草栽培生理与科学利用

探明了柱花草等重要豆科牧草适应南方酸性土壤普遍存在的低磷、铝毒的生理与分子机制。研发了主推牧草品种的高产栽培利用技术及林（果）草间作模式。针对滇桂黔石漠化生态脆弱地区，研发了"果上山，草盖地，藤盖石，畜吃草，粪还田"的综合治理模式，助力脱贫攻坚及乡村振兴成效显著。

四、人才培养与科技培训

协助原华南热带农业大学（现已并入海南大学）成立草业科学本科专业和硕士学位点，负责骨干教材的编写和出版。已培养草业科学专业本科生 600 余名、研究生 80 余名。

五、成果推广与科技服务

刘国道十分重视技术转移和成果转化工作，针对我国南方农区畜牧业以农户为单元等特点，带领团队利用"农民参与式"方法构建牧草推广体系，通过科技下乡活动，把新品种、新技术传递给农户。组织编写的大型科普读物《热带畜牧业发展实用技术丛书》（共 19 册，2015 年获农业农村部中华农业科普奖）特色鲜明、通俗易懂，深受农户喜爱，累计培训农民 4000 多人次，发放宣传册 5000 余册，得到地方科技部门的好评。所在单位连续十年获得海南科技活动月一等奖。

六、国际合作

不断深化和拓展与国际热区科研机构的合作，先后出访 70 余个国家与地区，组织承办国际学术会议 10 余次，组织开展热带农业国际培训班 79 期，培训了来自 90 多个国家的 3824 名学员。推动与联合国粮农组织（FAO）、国际热带农业中心（CIAT）、澳大利亚国际农业研究中心（ACIAR）等 10 余个国际组织和研究机构建立长期友好合作关系，推动所在单位 2014 年被 FAO 认定为"FAO 热带农业研究培训参考中心"；促成 CIAT 在所在单位设立合作办公室和联合实验室，共同创办国际学术刊物 *Tropical Grasslands-Forrajes Tropicales*（已被 SCI 收录），并推荐 CIAT 荣获 2019 年度海南省国际科学技术合作奖。承担国家自然科学基金地区合作项目、农业农村部引进国际先进农业科学技术项目等多项国际合作项目，通过项目引进国外技术 7 项、牧草种质资源 2406 份、外国专家 60 余人次，其中 2 名专家获得中国政府友谊奖、2 名专家获得海南省椰岛奖。团队所在单位于 2001 年被国家外国专家局授予"热带牧草选育"引智成果示范推广基地。

七、主要科技成果与科研业绩

在 *New Phytologist*、《草业学报》等杂志上发表中英文学术论文 460 多篇。出版《海南禾草志》《海南莎草志》《海南饲用植物志》《中国热带牧草品种志》等 18 部专著，并主编教材《热带牧草栽培学》《热带作物种质资源学》等 4 部，主编《南方农区畜牧业实用技术丛书》等科普丛书 3 套。以第一或者主要完成人获得包括农业农村部中华农业科技一等奖、中华农业科技团队奖、海南省自然科学特等奖、海南省科技进步奖一等奖、海南省科技成果转化奖一等奖在内的省部级科技奖励 30 余项（其中省部级一等奖 8 项）。以第一或者主要完成人选育热研 4 号王草等牧草新品种 29 个，获得 6 项国家发明专利授权、10 项国家实用新型专利授权。

Awardee of Region Innovation Prize, Liu Guodao

Liu Guodao was born in Tengchong City of Yunnan Province in June 1963. Liu Guodao is engaged in the research field of pratacultural science, and has done a series of pioneering research work in the collection, identification, evaluation and innovative utilization of tropical forage resources.

1. On tropical forage resources

After more than 30 years' efforts, there are more than 14100 tropical forage germplasm resources been collected, and Tropical Forage Germplasm Resources Nursery of the Ministry of Agricultural and Rural Affairs and Chinese Mid-term (backup) Forage Germplasm Preservation Database and Herbarium have been established. He internationally named five new species endemic to China (Hainan), and published one genus and 55 species newly recorded in Hainan.

2. On genetic breeding of tropical forage

He, as the first or the main completion person, has bred 29 officially recognized forage varieties, and obtained 2 new varieties protection rights. Among them, Reyan No.4 King Grass is the most important mowing grass in Southern China with an annual yield of 15000–25000 kg for fresh grass per mu, which has been selected to enter the Ten-Year Achievement Exhibition of Agricultural Development in China, and has become the main forage for house feeding and breeding in Southern China. Stylosanthes is the most important tropical legume forage in Southern China. There is a saying "Alfalfa in the North and Stylosanthes in the South". It has become the dominant grass and forage variety in the South. The new varieties have been popularized for more than 38 million mu, with remarkable economic, ecological and social benefits.

3. On cultivation physiology and scientific utilization of forage

He found out the physiological and molecular mechanisms for low phosphorus and aluminum toxicity of Stylosanthes and other important legumes adapted to acid soil in Southern China. He has developed the high yield cultivation and utilization technology of main forage varieties and intercropping mode of forest (fruit) and grass. Aiming at the ecologically fragile rocky desertification areas in Yunnan, Guangxi and Guizhou, a comprehensive management mode of "fruit tree planted in mountain, grass covering land, vine covering stone, livestock grazing grass, and manure returning to the field" was developed by him, with remarkable results to help poverty alleviation and rural revitalization.

4. On talent cultivation and science and technology training

He assisted the former South China University of Tropical Agriculture (now incorporated into Hainan University) to set up undergraduate and master degree programs in pratacultural science, and was responsible for the compilation and publication of key textbooks. More than 600 undergraduates and 80 postgraduates have been cultivated by him.

5. On achievements promotion and science and technology service

Prof. Liu attaches great importance to technology transfer and achievement transformation. In view of the characteristics of animal husbandry in Southern China, such as taking farmers as a unit, he led the team to build a forage extension system by using the "farmer participation" method, and passed new varieties and technologies to farmers through the activities of science and technology going to the countryside. The large-scale popular science reading series of *Practical Technologies for Tropical Animal Husbandry Development* (19 volumes in total) compiled by him won the Chinese Agricultural Science Popularization Award from the Ministry of Agriculture and Rural Affairs in 2015. These books have distinctive features, easy to understand, and deeply loved by farmers. By using these books of more than 5000 brochures distributed, more than 4000 farmer have been trained, which has been highly praised by local science and technology departments. His institution has won the First Prize of Hainan Science and Technology Activity Month for ten consecutive years.

区域创新奖获得者

王 爱 勤

　　王爱勤，1963年2月出生于甘肃省民勤县。1986年毕业于兰州大学化学系，获理学学士学位；1996—1999年毕业于中国科学院兰州化学物理研究所，获理学博士学位。1989年12月至今在中国科学院兰州化学物理研究所工作。2002年3—6月在日本大阪高等工业研究院作JSPS高级访问学者。现任甘肃省黏土矿物应用研究重点实验室主任，中国科学院兰州化学物理研究所环境材料与生态化学研究发展中心主任，甘肃省和江苏省凹凸棒石产业技术创新战略联盟理事长，中国非金属矿工业协会黏土矿物专业委员会副理事长，中国非金属矿工业协会专家委员会副主任。获第二届全国创新争先奖、首届陇原最美科技工作者、中国科学院院地合作先进个人等荣誉称号。发表学术论文500余篇，出版专著7部；申请发明专利168件，获授权国家发明专利82件；制定国家标准1项、行业标准2项；荣获国家级科技奖励2项、省部级科技奖励13项。自2014年连续6年入选Elsevier中国高被引学者榜单，自2017年连续3年入选全球高被引科学家榜单。

　　王爱勤长期从事黏土矿物功能材料研究，在凹凸棒石纳米棒晶无损解离、杂色凹凸棒石转白、伴生矿物同步转化、高附加值功能产品开发及其产业化等方面做出了一系列开创性研究工作。

一、从资源高值到环境材料应用

　　环境材料是生态恢复的基础材料，过去的工作缺少材料创新和配套。为此，从2000年开始，在国家"863"、中国科学院"西部行动"和国家农业转化资金等项目的支持下，王爱勤带领科技团队，根据西部土壤和气候特点，以高值化利用可再生的植物资源——淀粉和甘肃丰富的矿产资源——凹凸棒石黏土为背景，先后创新性地开发了凹凸棒石有机无机复合保水剂、淀粉发泡输水材料、植被多功能恢复剂和抗蒸腾新材料，分别在甘肃"读者林"基地、酒泉卫星发射基地、多条高速公路边坡和兰州市北山进行了应用试验，总结出了高盐碱、板结型和无上水条件土壤植树造林用新材料应用的成功经验，形成了"产品研发—产业生产—应用示范"的互动发展模式，达到了资源高值和生态恢复的双重目的。在生态恢复中，提出"源于自然，用于自然，融于自然"的理念，为我国节水农业发展、西部生态环境修复和扶贫攻坚做出了重要贡献。成果获 2010 年国家科技进步奖二等奖。

二、从黏土矿物到功能材料应用

凹凸棒石在我国主要分布在甘肃、江苏和安徽等地，探明储量占世界总量的 50%。但由于天然形成的凹凸棒石棒晶以棒晶束形式聚集，导致长期以来资源利用水平低、产品附加值不高。如何在不损伤棒晶长径比的前提下高效解离棒晶束，成为制约产业发展的关键共性问题。王爱勤带领团队以凹凸棒石黏土资源的高值化利用为目标，采用对辊处理－制浆提纯－高压均质－乙醇交换一体化工艺，高效无损解离了凹凸棒石棒晶束，棒晶达到纳米级分散，实现了凹凸棒石从矿物材料到纳米材料的根本性转变，突破了制约产业发展的关键共性技术瓶颈。在此基础上，系统开展了不同类型改性剂对凹凸棒石表面功能化改性研究，建立了高压均质和改性剂协同作用提高改性效率的新方法，实现了应用导向的凹凸棒石表面性质调控和功能化设计。从应用基础突破、关键技术发明到高值产品开发，形成了具有自主知识产权的技术创新链，形成了凹凸棒石纳米无机凝胶和油品高效脱色剂等高附加值产品。成果获 2015 年江苏省科学技术奖一等奖。

在上述研究基础上，利用棒晶束解离凹凸棒石纳米棒晶和孔道，通过表面构筑双吸附位点，攻克了凹凸棒石对玉米赤霉烯酮和呕吐毒素吸附的技术难题，与企业合作建成了国内首条全自动生产线，产品性能超过国外高端产品水平，打破了欧美产品的市场垄断。针对畜禽健康养殖对替抗产品的迫切需求，形成了具有自主知识产权的工艺包和技术创新链，成果转化产品产生了显著的经济和社会效益。所建立的技术体系显著提高了我国凹凸棒石的自主研发水平，在国内外同行中产生了重要影响，对带动凹凸棒石产品升级换代和推动凹凸棒石产业及相关行业创新发展起到了引领作用。

甘肃省凹凸棒石黏土资源极为丰富，远景总储量超过 10 亿吨，是典型的湖相沉积型矿物。因八面体位置上阳离子的类质同象取代较为普遍，晶体骨架中的镁部分被铁和铜等变价离子替代使其呈现杂色。由于"颜值"较低和伴生矿物较多，不具备功能导向的工业应用价值，严重制约了甘肃省凹凸棒石产业的规模发展。在充分研究凹凸棒石微观结构基础上，发明了杂色凹凸棒石结构性转白关键制备技术，利用既具有还原性、又具有酸性和离子络合能力的有机酸，选择性梯度溶出八面体中的致色离子，在转白的同时完整保留了凹凸棒石的规整孔道和纳米棒晶，解决了八面体溶蚀引起纳米棒晶损伤的技术难题，实现了在涂覆锂离子电池隔膜涂层和增韧补强塑料母粒中的应用；采用转白凹凸棒石，创制了凹凸棒石玛雅蓝和钴蓝纳米杂化颜料，实现了在高耐候防腐涂料和工程塑料等领域的推广应用；利用凹凸棒石伴生矿和八面体溶出离子，攻克了宏量制备纳米功能材料的技术难题，实现了伴生矿的高值利用和溶出离子的有效利用。成果获 2017 年甘肃省技术发明奖一等奖和 2018 年国家技术发明奖二等奖。

三、从平台建立到技术体系建设

凹凸棒石是我国的特色优势资源，如何高值利用一直是地方政府和业界共同关注的问题。为了创新驱动产业发展，先后组建了甘肃省黏土矿物应用研究重点实验室、甘肃省矿物功能材料制造业创新中心、甘肃省凹凸棒石产业技术创新战略联盟、中国科学院盱眙凹土应用技术研发与产业化中心和江苏省凹土材料产品检测技术重点实验室等平台，贯通了人才聚集平台、创新研发平台和检测服务平台，制定了 GB 29225—2012 国家标准、JC/T 2266—2014 和 JC/T 2412—2017 行业标准。在江苏和甘肃地方政府的支持下，形成了独具特色的产业集群和助推产业发展模式。

Awardee of Region Innovation Prize, Wang Aiqin

Wang Aiqin was born in Minqin County of Gansu Province in February 1963. He graduated from Lanzhou University with a Bachelor of Science degree in Department Chemistry in 1986. From December 1989 to present, He has been working in Lanzhou Institute of Chemical Physics(LICP), Chinese Academy of Sciences（CAS）, and he received his Ph.D in Physical Chemistry in 1999 from LICP, CAS. From March 2002 to June 2002, he worked as a senior Visiting Scholar of JSPS in Institute of Advanced Industrial Research in Osaka, Japan. He is the director of Key Laboratory of Clay Mineral Applied Research of Gansu Province, and the director of R&D Center of Eco-material and Eco-Chemistry of LICP, CAS. He is also the chairman of the Strategic Alliance of Attapulgite Industry Technology Innovation of Gansu and Jiangsu Provinces. He has won the second National Innovation Competition Award, the first Longyuan Most Beautiful Scientific and Technological Worker, Innovation Award of Chinese Industry–University– Research Cooperation and "Outstanding Member of Communist Party of China" of CAS, etc.

His research focuses on synthesis, characterization and application of clay mineral–based functional materials and their industrialization. To date, he has published more than 500 papers, and 7 monographs in domestic and foreign journals. He has applied 168 national invention patents, and 82 of them have been authorized by China. He has won 2 National Second Prizes and 13 Provincial or Ministerial Science and Technology Awards for his relevant researches. It has been selected into the Elsevier's List of Most Cited Chinese Researchers of Chemical Engineering for 6 consecutive years since 2014, and the List of Global Highly Cited Scientists for 3 consecutive years since 2017.

Wang Aiqin is engaged in the research of mineral functional materials, and has made a series of pioneering researches on the disaggregation attapulgite nanorod crystals, the whitening of variegated attapulgite, the synchronous transformation of the associated minerals, and the development and industrialization of high-value-added functional products. He and his group solved the key bottlenecks that restricted the high value utilization of natural attapulgite resources, and developed a series of high value-added products and realized their industrialization applications, such as attapulgite-based high-performance bleaching earth for palm oil, mycotoxin adsorbent, cobalt blue hybrid pigments, green hybrid antibacterial agent, etc. Furthermore, the established technique system significantly enhanced the level of the independent research and development of attapulgite in our country, and realized the synergetic development of attapulgite industry from the basic research to applied research to application development and industrialization. The obtained research achievements realized the leaping development of the research level of attapulgite in our country from "Following" to "Overtaking".

区域创新奖获得者

张 宗 亮

张宗亮，1963 年 5 月出生于山东省济南市。1984 年毕业于清华大学水利系，获学士学位；2008 年毕业于天津大学建筑工程学院，获管理学博士学位。自 1984 年在中国电建昆明院从事水利水电勘察设计科研工作至今，2003 年至今任院总工程师。2008 年当选全国工程勘察设计大师。兼任天津大学、河海大学教授，中国水力发电工程学会常务理事，中国岩石力学与工程学会常务理事，中国水力发电工程学会混凝土面板堆石坝专业委员会副主任委员，中国水利学会水工结构专业委员会副主任委员，云南省岩土力学与工程学会理事长等。

主持和组织完成国内外 70 座水电站（总装机容量 3700 万千瓦）的勘察设计科研工作，主持国家重点研发计划项目 1 项、省部级重大科技项目 5 项。在高坝工程、堰塞坝等工程技术及水利水电信息化方面取得系列创新成果。

一、特高心墙堆石坝技术创新——我国心墙堆石坝坝高提升 100 米

糯扎渡水电站心墙堆石坝高 261.5 米，比我国当时最高的小浪底提升了 100 米，对高心墙坝渗流、变形、坝坡稳定和泄洪、抗震安全等重大难题开展了系统研究。

首次提出特高心墙坝采用人工碎石掺砾土料和软岩堆石料筑坝成套技术，攻克了特高心墙坝变形控制和变形协调难题。发展了坝料静、动力本构模型和水力劈裂及裂缝计算分析方法，突破了特高心墙坝工程安全评价技术瓶颈。构建了特高心墙坝勘察设计技术和安全评价体系，建成我国首座 300 米级高心墙坝。研发了特高土石坝施工质量实时控制关键技术，开创数字大坝先例，保障了筑坝质量和大坝安全。建立了高水头大流量泄洪安全技术体系，解决了特高心墙坝泄洪安全难题。

创新成果在糯扎渡水电站成功应用，居国际领先水平。奠定了我国 300 米级心墙坝筑坝技术基础。核心技术在后续大渡河长河坝水电站、雅砻江两河口水电站、澜沧江如

美水电站等特高心墙坝工程中推广应用，经济社会效益显著。作为两河口水电站特咨团专家组组长、如美水电站特咨团专家，对多座特高心墙坝开展咨询工作，有力推动了我国特高心墙坝的成功建设和技术发展。

二、高混凝土面板堆石坝技术创新——我国面板堆石坝坝高跨越100米

2000年建成高178米的天生桥一级面板坝，实现了从100米级到200米级的跨越。作为项目设计总工程师，解决了高面板坝变形控制及面板结构抗裂等重大难题。

揭示了200米级高面板堆石坝变形规律，提出高面板坝采用分期蓄水等控制变形的协调措施，被国际著名土石坝专家库克先生称赞为"化有害变形为无害变形"。充分利用建筑物开挖料进行坝体分区和坝料设计，节省投资。提出面板坝渗流控制设计准则和自愈式止水系统。创新成果成功应用于天生桥一级面板坝，核心技术在乌江洪家渡、沅水三板溪、清江水布垭等高面板坝推广应用。主编《混凝土面板堆石坝设计规范》。

近10年来，主要依托古水240米高面板坝，对西部高海拔高寒强地震复杂条件下的300米级面板坝关键技术开展研究。揭示面板挤压破坏机理，提出工程对策措施；建立300米级面板坝设计准则、安全控制标准；研发变形协调控制技术和精细化数值模拟技术。创新成果纳入《混凝土面板堆石坝设计规范》，总体居国际领先水平，在大渡河猴子岩、黄河茨哈峡、新疆大石峡等推广应用。

三、堰塞坝技术创新——建成世界首座100米高堰塞坝水利枢纽

2014年云南鲁甸"8·03"地震造成红石岩堰塞湖，作为应急抢险专家组组长和设计总工程师，主持堰塞湖应急处置与综合整治设计研究；作为项目负责人，主持国家重点研发计划项目，对堰塞体形成过程与溃决机理、堰塞坝形态演变机理与安全评价等重大科学问题开展系统研究。

研发了堰塞体形成全过程数值模拟方法和双曲线冲刷侵蚀、溃口圆弧坍塌扩展计算模型，建立应急抢险指挥平台，攻克了应急抢险快速响应与科学决策的技术难题。提出尺寸效应分析方法和长期性态计算分析模型，开发了大型非线性接触三维有限元数值模拟软件，提出散粒料的动力Bouc-Wen修正模型，突破了堰塞坝静动力工作性态分析和安全评价的技术瓶颈。创建堰塞体综合勘察设计技术体系，建立应急处置全专业HydroBIM协同设计平台，开创了堰塞坝减灾兴利、整治利用的先例。研制了堰塞坝整治利用的关键材料和施工成套装备，解决了复杂环境下宽级配堰塞坝防渗结构施工关键技术难题。

创建"应急抢险—后续处置—整治利用"一体化技术体系，将红石岩建成具有防洪、供水、灌溉、发电等综合功能的世界首座堰塞坝水利枢纽工程。创新成果总体居国际领先水平，提升了西部强震区自然灾害防治技术水平。

四、水利水电工程信息化 BIM 技术创新——建立 HydroBIM 理论和技术体系

自 2005 年带领团队在国内率先开展水利水电工程信息化 BIM 技术研究，形成了具有自主知识产权的 HydroBIM 理论和技术体系，研发 HydroBIM 设计施工运行一体化综合平台，成功应用于百余项水利水电工程。获欧特克全球基础设施卓越设计大赛金奖 2 项，将水利水电 BIM 技术应用推进到国际领先水平。

编著《大国重器·糯扎渡卷》，入选国家重点出版基金项目；主编"水利水电工程信息化 BIM 丛书"，入选"十三五"重点出版项目。共主编出版专著 7 部，发表论文 85 篇，其中 SCI/EI 36 篇。

Awardee of Region Innovation Prize, Zhang Zongliang

Zhang Zongliang was born in Jinan City of Shandong Province in May 1963. He is the chief engineer in POWERCHINA Kunming Engineering Corporation Limited (hereafter referred to as KHIDI) and the National Master in Engineering Investigation and Design. He graduated from Department of Water Conservancy in Tsinghua University and then has been engaged in scientific and research work of investigation and design in the sector of water conservancy and hydropower projects in southwest of China for 37 years.

From 1984 to 1989, as the principal designer, Zhang participated in the tech-construction design and research of Lubuge Hydropower Project, which was a window for China's hydropower infrastructure projects opening to outside. From 1990 to 2000, as the chief design engineer and project manager, he chaired the design and research work of Tianshengqiao 1st Hydropower Project for 10 years. The dam height is 178 m, which was the highest concrete-faced rockfill dam in China (the second in the world) when it was completed, and realized the leap-forward development of dam height from 100 m to 200 m in China. From 2000 to 2014, as the chief design engineer and chief engineer of KHIDI, Dr. Zhang presided over the investigation, design and scientific research of Nuozhadu Hydropower Project for 15 years. The dam height of it is 261.5 m, which was the highest earth-rock dam in China (the third in the world), and an international milestone of rockfill dam project, leading the development of dam construction technology of super-high core wall dam in China. From 2014 to 2020, as the chief design engineer, he presided over the design and research of emergency rescue and development & utilization of Hongshiyan Barrier Dam which is with the dam height of 103 m. Dr. Zhang innovatively put forward the concept of "promoting the beneficial and eliminating the harmful, turning waste into wealth", and built the world's first barrier dam hydro-junction project. From 2003 to 2020, as the chief engineer of KHIDI, he chaired the design and research of Xiaowan, Guanyinyan, Huangdeng and other high dam projects, and created many milestone projects, ranking the first both at home and abroad, representing the world leading level of dam construction technology of similar dam types. Xiaowan Hydropower Project, with the dam hight of 294.5 m, was the highest concrete arch dam in China (the first in the world) when it was complected. And it is one of the international milestone projects of concrete arch dam and it is also a landmark project of China's super-high arch dam construction from following to catching up the international level. Besides, Dr. Zhang has achieved several innovations in the engineering fields of high dam and barrier dam, etc.

Zhang has won 6 second prizes of National Scientific and Technological Progress, 2 Excellent Prizes of FIDIC Engineering Projects and 2 Tien-Yow Jeme Civil Engineering Prizes. And he was elected as the National Master in engineering investigation and design. Dr. Zhang was awarded Guanghua Engineering Science and Technology Award, National Outstanding Engineer Award, Pan Jiazheng Award and National Dam Outstanding Engineer. He was listed in National Talents Project and in Leading Talents in Science and Technology in Yunnan Province. His team has also won the Excellent Scientific and Technological Innovation Team of National Enterprises. Dr. Zhang has been elected as the National Master in Engineering Investigation and Design for 12 years and he is a scientific and technological leading figure in the field of high earth-rock dam engineering investigation and design in China.

产业创新奖获得者

程 博 闻

程博闻，1963年1月出生于湖北省黄梅县。1983年本科毕业于天津纺织工学院纺化系，后留校任教；1989年获工学硕士学位；2003年获天津工业大学纺织工程工学博士学位。先后担任天津工业大学材料系主任、科技处处长、纺织学部主任、校长助理、副校长，其间被聘任为国家重点学科纺织科学与工程学科学术带头人、天津市非织造技术工程中心和高性能纤维及纺织复合材料国家地方联合工程研究中心主任。先后兼任纺织学报编委副主任，中国纺织工程学会副理事长和中国纤维素行业协会技术委员会副主任。2019年4月至今任天津科技大学副校长。

先后入选或获得"百千万人才工程"国家级人选、全国中青年突出贡献专家、全国纺织科技创新领军人才、中国纺织学术大奖、中国纺织学术带头人、全国优秀科技工作者、全国五一劳动奖章获得者、改革开放40年中国纺织行业突出贡献人物和全国创新争先奖等荣誉。

程博闻长期从事纤维新材料和产业用纺织品的科研与教学工作，围绕我国环境保护、医疗卫生、国防、先进能源等领域对高性能产业用纺织品及其应用技术的重大需求，以产业用纤维新材料为先导，以新型纤维集合体柔性复合材料关键制备技术为依托，以产业纺织品应用为重点，突出基础研究和交叉学科研究。先后承担完成了国家科技支撑、"973""863"、国家自然基金以及国防科工局等项目50余项，获国家科学技术进步奖二等奖3项，中国纺织工业联合会科技进步奖一等奖4项，上海市科技进步奖一等奖1项，天津市科技进步奖一等奖2项、二等奖2项，天津市技术发明奖二等奖2项，中国专利优秀奖2项，天津市专利金奖2项，中国纺织行业专利金奖1项。近5年发表SCI论文211篇，其中1区论文57篇，SCI论文他引总数1802次；授权中国发明专利85项。

一、建立以纺丝成网为核心技术的新型非织造材料制备体系，促进相关理论、技术与产业的发展

在新型非织造材料设计与开发方向，针对制约我国熔喷非织造材料制备技术的发展瓶颈，揭示了电荷储存机制、驻极材料过滤机理和保暖材料传质传热机制，攻克了纳米掺杂双组分熔喷耐久驻极纳微纤维非织造材料制备技术，实现了高效、低阻非织造过滤材料的产业化；开发了短纤插层复合熔喷非织造材料制备技术，实现了高弹耐压复合熔喷非织造过滤、吸油、保暖材料的产业化；研发了层间复合协同增效熔喷非织造材料制备技术，实现了复合熔喷非织造耐磨保暖材料的产业化；开发出了一步法熔喷微/纳交叠纤维非织造材料制备及纺粘/熔喷/纺粘集成技术，合成了纳米磁性多面体倍半硅氧烷（Fe_3O_4–POSS）驻极体，实现了兼具电、磁双驻极效应的高品质个体防护非织造材料的产业化，过滤防护材料产品远销欧美，在非典和甲流尤其是新型冠状病毒的重大公共突发事件中发挥了重要作用；系列保暖材料已装备全军部队，极大提升了我军寒冷环境下的单兵机动能力，显著提升了我国纺丝成网非织造技术和装备水平。

基于高速气流拉伸成形机理，首创（静电）溶液喷射纺规模化微纳米纤维生产成套装置，解决了传统微纳米纤维制备技术制备效率低的难题，实现了微纳米纤维规模化制备技术的突破，开发出适用于高效空气过滤器、质子交换膜、超级电容器电极等的纳米纤维制品，为我国环境治理、个体防护和新能源产业等领域提供了高性能纳米纤维材料；发明了静电溶喷技术，制备出柔性氧化铝纳微纤维（500～5000 nm）隔热材料，技术指标接近国外同类产品水平。

二、突破功能纤维一系列关键制备技术，建立了成套产业化集成技术，实现了国产功能纤维生产技术的提升

在纤维材料设计和制备方向，解决了纤维用纳米功能材料制备、多相体系纺丝成形、纤维加工等系列科学与技术难题，揭示了功能组分对纤维性能的影响规律，形成了功能纤维复合纺丝设备与生产线设计、生产、产品性能评价等成套产业化集成技术，实现了复合导电纤维的产业化，复合导电纤维技术指标均达到国际先进水平，打破了国外的技术封锁和垄断，填补了国内相关技术领域的空白，开发出多种导电纤维功能面料和制品，在 07 军服生产中得到了广泛应用，对我国新型功能纤维的开发具有重要的推动作用。

中空纤维反渗透膜技术属于膜领域中少数的"卡脖子"技术之一，技术难度大，在高端分离领域具有重大的战略意义。程博闻组织产学研交叉团队在膜天膜科技公司建成了国内首条具有自主知识产权的规模化制备中空纤维反渗透膜及膜组件的生产线，中空纤维反渗透膜产品进行了工业化应用。

电解水制氢是目前最具潜力的高效、清洁制氢技术。隔膜是水电解过程的关键材料。针对我国氢能源发展需求，开发聚苯硫醚（PPS）的非锂合成技术和液相提纯技术，实现

了隔膜用纤维级 PPS 树脂的产业化；研究 PPS 纤维熔融纺丝技术和涡流纺纱工艺，突破隔膜多级孔结构的力－温协同调控技术，实现了大尺寸织物型隔膜的规模化制备，成功替代了西方限制使用的传统石棉纤维水电解隔膜，成果已成功应用于某国防工程并推广到民用市场，整套民用设备出口到国外，为电能转化为清洁的氢能提供了关键材料。

三、推进专业、学科建设与人才培养，参与国家、区域和行业的发展规划研究

参与 2005 年我国最早开设非织造材料与工程专业，培养了一大批优秀本、硕、博毕业生，培养博士生获博士国家奖学金 8 人次、天津市大学生创新奖学金特等奖 3 人次、天津市优秀学生 1 人次；2017 届博士生厉宗洁的博士毕业论文获第八届"王善元优秀博士论文基金"、2019 年天津市优秀博士学位论文，2018 届博士生邓南平的博士毕业论文获中国纺织工程学会优秀博士学位论文、2019 年天津市优秀博士论文，2019 届博士生王航的博士毕业论文获中国纺织工程学会优秀博士论文。参与编写《生物基化学纤维生产及应用》《非织造布用粘合剂》《膜分离技术实用教程》等 9 部著作和教材；以纺织工程国家重点学科为依托，参与建成省部共建分离膜与过程国家重点实验室等多个国家级创新平台，积极参与国家、天津市和行业的相关领域发展规划和标准研究，为我国由纺织大国迈向纺织强国做出了应有贡献。

Awardee of Industrial Innovation Prize, Cheng Bowen

Cheng Bowen was born in Huangmei County of Hubei Province in January 1963. He obtained Master's and Doctor's degree of Textile Engineering from Tianjin Polytechnic University. He worked in Tianjin Polytechnic University from 1983, and successively served as director of Office for Science and Technology, director of School of Textiles, and Vice President of Tianjin Polytechnic University from April 2009 to April 2019. During the period, he was also appointed as Academic leader of State Key Discipline–Textile Science and Technology, director of Tianjin Nonwoven Technology Engineering Center, director of National–Local Joint Engineering Research Center, etc. Currently, he serves as Vice President of Tianjin University of Science and Technology.

Bowen Cheng has won honors of National Candidate of Talent Project, Outstanding Mid–aged Expert of National Talent Engineering, State Council Special Expert, National Textile Innovation Leading Talent, China Textile Academic Award, China Textile Academic Leader, Tianjin Outstanding Talents, Tianjin High–level Innovative Leading Talents of Science & Technology Innovation, National Outstanding Scientific & Technology Worker, National May 1st Labor Medal Winners, etc.

He has engaged in research and teaching in the area of novel fiber materials and industrial textiles for many years, focusing on the country's major demands for high—performance industrial textiles and their application technologies in the fields of environmental protection, healthcare, national defense, and advanced energy. He established a preparation system for novel nonwoven materials, and led the development of related theories, technologies, and industries. Meanwhile, he made a breakthrough in a series of key preparation technologies for functional fibers, and realized the improvements in preparation technology of domestic functional fibers. He has undertaken and completed more than 50 scientific projects, including National Key Technology R&D Program, National Basic Research Program of China (973 Program), National High Technology Research and Development Program of China (863 Program), National Natural Science Foundation of China, National Defense Foundation of China, etc., and won approximately 20 awards, such as National Science and Technology Progress, China Textile Industry Association Prize for Progress in Science and Technology, Shanghai Science and Technology Progress, Tianjin Science and Technology Progress, China's Patent Award, etc. He has published 211 SCI articles and achieved 85 authorized China invention patents in the past five years.

Bowen Cheng participated in the establishment of Nonwoven Materials and Engineering Major, national innovation platforms, development plan and standard research in related fields. He has made due contributions to China from Tex—giant to Tex—superpower.

产业创新奖获得者

贾振华

贾振华，1975 年 12 月出生于山东省博兴县。2008 年毕业于河北医科大学，获中西医结合博士学位。担任河北以岭医院及河北省中西医结合医药研究院院长，兼任中华中医药学会络病分会副主任委员兼秘书长、中国中西医结合学会血管脉络病专委会候任主任委员、世界中联络病专委会副会长兼秘书长。荣获中医药传承与创新"百千万"人才工程岐黄学者、国家高层次万人计划领军人才、科技部中青年科技创新领军人才、国家卫计委有突出贡献中青年专家、全国优秀科技工作者等荣誉称号。

贾振华始终致力于中医络病理论及其指导心肺疾病研究，在心、脑、（糖）肾等重大疾病微血管防治及病毒类呼吸系统传染病研究方面开展了系列工作并取得重大科研成果。

一、系统构建络病理论，建立"络病证治"体系，奠定络病学科理论基础

系统构建络病理论，在中医学术发展史上首次建立"络病证治"体系，奠定络病学科理论基础，提高多种难治性疾病临床疗效，获 2006 年国家科技进步奖二等奖。建立络病理论指导基于临床的成果转化平台——科技部络病研究与创新中药国家重点实验室、国家中管局络病重点研究室、国家中医临床重点专科、国家中管局区域诊疗中心、重大疑难疾病中西医协作临床试点单位。编写《络病学》专著并改编为教材，推动国内 28 所高校和新加坡仲景医学院开课；组织成立中华中医药学会、世界中联及中国中西医结合学会络病专委会，推动国内 28 个省市建立络病专委会；推动北京、陕西、湖北、辽宁、深圳等 10 余家络病重点学科、研究室、工作室的建立；出版《络病学》繁体版及英文版，建立欧洲、加拿大等海外络病研究团体。

二、参与脉络学说构建及其指导微血管病变防治取得重大突破，传承创新脉络学说营卫理论，指导开展心血管事件链系统干预

系统构建中医脉络学说，形成中医学指导血管病变防治新理论；建立"脉络－血管系统病"辨证诊断标准并成为学会标准；证实通络改善微血管血流灌注是治疗心、脑、（糖）肾重大疾病共性机制，明确通络治疗微血管病变的核心机制是保护微血管内皮细胞；采用国际标准完成 4 项循证研究，解决急性心梗无再流临床国际医学界重大难题，为心功能不全伴室早治疗提供新药物，填补窦缓伴室早快慢兼治、整合调律药物治疗空白，在国际标准治疗基础上明显提高慢性心衰临床疗效。"973"项目验收专家组评价该成果"首次形成指导微血管病变性重大疾病防治的新理论，取得中医药治疗微血管病变重大突破"。成果获 2019 年国家科技进步奖一等奖。

主持 2018 年国家重点研发计划，传承创新脉络学说，首先提出心血管事件链系统干预观点。选择心血管事件链关键环节重大疾病，开展通络药物逆转代谢综合征糖耐量异常 880 例、稳定冠状动脉易损斑块 220 例、干预急性心梗心血管事件 3796 例、预防射频消融术后房颤复发 920 例、改善慢性心衰预后 3080 例等 5 项循证研究，为首次以临床事件发生率为评价指标、以心血管事件链系统干预为研究内容且遵循国际规范的中药循证医学临床研究，为建立中医药参与心血管事件链系统干预方案提供了高质量的研究证据。

三、率先应用络病理论指导外感热病防治，研制治疗流感国家专利新药连花清瘟，成为中医药防治呼吸系统公共卫生事件品牌中药

开展基于络病理论指导流感等外感热病治疗研究。基于络脉空间位置分布，提出"阳络→经脉→阴络"的病机传变规律，揭示病邪由阳络传至经脉的病机特点及易传入脏腑阴络的传变规律，提出积极干预策略，制定连花清瘟组方：以东汉张仲景麻杏石甘汤与清代吴鞠通银翘散为基础方，卫气同治、表里双解，吸取明代吴又可治疗疫病用大黄经验，先证用药、截断病势，配伍红景天清肺化瘀、调节免疫，藿香芳香化湿、祛邪辟秽，体现积极干预组方特色。2003 年，军事医学科学院证实连花清瘟组方体外具有明显抑制 SARS 病毒作用，成为 SARS 期间通过国家药监局绿色通道获批的唯一专利中药。上市以来累计 23 次列入国家卫健委、国家中医药管理局发布的甲流、禽流感、中东呼吸综合征、新冠肺炎等病毒类传染性公共卫生事件诊疗方案或指南共识，成为应对此类公共卫生事件的代表性中成药。成果获 2011 年国家科技进步奖二等奖。

连花清瘟治疗甲型 H1N1 流感较西药磷酸奥司他韦更具优势。连花清瘟治疗指数明显高于奥司他韦，病毒核酸转阴时间与奥司他韦无差异，在减少疾病严重程度、退热、缓解咳嗽、乏力、头痛、肌肉酸痛等方面明显优于奥司他韦，治疗费用相当于奥司他韦的 1/8。被列入卫生部《甲型 H1N1 流感诊疗方案》，并作为国家工信部、解放军总后卫生部、北京市等作为防控流感储备用药，在防控疫情中发挥重大作用，入选《科技日报》

2009 年国际十大科技新闻。相关成果获 2011 年国家科技进步奖二等奖。

连花清瘟治疗新冠肺炎形成细胞—动物—临床完整证据链：体外抑制 SARS–CoV–2 病毒并有显著抗炎作用；有效抑制转基因新冠肺炎小鼠模型体重下降，改善肺部炎性损伤；常规治疗基础上加用连花清瘟可进一步改善发热、乏力、咳嗽等临床症状，缩短症状持续时间，明显改善肺部炎症（CT），提高临床治愈率，转重型率降低 50%。

推动治疗新冠肺炎适应证写入药品说明书；被列入国家卫健委《新型冠状病毒感染的肺炎诊疗方案》及 20 余省市的诊疗方案推荐用药；被列入《武汉方舱医院工作手册》，在武汉方舱医院及湖北省 1600 余家医院社区应用；疫情期间发货 2 亿余盒，相当于 8000 万人次使用，湖北疫区应用临床总结疗效确切；连花清瘟抗击新冠肺炎成果多次参与国际学术交流。

Awardee of Industrial Innovation Prize, Jia Zhenhua

Jia Zhenhua, born in Boxing County of Shandong Province in December 1975, was graduated from Hebei Medical University with a doctorate in integrated Chinese and Western medicines in 2008. Presently, Jia Zhenhua is the Vice Chairman and Secretary–General of Collateral Disease Branch of China Association of Chinese Medicine & Hebei Yiling Hospital, Vice Chairman of Special Committee on Vascular and Collateral Diseases of Chinese Association of Integrative Medicine, as well as Vice Chairman and Secretary–General of Special Committee on Collateral Disease of World Federation of Chinese Medicine Societies. He also wins various titles and prizes including Qihuang scholar under "Ten Million" Talents Project of Traditional Chinese Medicine Inheritance and Innovation, leading talent of National Special Support Program for High–Level Talents, young and middle–aged leading talent in scientific and technological innovation awarded by Ministry of Science and Technology, young and middle–aged expert with outstanding contribution awarded by National Health and Family Planning Commission, national outstanding scientific and technical worker, Youth Science and Technology Prize of China, and etc.

Jia Zhenhua has been devoted to conducting researches on TCM collateral disease theory and its guidance in cardiac–pulmonary diseases. Jia Zhenhua has won the first prize of National Science and Technology Progress Award for one time (the third principal investigator), the second prize of National Science and Technology Progress Award for two times (the first and the third principal investigator respectively) and the first prize of Provincial and Ministerial–Level Science and Technology Progress Award for two times (the first principal investigator).

Jia Zhenhua systematically constructs collateral disease theory and establishes system of "collateral disease syndrome and treatment" to lay a theoretical foundation for collateral disease subject. He won the second prize of National Science and Technology Progress Award in 2006

(the third principal investigator). He achieves significant effect in promoting collateral disease discipline construction.

Jia Zhenhua participated in construction of a collateral disease doctrine branch— collaterals doctrine and its guidance in prevention and treatment of microangiopathy. This project has obtained a major breakthrough, and won the first prize of National Science and Technology Progress Award in 2019 (as the third principal investigator). Undertaking the national key research and development plan, he inherit and innovate the theory of *Mailuoxueshuo*, which guides the intervention research of cardiovascular event chain disease.

Jia Zhenhua is the first person to use collateral disease theory in guiding prevention and treatment of externally contracted heat disease, and develops a national patented new drug for treating influenza Lianhua Qingwen. This drug becomes a branded Chinese medicine for prevention and control of respiratory—system public health event by TCM, and won the second prize of National Science and Technology Progress Award in 2011 (the first principal investigator).

产业创新奖获得者

李 晋 闽

李晋闽，1957年2月出生于福建省福州市。现任半导体照明联合创新国家重点实验室主任，国家半导体照明工程研发及产业联盟研发执行主席。1991年获中国科学院西安光学精密机械研究所光学专业理学博士学位，曾任中国科学院半导体研究所所长。2006起担任"十一五""十二五""863"重大项目"半导体照明工程"总体专家组组长、"十三五"国家重点研发计划"战略性先进电子材料"重点专项编制专家组成员。

李晋闽主要从事新型半导体材料与器件的研究工作。作为国家半导体照明工程的建议者、推动者和实践者之一，他针对产业主流技术存在的问题，在核心关键技术上取得突出成就，其代表性成果有力地支撑了产业的形成和发展，曾先后获得国家科技进步奖一等奖、国家技术发明奖二等奖、北京市科学技术奖、中国产学研合作突出贡献奖等奖项。在第三代半导体材料核心技术及产业化应用领域做出了一系列开创性成果。

一、半导体照明材料和物理研究奠定了技术发展的基础

李晋闽揭示了微纳米图形衬底在外延过程中位错弯曲、闭合和阻断的动力学规律及有效抑制位错密度的物理机制，提出3D-2D交替调控生长模型，实现位错湮灭，获得了高质量氮化镓外延材料。基于该技术的大功率LED器件稳态发光效率超过200lm/W，材料质量达到国际最好水平。论文发表在APL、JAP等期刊，SCI他引473次，在JAP近5年刊发的文章中被引用率位于前5%。

在国际上首次提出并建立了一种金属极性面3D极化诱导空穴气的物理模型和技术，通过控制p型铝镓氮层中铝组分渐变，利用极化效应诱导出3D空穴气，在p型铝镓氮材料中获得了高达$2.6 \times 10^{18} cm^{-3}$的空穴浓度，相比传统方法空穴浓度提升一个数量级，是氮化物p型掺杂的关键性突破。2014年诺贝尔物理学奖获奖者、美国加州大学中村修二教授评价该工作"是一项重要的科研成就，对发展高亮度半导体照明器件具有重要

意义"。

提出"缺陷共振态 p 型掺杂"这一宽禁带半导体材料 p 型掺杂新方法。通过周期性结构中受主缺陷能级间的相互耦合，完成受主能级从局域态向共振态的转换，实现高效氮化物 p 型掺杂。该方法基于能带"剪裁"，具有普适性，也为其他宽禁带半导体材料的 p 型掺杂提供了新途径。该方法实现 Mg 受主高效离化，空穴浓度达 $3 \times 10^{18}/cm^3$，同时保证了较高的空穴迁移率，电阻率达 $0.136\Omega \cdot cm$，与传统掺杂方法相比降低了一个数量级，为同期国际最好指标。为高效氮化物 LED 产业化技术提供了原创性方法。

二、半导体照明核心器件研究技术创新支撑了产业发展

1. 在国内率先研发 PVD-AlN 缓冲层技术，大大改善氮化物材料质量，成为半导体照明芯片不可或缺的关键技术

通过 PVD-AlN 缓冲层技术，在微米图形衬底上开展外延技术开发，掌握了小间距微米图形衬底上 PVD-AlN 缓冲层的工艺优化条件，使外延氮化物材料的螺位错密度降低至 $2 \times 10^7/cm^3$ 以下。此外，采用 PVD-AlN 缓冲层技术，可节约 GaN 基 LED 的外延生长时间，节省生产成本 15% 以上，已成为半导体照明外延芯片产业界不可或缺的关键技术。

2. 提出全向宽谱光子耦合增强光学薄膜结构，解决了 GaN 基 LED 光提取效率低的关键难题

受限于 GaN 材料的物理性质，只有约 4% 的光可通过平整的氮化镓／空气界面出射，光提取一直是半导体照明器件效率提升的瓶颈。李晋闽提出了一种膜层界面融合、中心波长延展的宽光谱全向膜系结构及制备技术，阐明了高折射率、多光学界面体系的光子传输过程并实现了有效调控，器件光提取效率提高 1.6 倍，解决了 GaN 基 LED 光提取效率低的关键难题。美国工程院院士、佐治亚理工学院 C.P.Wong 教授认为"这是 GaN 基 LED 光提取领域突破性的进展，是提升 LED 提取效率的有效手段"。

三、引领国际标准制定，提升产业国际影响力

1. 突破 LED 光源模组规格接口共性关键技术

半导体照明技术作为新兴技术，国内外均无现成标准可循。灯具模组规格种类繁多、不能互换，严重制约照明产品规模化推广应用。

针对上述难题，围绕路灯、隧道灯等主要照明产品的光学、机械、热学、电气等接口及涉及专利开展调研和技术分析，设计出 LED 光源产品规格接口，并开展合规性测试。从光源模组产品可替代性出发，制作具有统一规格接口的标准化模组，提升通用性和互换性，降低维护成本，推动标准化 LED 光源模组的大规模应用。制定出 LED 规格接口的团体标准，成为中国首个获得标准创新贡献奖的团体标准。转化为上海、湖南、四川等地方标准，在各地照明工程招标中获得广泛采用。截至 2016 年年底，符合标准的 LED 路灯模组销售量已超过 400 万只；2017 年上升为国家标准，并被推荐为国际半导体照明联

盟标准。

2. 制定系列标准，抢占国际标准话语权

随着半导体照明技术成熟度的提高，迫切需要开展规格化标准化应用技术、核心器件共性关键技术、低成本高可靠系统集成技术、超越照明技术等研究，来抢占半导体照明产业制高点。根据产业需求，李晋闽团队发布了《LED 照明产品加速衰减试验方法》《LED 照明产品检验试验规范》《寒冷地区 LED 道路照明产品标准》《家居智能照明通信模块接口规范》等一系列标准，开发出智能化照明控制系统，支撑技术规范和国家标准的研究与制定，引领制定国际标准，抢占国际标准话语权。

以上标准既结合产业现状，又兼顾未来技术发展趋势，获得产业界广泛认可。项目发布了以规格接口为代表的一系列标准，包括团体标准 15 项，其中 4 项转化为国家标准、3 项推荐为国际标准，为半导体照明产品的规模化应用与推广扫清了障碍，为提高我国半导体照明产业国际竞争力发挥了重要的促进作用。

基于上述创新成果，形成了具有自主知识产权的全套技术，关键技术指标处于国际领先水平，支撑了我国半导体照明产业的快速发展。

Awardee of Industrial Innovation Prize, Li Jinmin

Li Jinmin was born in Fuzhou City of Fujian Province in February 1957. He is the director of State Key Lab of Solid-State Lighting and the executive chairman of China Solid-State Lighting Alliance. From 1991 to 1993, he was a post-doctoral researcher in the Institute of Semiconductors, CAS. Since then, he started his professional researches and was mainly focused on the study of novel semiconductor materials in ISCAS. In the next following years from 1995 to 2002, acting as director of material science center of ISCAS, director assistant and academic committee number of ISCAS, he was engaged in the research work on novel semiconductor materials, presiding over and accomplishing the construction of "national novel semiconductor materials research center" of "north microelectronic base" which was one of the key items in national scientific and technological projects. He was responsible for the major and key programs of National High-Tech Research and Development Plan.

As one of the advisers, promoters and practitioners of the National Semiconductor Lighting Project, Prof. Jinmin Li has made outstanding achievements in key technologies of semiconductor lighting, which strongly supported the formation and development of the industry. He has won the first prize of National Science and Technology Progress Award, the second prize of National Technology Invention Award, Beijing Science and Technology Award, China Industry-University-Research Cooperation Innovation Achievement Award, and Outstanding Contribution Award, etc.

For more than ten years, Prof. Jinmin Li has been committed to the development of research and industrial promotion in the field of semiconductor lighting, which has promoted the launch and implementation of National Semiconductor Lighting Project. He is the chief scientist of National Basic Research Program of China. As the main planner and participant, he promoted the establishment of International SSL Alliance in China. It is the first international organization to establish strategic emerging industries in China, and Jinmin Li is the sole representative from mainland China in the advisory committee. Prof. Jinmin Li has an important influence on the academic and industrial circles at home and abroad. He has made outstanding contributions to the research and application of semiconductor lighting in China.

产业创新奖获得者

凌　祥

凌祥，1967年6月出生于江苏省东台市。1988年毕业于南京化工学院并留校工作；2002年获得化工机械博士学位。2005年被评为全国化工优秀科技工作者，2007年被评为教育部"新世纪优秀人才支持计划"人选，2009年入选国家新世纪百千万人才工程，2014年被评为教育部"长江学者奖励计划"特聘教授，2017年、2019年入选中国工程院第二轮院士候选人，2020年获得全国创新争先奖。2012年以来，先后担任中国机械工程学会换热器专业委员会副主任委员，中国化工学会化工机械专业委员会副主任委员，中国化工节能技术协会常务理事，江苏省机械工程学会副理事长，江苏省能源研究会副理事长，江苏省过程强化与新能源装备技术重点实验室主任，江苏省流程工业节能技术与装备工程实验室主任，《储能科学与技术》《石油化工设备》等编委。

凌祥长期从事传热强化理论与节能装备技术研究。针对流程工业实现高能源利用率的重大需求，围绕高效低耗节能技术和严苛环境下节能装备研制两大难题做出了一系列开创性的研究工作。

一、在传热强化理论方面，提出扩缩变流强化传热理论，解决了高效传热与减阻同时实现的难题，为高效节能装备研发奠定了理论基础

流程工业传统余热回收装置传热系数较低，特别在气－气换热中余热回收效果较差。凌祥发明了扩缩变流紧凑变截面流道结构，揭示了其内部纵向涡与横向涡强化传热的机制，提出了扩缩变流强化传热理论。研制出错逆流结构翅片板和超长内翅片管两种扩缩变截面换热器，加热炉余热回收应用实践表明：能源利用率比世界最好的德国林德公司提高3%～4%。研究成果已应用于扬子石化等企业的高能耗系统。开发的新型紧凑换热器打破瑞典Alfalaval等世界领先企业的长期技术垄断；可统计的节能约260万吨标准煤。

二、在节能装备关键技术方面，提出镍基扩散钎焊工艺，发明了扩缩变流节能装置，解决了传统装备不耐高温和腐蚀、难于大型化等难题

开发的钎焊扩缩变流余热回收装置面临耐高温和抗腐蚀性能差、强度低且无法大型化的难题。为此，提出了镍基扩散钎焊大型化制造新工艺，建成了大型耐高温紧凑式换热装置连续生产线，耐温可达 850℃。研制成功世界最大高炉鼓风除湿的铝合金表冷器（迎风面积 4m×6m），传热系数提高 2 倍，高炉吨铁焦比消耗降低 8%，达到国际先进水平。

三、在环保装备关键技术方面，提出了玻璃冲击表面强化抗应力腐蚀和疲劳新技术，攻克了 MVR 高通量废水处理系统寿命短的难题，发明了油气回收的扩缩变流吸附耦合一体化新装置，解决了有机废气处理中变流量、不连续导致回收系统易爆的难题

流程工业中蒸发过程能耗较高，如何实现这些过程的高效低耗是急需解决的瓶颈问题。蒸汽压缩自循环（MVR）蒸发是一种高效节能的蒸发技术，但核心装备蒸汽压缩机的叶轮长期在严苛的高速旋转和腐蚀条件下运行，寿命短。提出将玻璃冲击表面强化和扩缩变流强化蒸发技术应用到 MVR 蒸发系统，突破了大处理量蒸汽再压缩废水蒸发系统疲劳、寿命短的难题。研制出国产最大的 MVR 蒸发装置，成功应用于川宁生物制药的 1200 吨 / 天废水处理，打破了国外技术壁垒。

发明油气回收的扩缩变流深冷吸附耦合一体化新装置，将"深冷 + 吸附、加热 + 解吸"四个过程集成在同一个通道内同时完成，缩短了工艺流程，油气回收率达 99% 以上，排放低于 40mg/Nm³，比传统方法能耗降低 20%，解决了催化氧化燃烧等方法因变流量、不连续导致回收系统易爆的重大难题。

成果累计应用于全国 200 多家大型石化和冶金企业的特大型耗能系统，节能效果显著，取得了重大的经济社会效益。

Awardee of Industrial Innovation Prize, Ling Xiang

Ling Xiang was born in Dongtai City of Jiangsu Province in June 1967. Ling Xiang has long been engaged in the research of heat transfer enhancement theory and energy-saving equipment technology. Aiming at the great demand of process industry to realize high energy efficiency, a series of pioneering researches have been done centering on the two major problems of high efficiency and low energy saving technology and the development of energy saving equipment under harsh environment.

（1）It was found that the energy efficiency was 3% ～ 4% higher than that of Linde Group.

And these devices have applied in the high energy consumption systems of enterprises such as Sinopec Yangzi Petrochemical Co., Ltd. The developed new compact heat exchanger break the long-term technological monopoly of world leading companies such as Alfalaval in Sweden and with this technology, the energy saved has reached to 260×10^4 tons of standard coal.

(2) A new large-scale manufacturing process using nickel-based diffusion brazing was proposed, and a continuous production line of large-scale compact heat exchange devices was built. The device can withstand high temperature up to $850°C$. What's more, the largest aluminum alloy surface cooler (windward area $4m \times 6m$) for blast furnace dehumidification in the world has been successfully developed. The practice shows that the heat transfer coefficient is increased by 2 times and the iron coke ratio consumption of blast furnace is reduced by 8%, reaching the international advanced level.

(3) Developed the largest internal MVR evaporation device successfully applied it to the 1200 tons/day wastewater treatment of Chuanning Biopharmaceuticals, breaking the technical barriers of foreign countries. In the process of oil production, storage, transportation, and use, nearly 2 million tons of organic waste gas (oil gas) are discharged into the atmosphere each year, and its components are complex, variable and discontinuous. Conventional oil gas treatment methods have the problem of high energy consumption. Therefore, a novel integrative device for oil gas recovery with combining expansion-contraction and absorption was invented. It integrated four processes of deep cryogenic, absorption, heating, and desorption and made them completed simultaneously in a single channel. The technological process is shortened, the oil gas recovery rate is over 99%, the emission is less than $40mg/Nm^3$, and the energy consumption is reduced by 20% compared with the traditional method. It solves the major problem that the recovery system is explosive due to the variable flow and discontinuity in catalytic oxidation combustion methods.

The results have been applied to the oversize energy-consuming systems of more than 200 large-scale petrochemical and metallurgical enterprises in China. The energy saving effect is remarkable and significant economic and social benefits have been obtained.

产业创新奖获得者

路 建 美

路建美，女，1960年10月出生于江苏省宜兴市。1999年获浙江大学高分子物理与化学专业博士学位。1989—1999年任苏州大学化工教研室主任，1999—2002年任苏州大学化学化工学院院长，2003—2006年任常州大学副校长，2006—2017年任苏州大学副校长，2017年至今任苏州大学党委副书记、副校长。俄罗斯工程院院士、中国化工学会会士、英国皇家化学会会士，科技部国家重点研发计划纳米专项总体专家组成员。

路建美长期致力于海上溢油污染快速处置和低浓度污染物深度治理的创新研发，形成了以三维网络吸附材料为核心的治理与检测特色方向。发表SCI论文371篇，他引超过9200次；主编和参编专著3部，国内外特邀报告40次、共同发起国际会议6次；授权发明专利105项（美国专利18项），转让专利11项、成果产业化32项。在美国墨西哥湾、大连等国内外工程应用320余项，有力地推动了我国环境化学工程技术的发展。

一、以亲油 / 亲水基团协同调控表面浸润性创制三维网络高吸油材料

突发性溢油事故易造成重大环境灾难，源于缺乏从油水体系中高效回收溢油的技术。吸附材料回收溢油被认为是最有效的技术，但经国内外几十年研究仍存在吸附速度慢（4～6小时）、倍率低（2～3倍）及强度低（粉末状）的问题，工程化应用困难。路建美依据固液界面理论，提出吸附材料表面亲油亲水性是改变其吸油速度的关键，设计了近千种亲油亲水单体并进行均聚和组合共聚，揭示了亲油亲水基团协同的材料表面浸润性调控吸附速度的机制，实现对油2～11秒超快吸附，该论文被 Materials View 网站评为十大热点文章；提出了以"刚柔并济"交联剂构建三维网络结构吸附材料的新思路，调控交联剂柔性链长短提高三维网络的弹性，实现吸油倍率高达15～30倍；调控交联剂刚性基团提升材料强度，实现50MPa拉力下材料不断裂、材料反复使用100次后性能无衰减。针对工程化应用，攻克表面快速交联生产纤维状吸油材料的难题，开发了纤维编织成海绵状吸油材料的新装备，建成投产 400 吨 / 年生产线，同时研发了"吸附 / 脱附"循环装备用于溢油应急处置。

上述成果以技术占股 70% 组建科技企业，在美国墨西哥湾和大连 716 等 40 余起重大溢油事故中成功应用，处置区域溢油回收率大于 95%，与美国墨西哥湾溢油处置的美国水下工程技术公司签订北美唯一销售代理权。在克拉玛依油田等建成 500 吨 / 天含油废水净化设备 10 套并成功运行，处理后的水体中含油量小于 3 ppm。2010 年被环保部列入《国家先进污染防治示范技术名录》，2012 年被中石油和中海油列为指定应急产品；国家科技部 2011 年度科技报告称"该成果突破了高效吸附技术，参与处置了大连原油泄漏、江苏盱眙原油管道泄漏等多起有重大影响的水面溢油事故应急救援"；应邀在联合国西北太海洋环境应急与防备会议上作特邀报告。研究的均聚吸附材料与聚丙烯等制备互穿网络纤维及其应用获 2013 年国家科技进步奖二等奖；创建的共聚三维网络空间吸附材料及其在水面溢油应急处置技术获 2014 年国家技术发明奖二等奖。

二、以三维网络限域提升分子有效碰撞发明"强化富集 / 催化降解"双功能材料

针对传质效率低，借助 COMSOL 研发确认了吸附材料内长 / 短酯基比例为 2∶8 时对复杂低浓度污染物富集能力最强，比活性炭提升 20 倍，实现对低浓度污染物在三维网络限域内的快速高容量富集。俞书宏院士发表的 *Adv. Mater.* 综述通过对三十余种吸附材料的性能对比，显示该材料吸附能力最强。提出对富集后的污染物原位催化降解的新思路，将贵金属、过渡金属及其氧化物等组成多元催化剂，并嵌入吸附材料三维网络形成"强化富集 / 催化降解"双功能新材料，实现三维网络限域内污染物分子与催化剂碰撞概率的极大提升并原位瞬时催化成 CO_2 和 H_2O 等无害物排出。张洪杰院士在 *Chem. Soc. Rev.* 综述中评价该类催化剂是提升反应效率的有力途径；路建美受邀在 *Adv. Mater.* 上撰写关于双功能材料及其环境治理应用的综述；韩国两院院士河昌植在 *Adv. Funct. Mater.* 上发文评价其"开创了污染物强化富集 / 快速降解的新技术"；双功能材料研究论文入选英国皇家化学会世界百名材料学女科学家专刊。开发了以双功能材料为核心的低浓度污染物智能化净化装备，并在全国 15 个省份 VOCs 治理中应用 280 套，在海洋工程装备和船舶涂装市场占有率分别达 90% 和 80%，VOCs 处理可低至 0.48 mg/m³，远低于各地最严排放标准，综合治理成本仅为活性炭吸附技术的 20%。成果"多元催化剂嵌入法富集去除低浓度 VOCs 增强技术及应用"获 2019 年国家技术发明奖二等奖。

三、以跨尺度方法创建多电信号材料快速高敏检测多组分污染物的变革性技术

提出用多电信号响应材料快速高敏检测 VOCs 的创新思想。发明分子尺度内电荷陷阱数量调控的三电信号响应材料，美国化学工程等三大网站专题报道称"中国人突破双电信号、实现三电信号"，美国宾州大学阿加沃教授称"世界上第一个稳定的三电信号响应器件"；创立多电信号响应材料的分子共轭结构、分子间氢键和热处理方法协同调控薄膜

表面形貌以及薄膜内分子间有序堆积的新方法，任咏华院士在JACS文章中评价其"为器件性能提升提供了一种有效方法"。发明的多电信号传感器件被应用于污染物检测，响应时间从国际报道的3秒缩短至1秒，灵敏度从国际报道的100 ppb提高到1 ppb，产品已成功在280套VOCs治理装备中实现在线稳定检测。成果"多尺度体系构筑稳定多机制材料"获2017年教育部化工学科自然科学奖一等奖。

Awardee of Industrial Innovation Prize, Lu Jianmei

Lu Jianmei, female, was born in Yixing City of Jiangsu Province in October 1960. After receiving BS from Soochow University in 1982 and Ph.D from Zhejiang University in 1999, she worked as a full professor in College of Chemistry, Chemical Engineering & Material Sciences in Soochow University. She was vice president of Changzhou University from 2003 to 2006, vice president of Soochow University from 2006 to 2017, and vice secretary and vice president of Soochow University from 2017 to 2020. Currently, she is an academician of the Russian Academy of engineering, a member of the Chinese Society of Chemical Engineering, a member of the Royal Chemical Society of the United Kingdom, and a member of the overall expert group for the National Key Research and Development Program of the Ministry of Science and Technology.

Over the past 30 years, her research focuses in the precise design of functional molecules and materials for environment remediation and pollutant detection. She published 371 papers as corresponding author or the first author in SCI-indexed journals, including *Nature Commun., J. Am. Chem. Soc. Angew. Chem. Int. Ed.* and *Adv. Mater.* She was awarded with 105 invention patents, including 18 registered in US and 32 had been either licensed or commercialized. She leads the construction of two national platforms of the Ministry of Science and Technology, the National Development and Reform Commission.

She proposed and developed a concept of synergetic coupling of rigid and loose chains with cross-linkers for bonding hydrophilic groups-rich polymer chains to build 3D porous polymer networks toward boosting oil absorption, demonstrating that the hydrophilic/lipophilic groups of the designed materials can synergistically tune the wettability, greatly enhance the oil absorption rate and shorten the saturation time. This innovative 3D porous networked polymer had been commercialized as an oil absorbent material and successfully applied in more than 40 oil spill accidents, such as US Gulf of Mexico oil spill, Dalian oil spill (China) and Huangdao oil pipe explosion (China). To recognize the contribution to the new materials to recycle highly concentrated oil pollutants, she was awarded by the First Price of National Science and Technology Progress Award in 2013 and the Second Prize of National Technological Innovation Award in 2014.

She further developed "enhanced enrichment/catalytic degradation" dual-functional materials by grafting nanocatalysts into 3D polymeric networks for removal of low-concentrated volatile organic compounds (VOCs) in air. Multifunctional nanocatalysts were designed and embedded into 3D porous polymeric materials rapidly react with low-concentrated VOCs *in-situ* degrading to CO_2 and H_2O, demonstrating prominent merits of a much lower concentration limit and lower reaction temperature than that of the current industrial technologies. This innovated technology has been commercialized and benefited 101 companies to establish 280 VOCs governance projects in 15 provinces across the country. Based on this innovation, she won the second prize of National Technological Invention Award in 2019 again.

In addition, for the first time she discovered the ternary resistive memory property for small organic molecules and successfully applied it to pollutant detection. By linking various electron donating/withdrawing functionalities with conjugated molecules, she observed multi-level resistive switching between the charge traps under electric fields for a ternary organic memory. This unique contribution was commented as a breakthrough by American Chemical & Engineering website. Furthermore, these ternary resistive memory molecules were for the first time used for gas sensing. In contrast to traditional inorganic chemiresistors with a limited ability to detect only single gasous component, she discovered that various functional groups as the charge traps in conjugated molecules were able to selectively bind different gas molecules, achieving multiple gas recognition. In consequence, she won a First Price of Natural Science Award from the Ministry of Education of China.

产业创新奖获得者

王　琪

　　王琪，女，1949年7月出生于四川省自贡市。中国工程院院士，塑料加工工程专家，四川大学教授，博士生导师，教育部"长江学者奖励计划"特聘教授。1989年获四川大学高分子材料专业工学博士学位。1989年12月—1992年3月在加拿大Laval大学高分子科学工程中心做博士后。1984年7月至今任四川大学高分子研究所教师，历任高分子材料工程国家重点实验室（四川大学）主任、四川大学"211工程"子项目建设组组长、四川大学"985工程"科技创新平台首席科学家、国际聚合物加工学会国际（中国）代表等。现任《高分子材料科学与工程》主编、*Sustainable Materials*主编，中国塑料加工工业协会专家委员会副主任，英国Bradford大学荣誉客座教授，四川大学塑料先进制造加工超前部署学科首席科学家，高分子材料工程国家重点实验室（四川大学）学术委员会副主任等。

　　王琪带领团队长期围绕国家重大需求和学科前沿开展研究工作，致力于塑料加工新理论新技术新装备和环境友好高分子材料的研究和工程化应用，取得系列具有自主知识产权的重要创新成果，攻克了塑料加工领域的诸多世界难题，为我国塑料加工行业科技进步和产业创新发展做出突出贡献。

一、固相力化学加工新技术新装备

　　针对传统塑料加工装备不能加工交联型塑料，传统粉碎装备难以规模化制备聚合物基微纳米功能复合材料、难以有效回收利用废旧塑料橡胶和规模化高值化利用天然生物质材料等难题，王琪及其研究团队发明了以剪切力为主的固相力化学加工装备，并实现产业化应用。

　　建立和发展固相力化学加工理论，发明了有独特三维剪结构的固相力化学加工系列装备，具有粉碎、分散、混合、力化学多重功能，克服了常规加工装备的局限，实现了室温超细粉碎黏弹性塑料，粉碎粒度可达微纳米级；实现无机功能填料在塑料基体中的微纳米分散、混合；实现了交联型塑料、橡胶部分解交联，使其可再热塑加工，攻克了常规塑料加工装备不能解决的三大难题，规模化制备了高分子微纳米功能复合材料，解决高端制造微型加工和3D打印加工缺乏功能材料的难题，制备了常规加工方法难以制备的微型功能器件和形状复杂的功能器件，如重量仅0.002克高强耐高温的玻纤增强聚醚醚酮微型功能器件等；实现了共混复合型、交联型废弃塑料橡胶的高效粉碎和均一化改性，由复合粉体的粒径和粒径分布调控制品相畴结构和性能，解决了传统回收技术要求组分相容、黏度匹配因而需分类分离的难题；通过应力解交联，赋予交联型废弃塑料橡胶热塑加工性，解决其不能二次加工的难题。实现难再生废弃塑料橡胶（如废弃电路板、汽车拆解尾料、废弃交联电缆料、废弃人造草坪）高值高效回收利用，制备了高性能土工膜、土工格栅、木塑制品、防水卷材等；高值化固相利用纤维素、贝壳等天然生物质材料。建成废旧塑料回收利用生产线，引领我国废弃塑料高效高值回收利用产业创新，促进了塑料加工产业的可持续发展。

二、旋转挤出加工新技术新装备

我国塑料管年产量居世界首位。常规挤出加工塑料管环向强度低，易开裂。王琪带领研究团队通过分析天然管竹子竹纤维轴向排列，发现纵向破裂易、横向破裂难的特点，提出通过旋转挤出加工形成偏离轴向增强相提高塑料管性能的学术思想。建立了旋转挤出流变学模型，阐明增强相偏离轴向的角度由旋转方式、速度、口模中的位置决定；研究了内外壁双冷温度场定构偏离轴向增强相的机理。

发明了塑料管旋转挤出加工新装备，可实施芯棒和口模多种组合旋转，调控环向应力；在具空心结构的芯棒中通入冷却介质，调控管内温度梯度，构建了不同于传统挤出加工的应力场和温度场，在塑料管中形成和定构不同层次的偏离轴向的增强相结构，大幅度提高其性能。通过旋转挤出加工制备了聚乙烯、聚丙烯、聚丁烯等系列高性能塑料管，如旋转挤出使聚乙烯管环向强度提高78%、耐慢速应力开裂性能提高5倍。建成塑料管旋转挤出生产线，制备了目前耐压等级最高的聚乙烯管，推动了我国塑料管加工产业的发展。

三、聚乙烯醇热塑加工新技术

我国聚乙烯醇（PVA）产能世界第一。但其熔点（225℃）与分解温度（200～250℃）十分接近，不能熔融加工，溶液法不能生产三维塑料制品，使其应用受限，严重约束PVA工业发展。王琪带领研究团队发明了与PVA有互补结构的含氮化合物/水系列改性剂，可与PVA氢键分子复合，获得60～100℃的热塑加工窗口，攻克了PVA不能热塑加工的世界难题；建成世界首套PVA熔融纺丝装置，制备了传统PVA湿法纺丝不能得到的高强高模纤维、功能复合纤维、粗旦纤维和异形纤维等，达到国际领先水平；首次实现 PVA 挤出、注塑、中空吹塑等，开辟了 PVA 作为新型环保型塑料应用的新领域，推动了我国 PVA 工业产业创新。

四、环境友好无卤阻燃塑料制备和加工新技术

塑料无卤阻燃关系人民生命财产安全和环境友好。传统阻燃塑料存在大量使用含卤阻燃剂并劣化加工和力学性能等问题。王琪带领研究团队发明分子复合超低黏度合成新型无卤阻燃剂三聚氰胺氰尿酸盐新技术，体系黏度比传统技术降低 2 个数量级，溶剂用量减少 80%，反应时间缩短 75%，开发了一步法旋转闪蒸清洁生产新装置及工艺；发明了反应性挤出加工制备无卤阻燃塑料新技术，一步法实现常规反应釜方法难以合成的无卤阻燃剂原位合成、成纤及阻燃塑料制备，解决传统合成法毒性大、反应温度高及难以兼顾阻燃与力学性能的难题；攻克泡沫塑料无卤阻燃世界难题，制备了无卤阻燃聚苯乙烯、聚乙烯醇泡沫塑料。建成万吨级阻燃剂和阻燃塑料生产线，推动了我国环保型阻燃塑料领域的产业创新。

研究成果获国家技术发明奖二等奖 2 项，中国发明专利金奖 1 项，省部级特等奖 1 项、一等奖 3 项；获授权发明专利 60 余项；发表学术论文 440 余篇、学术会议论文 340 余篇。获何梁何利基金科学与技术创新奖、中国塑料加工业三十年"中国塑料行业杰出人物"等奖项及荣誉。

Awardee of Industrial Innovation Prize, Wang Qi

Wang Qi, female, was born in Zigong City of Sichuan Province in July 1949. She is the Academician of Chinese Academy of Engineering, an expert in the field of plastic processing engineering and a professor of Sichuan University, China.

Prof. Qi Wang received her Ph.D majored in polymer material from Sichuan University, China, in June 1989, did post-doctoral research in Laval University, Canada, from December 1989 to March 1992. Since July 1984, she has been the staff of Polymer Research Institute of Sichuan University, China, acted as the Director of the State Key Laboratory of Polymer Materials Engineering, Leader of subproject construction team of "211" Project of Sichuan University, Chief Scientist of Science and Technology Innovation Platform of "985" Project of Sichuan University, International Representative of Polymer Processing Society, etc. She is currently the Editor-in-Chief of "Polymer Materials Science & Engineering" and "SusMat" (Sustainable Materials, an international journal co-established by Wiley and Sichuan University), Deputy Director of Expert Committee of China Plastics Processing Industry Association, Honorary Visiting Professor of Bradford University of UK, Principal Scientist of Advanced Plastics Manufacturing and Processing Discipline of Sichuan University, Deputy Director of Academic Committee of State Key Laboratory of Polymer Materials Engineering (Sichuan University), etc.

Professor Qi Wang is engaged in the scientific research on novel technologies and equipment for polymer processing and industrialization. She invented novel polymer processing technologies and equipment based on solid state mechanochemistry, realizing the efficient recycling of waste plastics and rubbers, providing a novel way to solve the environmental pollution caused by waste plastics. Prepared micro–nano functional polymer based composites devices and realized their micro–processing and 3D printing to produce novel polymer functional devices. Invented novel polymer processing technologies and equipment of rotation extrusion, fabricated high performance plastic pipes and functional micro–tubes. Realized the thermoplastic processing of polyvinyl alcohol, opening its new application as an eco–friendly plastic. Invented novel halogen–free flame retardant plastics and polymer foams, etc. A lot of her research achievements are at word–leading level and successfully applied in industrials, making remarkable contributions to the innovation and the development of plastic processing industry in China. She has gotten 2 The Second Prize of National Technology Invention Award, 1 Golden Award for Chinese Outstanding Patented Invention, 1 Grand Prize and 3 First Prize of provincial and ministerial–level, 60 granted patents and more than 440 published journal papers, etc.

产业创新奖获得者

魏世忠

魏世忠，1966年6月出生于河南省滑县。教授，博士生导师。2005年毕业于西安交通大学材料学院，获工学博士学位。1985年至今在河南科技大学工作，任河南科技大学副校长、金属材料磨损控制与成型技术国家地方联合工程研究中心主任、摩擦学与材料防护教育部工程研究中心主任、教育部"长江学者和创新团队发展计划"创新团队带头人、中原学者科学家工作室首席科学家、美国密歇根大学访问教授、河南省特聘教授等。兼任中国材料与试验团体标准委员会综合标准领域委员会金属材料磨损控制与成型技术委员会主任委员、钢铁耐磨材料产业技术创新战略联盟副理事长、TMS高级会员、SME高级会员等。百千万人才工程国家级人选，国家有突出贡献中青年专家。以第一完成人获国家科技进步奖二等奖2项、省部级一等奖4项，授权国家发明专利45件，发表论文318篇，出版专著5部。

魏世忠长期从事材料冶金成型技术研究和产业化应用。研发出高钒高耐磨合金及复合成型技术、大型铸锻件制造技术和陶瓷强化钨钼合金等原创性成果，在冶金、矿山、能源、高能物理、军工等领域实现工程化应用，助推了我国装备制造业发展。创建和领导的科研团队在国际金属材料磨损控制领域有一定影响。

一、研制出高钒高耐磨合金及复合成型技术，实现耐磨材料升级换代

材料的耐磨性主要由耐磨相和基体的硬度决定。碳化钒是目前硬度最高的碳化物之一，密度与钢接近，凝固时不易偏析，是最理想的耐磨相。但凝固成型时，碳化钒四种结构并存、共同结晶，不能达到或接近理论硬度，致使以碳化钒为耐磨相的金属耐磨材料一直没有得到广泛应用。通过十几年深入研究，魏世忠解决了碳化钒的结构控制、凝固成型、磨损稳定性控制、双金属冶金复合技术集成等问题，研制出了高钒高耐磨合金及其成型技术，确定了高钒合金的耐磨相结构类型，提出凝固控制方法。

发现碳化钒四种结构中碳和钒原子比为 1∶1 的碳化钒硬度最高，且与基体存在共格关系；采用原子置换控制技术，解决了碳化钒多种结构并存难题，研制出碳化钒弥散分布的高钒耐磨合金。研究碳化钒与奥氏体基体匹配的储能效应机制，控制了磨损稳定性；阐明了高钒合金相组成与耐磨性的内在关联，解决了耐磨材料不同工况的冲击磨损突变问题，实现了高钒合金服役安全稳定。发明了高钒合金与低合金钢的液－液复合成型技术和局部自熔复合成型技术；采用控量、控温及随流液面保护技术，实现了不同金属液－液熔合；发明了半连续复合铸造高钒合金与低合金钢的液－固复合技术。采用电磁感应定量给热均匀化方案，解决了液－固复合非稳态凝固过程组织控制和应力诱发裂纹的技术难题，实现了高钒合金与不同金属的冶金复合。

技术成果获 2013 年国家科学技术进步奖二等奖，为"国家新重机工程"等重大工程提供了关键耐磨部件，推动近 50 家企业产品升级，其中轧钢复合金属导卫占全国市场的 60%。

二、开发重型装备大型铸锻件制造技术，推动我国跻身世界一流大型铸锻件制造强国

重型装备核心部件的性能决定了装备的整体水平。重型装备向大型、高效、连续、应用条件苛刻化的发展趋势要求大型铸锻件高致密、无缺陷。魏世忠通过建立材料数据库、协同仿真建模、完善凝固及成形理论，解决了长时凝固、多通道补缩、大变形等制造过程中的关键难题，研制出冶－铸－锻－热整套集成制造技术。

研制出高纯钢冶炼、钢锭组织成分控制技术和短流程双真空浇注设备；开发出精炼炉高真空软吹氩、复合变质细晶技术，研制出浸入式水口、真空精炼中间包、吹氩引流与打散等浇注技术。提出了局部磨损大型铸件同时凝固、共同补缩浇注系统的设计理念和冒口设计准则；开发出带包浇注"全开放"工艺系统，发明了堵截式浇注控制技术，制定出多包合浇、长时凝固大型铸件冒口设计工艺，确保了大型铸件的致密化，确定了大型锻件控形控性工艺参数设计原则。通过建立材料高温变形损伤演化模型，提出了含有耐磨相的大型锻件高温断裂判据，计算出材料塑性变形的临界损伤值，实现了大型锻件无缺陷近净成形。研究尺寸－温度－相变的相互作用，构建了大型锻件淬火冷却过程的非稳态温度场模型，制定了差温热处理工艺；开发出差温热处理技术及装备，实现了大型锻件组织和性能梯度的可控分布。

技术成果获 2016 年国家科学技术进步奖二等奖。成果已应用到澳洲铁矿、巴西基若水电站、三峡工程、红沿河核电站等重大工程，创造了多项大型铸锻件的世界之最，使我国跻身于世界一流大型铸锻件生产强国。

三、开发自生陶瓷强化高性能钨钼合金，推动了高端钨钼合金的发展

钨钼合金广泛应用于航空航天、电子信息、军工、核能等领域，要求具有良好的力学、耐磨、耐冲蚀等性能。魏世忠通过发明自生纳米陶瓷钨钼复合粉体制备技术，解决

了陶瓷相原位自生难、分布不均、尺寸大的共性技术难题。发明了液液掺杂＋共沉淀＋共分解一体化制备方法，实现在液相中各组元分子级均匀混合，使纳米陶瓷颗粒在钨钼颗粒表面原位自生。发明了纳米陶瓷和基体晶体学关系调控技术，提升钨钼合金性能，发明了模板剂法前驱体引导定向技术，控制了纳米陶瓷相生长过程中的球形化，实现了球形陶瓷相与基体界面共格，大幅度提高界面结合强度和耐磨耐冲蚀性能。发明了纳米陶瓷钨钼合金烧结及成形技术，解决了烧结过程晶粒易长大、轧制时陶瓷与基体非协调性变形导致内部裂纹萌生的问题；计算出烧结温度、烧结时间、变形温度、变形量临界条件，制订出低温短时烧结和低温多道次小变形轧制工艺。

技术成果获2016年中国有色金属工业科学技术奖一等奖和2018年河南省科学技术进步奖一等奖。研制的钨钼合金成功应用于欧洲大型强子对撞机直线粒子加速器，钨钼合金高温屏蔽部件应用于中核集团等，成果有力提升了我国钨钼产品的国际竞争力。

Awardee of Industrial Innovation Prize, Wei Shizhong

Wei Shizhong was born in Huaxian of Henan Province in June 1966, a professor and doctoral supervisor. In 2005, he graduated from the school of materials science and engineering of Xi'an Jiaotong university with a doctorate in engineering. Now he is the vice-president of Henan university of science and technology, a director of the national joint engineering research center for abrasion and molding of metal material, a director of the engineering research center for tribology and material protection, ministry of education, a leader of the "Changjiang Scholars and innovative team development program", the ministry of education, a chief scientist of "Zhongyuan Scholars" and scientists studio, visiting professor at the University of Michigan. He is also the special government allowance expert of the State Council. He has won 2 second prizes of "National Science and Technology Progress Award", 4 first prizes of provincial award. He has authorized 45 national invention patents, published 5 monographs and 318 papers, of which 125 are included by SCI/EI.

Professor Wei Shizhong has been engaged in the research and industrialization of material metallurgy forming technology for long time. Developed original achievements have realized the engineering applications in metallurgy, mining, energy, high-energy physics, military and other fields, which boosts manufacturing development of China's equipment. The scientific research team he created and led has a certain influence in the field of international metal material wear control.

The high-vanadium high-wear-resistant alloy and composite molding technology have been developed, realizing the upgrading of wear-resistant materials, which has won the second prizes of "National Science and Technology Progress Award" in 2013.

The manufacturing technology for large-scale castings and forgings of heavy equipment have been developed, promoting China to become a world-class country of large-scale casting and forging manufacturing, which has won the second prizes of "National Science and Technology Progress Award" in 2016.

The self-generated ceramics to strengthen high-performance tungsten-molybdenum alloys have been developed, promoting the progress of high-end tungsten-molybdenum alloys, which has won the first prize of "China Nonferrous Metal Industry Science and Technology Award" in 2016 and first prize of "Henan Province Science and Technology Progress Award" in 2018.

产业创新奖获得者

曾　毅

曾毅，1965年5月出生于四川省古蔺县。1986年毕业于北京工业学院自动控制系，获工学学士学位；1995年毕业于南京理工大学兵器系统工程专业，获工学硕士学位。1986—1987年在中国兵器工业第201研究所工作；1987—2011年在中国兵器科学研究院工作，先后担任规划计划处处长、副院长、院长；2011—2018年12月任中国兵器工业集团有限公司副总经理；2018年12月至今任中国电子信息产业集团有限公司董事、党组副书记。先后兼任某领域专家委员会主任委员、首席科学家，中国卫星导航系统专家委员会委员，中国兵工学会副理事长，中国指挥与控制学会名誉理事长，中国电子学会高级会员等。

曾毅从事科技创新30余年，在科技发展战略与顶层设计、重大项目综合论证与工程研制、关键技术攻关与创新等方面开展了系列工作。荣获国家科技进步奖一等奖、国防科学技术进步奖一等奖、国防科学技术进步奖二等奖、国防科学技术工业委员会个人一等功、国家高新武器装备发展建设工程银奖等奖项。

一、主持研究制定某领域科技战略与规划

分析研判新技术革命发展态势，系统构建信息主导、体系创新、前沿突破的科技创新战略。加强技术发展顶层设计，多次主持研究制定技术发展战略及发展规划，论证实施一批重点项目，积极推动从机械化向机械化信息化复合发展、网络化智能化融合创新的转型升级。

二、突破重大技术领域瓶颈

针对我国某技术领域发展滞后的局面，体系化推进基础理论、工程研制、先进制造、试验手段、安全标准等技术攻关，实现了规模化应用，创新研究与国际保持同步，缩短

了我国该技术领域的发展差距。把握信息化战争的本质特征，率先探索开展体系建设，确定了分布式、大协同的总体架构，形成了以智能操控为核心的技术路径，初步实现了由"集成"向"解耦"的本质转变，推动了新一代技术体系的构建。创新研制模拟训练与仿真系统，构建瞬态实时模拟训练平台，提升了训练与评估的水平。系统提出"快、融、控、虚、防、智、称"的未来演变趋势，以智能化为核心谋划构建智能体系，推动融合创新、跨域发展。

三、主导研制多项新型项目

先后担任十余项重点项目行政总（副总）指挥，开展总体方案论证、关键核心技术攻关、工程研制与试验验证，初步实现了由跟踪仿研向自主创新的提升。某工程突破了多项核心关键技术，主要性能达到较高水平。某工程首次开展整体发展体系构想，建立跨部门协同、多技术集成的创新模式，主要性能达到较高水平。以工程研制为牵引，组织开展多项重大关键技术攻关，某项技术在国内率先实现工程化应用，形成从基础材料、核心器件到整机研发生产的自主可控产业链，等等。

四、构建北斗高精度服务

主持完成国家北斗地基增强系统研制建设，创新提出"国家主导、企业主体、市场运作、走出国门"的北斗推广应用发展思路，组织攻克了北斗高精度定位算法、海量数据接入存储、大规模分布式计算、高并发实时处理等一系列核心技术，建成了全国产化的北斗地基增强系统"全国一张网"，构建北斗高精度"一个服务平台"，实现了北斗实时米级、分米级、厘米级和后处理毫米级定位服务的全国陆地疆域覆盖，在国土资源、交通运输、海洋渔业等国民经济重要领域以及智能手机、智能网联汽车、无人机、共享单车等大众消费领域迅速推广应用，取得了良好的经济社会效益，实现了北斗高精度服务从无到有、快速发展。

Awardee of Industrial Innovation Prize, Zeng Yi

Zeng Yi was born in Gulin County of Sichuan Province in May 1965. He graduated from Beijing Institute of Technology in 1986, with Bachelor's Degree in automatic controlling. He obtained his Master Degree of Engineering in weapon system engineering from Nanjing University of technology. From July 1986 to October 1987, he worked in the No.201 Research Institute of China Ordnance Industry. From October 1987 to March 2011, he worked in the China Academy of Ordnance Science, and took various positions as Director of Planning Division, Deputy General Manager, and General Manager. From March 2011 to December 2018, he served as the Vice

President of China Ordnance Industry Group Co., Ltd. From December 2018 to now, he has served as the Board Director and Deputy Secretary of CPC Party Committee of China Electronics Corporation (CEC).

Zeng Yi, has been the Chief Scientist and Chairman of the Experts Committee for some field, member of the Experts Committee of China's Satellite Navigation System, Vice president of China Ordnance Industry Association, Honorary Chairman of China Command and Control Society, and senior member of China Electronics Society.

Mr. Zeng Yi has been engaged in the innovation of science and technology (S&T in short hereinafter) for more than 30 years, and has carried out a series of major research work in the fields of S&T development strategy and top-level designing, comprehensive assessment of major projects and engineering development, and R&D of some key technology with cutting-edge innovation, etc.

1. Chairing the formulation of S&T development strategy and planning for some industry

With analyzing and judging the development trend of new technological revolutions, and systematically building technological innovation strategies featuring information dominance, system innovation, and cutting-edge breakthroughs, and strengthening the development of top-level technology designing, Mr. Zeng Yi has chaired the tasks of formulating technology development strategies and development plans; led the demonstration and implementation of some key projects; and positively promoted the transfer of industrial technology from mechanization to mechanization-informatization complex development, as well as the transformation and upgrading of network and intelligence integration and innovation.

2. Breaking through the bottleneck in major technological fields

As for the inadequate development of the technical field in China, Mr. Zeng Yi systematically promote basic theories, engineering designing, advanced manufacturing, testing methods, safety standards and other technology research, and realize large-scale application and maintain the synchronization of the research in this field with the international level, shortening the development gap between China and that of the world. He managed to grasp the essential characteristics of informatization, took the lead in exploring system construction, and determined the distributed and coordinated overall architecture, so as to form the technology path with intelligent control as its core, and initially realized the essential transformation from "integration" to "decoupling", and promoted the construction of a new generation of technology system. He innovated and developed simulation training and simulation systems. By building a real timing simulation training platform, it greatly improved the informatization level of training and evaluation. He systematically proposed the future evolution trend featuring "quickness, integration, control, virtualness, defense, intelligence and balance". He planned to build equipment system with intelligent trend as the core, planning the construction of intelligent system, and promote the integrated and innovative cross-domain development of industrial technologies.

3. Leading the development of some new type projects

Mr. Zeng Yi had served as the executive chief (or deputy chief) of more than ten key projects, organized the demonstration of the overall plan, key core technology research, engineering development and test verification, and basically realized the leap-forward improvement of industry technology from tracking and imitating to independent innovation. Many core key technologies of the project were broken through, with relatively high level of main performance. The concept of an overall development system for a new type of project was formed for the first time, an innovative model of cross-department coordination and multi-technology integration was established, and the leading level in performance was achieved. It took the development of engineering designing as the driving force, organized and carried out a number of major technological researches, and took the lead in engineering application of a technology in China, forming an independent and controllable industrial chain from basic materials, core devices to the development and production of complete machines, etc.

4. Constructing the high-precision service of Beidou

Mr. Zeng Yi presided over the completion of the development and construction of the National Beidou Ground Enhancement System, innovatively proposed the Beidou promotion and application development ideas of "State-led, Enterprise-based, Market-oriented, and Going abroad", and organized and solved a series of core technologies such as Beidou high-precision positioning algorithm, mass data access storage, large-scale distributed computing, high concurrent real-time processing and so on. In consequence, the national industrialized Beidou Ground Enhancement System "One Network all over the Country" was built, forming Beidou's high-precision "single service platform", and the national land coverage of Beidou real-time meter-level, decimeter-level, centimeter-level and post-processing millimeter-level positioning services was realized, and its applications were quickly promoted in important areas of the national economy such as land resources, transportation, marine fisheries, as well as mass consumption fields such as smart phones, smart connected vehicles, unmanned drones, shared bicycles, etc. The system had achieved good economic and social benefits. Beidou's high-precision service had developed rapidly from scratch, accompanied with many competitive advantages.

Mr. Zeng Yi is entitled to the special government allowance of the State Council. He has won many awards, including the first prize of the National Science and Technology Progress Award, the first prize of the National Defense Science and Technology Progress Award, the second prize of the National Defense Science and Technology Progress Award, the first-class personal contribution of the National Defense Science, Technology and Industry Committee, Silver Award of National New and High Weapon Equipment Development and Construction Project, and published many papers.

产业创新奖获得者

赵 元 富

赵元富，1962年11月出生于江西省进贤县。1983年、1986年、1989年分别获浙江大学半导体物理与器件专业学士学位、西安电子科技大学半导体物理与器件专业硕士学位和陕西微电子学研究所计算机设备与器件博士学位。博士毕业后进入航天七七一所工作，先后任工程师、高级工程师、研究员。1996—1998年在美国斯坦福大学和范德堡大学做访问学者。归国后历任航天七七二所所长助理、副所长、所长；现任航天科技集团九院科技委副主任，博士生导师。国防科技创新特区自主可控推进委员会委员、抗核和辐射加固技术专家组成员、国防科技工业科学技术委员会电子领域组电子基础专业组组长、国家重点研发计划"光电子与微电子器件及集成"重点专项总体专家组成员、上海证券交易所第一届科技创新咨询委员会委员、中国半导体行业协会常务理事。

赵元富长期致力于集成电路研究，是我国抗辐射加固集成电路技术的主要带头人。作为技术首席，负责国家"973"计划2项，主持自然科学基金、重大科技专项等计划中的多个项目，带领团队攻克了抗辐射加固集成电路的重大技术难题，为我国航天集成电路自主可控、产业创新做出重大贡献。

一、走出了中国特色的抗辐射加固集成电路技术路线

集成电路应用于太空辐射环境，受单粒子和总剂量等辐射效应影响严重，是航天器在轨故障的主要来源。抗辐射加固集成电路技术是航天领域的核心基础技术，受到西方技术强国的严格封锁和禁运。

集成电路抗辐射加固技术路线主要有工艺加固和设计加固两类。经系统论证技术基础和发展趋势，赵元富团队认为设计加固技术路线更适合我国实际情况，并针对设计加固面临的单粒子翻转等重大技术难题，提出单粒子翻转时域测试方法，通过揭示单粒子翻转的时空交织机理，获取了单粒子翻转数量和位置随时间的变化关系，首次实时区分

了单粒子的直接翻转和间接翻转；提出错峰控制的双模交叉耦合单粒子翻转加固方法，实现了双冗余延迟滤波和光电流淬熄，同步解决了单粒子直接翻转和间接翻转的加固难题。

研究成果提升了我国在抗辐射加固集成电路领域的国际学术影响力。2018年，赵元富促成了该领域重要国际学术会议——元器件和系统辐射效应论坛首次走出欧洲、在北京召开，并担任大会主席。原美国辐射效应委员会主席Galloway教授评价"美国、欧洲和俄罗斯高度认可赵元富及其团队在辐射效应和加固技术方面的研究成果"。

二、谱系化研制了抗辐射加固集成电路产品

在系统攻克单粒子翻转、单粒子闩锁等重大技术难题和突破总剂量加固等多项关键技术的基础上，开发了抗辐射加固单元库，构建了研制平台，成谱系研制成功FPGA、微处理器、专用电路、总线、转换器和存储器等各类产品数百款，实现了抗辐射加固集成电路的跨越发展。

成功研制的主要核心芯片包括：①首款单粒子加固FPGA。单粒子加固FPGA是世界航天领域的研究热点，针对单粒子加固引发上电浪涌电流大的技术瓶颈，提出了基于微压差诱导方法的多阈值非对称配置存储器结构，使上电浪涌电流从5～8A降低到小于250mA。②国内首款抗辐射加固微处理器。微处理器的核心地位和复杂性使其成为抗辐射加固集成电路的典型代表，针对单粒子攻击导致锁相环时钟输出紊乱的重大加固难点，提出了双模自切换时钟生成方法，锁相环单粒子功能错误率降低4个数量级。③抗辐射加固百万门级专用电路。针对我国多颗卫星使用进口FPGA在轨频繁发生单粒子故障的严峻局面，在国内率先研制成功9款抗辐射加固百万门级专用电路，产品已随数十颗卫星上天，在轨最长超过9年，均未发生单粒子故障，为卫星稳定可靠工作发挥了关键作用。

三、实现抗辐射加固集成电路批量应用与出口

抗辐射加固集成电路产品应用覆盖了国内重点航天工程，包括北斗导航、载人航天、探月和军事卫星等，用户单位涉及航天科技、中国科学院和中国电科等所属企业近百家，大幅提升了航天集成电路国产化水平，为我国航天元器件自主可控做出了突出贡献。以北斗三号卫星为例，星上所有电子设备均使用了赵元富团队研制的产品，单颗卫星用量超过1500只，为北斗三号卫星核心元器件100%国产化发挥了关键作用。航天七七二所已成为国内航天型号抗辐射加固集成电路的主要供应商。

抗辐射加固集成电路实现了从被禁运到出口的重大转折。2014年出口俄罗斯，是我国抗辐射加固集成电路首次进入国际市场。产品经法国泰雷兹公司严格检验后认证合格，使中国抗辐射加固集成电路首次进入欧洲航天供应链，已出口法国、德国、瑞士和西班牙等国。

赵元富带领团队通过技术发明、平台开发、产品研制和型号应用的系统创新，走出

了中国特色的抗辐射加固技术路线，改变了国际抗辐射加固集成电路的供应格局。作为第一完成人，获国家技术发明奖一等奖 1 项、省部级科技一等奖 7 项；作为团队技术负责人，集体获国家科技进步奖特等奖 1 项，授权发明专利 97 项，发表学术论文 137 篇。入选国家百千万人才工程，获钱学森杰出贡献奖、航天功勋奖、中国青年科技创业奖等多个奖项，以及北斗二号卫星工程建设突出贡献个人、做出突出贡献的中国博士学位获得者、国防科技工业有突出贡献中青年专家等多项荣誉。

Awardee of Industrial Innovation Prize, Zhao Yuanfu

Zhao Yuanfu, born in Jinxian County of Jiangxi Province in November 1962, is now the Vice Director of Science and Technology Committee in the 9th Academy, CASC, a professor, a Ph.D supervisor, and a main leader on radiation-hardened integrated circuits (ICs) technology in China. He graduated from Zhejiang University (1983), Xidian University (1986) and Shaanxi Microelectronics Institute (1989) for BS, MS and Ph.D degree, respectively. He successively worked at the 771 institute of the Aerospace Industry Corporation and the 772 institute of the 9th Academy, CASC. From 1996 to 1998, he studied and worked at Stanford University and Vanderbilt University as a visiting scholar. From 1999 to 2016, Dr. Zhao served as the director of the 772 institute where he devoted himself to developing both technology and industrialization of radiation-hardened ICs. As the principle investigator, he has been in charge of two National 973 Projects, and hosted many projects such as significant programs funded by National Natural Science Foundation of China and the Special Scientific and Technological Project, most of which are about radiation effects and radiation hardening. He has led his research group to overcome technical difficulties in radiation hardening of ICs, developed a technical route of radiation-hardened ICs with Chinese characteristics, and made outstanding contribution to the localization of radiation-hardened ICs. The products from his group have been widely applied in national major projects such as Beidou Navigation System, Manned Space Flight and Lunar Exploration, and played a key role in core chips' autonomy and control in China's space engineering. The products have been also exported in batch to Russia, France, Germany, Switzerland and Spain, which is the first time for China's radiation-hardened ICs to be sold overseas, and achieves a major turning point from being embargoed to exporting. Dr. Zhao won the First Prize of National Technology Invention Award in 2018 and 7 First Prizes of Provincial/Ministerial Science and Technology Award as the first person. He also won a National Science and Technology Progress Award- Special Award as the technical leader of the 772 institute. He has been granted 97 invention patents, and has published 137 academic papers. He is the advisor for 9 Ph.D students/post-doctors, and 26 master students.

产业创新奖获得者

朱 衍 波

朱衍波，1970年12月出生于浙江省舟山市。1992年毕业于北京航空航天大学微波与电磁场专业，1995年和2009年分别于北京航空航天大学获得工学硕士和博士学位。1995年在北京卫星信息工程研究所任工程师；1996年至今在民航数据通信有限责任公司工作，先后担任公司总工程师、副总经理；2009年至今担任国家空管新航行系统技术重点实验室副主任；2017年至今担任民航协同空管技术与应用重点实验室主任。朱衍波是国际民航组织航空通信、航空导航、无人机等多个专家组专家，中国指挥与控制学会空管专业和指控网络专业委员会委员，中国航空学会航电与空管分会委员，民航中长期科技规划战略研究空管专家组组长，国家空管委办公室国家空管专家。

朱衍波长期从事民航空管系统与技术研究，在航空通信导航监视与数字化协同管制等方面做了大量基础性和开拓性工作。主持国家级民航科研与工程项目40余项，通过产学研用相结合，主持建成了中国民航数字化协同管制服务网、中国民航飞行运行监控系统、基于精确定位的航空协同监视系统等多个重大基础设施，为推动我国民航空管技术进步与产业升级做出突出贡献，近3年创造经济效益逾20亿元。获国家技术发明奖一等奖、国家科技进步奖一等奖各1项，国家科技进步奖二等奖2项；发表SCI论文27篇、EI论文46篇，获授权国家发明专利120余项，参与制定行业标准10项。获中国青年科技奖，是全国民航空管系统优秀共产党员和科技创新先进个人，荣立民航空管系统二等功；创建了民航协同空管领域唯一的重点实验室，带领的团队入选民航科技重点领域创新团队。

一、主持建成中国民航数字化协同管制服务网

针对民航繁忙机场和航路高密度安全运行的急需，在国家科技支撑计划的支持下，带领团队创建了空地一体的数字化协同管制技术构架，突破了复杂管制业务数字协同、

广域飞行威胁精准识别等技术；主持建成了中国民航数字化协同管制服务网，已在全国全部52个管制单位投入运行，服务全国98%以上的航班量，成为保障复杂空域高密度运行的重大基础设施，实现了中国民航数字化协同管制服务从无到有的跨越式发展，为提升民航航班运行正常性发挥了重要作用。相关成果获国家科技进步奖二等奖，个人荣立民航空管系统二等功。

二、主持研制基于精确定位的航空协同监视系统

针对西部、洋区等无雷达覆盖地区的空管安全保障问题，在国家"863"计划的支持下，提出了基于我国国情的GNSS地基区域完好性监测系统的概念，设计了支持多时空基准的多元监视信息一致性处理和互校方法，主持研制了基于精确定位的航空协同监视系统（ADS-B），主持建成了全国ADS-B网络一级数据中心系统，应用于全国民航管制单位、航空公司及航空安全相关保障部门，解决了高原、海洋等无雷达覆盖地区的安全高效飞行保障难题，有力支撑了我国西部地区由程序管制向类雷达管制的过渡，提升了航空公司的运行监控能力。相关成果获国家技术发明奖一等奖。

三、主持研制中国民航首套飞行运行监控系统

针对民航跨区域、多机场、高密度航班的协同指挥与调控问题，在国家科技支撑计划的支持下，突破了多业务高效共享、全网络广域调控、多机场关联调配等关键技术，主持研制了中国民航首套飞行运行监控系统，实现了民航航班运行的"统一计划、统一态势、统一调配、统一指挥"。带领团队承担民航局空管局"中国民航运行保障系统"和"中国民航空中交通流量管理一期工程"等项目的建设与运行，在全国民航各级空管单位投入使用，服务于中国民航运行监控中心、空管局运行管理中心以及北京、上海、广州等地区空管部门的民航飞行运行监控与管制指挥，有效提高了民航飞行运行效率和应急保障能力。相关成果获国家科技进步奖二等奖。

四、积极推动中国民航空管技术国际化

作为民航局的国际民航组织航空通信、航空导航、无人机专家组专家，积极参与国际民航事务，努力推动北斗卫星导航系统国际标准化。结合中国民航的实际需求，将国际先进技术和标准转化为中国民航发展的知识和技术储备，积极促进新技术在国内的论证和试验。与美国斯坦福大学、波音公司、柯林斯公司、霍尼韦尔公司和法国空客公司、泰雷兹公司、西班牙英德拉公司等国际知名空管研究机构及企业保持紧密的技术交流与合作关系。作为国际航空标准组织RTCA、ARINC、EUROCAE和CANSO等会员，为加快国内空管新技术的跨越式发展提供重要的技术资源；同时，积极推动中国民航空管新技术的国际化。获2017年民航"空管榜样"荣誉称号和2019年空管系统优秀共产党员荣誉称号。

Awardee of Industrial Innovation Prize, Zhu Yanbo

Zhu Yanbo was born in Zhoushan City of Zhejiang Province in December 1970. In 2009, he received his doctor's degree from School of Electronic and Information Engineering, Beihang University. In 1995, he worked as an engineer in Beijing Institute of Satellite Information Engineering. From 1996 to now, he has worked in Aviation Data Communication Corporation (ADCC) first as the chief engineer and later as the deputy general manager. He has served as the deputy director of the National Key Laboratory of CNS/ATM since 2009, and the director of the Key Laboratory of Collaborative ATM Technology and Application of CAAC since 2017. He is an expert for several panels of the International Civil Aviation Organization (ICAO), including the Communications Panel (CP), Navigation Systems Panel (NSP) and Remotely Piloted Aircraft Systems Panel (RPASP). He is also a member of Air Traffic Management Specialized Committee of the Chinese Institute of Command and Control (CICC), as well as Technical Committee of Avionics and Air Traffic Management of Chinese Society of Aeronautics and Astronautics (CSAA).

Zhu Yanbo has done extensive fundamental and pioneering works in the research field of civil aviation air traffic management system, including aviation communication, navigation, surveillance and collaborative air traffic management. He has hosted and completed more than 40 projects supported by national and civil aviation R&D funds. Through the combination of the efforts of enterprises, universities and research institutions, he has presided over the developments of the Civil Aviation Digitalized and Collaborative Air Traffic Control (ATC) Service Network, Air Traffic Operation Monitoring System, Automatic Dependent Surveillance-Broadcast (ADS-B) Network and other major infrastructures in China, which greatly contribute to the advancement of technical progress of China's ATM system. He has been awarded the first prize of National Technology Invention for once, the first prize of National Science and Technology Progress Award for once, and the second prize of National Science and Technology Progress Award for twice. He has 27 SCI papers and 46 EI papers published, and he has declared at least 120 national invention patents, as well as the formulation of 10 industry standards.

1. Presided over the development of the digitalized and collaborative ATC service network

In response to the urgent need for high-density and safe operation of civil aviation's busy airports and airways, Zhu led the team to build an air-ground digitalized and collaborative ATC service Network with the support of the national science and technology support plan. Serving as a major infrastructure to ensure high-density operations in complex airspace, the network has been deployed in all 52 ATC units across the country and serves more than 98% of the national airlines' fleets. The Digitalized and Collaborative ATC Services is playing an important role in the quality and safety enhancement of the civil aviation operations.

2. Presided over the development of National Automatic Dependent Surveillance-Broadcast (ADS-B) Network

Aiming at the air traffic control safety issue in non-radar areas, especially the western and oceanic areas, with the support of the National 863 Program, Zhu presided over the development of Automatic Dependent Surveillance-Broadcast (ADS-B) system, and the establishment of national ADS-B network. Through the applications to nationwide ATC units, airlines and airports, flight safety and efficiency in non-radar areas (e.g., plateaus and oceans) can be guaranteed and monitoring capabilities of airlines can be improved, marking a significant shift from the procedural control to radar-like control in western China.

3. Presided over the development of air traffic operation monitoring system of China's Civil Aviation

Focused on the issue of collaborated command and control of flight operations with internal characteristics of cross regions, multiple airports, and high-density, with the support of the national science and technology support plan, Zhu has made breakthroughs in key technologies such as multi-service efficient sharing, full network wide-area control and multi-airport related deployment. He presided over the development of air traffic operation monitoring system of China's civil aviation to achieve "consolidated plan, common situation awareness, unified regulation, and uniform control" in air traffic operations. The system has been put into use in all levels of civil aviation air control units across the country as well as the operation management center of the Civil Aviation Administration of China.

附　　录

APPENDICES

何梁何利基金评选章程

（2020 年 5 月 27 日何梁何利基金信托委员会全体会议通过）

一、总　　则

第一条　何梁何利基金（以下称"本基金"）由何善衡慈善基金会有限公司、梁銶琚博士、何添博士、利国伟博士之伟伦基金有限公司于 1994 年 3 月 30 日捐款成立。2005 年 10 月 24 日经香港高等法院批准。基金捐款人，除了何善衡慈善基金会有限公司及利国伟博士之伟伦基金有限公司外，梁銶琚慈善基金会有限公司和何添基金有限公司各自分别为已故梁銶琚博士及已故何添博士之遗产承办人指定之慈善机构，以便根据本基金信托契约之条款行使有关权力或给予所需批准。

第二条　本基金的宗旨是：

（一）促进中国的科学与技术发展；

（二）奖励取得杰出成就和重大创新的科学技术工作者。

第三条　本基金依法登记设立何梁何利基金（香港）北京代表处，负责何梁何利基金科学技术奖评选工作，执行基金在中国内地的相关业务。

何梁何利基金（香港）北京代表处的业务主管部门为中华人民共和国科学技术部。

二、评奖条件

第四条　本基金奖励和资助致力于推进中国科学技术取得成就及进步与创新的个人。

第五条　本基金奖励和资助具备下列条件的中华人民共和国公民：

（一）对推动科学技术事业发展有杰出贡献；

（二）热爱祖国，积极为国家现代化建设服务，有高尚的社会公德和职业道德；

（三）在我国科学技术研究院（所）、大专院校、企业以及信托委员会认为适当的其他机构从事科学研究、教学或技术工作已满 5 年。

第六条　获奖候选人须由评选委员会选定的提名人以书面形式推荐。

提名人由科学技术领域具有一定资格的专家包括海外学者组成。

三、奖　　项

第七条　本基金设"何梁何利基金科学与技术成就奖""何梁何利基金科学与技术进步奖""何梁何利基金科学与技术创新奖"，每年评奖一次。

第八条　何梁何利基金科学与技术成就奖授予下列杰出科学技术工作者：

（一）长期致力于推进国家科学技术进步，贡献卓著，历史上取得国际高水准学术成就者；

（二）在科学技术前沿，取得重大科技突破，攀登当今科技高峰，领先世界先进水平者；

（三）推进技术创新，建立强大自主知识产权和自主品牌，其产业居于当今世界前列者。

何梁何利基金科学与技术成就奖获奖人每人颁发奖励证书和奖金100万港元。

第九条　何梁何利基金科学与技术进步奖授予在特定学科领域取得重大发明、发现和科技成果者，尤其是在近年内有突出贡献者。

何梁何利基金科学与技术进步奖按学科领域分设下列奖项：

（一）数学力学奖

（二）物理学奖

（三）化学奖

（四）天文学奖

（五）气象学奖

（六）地球科学奖

（七）生命科学奖

（八）农学奖

（九）医学药学奖

（十）古生物学、考古学奖

（十一）机械电力技术奖

（十二）电子信息技术奖

（十三）交通运输技术奖

（十四）冶金材料技术奖

（十五）化学工程技术奖

（十六）资源能源技术奖

（十七）生态环保技术奖

（十八）工程建设技术奖

何梁何利基金科学与技术进步奖获奖人每人颁发奖励证书和奖金20万港元。

第十条　何梁何利基金科学与技术创新奖授予具有高水平科技成就而通过技术创新和管理创新，创建自主知识产权产业和著名品牌，创造重大经济效益和社会效益的杰出贡献者。

何梁何利基金科学与技术创新奖分设下列奖项：

（一）青年创新奖

（二）产业创新奖

（三）区域创新奖

何梁何利基金科学与技术创新奖获奖人每人颁发奖励证书和奖金20万港元。

第十一条　本基金每年各奖项名额如下：

何梁何利基金科学与技术成就奖不超过 5 名；何梁何利基金科学与技术进步奖、何梁何利基金科学与技术创新奖总数不超过 65 名（原则上科学与技术进步奖和科学与技术创新奖名额的比例为 3 比 1 至 2 比 1）。而奖金总额不超过该年度信托委员会审议通过的奖金总额。

具体名额根据年度资金运作情况和评选情况确定。

四、评选委员会

第十二条　本基金成立由各相关领域具有高尚道德情操、精深学术造诣、热心科技奖励事业的专家组成的评选委员会。

评选委员会委员经过信托委员会批准、颁发聘任书后，独立行使职能，负责评选工作。

第十三条　评选委员会委员最多不超过 24 人，其中主任一人、副主任二人、秘书长一人，由内地学者和海外学者出任。

评选委员会委员内地学者和海外学者的比例，原则上每四名委员中，内地学者为三人，海外学者为一人。

评选委员会主任、副主任由基金信托契约补充条款规定的信托委员兼任。其中主任由补充契约所指明的与科技部有关的信托委员兼任，副主任二人分别由补充契约所指明的与教育部有关的信托委员和补充契约所指明的国际学者信托委员兼任。评选委员会秘书长由信托委员会任命并征得捐款人同意的人选担任。

评选委员会委员实行任期制，一任三年，可以连聘连任。

评选委员会委员原则上每三年更换四分之一（不包括主任、副主任及秘书长）。

此外，评选委员会委员的聘任，贯彻相对稳定和适度更新的原则。其办法由评选委员会制定。

评选委员会办公室设在北京，挂靠科学技术部。

第十四条　评选委员会根据评选工作需要，可组织若干专业评审组、奖项评审组，根据提名人的提名推荐材料对被提名人进行初评，产生获奖候选人，提交评选委员会终评。

专业评审组、奖项评审组的评委由评选委员会任命。

第十五条　本基金各奖项获奖人由评选委员会会议评定。

何梁何利基金科学与技术进步奖、何梁何利基金科学与技术创新奖的获奖人，由评选委员会根据专业评审组、奖项评审组的评选结果，评选审定。

何梁何利基金科学与技术成就奖获奖人，由评选委员会全体会议根据评选委员提名评选产生。评选委员会设立预审小组，必要时对候选人进行考察和听证。

第十六条　评选委员会会议贯彻"公平、公正、公开"原则，实行一人一票制，以无记名形式表决确定获奖人。何梁何利基金科学与技术进步奖、何梁何利基金科学与技术创新奖的候选人，获半数赞成票为获奖人。何梁何利基金科学与技术成就奖的候选人，获三分之二多数赞成票为获奖人。

第十七条　评选委员会在评定获奖人名额时，应适当考虑奖种、学科和区域之间的平衡。

五、授　　奖

第十八条　评选委员会评选结果揭晓前须征求获奖人本人意愿，并通知捐款人及信托委员会。遵照捐款人意愿，获奖人应承诺于获奖后，继续在国内从事科学研究和技术工作不少于三年。

第十九条　本基金每年适当时候举行颁奖仪式，由评选委员会安排向何梁何利基金各奖项获得者颁发证书和奖金，并通过新闻媒体公布获奖人员名单及其主要贡献。

六、出版物和学术会议

第二十条　本基金每年出版介绍获奖人及其主要科学技术成就的出版物。

出版物的编辑、出版工作由评选委员会负责。

第二十一条　本基金每年举办学术报告会、研讨会，由评选委员会委员、获奖人代表介绍其学术成就及相关学科领域的进展。

根据基金财政状况，本基金各专业领域专题学术讨论会可在海外举办。

本基金学术论坛由评选委员会负责组织。

七、附　　则

第二十二条　本基金评选委员会每年例会一次，总结当年工作，部署下一年度工作，研究和决定重大事宜。

第二十三条　本章程由本基金评选委员会解释。

第二十四条　本章程自 2020 年 5 月 27 日施行。

REGULATIONS OF HO LEUNG HO LEE FOUNDATION ON THE EVALUATION AND EXAMINATION OF ITS PRIZES AND AWARDS

(Adopted at the Plenary Meeting of the Trust Board on May 27, 2020)

I General Provisions

Article 1 Ho Leung Ho Lee Foundation (hereinafter referred to as " the Foundation") was established on March 30, 1994 in Hong Kong with funds donated by the S H Ho Foundation Limited, Dr. Leung Kau–Kui, Dr. Ho Tim and Dr. Lee Quo–Wei's Wei Lun Foundation Limited. With the approval of the High Court of Hong Kong, apart from S H Ho Foundation Limited and Wei Lun Foundation Limited (donors of the Foundation), Leung Kau–Kui Foundation Limited and Ho Tim Foundation Limited have respectively been nominated by the estates of the late Dr. Leung Kau–Kui and Dr. Ho Tim to and they can as from October 24, 2005 exercise the powers or give the necessary approvals under the terms of the Foundation's trust deed.

Article 2 Purposes of the Foundation are:

(1) To promote the development of science and technology in China.

(2) To reward the scientific and technical personnel with outstanding achievements and great innovations.

Article 3 The Beijing Representative Office of the Ho Leung Ho Lee Foundation (Hong Kong) is established through registration in accordance with the law. It is responsible for selecting the winners of science and technology prizes and awards granted by the Ho Leung Ho Lee Foundation, and carries out the works related to the Foundation on the mainland of China.

The Ministry of Science and Technology of the People's Republic of China acts as the competent authority responsible for the work of the Beijing Representative Office of the Ho Leung Ho Lee Foundation (Hong Kong).

II Criteria for Awards

Article 4 The Foundation shall grant awards and prizes to individuals who are devoted to the achievements, progress and innovations of China's science and technology.

Article 5 The Foundation shall grant awards and prizes to the citizens of the People's Republic of China who meet the following criteria:

(1) Having made outstanding contributions in promoting the development of science and technology.

(2) Being patriotic, vigorously working for the modernization drive of the country, and preserving lofty social morality and professional ethics.

(3) Being with at least five years of scientific researches, teaching or technical working experience in China's science and technology research institutes, institutions for higher learning and universities, enterprises and other organizations which the Board of Trustees regards as appropriate.

Article 6　Candidates for the awards and prizes of the Foundation shall be recommended in writing by nominators identified by the Selection Board.

Nominators should be qualified experts (including those overseas) in various fields of sciences and technology.

III　Awards and Prizes

Article 7　The Foundation sets three annual prizes. They are the Prize for Scientific and Technological Achievements of Ho Leung Ho Lee Foundation, the Prize for Scientific and Technological Progress of Ho Leung Ho Lee Foundation, and the Prize for Scientific and Technological Innovation of Ho Leung Ho Lee Foundation.

Article 8　The Prize for Scientific and Technological Achievements of Ho Leung Ho Lee Foundation shall be awarded to the outstanding science and technology personnel as follows:

(1) Those who have devoted to scientific and technological progress in China for a long time, having made significant contributions and world-class academic achievements.

(2) Those who have made great breakthroughs in the frontline of science and technology, attaining high levels in science and technology and leading the trend in specific areas in the world.

(3) Those who have made great efforts in pushing forward the technology innovation and have built up powerful self intellectual property and brand of its own so that its industry ranks the top of today's world.

Each winner of the Prize for Scientific and Technological Achievements of Ho Leung Ho Lee Foundation will receive a certificate and the amount of the prize of HK $ 1000000.

Article 9　The Prize for Scientific and Technological Progress of Ho Leung Ho Lee Foundation is for those who have made important inventions, discoveries and achievements in specific subject areas, especially having remarkable contributions in recent years.

The following prizes of the Prize for Scientific and Technological Progress of Ho Leung Ho Lee Foundation are set up by subjects:

(1) Award for Mathematics and Mechanics

(2) Award for Physics

(3) Award for Chemistry

(4) Award for Astronomy

(5) Award for Meteorology

(6) Award for Earth Sciences

(7) Award for Life Sciences

(8) Award for Agronomy

(9) Award for Medical Sciences and Materia Medica

(10) Award for Paleontology and Archaeology

(11) Award for Machinery and Electric Technology

(12) Award for Electronics and Information Technology

(13) Award for Communication and Transportation Technology

(14) Award for Metallurgy and Materials Technology

(15) Award for Chemical Engineering Technology

(16) Award for Resources and Energies Technology

(17) Award for Ecology and Environmental Protection Technology

(18) Award for Engineering and Construction Technology

Each winner of the Prize for Science and Technological Progress of Ho Leung Ho Lee Foundation will be awarded a certificate and the amount of the prize of HK $ 200000.

Article 10   The Prize for Scientific and Technological Innovation of Ho Leung Ho Lee Foundation is for the outstanding contributors who have made high level achievements in science and technology, created industry with self intellectual property and famous brands through technology and management innovation, and thus have created great economic and social benefits for the society.

The following prizes of the Prize for Scientific and Technological Innovation of Ho Leung Ho Lee Foundation are set up:

(1) Award for Youth Innovation

(2) Award for Industrial Innovation

(3) Award for Region Innovation

Each winner of the Prize for Scientific and Technological Innovation of Ho Leung Ho Lee Foundation will be awarded a certificate and the amount of the prize of HK $ 200000.

Article 11   Annual quotas of awardees of each prize of Ho Leung Ho Lee Foundation are as follows:

There should be no more than 5 awardees each year for the Prize for Scientific and Technological Achievements of Ho Leung Ho Lee Foundation; and the total number of the winners of the Prize for Scientific and Technological Progress of Ho Leung Ho Lee Foundation and the Prize for Scientific and Technological Innovation of Ho Leung Ho Lee Foundation should be no more than 65 (The proportion of the awardees of the Prize for Scientific and Technological Progress of Ho Leung Ho Lee Foundation and the Prize for Scientific and Technological Innovation of Ho Leung Ho Lee Foundation is in principle from 3 to 1 to 2 to 1). And the total amount of all the Prizes awarded should not exceed the total amount of prize moneys of the year as approved by the Board of Trustees for that year.

The number of winners of each prize should be decided according to the situation each year of the operation of the Foundation's funds and the results of evaluation and selection for the year.

IV   Selection Board

Article 12   A Selection Board shall be constituted under the Foundation, consisting of scholars who are highly respected in ethics, with accomplishments in academic researches and devotion to the work of award of science and technology prizes.

Members of the Selection Board shall independently exercise the powers and are responsible for the evaluation work after they have been appointed with the approval of the Board of Trustees and received the letters of appointment.

Article 13   The total number of the members of the Selection Board should be no more than 24. Among them, there will be one Chair, two Vice Chairs and one Secretary-General. Both local and overseas scholars could be members of the Selection Board.

For every four members of the Selection Board, the ratio between local and overseas scholars should in principle be 3 to 1.

The Chair and the two Vice Chairs of the Selection Board should also be members of the Board of Trustees as stated in the Foundation's Supplemental trust deed. Among them, the Chair should be the member of the Board of Trustees who is related, as stated in the Foundation's Supplemental trust deed, to the Ministry of Science and Technology. And the two Vice Chairs should respectively be the member of the Board of Trustees who is related, as stated in the Foundation's Supplemental trust deed, to the Ministry of Education and the international scholar member of the Board of Trustees as mentioned in the Foundation's Supplemental trust deed.

Secretary General of the Selection Board should be appointed by the Board of Trustees with the agreement of the donors as well.

A system of the set term of office is instituted for members of the Selection Board. Each term of office of the members of the Selection Board is 3 years. A member of the Selection Board may serve consecutive terms.

In principle, the members of the Selection Board shall be altered a quarter every 3 years (except Chair, Vice Chair and Secretary General.)

Besides, the appointment of the members of the Selection Board should be in line with the principles of comparative stability and proper renewal. The Selection Board will be responsible for formulation of the ways of selection.

The office of the Selection Board is located in Beijing and affiliated to the Ministry of Science and Technology of China.

Article 14　Several specific professional evaluation panels or prize evaluation panels may be set up under the Selection Board when it is necessary. The first round of evaluation is done according to recommendation materials submitted by the nominators with a candidate list as the results. This list will be submitted to the Selection Board for a final evaluation.

Members of the professional evaluation panels and prize evaluation panels shall be appointed by the Selection Board.

Article 15　Winners of the prizes of the Foundation are evaluated and decided by the Selection Board.

The Selection Board shall evaluate and determine the winners of the Prize for Scientific and Technological Progress of Ho Leung Ho Lee Foundation and the Prize for Scientific and Technological Innovation of Ho Leung Ho Lee Foundation on the basis of results of the work of the professional evaluation panels or the prize evaluation panels.

The Prize for Scientific and Technological Achievements of Ho Leung Ho Lee Foundation should be decided on a plenary meeting of the Selection Board and on the basis of the nomination of the Selection Board. The Selection Board may set up preliminary evaluation panel to exercise the right of examination and hearing of the candidates when necessary.

Article 16　The Selection Board shall work with the principles of "Fairness, Justness and Openness" and "One Member One Vote". Decisions on winners of prizes of the Foundation are made in a way of anonymous ballot by the members of the Selection Board. The endorsement of at least half of the members of the Selection Board is a must for a candidate to win the Prize for Scientific and Technological Progress of Ho Leung Ho Lee Foundation and the Prize for Scientific and Technological Innovation of Ho Leung Ho Lee Foundation; while at least two-third of favorable votes of the total number is a must for candidates to win the Prize for Scientific and Technological Achievements of Ho Leung Ho Lee Foundation.

Article 17　The Selection Board should take the balance between types of prize, between subjects and between regions into consideration in the process of evaluation.

V　Awarding

Article 18　The Selection Board must ask for the winners' willingness prior to any public announcement of the results of evaluation and selection, and notify both the donors and the Board of Trustees. According to the wishes of the donors, the winners are required to stay in China and continue to carry on scientific researches or technological work for no less than 3 years after receiving the prizes.

Article 19　An award granting ceremony will be held each year at a proper time, in which the winners shall be granted with certificates and prizes as arranged by the Selection Board. The list of awardees and their major contributions will be publicized through media.

VI Publications and Academic Seminars

Article 20   The Foundation shall make a publication yearly to introduce the awardees and their major scientific and technological achievements.

The Selection Board is responsible for editing and publication of the publications.

Article 21   The Foundation shall organize academic seminars every year, in which members of the Selection Board and representatives of the awardees introduce their academic achievements and updated progress in the related areas and make relevant reports where appropriate.

Should the financial situation of the Foundation permits, the academic seminars of specific subjects of the Foundation may be held abroad.

The Selection Board is responsible for the organizing academic forums of the Foundation.

VII Supplementary Provisions

Article 22   The Selection Board of the Foundation holds a meeting annually to summarize the work of the year, to plan the work of the following year and to study and decide on the relevant important issues.

Article 23   The Selection Board of the Foundation shall have the right of explanation of the Articles of this regulation.

Article 24   This regulation becomes effective on May 27, 2020.

关于何梁何利基金获奖科学家
异议处理若干规定

（2009 年 5 月 20 日何梁何利基金信托委员会会议通过）

一、总　　则

为了正确处理对何梁何利基金获奖人提出异议的投诉事件，弘扬科学精神，崇尚科学道德，抵御社会不正之风和科研不端行为，提升何梁何利基金科学与技术奖的权威性和公信力，制定本规定。

二、基本原则

处理对获奖人投诉事件，贯彻以事实为依据，以法律为准绳的原则，遵循科学共同体认同的道德准则，区别情况，妥善处置。

三、受　　理

涉及对获奖科学家主要科技成果评价、知识产权权属以及与奖项有关事项提出异议的署名投诉信件，由评选委员会受理，并调查处理。

匿名投诉信件，原则上不予受理。但涉及获奖人因科研不端行为受到处分、学术资格被取消或与其学术著作、奖项评选相关重要情况的，应由评选委员会跟进调查核实处理。

四、调　　查

评选委员会受理投诉后，由评选委员会秘书长指定评选委员会办公室专人按以下工作程序办理：

1. 将投诉信函复印件送交该获奖人的专业评审组负责人，征求意见。

2. 专业评审组负责人有足够理由认为投诉异议不成立，没有必要调查的，评选委员会秘书长可决定终止处理。

专业评审组负责人认为投诉异议有一定依据，有必要进一步调查的，由评选委员会办公室向获奖人所在部门或单位发函听证。

3. 获奖人所在部门或单位经调查，认为投诉异议不成立或基本不能成立的，应请该单位出具书面意见。评选委员会秘书长可据此决定终止处理。

获奖人所在部门或单位根据投诉认为获奖人涉嫌科研不端行为的，评选委员会应建议该部门或单位根据国家有关规定调查处理，并反馈查处信息。

4. 调查结果应向信托委员会报告。

五、处理决定

获奖人所在部门或单位经调查认定获奖人确属科研不端行为，并做出相应处理的，评选委员会秘书长应当参照《中华人民共和国科学技术进步法》第七十一条规定，提出撤销其奖励决定（草案），经评选委员会主任批准后，提交信托委员会审议。

六、公　　告

因获奖人科研不端行为，撤销其奖励的决定经信托委员会审议通过后，由评选委员会在何梁何利基金年报上公告，并通知本人，返回奖励证书、奖金。

信托委员会对获奖人撤销奖励的决定是终局决定。

七、附　　则

本规定自 2009 年 6 月 1 日起试行。

附:《中华人民共和国科学技术进步法》第七十一条:

"违反本法规定，骗取国家科学技术奖励的，由主管部门依法撤销奖励，追回奖金，并依法给予处分。

违反本法规定，推荐的单位或者个人提供虚假数据、材料，协助他人骗取国家科学技术奖励的，由主管部门给予通报批评；情节严重的，暂停或者取消其推荐资格，并依法给予处分。"

REGULATIONS ON HANDLING THE COMPLAINT LODGED AGAINST THE PRIZE-WINNER WITH HO LEUNG HO LEE FOUNDATION

(Adopted at the Meeting of the Board of Trustees on May 20, 2009)

I General Principle

For the purpose of handling properly the objection lodged against the prize-winner with Ho Leung Ho Lee Foundation, promoting scientific spirits and upholding scientific ethics, preventing social malpractice or misconduct in scientific research, and improving the public credibility and authority of Ho Leung Ho Lee Foundation with respect to awards for science and technology, the Selection Board hereby formulates the regulations as stipulated below.

II Basic Principle

The Selection Board shall handle the complaint lodged against any prize-winner in accordance with the principle of taking the facts as the basis and taking the law as the criterion, and deal with each case properly by following the moral standard recognized by the scientific community.

III Acceptance

For any duly signed letter of objection against a prize-wining scientist with respect to the appraisal of his major scientific and technological achievement, the ownership of intellectual property right and other prize-related matter, the Selection Board shall be responsible for acceptance of the letter of objection and for further investigation and handling thereof.

The Selection Board shall, in principle, not accept a letter of objection written or sent in an anonymous manner. However, if it is mentioned in the letter of objection that, due to misconduct of the prize-winner in the scientific research, the discipline measure is imposed against him, or his academic qualification is cancelled, or there is any other important matter concerning his academic publication and prize selection, such a letter of objection must be accepted by the Selection Board, followed by further investigation, verification and handling.

IV Investigation

Upon acceptance of a letter of objection, the Secretary General of the Selection Board shall designate a special person in the Office of Selection Board to handle the letter of objection according to the procedures as follows:

1. A copy of the letter of complaint shall be sent to the person-in-charge of the specialized evaluation team determining to grant the award to the prize-winner for soliciting his comment.

2. When the person-in-charge of the specialized evaluation team concludes with sufficient reason that the objection cannot be established and it is not necessary to make further investigation, the Secretary General of the Selection Board can make a decision as to terminate the handling of the letter of objection.

When the person-in-charge of the specialized evaluation team deems that the objection can be established on basis of facts but should be proved by further investigation, the office of the Selection Board shall issue a notification to the working unit of the prize-winner to request his presence at a hearing to be held.

3. If the working unit of the prize-winner deems that the objection cannot be established or basically cannot be established after investigation, the working unit is obligated to produce a formal document in writing to state its opinion. Then the Secretary General of the Selection Board has the right to make a decision as to the termination of the handling of the letter of objection.

In case the working unit of the prize-winner deems that the prize-winner commits malpractice or misconduct in proof of the letter of objection, the Selection Board is obligated to propose that the working unit carry out investigation in accordance with government regulations before making a response by sending a feedback to the Selection Board.

4. The investigation results should be reported to Ho Leung Ho Lee Foundation's Board of Trustees.

V Decision

Once the working unit of the prize-winner proves with further investigation that the prize-winner commits malpractice or misconduct, and takes discipline measure against the prize-winner, the Secretary General of the Selection Board should draft a proposal, in accordance with Article 71 of the *Law of the PRC on, Science and Technology Progres*s, on withdrawal of the prize awarded to the prize-winner. The proposal needs to be further approved by the Director of the Selection Board before being submitted to Ho Leung Ho Lee Foundation's Board of Trustees for deliberation.

VI   Announcement

The Selection Board shall announce its decision with respect to withdrawal of the prize from the prize-winner, due to his malpractice or misconduct, in its annual report with approval of the Ho Leung Ho Lee Foundation's Board of Trustees, and shall notify the prize-winner that the prize and prize-winning certificate are to be cancelled. The decision to withdraw the prize from the prize-winner made by Ho Leung Ho Lee Foundation's Board of Trustees shall be final.

VII   Appendix

These regulations shall enter into trial implementation on June 1, 2009.

Appendix: Article 71 of the *Law of the People's Republic of China on Science and Technology Progress* stipulates as follows:

The competent authority shall, in accordance with law, withdraw a prize and a bonus and take disciplinary action against anyone who is engaged in fraudulent practice for winning the National Science and Technology Prize.

For anyone or any working unit, which offers false data, false material, or conspire with others in fraudulent practice for winning the National Science and Technology Prize, the competent authority shall circulate a notice of criticism of such malpractice or misconduct; if the circumstances are serious, the competent authority shall suspend or cancel the working unit's eligibility for recommendation of any prize-winning candidate, and shall punish it in accordance with law.

关于何梁何利基金评选工作
若干问题的说明

何梁何利基金是由香港爱国金融实业家何善衡、梁铣琚先生、何添先生、利国伟先生于 1994 年 3 月 30 日在香港创立的，以奖励中华人民共和国杰出科学技术工作者为宗旨的科技奖励基金。截至 2010 年，已有 901 位获奖科学家获得此项殊荣。经过 16 年的成功实践，何梁何利基金科技奖已经成为我国规模大、层次高、影响广、在国内外享有巨大权威性和公信力的科学技术大奖。为便于科技界、教育界和社会各界进一步了解基金宗旨、基本原则、评选标准和运行机制，在 2010 年 10 月颁奖大会期间，何梁何利基金评选委员会秘书长段瑞春就基金评选章程、评选工作以及社会各界所关心的有关问题，做了如下说明。

一、什么是何梁何利基金评选章程？

何梁何利基金评选章程是评选工作的基本准则。评选章程以基金《信托契约》为依据，由何梁何利基金信托委员会全体会议审议通过和发布。第一部评选章程诞生于 1994 年 3 月 30 日基金成立之时，保障了评选工作从一开始就步入科学、规范、健康的轨道运行。1998 年 5 月 11 日适应香港九七回归和国内形势发展，对评选章程做过一次修订。2007 年 5 月 15 日基金信托委员会会议决定再次修改评选章程，其主要目的，一是根据 2005 年 10 月 12 日香港高等法院批准生效的《补充契约条款》，对评选章程有关条款做相应修改，使之与基金《信托契约》及其《补充契约条款》保持一致。二是将评选委员会适应我国创新国策、改革评选工作的成功经验上升为章程，使之条文化、规范化、制度化，进一步提升各奖项的科学性、权威性。

二、根据《补充契约条款》，评选章程做了哪些重要修改？

何梁何利基金是依据香港法律创立的慈善基金。当初，根据香港普通法原则，实行信任委托制度，由捐款人与信托人签订《信托契约》，经香港终审法院批准成立。信托委员会是基金的最高权力机构，决定基金投资、评选和管理等重大事项。自 1994 年 3 月基金成立以来，当年四位创立者中，梁铣琚先生、何善衡先生、何添先生都在九旬高寿与世长辞。我们永远缅怀他们的崇高精神。由于他们的离去，《信托契约》有关捐款人的权利与义务主体出现缺位，从法律意义上影响到基金决策程序的进行。2005 年 10 月，经香港高等法院批准《信托契约补充条款》将基金"捐款人"统一修订为原捐款人或者其遗产承办人指定的慈善基金，从而实现了捐款人从老一辈爱国金融家向其下一代的平稳过渡。依据此项修订，现基金捐款人为 4 个法人，即何善衡慈善基金有限公司、梁铢琚慈善基金有限公司、何添基金有限公司、利国伟先生和其夫人的伟伦基金有限公司。为此，评选章程也做了相应修改。

三、何梁何利基金奖励对象应当具备什么条件？

何梁何利基金奖励对象为中华人民共和国公民，获奖人应具备下列三个条件：一是对推动科学技术事业发展有杰出贡献；二是热爱祖国，有高尚的社会公德和职业道德；三是在国内从事科研、教学或技术工作已满 5 年。

1994 年 3 月 30 日，何梁何利基金成立时，香港、澳门尚未回归祖国。鉴于当时历史状况，评选章程关于奖励对象为中华人民共和国公民的规定，仅适用祖国内地科技工作者，不包括在香港、澳门地区工作的科技人员。在"一国两制"的原则下，香港和澳门先后于 1997 年 7 月 1 日和 1999 年 12 月 20 日回归祖国。祖国内地与港澳特区科技合作与交流出现崭新局面。而今，香港、澳门特别行政区科技人员，是中华人民共和国公民中的"港人""澳人"，符合章程的要求。为此，自 2007 年起，何梁何利基金奖励对象扩大到符合上述条件的香港特别行政区、澳门特别行政区科学技术人员。

四、现行评选章程对基金奖项结构是如何规定的？

在中央人民政府和香港特区政府的关怀和指导下，16 年来，何梁何利基金已经形成了科学合理的奖项结构和严谨、高效、便捷的评选程序。始终保持客观、公正、权威和具有公信力的评选纪录。现行评选章程规定基金设"科学与技术成就奖""科学与技术进步奖""科学与技术创新奖"。

每年，"科学与技术成就奖"不超过 5 名，授予奖牌、奖金 100 万港元；"科学与技术进步奖"和"科学与技术创新奖"总数不超过 65 名，分别授予相应的奖牌、奖金 20 万港元，其中，"科学与技术进步奖"和"科学与技术创新奖"的数量按 3∶1 至 2∶1 的比例，由评选委员会具体掌握。

五、"科学与技术成就奖"的评选标准是什么？

根据评选章程，符合下列三类条件的杰出科技工作者，均可获得"科学与技术成就奖"。一是长期致力于推进国家科学技术进步，贡献卓著，历史上取得国际高水平学术成就者；二是在科学技术前沿，取得重大科技突破，攀登当今科技高峰，领先世界先进水平者；三是推进技术创新，建立强大自主知识产权和自主品牌，其产业居于当今世界前列者。符合上述标准的获奖人选，既包括毕生奉献我国科技事业、其卓越成就曾达到世界一流水平的资深科学家，也包括以科学研究或技术创新领域的重大突破或突出业绩，使我国取得世界领先地位的中青年杰出人才。在征求意见过程中，我国科技界对此普遍赞同，认为这样修订丝毫没有降低了标准，而是使基金的科技大奖进一步向国际规范靠拢，为在研究开发和创新第一线拔尖人才的脱颖而出注入强大精神动力，也使基金科技奖励更加贴近建设创新型国家的主旋律。

六、"科学与技术进步奖"的评选标准是怎样规定的？

评选章程规定，"科学与技术进步奖"授予在特定学科领域取得重大发明、发现和科技成果者，尤其是在近年内有突出贡献者。需要说明的，一是这里所说的"特定学科"包括：数学力学、物理学、化学、天文学、气象学、地球科学、生命科学、农学、医学和药学、古生物学和考古学、机械电力技术、电子信息技术、交通运输技术、冶金材料技术、化学工程技术、资源环保技术、工程建设技术等17个领域，每一领域设一个奖项。原评选章程用"技术科学奖"涵盖了机电、信息、冶金、材料、工程、环保等技术领域，修订后的章程从学科领域之间平衡考虑，将其分别设立奖项。二是"科学与技术进步奖"评选政策，重在考察被提名人"近年内"的突出贡献。所谓"近年内"是指近10年内。三是随着科学技术飞速发展，新兴学科、交叉学科、边缘学科层出不穷。这些学科的被提名人宜按其最主要成就、最接近学科领域归类。关注新兴、交叉、边缘学科优秀人才，是评选委员会的一项政策。有些确实需要跨学科评议的特殊情况，将作为个案协调处理，但不专门设立新兴学科、交叉学科、边缘学科等奖项。

七、"科学与技术创新奖"的评选标准是怎样规定的？

设立"科学与技术创新奖"是基金评选工作的重要改革。评选章程规定："科学与技术创新奖"授予具有高水平科技成就而通过技术创新和管理创新，创建自主知识产权产业和著名品牌，创造重大经济效益和社会效益的杰出贡献者。这里需要说明的是，创新，是一个经济学的范畴，指的是有明确经济、社会目标的行为。有人解释为"科学思想在市场的首次出现"。何梁何利基金为适应我国提高自主创新能力，建设创新型国家的重大决策设立这个奖项，评选章程所称的"科学与技术创新"，第一，要以高水平的科学技术成就为起点，实现科技成果转化为现实生产力，完成科技产业化的过程。第二，就创新活动而言，是指在高水平科技成就基础上的技术创新和管理创新，包括原始创新、集成创新和在他人先进技术之上的再创新，但应有自主知识产权产业和著名品牌，创造出重大经济效益和社会效益，对于创新成果在教育、节能环保、生态平衡、国家安全、社会公益事业等领域产生的巨大社会效益，将和可计量的经济效益一样，获得评选委员会的认可。第三，任何一项重大创新都是团队作战的成果，"科学与技术创新奖"的得主，可以是发挥核心作用的领军人物，也可以是实现技术突破的关键人物。当然，这里所说的领军人物本身要有科技成就，而不只是行政管理和组织协调工作。

八、怎样理解"科学技术创新奖"所分设的奖项？

根据评选章程，"科学技术创新奖"分设青年创新奖、产业创新奖和区域创新奖等三个奖项。青年创新奖授予在技术创新和管理创新方面业绩突出、年龄不超过45周岁的优秀科技人才；区域创新奖授予通过技术创新、管理创新和区域创新，对区域经济发展和技术进步，尤其是对祖国内地、边远、艰苦地区和少数民族地区发展做出突出贡献的人物；产业创新是指通过创新、创业，大幅度推进技术进步和产业升级，包括对传统产业技术改造和新兴产业的腾飞跨越做出贡献的优秀人才。分设上述三个奖项，是评选政策的安排，其本身并不是相互独立的创新门类。因此，"科学技术创新奖"仍然按照创新奖的基本要求统一评选，适当注意三类奖项的结构平衡，不按区域创新奖、产业创新奖、青年创新奖分组切块进行评审。

九、"科学与技术进步奖"和"科学与技术创新奖"评选标准有何差别？

从原则上讲，"科学与技术进步奖"按照学科领域设置，"科学与技术创新奖"基于创新业绩设置，二者有交叉和关联之处，又有重要区别，评选标准的政策取向和侧重有所不同。《评选章程》要求"科学与技术进步奖"获奖人必须是重大发明、发现和科技成果的完成人或主要完成人。而"科学与技术创新奖"的获奖人是在高水平科技成就基础上的创新实践者。前者，重在考察其发明、发现和其他科技成就的水平及其在国内国际的学术地位；而后者，重点考察其产业高端技术创新和管理创新的业绩，包括经济社会效益、自主知识产权和著名品牌建设。当然，"科学与技术创新奖"得主的领军人物本身要有高水平的科技成就，而不只是战略决策、行政管理和组织协调工作。

十、"科学与技术进步奖""科学与技术创新奖"获奖人能否获得"科学与技术成就奖"？

何梁何利基金的宗旨是鼓励我国优秀科学技术工作者，无所畏惧地追求科学真理，勇攀当代科学技术高峰。已经获得"科学与技术进步奖""科学与技术创新奖"的科技工作者，在获奖后，再接再厉，开拓进取，在科学技术前沿取得新的重大科技突破，领先世界先进水平者；或者在产业高端做出新的重大技术创新，建立强大自主知识产权和自主品牌，使得我国产业跃居当今世界前列者；如果在前次获奖后取得的新的杰出成就达到"科学与技术成就奖"标准，可以推荐为"科学与技术成就奖"被提名人的人选，按照《评选章程》规定程序参评，也有望摘取"科学与技术成就奖"的桂冠。

十一、评选委员会按照怎样的程序进行各奖项评选工作？

每年，基金评选委员会按照下列程序开展评选工作：

（一）提名

每年年初，评选委员会向国内外2000多位提名人发去提名表，由其提名推荐获奖人选，并于3月31日前将提名表返回评选委员会。评选办公室将对提名材料进行形式审查、整理、分组、印刷成册。

（二）初评

每年7月中旬，评选委员会召开当年专业评审会，进行"科学与技术进步奖""科学与技术创新奖"的初评。其中，"科学与技术进步奖"初评，按照学科设立若干专业评审组进行；"科学与技术创新奖"成立一个由不同行业和领域专家组成的评审组进行初评。经过初评，以无记名投票方式，产生一定差额比例的候选人，提交评选委员会会议终评。

（三）预审

根据《评选章程》，"科学与技术成就奖"候选人由评选委员会委员在初评结束后提名。每年8月，评选委员会成立预审小组进行协调、评议，必要时进行考察和听证，产生"科学与技术成就奖"候选人，并形成预审报告，提交评选委员会会议终评。

（四）终评

每年9月中旬评选委员会召开全体会议进行终评。对候选人逐一评议，最后，根据基金信托委员会确定的当年获奖名额，进行无记名投票表决。"科学与技术进步奖""科学与技术创新奖"的候选人，获半数以上赞成票为获奖人。"科学与技术成就奖"的候选人，获三分之二多数赞成票为获奖人。

（五）授奖

每年10月的适当时候，何梁何利基金举行颁奖大会，向获奖人颁发奖牌、奖金。

十二、何梁何利基金获奖人有哪些权利和义务？

《世界人权宣言》宣布："人人对他所创造的任何科学、文学或艺术成果所产生的精神的和物质的权利，享有受保护的权利。"知识产权是精神权利和经济权利的总和，其本原和第一要义，是给人的智慧、才能和创造性劳动注入强大精神动力。科技奖励是确认和保护精神权利的重要制度，何梁何利基金"科学与技术成就奖""科学与技术进步奖""科学与技术创新奖"获奖人的权利是，享有何梁何利基金获奖科学家的身份权、荣誉权；享有接受何梁何利基金颁发的奖金的权利，该奖金个人所有；有从第二年起成为基金提名人，向基金提名推荐被提名人的权利。根据基金《信托契约》和评选章程，获奖人有义务在获得基金奖励后继续在中华人民共和国从事科学与技术工作不少于三年，为我国科技进步与创新做出更多贡献。

十三、评选委员会委员和专业评委是怎样产生的?

评选委员会是何梁何利基金评选工作的执行机构,通过全体会议审议、决定各奖项获奖人,行使最终评选决定权。根据评选章程,评选委员会由最多不超过20名委员组成。评选委员会主任由科技系统的信托委员担任,副主任委员两人,分别由教育部系统的信托委员和补充契约所指明的国际学者信托委员担任。评选委员会秘书长由信托委员会任命并征得捐款人代表同意的人选担任。

评选委员会委员由信托委员会任命,委员名单通过何梁何利基金出版物、网站公布。

按《评选章程》规定,评选委员会委员的聘任条件是:第一,要具备高尚道德情操,能够公正履行评选委员的职责;第二,要具备精深学术造诣,能够对其所属领域科技成就做出科学性和权威性评价;第三,要热心祖国科技奖励事业,愿意为之做出无私奉献;第四,评选委员会委员的结构配置,原则上每一领域有一名委员,国内评委和海外评委按照三比一的比例安排;第五,评选章程还规定了评选委员会委员的更新和替换制度,以保障评选委员会的生机和活力。

每年7月何梁何利基金召开专业评审会议,进行初评。初评是评选工作的第一道关口。其十多个"科学与技术进步奖"评审组和"科学与技术创新奖"的专业评委,由评选委员会根据工作需要,从250人左右的评审专家库或历年获奖科学家中,按《评选章程》规定的上述条件遴选。

十四、怎样理解基金公平、公正、公开的评选原则?

科学精神的精髓是求实、求是、求真。科技奖励评选工作必须坚持以诚信为本,践行实事求是的方针。何梁何利基金从一开始就贯彻"公平、公正、公开"的评选原则,保持良好的评选记录,得到社会各界的高度评价和充分肯定。所谓公平,体现在所有被提名者,不论职务、职位、学衔、资历,也不论年龄、民族、性别,在评选章程确定的评选标准面前一律平等。所谓公正,是指评选工作严格按照章程确定的评选标准和评选程序进行,无论初评的专业评委,还是终评的评选委员会委员,有权做出独立判断,按一人一票的制度行使表决权,最终依据评委共同体的意志决定获奖人,不受任何单位或个人的干扰。所谓公开,是指何梁何利基金评选章程、评选标准及其解释、评选委员会委员、逐年获奖人材料等,通过年报、网站等向社会公开,接受社会公众的监督和指导。自2006年起,评选委员会在部分省市和部门建立联络员,加强同社会各界的联系。何梁何利基金评选实践经验凝练到一点,就是贯彻"公平、公正、公开"的评选原则,是何梁何利基金的指导方针,是评选委员会的工作纪律,是基金的立业之本、权威之根、公信力之源泉,是一个具有国内和国际影响力的科技大奖的生命线。今后,基金将一如既往恪守"三公"原则,本着对科学负责、对基金负责、对科技共同体负责的精神,做好评选工作，使何梁何利基金科学与技术奖经得起历史的检验。

十五、何梁何利基金有无异议处理程序？

为了弘扬科学精神，崇尚科学道德，抵御社会不正之风和科研不端行为，提升何梁何利基金科学与技术奖的权威性和公信力，基金于2009年5月20日制定并发布了《关于何梁何利基金获奖科学家异议处理若干规定》，自发布之日起试行。

根据该项决定，凡涉及对获奖科学家主要科技成果评价、知识产权权属以及与奖项有关事项提出异议的署名投诉信件，由评选委员会受理，并调查处理。匿名投诉信件，原则上不予受理。但涉及获奖人因科研不端行为受到处分、学术资格被取消或与奖项评选相关重要情况的，应跟进调查核实，酌情处理。

评选委员会的处理原则是，以事实为依据，以法律为准绳，遵循科学共同体认同的道德准则，区别情况，正确处置。经调查，认定获奖人确属科研不端行为，将参照《中华人民共和国科学技术进步法》第七十一条规定，报基金信托委员会审议并做出相应的处分决定，直至公告撤销其奖励的决定，并通知本人，返回奖励证书、奖金。

十六、何梁何利基金未来发展目标是什么？

在中央人民政府和香港特别行政区政府的指导下，在我国科技界、教育界和社会各界的共同努力下，何梁何利基金已经成为我国规模大、权威性高、公信力强的社会力量奖励，成为推进我国科技进步与创新的强大杠杆，在国内外影响和声誉与日俱增。在历年颁奖大会上，党和国家领导人亲临颁奖，发表重要讲话，给予基金同人极大鼓舞和力量。何梁何利基金同人将不负众望，不辱使命，承前启后，继往开来，在新的起点上总结经验，开拓创新，突出特色，丰富内涵，朝着办成国际一流的科技奖励的方向迈进，为祖国的科技进步和创新，为建设富强民主、文明和谐的社会主义现代化国家而不懈努力！

EXPLANATIONS ON SEVERAL ISSUES ON THE SELECTION WORK OF HO LEUNG HO LEE FOUNDATION

Ho Leung Ho Lee Foundation ("the Foundation") is a scientific and technological award foundation established on March 30, 1994 in Hong Kong by patriotic Hong Kong financial industrialists Ho Sin Hang, Leung Kau-Kui, Ho Tim, Lee Quo-Wei for the purpose of awarding prominent scientific and technological workers of the People's Republic of China. Up to 2010, there were 901 scientists who received this special honor. Within the 16 years of successful practice, HLHL Foundation Scientific and Technological Awards have become major scientific and technological awards of large scale, high standard and extensive influence in China that enjoy enormous prestige and public trust both domestically and abroad. In order for the circle of science and technology, the circle of education, and other various social circles to further understand the Foundation's purpose, basic principles, award selection criteria and operation mechanisms, Mr. Duan Ruichun, secretary general of the Selection Board of HLHL Foundation, made the following explanations during the awards ceremony in October 2010 with respect to the Foundation's selection regulation, selection work and other issues that various social circles are concerned about.

I. What is the Regulation of Ho Leung Ho Lee Foundation on the Selection of the Award Winners of its Prizes?

The Regulation of Ho Leung Ho Lee Foundation on the Selection of the Award Winners of its Prizes ("Selection Regulation") is the fundamental guideline of the award selection work. The Selection Regulation is based on the Foundation's Trust Agreement and deliberated, adopted and published by the plenary meeting of HLHL Foundation Broad of Trustees. The birth of the first selection regulation on March 30, 1994, the very day when the Foundation was established, guaranteed the operation of the selection work in a scientific, regulated and healthy track from the very beginning. On May 11, 1998, a revision was made to the Selection Regulation to adapt to the return of Hong Kong to China and the development of domestic situation. On May 15, 2007, it was resolved at the meeting of the Foundation's Broad of Trustees that another revision would be made to the Selection Regulation. The main purpose of the revision was that, on the one hand, relevant modifications would be made to certain terms and conditions in the Selection Regulation in accordance with the Supplementary Terms to the Trust Agreement which took effect upon approval by the Hong Kong SAR High Court on October 12, 2005 so that the Foundation's Trust Agreement became consistent with its Supplementary Terms to the Trust Agreement while, on the other hand, the successful experience of the Selection Board in adapting to China's national innovation policy and reforming its selection work was elevated to become part of the selection regulation so that the experience was embodied in agreement terms, standards and systems to further improve the scientific and authoritative features of different award categories.

II. What are the Important Modifications to the Selection Regulation Made in Accordance with the Supplementary Terms of the Trust Agreement?

HLHL Foundation is a charity foundation established in accordance with the laws of the Hong Kong SAR. In its early days, the trust system was established in accordance with the principles in Hong Kong's common law and the foundation was established upon the approval of the Hong Kong Supreme Court after the donors and the trustees signed the Trust Agreement. The Board of Trustees is the supreme body of power of the Foundation that decides on major matters of the foundation in investment, award selection and management. After the foundation was established in March 1994, Mr. Ho Sin Hang, Mr. Leung Kau-Kui and Mr. Ho Tim of the four founders, whose sublime and noble spirits we will all cherish forever, passed away in their nineties. Due to their decease, the main parties to the rights and obligations of donors in the Trust Agreement became absent, which affected the operation of the Foundation's decision-making procedures in terms of law. In October 2005, it was uniformly revised in the Supplementary Terms of the Trust Agreement, upon the approval of the Hong Kong SAR High Court, that the "donors" of the Foundation became the charity foundations designated by the original donors or their estate administrator. Thus a peaceful and smooth transition was achieved with respect to donors from the old generation patriotic financers to the charity foundations run by their next generation. According to the revision, the current donors of the Foundation are four legal persons, namely the S. H. Ho Foundation Limited, the Leung Kau-Kui Foundation Limited, the Ho Tim Foundation Limited, and the Wei Lun Foundation Limited of Mr. Lee Quo-Wei and his wife. And the relevant modifications were made to the Selection Regulation accordingly.

III. What Conditions Need the Winners of the Awards of HLHL Foundation Have?

The winners of the awards of HLHL Foundation shall be the citizens of the People's Republic of China. And they also need to meet the following three conditions: First, they shall have made prominent contributions in the development of the undertakings in science and technology. Second, they shall love the motherland and exhibit noble social ethics and good professional ethics. Third, they shall have engaged in scientific and technological research work, teaching work or technical work for no less than five years in China.

When HLHL Foundation was established on March 30, 1994, Hong Kong and Macao were not returned to the motherland yet. In view of the historical situation then, the provision in the Selection Regulation that the winners of the awards shall be citizens of the People's Republic of China only applied to scientific and technological workers in China's mainland and scientific and technological workers in Hong Kong and Macao were excluded. Then Hong Kong and Macao were returned to the motherland under the principle of "one country, two systems" respectively on July 1st, 1997 and December 20, 1999. And a brand new situation emerged in the cooperation and exchange between the mainland of China and the Hong Kong and Macao SARs. Now, the scientific and technological workers in the Hong Kong and Macao SARs are " Hong Kong people" and " Macao people" among the citizens of the People's Republic of China and thus meet the conditions in the Selection Regulation. Therefore, the scope of the scientists eligible to the awards of HLHL Foundation was expanded from 2007 to include scientific and technological personnel in the Hong Kong and Macao SARs who meet the above conditions.

IV. What are the Provisions on the Structure of the Award Categories in the Prevailing Selection Regulation?

Under the care and guidance of the Central People's Government and the government of the Hong Kong SAR, HLHL Foundation has formed during 16 years a scientific and rational structure of the award categories and a selection regulation of meticulousness, high efficiency, convenience and swiftness. It has always retained its objective, fair, authoritative selection performance and won good public trust. As provided in the prevailing Selection Regulation, the Foundation sets up the Prize for Scientific and Technological Achievements, the Prize for Scientific and Technological Progress, and the Prize for Scientific and Technological Innovation.

Each year there will be no more than five winners of the Prize for Scientific and Technological Achievements. Each of them will be given a medal and a prize of HKMYM one million. The total number of the winners of the Prize for Scientific and Technological Progress and the Prize for Scientific and Technological Innovation will not exceed 65. Each winner will be given a corresponding medal and a prize of HKMYM 200000. Among these, the proportion of the winners of the Prize for Scientific and Technological Progress to those of the Prize for Scientific and Technological Innovation will range from 3 : 1 to 2 : 1. The proportion will be determined by the Selection Board on the basis of specific situation.

V. What are the Selection Criteria on the Prize for Scientific and Technological Achievements?

According to the Selection Regulation, all outstanding scientific and technological workers who meet the following three conditions are eligible to be honored with the Prize for Scientific and Technological Achievements. The first condition is that the scientist has been committed for a long time to promoting the scientific and technological achievements of the state in China and he or she has made eminent contribution and obtained high−level international academic achievements in his career. The second condition is that the scientist has obtained major scientific and technological breakthroughs in the frontiers of science and technology, mounted the peak of the science and technology of the present age, and obtained achievements of a world−leading standard. Third, the scientist has promoted technological innovation and established powerful independently−owned intellectual property and brand. And the industry in which the scientist works is one of the leading industries in the world. The candidates who meet the above standards include both senior scientists who have devoted their whole life to Chinese scientific and technological undertakings and obtained eminent achievements that were once first−rate in the world and youth and middle−aged outstanding talents who have made major breakthroughs or prominent achievements in the area of scientific and technological research and technical innovation so that China got a world−leading position in the area. During the process of opinion solicitation, the Chinese scientific and technological circle expressed general approval of the revision and indicated that such revision lowered the standard by not a slight bit while pushing the Foundation's awards one step further and closer to international standards. It injected powerful spiritual impetus for top−level talents to excel in the frontline of research and development and innovation. The revision also drew the Foundation's scientific and technological awards more closer to the mainstream ideology of building an innovative country.

VI. What are the Provisions on the Selection Criteria of the Prize for Scientific and Technological Progress?

It is provided in the Selection Regulation that the Prize for Scientific and Technological Progress will be honored to scientists who have made major inventions, discoveries and scientific and technological results in particular disciplinary areas, particularly those who have made prominent contributions in recent years. First, it needs to be noted that the "particular disciplines" stated here include 17 disciplines, namely mathematics and mechanics, physics, chemistry, astronomy, meteorology, earth sciences, life sciences, agronomy, medical sciences and materia medica, paleontology and archeology, technology of machinery and electronics, information technology, communication and transportation technology, metallurgical materials technology, chemical engineering technology, resources and environment protection technology, and engineering and construction technology. One award category is established for each of these areas. In the original selection regulation, the Award of Technical Sciences is set up to cover various technical areas including machinery, electronics, information, metallurgy, material science, engineering and environment protection. The revised procedure sets up different award categories for these areas out of the consideration on the balance between various disciplinary areas. Second, the selection policy on the Prize for Scientific and Technological Progress focuses on examining and reviewing the prominent contribution of the nominees "within recent years" . And "within recent years" refers to within the recent ten years. Third, as emerging disciplines, interdisciplines, and fringe disciplines come up one after another with the rapid development of science and technology, the nominees from these disciplines should desirably be classified according to their most important achievements and the closest disciplines to which these belong. To pay more attention to the excellent talents from emerging disciplines, interdisciplines and fringe disciplines is one policy of the Selection Board. The special cases that truly need cross–disciplinary review and deliberation will be processed through coordination as separate cases. But no prize category will be established particularly for emerging disciplines, interdisciplines and fringe disciplines.

VII. What are the Provisions on the Selection Criteria of the Prize for Scientific and Technological Innovation?

Setting up the Prize for Scientific and Technological Innovation is an important reform of the Foundation's selection work. It is provided in the Selection Regulation that " the Prize for Scientific and Technological Innovation will be awarded to scientists who have high–level scientific and technological accomplishments and who have established an industry with independently owned intellectual property and famous brand, created significant economic and social benefits, and made prominent contribution". It needs to be noted here that, as a term in economics, innovation refers to acts with specific economic and social goals. Some people defines it as the "first presence of an idea in science on the market". HLHL Foundation set up the innovation award to adapt to China's important decision to improve the ability to independent innovation and build an innovative country. For the purpose of the Selection Regulation, to make "scientific and technological innovation" first needs to make high–level scientific and technological achievements as its starting point to realize the transformation of scientific and technological achievements into real productive force and complete the process of scientific and technological industrialization. Second, innovation activities refer to technological and managerial innovations on the basis of high–level scientific and technological achievements. These include original innovation, integration innovation and re–innovation on the basis of other people's advanced technology. And such innovations should create independently–owned intellectual properties and famous brands and create significant economic and social benefits. Besides, the Selection Board also accepts and approves, in the same way as measurable economic benefits, the enormous social benefits created by innovation results in the areas of education, energy preservation and environment protection, ecological balance, national security, and social public interest undertakings. Third, as any major innovation is the result of teamwork, the winner of the Prize for Scientific and Technological Innovation may be either a leading person that plays the key role or a key person who has achieved technical breakthroughs. Naturally, the leading person here needs to have his or her own scientific and technological accomplishments in addition to conducting administrative management, organization and coordination work.

VIII. How should the Award Categories Set Up in the Prize for Scientific and Technological Innovation be Understood?

In accordance with the Selection Regulation, the Prize for Scientific and Technological Innovation includes three award categories of the Award for Youth Innovation, the Award for Region Innovation and the Award for Industrial Innovation. The Award for Youth Innovation will be given to excellent scientific and technological talents not older than 45 years old who have achieved prominent performance in technical and managerial innovation. The Award for Region Innovation will be given to people who have made prominent contributions to regional economic development and technological progress through technical, managerial and regional innovations, particularly those who have made contributions to China's inland, remote regions, regions of harsh conditions, and regions of ethic minorities. The Prize for Industrial Innovation will be given to excellent talents who have made contributions through innovation and entrepreneurship to greatly promote technical progress and industrial upgrading, which include both the technical transformation of traditional industries and the leap-forwards of emerging industries. The above three award categories are set up according to the arrangement in selection policy. These do not define mutually-independent types of innovation. Therefore, the selection of the winners of the Prize for Scientific and Technological Innovation will be conducted as a whole part in accordance with the basic requirements on the Prize while proper attention will be paid to retain the structural balance between these three award categories. Selection and evaluation will not be conducted in a manner that the Award for Region Innovation, the Award for Industrial Innovation and the Award for Youth Innovation are separated and form different groups.

IX. What are the Differences in the Selection Criteria of the Prize for Scientific and Technological Progress and the Prize for Scientific and Technological Innovation?

In principle, the Prize for Scientific and Technological Progress has award categories set up in accordance with different disciplines while the Prize for Scientific and Technological Innovation has award categories based on innovation results. The two prizes have overlaps and connections while there are important differences between them. And the policy orientations and stresses in their selection criteria are also different. The Selection Regulation requires that the winners of the Prize for Scientific and Technological Achievements must be completers or major completers of major inventions, discoveries and scientific and technological research results while the winners of the Prize for Scientific and Technological Innovation are scientists in innovative practices on the basis of high-level scientific and technological achievements. The former focuses on examining the standard and value of a scientist's invention, discovery or other scientific and technological achievement and its domestic and international academic status. The latter focuses on examining a person's performance in high-end industrial technical and managerial innovations, including economic and social benefits, independently-owned intellectual properties and building of famous brands. Naturally, the winners of the Prize for Scientific and Technological Innovations need to have high-level scientific and technological achievements as leading persons in addition to just conducting strategic decision making, administrative management, organization and coordination work.

X. Can the Winners of the Prize for Scientific and Technological Progress and the Prize for Scientific and Technological Innovation Be Honored with the Prize for Scientific and Technological Achievements?

The purpose of HLHL Foundation is to encourage excellent Chinese scientific and technological workers to dauntlessly pursue the truth of science and courageously mount the peaks in modern science and technology. The scientific and technological workers who have won the Prize for Scientific and Technological Progress and the Prize for Scientific and Technological Innovation may continue to forge ahead and break new grounds. And they may achieve new important breakthroughs in the frontiers of science and technology and lead in the cutting edge area of the world. Or they may make new important technical innovations in the high-end areas of an industry and create powerful independent intellectual properties and independent brands so that China's relevant industries become industrial leaders in the world. If such scientists' new outstanding achievements obtained after the previous prize winning meet the criteria for the Prize for Scientific and Technological Achievement, these scientists may be recommended as candidates to be nominated to the Prize for Scientific and Technological Achievements. They will participate in the evaluation in accordance with the procedures as provided in the Selection Regulation. And it is hopeful that they may become the laureates of the Prize for Scientific and Technological Achievements.

XI. In Accordance with What Procedures Will the Selection Board Conduct the Selection Work for Various Award Categories?

Each year, the Foundation's Selection Board will carry out selection work in accordance with the following procedure:

A. Nomination. In the beginning of each year, the Selection Board will send nomination forms to over 2000 domestic and foreign nominators. The nominators will recommend candidates for award winners and return the nomination form to the Selection Board by March 31st. The Selection Office will conduct the formal examination, arranging, assorting, and printing of the nomination materials and bind them into booklets.

B. Preliminary Evaluation. In the middle of July each year, the Selection Board will hold the year's specialized evaluation meeting and conduct the preliminary evaluation for the Prize of Scientific and Technological Progress and the Prize for Scientific and Technological Innovation. In the preliminary evaluation, that of the Prize for Scientific and Technological Progress will be conducted with a number of specialized evaluation groups formed according to different disciplines. The preliminary evaluation of the Prize for Scientific and Technological Innovation will be conducted by an evaluation group consisting of experts from different industries and areas. After the preliminary evaluation, candidates will be determined with a proportion of competitive selection by means of secret ballot and submitted to the meeting of the Selection Board for final evaluation.

C. Preliminary Review. In accordance with the Selection Regulation, the candidates of the Prize for Scientific and Technological Achievements will be nominated by the members of the Selection Board upon the conclusion of the preliminary evaluation. Each August, the Selection Board will form a preliminary evaluation group to conduct coordination and evaluation. Inspection tours and hearings will be made when necessary. Then the candidates for the Prize for Scientific and Technological Achievements will be determined and a preliminary review report will be prepared and submitted to the meeting of the Selection Board for final evaluation.

D. Final Evaluation. In the middle of September each year, the Selection Board will hold a plenary meeting to conduct final evaluation. Candidates will be evaluated one by one. And finally a secret ballot will be made on the selection in accordance with the numbers of prize winners of the year determined by the Trust Board of the Foundation. The candidates for the Prize for Scientific and Technological Progress and the Prize for Scientific and Technological Innovation will become prize winners with over half of the votes in favor. The candidates for the Prize for Scientific and Technological Achievements will become prize winners with over two thirds of the votes in favor.

E. Award Ceremony. At a proper time in October each year, HLHL Foundation will hold an award ceremony to present medals and prizes to the winners.

XII. What Are the Rights and Obligations of the Winners of the Awards of HLHL Foundation?

The *Universal Declaration of Human Rights* states that "Everyone has the right to the protection of the moral and material interests resulting from any scientific, literary or artistic production of which he is the author. " Intellectual property rights are the sum of both spiritual and economic rights. Its origin and primary significance is to inject powerful spiritual drive to people's wisdom, talent and creative labor. Scientific and technological awards are important systems to recognize and protect spiritual rights. The rights of the winners of the Prize of Scientific and Technological Achievements, the Prize for Scientific and Technological Progress, and the Prize for Scientific and Technological Innovation of HLHL Foundation are the enjoyment of the right of status and the right of honor of the prize-winning scientists of HLHL Foundation, the enjoyment of the right to accept the prize money granted by HLHL Foundation which shall be owned personally by the prize winners, and the right to become a nominator of the Foundation from the year next to the prize winning to recommend nominees to the Foundation. In accordance with the Foundation's Trust Agreement and Selection Regulation, the prize winner is obligated to continue to engage in scientific and technological work in the People's Republic of China for three years after prize winning so as to make more contribution to China's scientific and technological advancement and innovation.

XIII. How are the Members of the Selection Board and the Specialized Evaluators Selected?

The Selection Board is the implementing body of the selection work of HLHL Foundation. It conducts deliberation through plenary meeting, decides on the winners of the award categories, and exercises the right of decision in final evaluation. In accordance with the Selection Regulation, the Selection Board consists of no more than twenty members at the most. The chairman of the Selection Board shall be a member of the Board of Trustees for the circle of science and technology. The two vice chairmen of the board shall be a member of the Board of Trustees from the bodies under the Ministry of Education and a member of the Board of Trustees who is an international scholar as specified in the Supplementary Terms to the Trust Agreement. The secretary general of the Selection Boards shall be appointed by the Board of Trustees upon the consent of the representatives of the donors.

The members of the Selection Board are appointed by the Board of Trustees. And the list of such members will be published through the publications and website of HLHL Foundation.

As provided in the Selection Regulation, the conditions for the appointment of a member of the Selection Board are: First, the person needs to have noble ethics and the ability to fairly perform the duties of the member of the Selection Board. Second, the person needs to have sophisticated academic accomplishment and the ability to make scientific and authoritative evaluation on the scientific and technological achievements in his or her own specialized field. Third, the person needs to have enthusiasm on the motherland's undertakings in scientific and technological awards and the willingness to make selfless contributions to these undertakings. Fourth, with respect to the structural distribution of the members of the Selection Board, there shall be one member from each area in principle and the proportion between domestic and overseas members shall be 3 : 1. Fifth, the Selection Regulation provides for the renewal and replacement system of the members of the Selection Board so as to ensure the liveliness and vigor of the board.

Each July, HLHL Foundation holds a specialized evaluation meeting to conduct the preliminary evaluation. The preliminary evaluation is the very first step in the selection work. About a dozen of evaluation groups for the Prize for Scientific and Technological Progress and the specialized evaluators of the Prize for Scientific and Technological Innovation will be selected by the Selection Board on the basis of working needs and in accordance with the above conditions as provided in the Selection Regulation from an evaluation expert pool containing about 250 persons or the prize winners in previous years.

XIV. How should People Understand the Foundation's Selection Principles of Fairness, Justice and Openness?

The essence of the scientific spirit is to be practical, honest and truth-seeking. The selection work for the scientific and technological awards must adhere to the principle of sincerity and follow the guideline of doing things with a realistic and pragmatic approach. HLHL Foundation persistently carries out the selection principle of fairness, justice and openness from the very beginning. It retains good selection records and wins high praises and full recognition from various social circles. The principle of fairness is embodied in the provision that all the nominees, regardless of their jobs, positions, academic titles or work experiences and also their age, ethnic group or gender, are equal with respect to the selection criteria determined in the Selection Regulation. The principle of justice refers to the provision that the selection work is carried out strictly in accordance with the selection criteria and procedures determined in accordance with the Selection Regulation. Any person as either a specialized evaluator in the preliminary evaluation or a member of the Selection Board in final evaluation has the right to make independent judgment and exercise the right to vote under the system of one vote for one person. The prize winners are eventually determined according to the common will of all the evaluators free from the intervention of any entity or individual. The principle of openness refers to the practice that HLHL Foundation's Selection Regulation, Selection Criteria, and their explanations and the information about the members of the Selection Board and the prize winners of different years are published to the society through annual report and website to receive supervision and guidance from the public in the society. From 2006, the Selection Board has appointed liaison persons in some governmental departments, provinces and cities to strengthen its contact with various social circles. One viewpoint that can summarize the practical experience of the award selection of HLHL Foundation is to carry out the selection principle of "fairness, justice and openness." It is the guideline of HLHL Foundation, the working discipline of the Selection Board, and the cornerstone of the Foundation, the root of its authoritativeness and the source of its public trust. It is the lifeline of this major scientific and technological award with both domestic and international influence. From now on, the Foundation will adhere to this three-word principle as always. It will carry out the selection work well with the spirit of being responsible to science, to the Foundation, and to the scientific and technological community so that the scientific and technological awards of HLHL Foundation can stand the test of the history.

XV. Does HLHL Foundation Have Dispute Handling Procedures?

With a view to carrying forward the spirit of the science, advocating the ethics of the science, guarding against the unhealthy tendencies in the society and the improper conducts in scientific and technological research, and enhancing the authoritativeness and public trust of HLHL Foundation's scientific and technological awards, the Foundation formulated and published on May 20th, 2009 *Several Provisions on Handling the Disputes on the Prize-Winning Scientists of Ho Leung Ho Lee Foundation*. It took effect from the date of publication.

In accordance with the resolution on the document, the Selection Board will accept, investigate and handle all the signed complaint letters on the disputes with respect to the evaluation of the main scientific and technological research results, the ownership of relevant intellectual properties, and the matters about award categories related to a prize-winning scientist. In principle, anonymous complaint letters will not be accepted and handled. However, where such anonymous complaint letters involve the information that a prize winner has been punished due to improper conducts in scientific and technological research, that his academic title or qualification was cancelled, or other information related to the award evaluation, follow-up action shall be taken to investigate and verify. Such disputes shall then be handled according to actual situation.

The complaint handling principle of the Selection Board is to take facts as the basis and the law as the criterion, follow the ethical principles commonly accepted by the science community, distinguish different situations, and handle correctly. Where it is determined upon investigation that a prize winner really involves in improper conducts in scientific and technological research, the case will be referred to the Board of Trustees of the Foundation for deliberation with reference to the provisions in Article 71 of the *Law of the People's Republic of China on*, *Science and Technology Progress*. The board will make resolutions on corresponding punishment up to that of a public announcement to cancel its reward. The person involved will be notified of the decision and required to return his certificate and prize money.

XVI. What are the Goals of HLHL Foundation on Its Future Development?

Under the guidance of the Central People's Government and the government of the Hong Kong SAR and with the joint efforts of China's scientific and technological circle, education circle and various social circles, HLHL Foundation has already become an awarding organization founded with social resources that is of large scale, high authoritativeness, and strong public trust in China. It becomes a powerful lever to push forward China's scientific and technological advancement and innovation. Its domestic and foreign influence and reputation also grow constantly. China's state and CPC leaders attended in person the award ceremonies in the previous years. They presented the awards and delivered important speeches to give great encouragement and power to our colleagues working with the Foundation. The people of HLHL Foundation will live up to the expectations of the people and their own commitment. They will build on the past and usher in the future. They will summarize their experiences and move on from a new starting point. They will explore and innovate, highlight the Foundation's features, enrich its connotations, and advance in the direction of making it an internationally first—rate scientific and technological award. They will work hard and relentlessly for the motherland's scientific and technological advancement and innovation and for building China into a wealthy, democratic, civilized and harmonious socialist modern country!

关于何梁何利基金（香港）北京代表处公告

（2019 年 11 月 20 日北京市公安局批准）

何梁何利基金是香港爱国金融家何善衡、梁銶琚、何添、利国伟先生基于崇尚科学、振兴中华的热忱，各捐资 1 亿港元于 1994 年 3 月 30 日在香港注册成立的社会公益性慈善基金。其宗旨是奖励中华人民共和国杰出科学技术工作者，服务祖国科技进步与创新伟业。

根据《中华人民共和国境外非政府组织管理法》，经申请，并经北京市公安局批准，何梁何利基金（香港）代表处自 2019 年 11 月 20 日在北京宣告成立。

何梁何利基金（香港）代表处负责基金在中国境内开展活动，执行评选委员会指定提名、初评、终评和颁奖大会等日常事务。举办基金学术论坛、图片展。出版《何梁何利奖》等刊物。

特此公告。

何梁何利基金（香港）北京代表处

2020 年 1 月 1 日

PUBLIC ANNOUNCEMENT OF THE BEIJING REPRESENTATIVE OFFICE OF THE HO LEUNG HO LEE FOUNDATION (HONG KONG)

(Approved by Beijing Municipal Public Security Bureau on November 20, 2019)

With their fervor for advocating science and rejuvenating the Chinese nation, four patriotic financial industrialists in Hong Kong—Mr. Ho Sin-Hang, Mr. Leung Kau-kui, Mr. Ho Tim and Mr. Lee Quo-Wei—each donated 100 million HK dollars to register the establishment of the Ho Leung Ho Lee Foundation in Hong Kong on March 30, 1994. The Ho Leung Ho Lee Foundation is aimed to reward the outstanding science and technology workers of the People's Republic of China and to serve the great undertaking of advancing scientific and technological progress and innovation in the motherland.

The Ho Leung Ho Lee Foundation submitted an application in accordance with *The Law of the People's Republic of China on Administration of Activities of Overseas Nongovernmental Organizations in the Mainland of China*. With the approval of the application by the Beijing Municipal Public Security Bureau, the Beijing Representative Office of the Ho Leung Ho Lee Foundation (Hong Kong) was announced to be established on November 20, 2019 in Beijing.

The Beijing Representative Office of the Ho Leung Ho Lee Foundation (Hong Kong) is responsible for conducting activities of the Ho Leung Ho Lee Foundation in the mainland of China, and handling day-to-day affairs of the Selection Board of Ho Leung Ho Lee Foundation such as designating nominees, holding preliminary and final evaluations, and holding the awarding ceremony of the Ho Leung Ho Lee Foundation. It is also responsible for organizing academic forum and photo exhibition of the Ho Leung Ho Lee Foundation, and publishing periodicals including the *Ho Leung Ho Lee Prize*.

The public announcement is hereby given.

Beijing Representative Office of the
Ho Leung Ho Lee Foundation (Hong Kong)
January 1, 2020

何梁何利基金捐款人简历

捐款者何善衡慈善基金会有限公司之创办人

何 善 衡

何善衡博士，1900 年出生，广东番禺市人。

何博士于 1933 年创办香港恒生银号，其后又创办恒昌企业及大昌贸易行。1952 年恒生银号改为有限公司，1959 年改称恒生银行，何氏一直担任董事长一职。1983 年，于恒生银行成立 50 周年时，何氏因年事关系，改任恒生银行名誉董事长至病逝。

何博士经营之业务包括银行、贸易、信托、财务、酒店、保险、地产、船务、投资等。

何博士热心慈善公益不遗余力。1970 年设立何善衡慈善基金会，资助国内外慈善事业，包括地方建设、教育、医疗、科学等，帮助社会造就人才，尤其对广州市及其家乡一带贡献很多。1978 年创办恒生商学书院，免费提供教学，并曾任多所学校校董。1971 年获香港中文大学荣誉社会科学博士衔，1983 年获香港大学荣誉法律博士衔，1990 年及 1995 年分别获广州市中山大学荣誉顾问衔及名誉博士学位，1993 年获广州市荣誉市民及番禺市荣誉市民称谓。

何善衡博士于 1997 年 12 月 4 日在香港病逝，享年 97 岁。

梁 銶 琚

梁銶琚博士，1903 年出生，广东顺德人。

梁博士为恒昌企业之创办人，曾任恒生银行董事、大昌贸易行副董事长，亦为美丽华酒店企业有限公司、富丽华酒店有限公司、Milford 国际投资有限公司等董事以及恒生商学书院校董等。

梁博士早年在穗、港、澳等地经营银号和贸易，为大昌贸易行创办人之一，为工作经常往返国内各大商埠及海外大城市，或开设分行，或推进业务，并与合伙股东制订运作规章，积极培育人才；梁博士领导华商参与国际贸易，并于20世纪60年代协助香港政府重新厘定米业政策，对香港的安定繁荣有卓越贡献。

梁博士宅心仁厚，精于事业，淡薄声名，热心公益。数十年来对社会福利、教育、医疗事业捐助良多，堪称楷模。较为显著者包括捐款建成纪念其先父之圣高隆庞女修会梁式芝书院，纪念其先母之保良局梁周顺琴学校，香港大学梁铢琚楼，香港中文大学梁铢琚楼，香港浸会学院"梁铢琚汉语中心"，岭南学院梁铢琚楼，广州中山大学捐建两千两百座位的梁铢琚堂与梁李秀娱图书馆，赞助杨振宁博士倡议之中山大学高级学术研究中心基金会及中国教育交流协会留学名额，为清华大学设立"梁铢琚博士图书基金"，中国人民解放军第四军医大学"梁铢琚脑研究中心"，清华大学建筑馆——梁铢琚楼。

在香港的其他教育捐助包括：顺德联谊总会梁铢琚中学，顺德联谊总会梁李秀娱幼稚园（屯门），顺德联谊总会梁李秀娱幼稚园（沙田），香港励志会梁李秀娱小学，恒生商学书院，劳工子弟学校新校，九龙乐善堂陈祖泽学校礼堂，乐善堂梁铢琚学校，乐善堂梁铢琚书院，香港大学黄丽松学术基金，香港女童军总会沙田扬坑营地及梁李秀娱花园；在医疗卫生方面包括：医务卫生署土瓜湾顺德联谊总会梁铢琚诊所，香港防癌会，香港放射诊断科医生协会，玛丽医院"梁铢琚糖尿病中心"，玛丽医院放射学图书博物馆教学资料和医院员工的福利，香港大学医院在山东省为胃癌研究工作经费，支持张力正医生在葛量洪医院的心脏病手术和医疗的发展经费及捐助圣保禄医院设立心脏中心并以"梁铢琚心脏中心"命名；在社会福利捐献包括：九龙乐善堂梁铢琚敬老之家，东区妇女福利会梁李秀娱晚晴中心，香港明爱，西区少年警讯活动及跑马地鹅颈桥区街坊福利会等；向宗教团体的捐助包括：资助基督教"突破机构"开设青年村——信息站，赞助"志莲净苑"重建基金及大屿山"宝莲禅寺"筹募兴建天坛大佛基金等。

多年来，梁博士对家乡顺德的地方建设、科技教育、医疗事业亦大量资助，其中包括捐资成立国家级重点中学梁铢琚中学，中学的科学楼并增置教学仪器，北头学校，梁铢琚图书馆及图书，增设杏坛医院230张病床、独立手术室及分科设备仪器等，杏坛康乐活动中心，北头大会堂及北头老人康乐中心，北头乡每户开建水井一口，修葺北头主路及河道两岸，北头乡蚕房四座，梁铢琚夫人保健中心（即妇产幼儿医院），梁铢琚夫人幼儿园及梁铢琚福利基金会。

1987年梁博士荣获香港中文大学颁授荣誉社会科学博士学位，1990年被广州中山大学聘为名誉顾问，1992年获顺德市（今顺德区）颁授为首位荣誉市民，1994年国务院学位委员会批准清华大学授予梁博士名誉博士学位；同年4月，国务院总理李鹏为梁博士题词"热心公益，发展教育"，以赞扬其贡献。1995年6月21日，香港大学向已故梁铢琚博士追授名誉法学博士文凭。

在海外方面，梁博士亦曾捐助英国牛津大学、苏格兰Aberdeen大学医学院与加拿大多伦多颐康护理中心。

梁铢琚博士于1994年11月10日在香港病逝，享年91岁。

何 添

何添博士于 1933 年加入香港恒生银行有限公司（前为恒生银号），于 1953 年任董事兼总经理，1967—1979 年任恒生银行副董事长。何添博士于 2004 年 4 月退任恒生银行董事，同时获该行委任为名誉资深顾问。何添博士曾任多个上市公司董事职位，包括美丽华酒店企业有限公司（董事长）、新世界发展有限公司、新鸿基地产有限公司、熊谷组（香港）有限公司及景福集团有限公司。

何添博士积极参与公职服务，他为香港中文大学联合书院永久校董、香港中文大学校董会校董、恒生商学书院校董、邓肇坚何添慈善基金创办人之一、香港何氏宗亲总会永久会长、旅港番禺会所永久名誉会长及金银业贸易场永远名誉会长。

何添博士于 1982 年获香港中文大学颁授荣誉社会科学博士学位；1997 年获香港城市大学颁授名誉工商管理学博士学位；1999 年获香港大学颁授荣誉法律博士学位；于 1988 年、1993 年、1995 年及 2004 年分别获广州市、番禺市、顺德市及佛山市授予荣誉市民的称号；又于 1996 年 11 月出任中华人民共和国香港特别行政区第一届政府推选委员会委员。

何添博士于 2004 年 11 月 6 日在香港病逝，享年 95 岁。

捐款者伟伦基金有限公司之创办人
利 国 伟

利国伟博士于 1946 年加入香港恒生银行有限公司（前为恒生银号），1959 年 12 月任该行董事，1976 年 1 月任副董事长，1983—1996 年 2 月做执行董事长，1996 年 3 月至 1997 年 12 月任非执行董事长，1998 年 1 月至 2004 年 4 月任名誉董事长，退任后续任名誉资深顾问。

在公职方面，利国伟博士 1963—1982 年为香港中文大学司库，1982—1997 年为该大学校董会主席，并于 1994 年 11 月 30 日起被该校委为终身校董。利博士亦曾先后任香港李宝椿联合世界书院创校主席及名誉主席。此外，亦曾任江门市五邑大学名誉校长。

利国伟博士曾先后任香港行政局议员 7 年，立法局议员 10 年，银行业务咨询委员会委员 14 年，教育委员会主席 7 年，教育统筹委员会主席 5 年。

利国伟博士历年获香港及海外多所大学颁授荣誉博士学位，这些学校分别为香港中文大学（1972）、英国赫尔大学（University of Hull）（1985）、英国伯明翰大学（University of Birmingham）（1989）、香港大学及香港城市理工学院（即现时之香港城市大学）（1990）、香港理工学院（即现时之香港理工大学）及香港浸会学院（即现时之香港浸会大学）（1992）、英国伦敦市政厅大学（London Guildhall University）（1993）、清华大学及香港公开进修学院（即现时之香港公开大学）（1995）。利博士于 1971 年及 1995 年分别获选为英国银行学会及美国塔夫斯大学（Tufts University）院士，并于 1991 年、1993 年、1995 年、1996 年及 2003 年分别获选为英国牛津大学圣休学院（St Hugh's College, Oxford University）、爱丁堡皇家医学院（Royal College of Physicians of Edinburgh）、香港心脏专科学院、香港内科医学院以及英国剑桥李约瑟研究所荣誉院士，并于 1993 年获广州市政府、开平市政府及江门市政府颁授荣誉市民名衔。此外，利博士在南华早报及敦豪国际（香港）有限公司主办之 1994 年香港商业奖中获商业成就奖。利博士于 1995—2003 年受聘为中国老教授协会名誉会长，并于 1997 年荣获香港特别行政区政府颁授"大紫荆勋章"，2006 年获香港证券专业学院授予荣誉会员衔。

多年来，利国伟博士对其原籍之开平地方建设、教育及医疗事务多所资助，对江门市亦捐赠不少。此外，对清华大学、上海市和广州市之其他机构亦分别做出捐献。

利国伟博士于 2013 年 8 月 10 日在香港病逝，享年 95 岁。

BRIEF INTRODUCTION TO THE DONORS TO
HO LEUNG HO LEE FOUNDATION

Brief Biography of Dr. S. H. Ho

Dr. S. H. Ho, the founder of the S. H. Ho Foundation Ltd. which donated to Ho Leung Ho Lee Foundation, born in 1900, was a native of Panyu, Guangdong Province. He cofounded Hang Seng Ngan Ho in Hong Kong in 1933 and later, the Hang Chong Investment Co Ltd. and the Dah Chong Hong Ltd. In 1952, Hang Seng Ngan Ho was incorporated and in 1959, was renamed Hang Seng Bank Ltd. From 1960 until 1983, Dr. Ho served as Chairman of the Bank. In 1983, on the 50th anniversary of the Bank, he became its Honorary Chairman until he passed away.

Dr. Ho was involved in a wide range of businesses, including banking, trade, trusteeship, financing, hotels, insurance, property, shipping and investment.

Dr. Ho was a philanthropist who was committed to promoting charitable causes. In 1970, he founded the S. H. Ho Foundation Ltd to support charitable causes in China and overseas, including regional construction, education, medical services, scientific research and the training of new talent. His contributions to Guangzhou and his homeland were particularly notable. In 1978, he founded the Hang Seng School of Commerce to provide free education to aspiring youths. He also sat as director on many school boards. In 1971, he was conferred the Honorary Degree of Doctor of Social Science by The Chinese University of Hong Kong and in 1983, an Honorary Degree of Doctor of Laws by The University of Hong Kong. In 1990, he became an Honorary Adviser to the Zhongshan University in Guangzhou and was conferred the Honorary Doctorate's degree by that University in 1995. He was made an Honorary Citizen of Guangzhou and of Panyu in 1993.

Dr. S. H. Ho passed away peacefully in Hong Kong on December 4, 1997 at the age of 97.

Brief Biography of Dr. Leung Kau-Kui

The late Dr. Leung Kau-Kui was born in 1903, a native of the City of Shunde in Guangdong Province. Dr. Leung made his mark in the businesses of foreign exchange and trading in Guangzhou, Hong Kong and Macau early in his career. He was a pioneer in leading Chinese businessmen to participate in international trades.

Throughout his career, Dr. Leung held directorships in various companies. He was a director of the Hang Seng Bank, founder of Hang Chong Investment Co. Ltd., and one of the founders and Vice-Chairman of the Dah Chong Hong Ltd. —a leading Chinese-owned trading firm in Hong Kong during the colonial days. He was also a director of Miramar Hotel and Investment Co. Ltd. Furama Hotel Co. Ltd., Milford (International) Investment Co. Ltd., and a director of the Hang Seng School of Commerce.

Dr. Leung travelled regularly and extensively to cities in China and overseas to set up branches for Dah Chong Hong Ltd. as well as to promote and develop businesses for his partners. During the 60's, he helped to restructure the import procedures of rice to Hong Kong from Thailand contributing significantly to the stability and prosperity of Hong Kong.

Benevolent, enterprising and self-effacing, Dr. Leung was a committed contributor to charitable causes. He gave generously to education, medical social services and religious organisations. Among the charitable causes which he had supported were: the Missionary Sisters St. Columban Leung Shek Chee College in memory of his late father, the Po Leung Kuk Leung Chou Shun Kam Primary School in memory of his late mother, The University of Hong Kong's KK Leung Building, The Chinese University of Hong Kong's Leung Kau-Kui Building, Lingnan College's Leung Kau-Kui Building, the Hong Kong Baptist College's (now the Hong Kong Baptist University) School of Continuing Education Leung Kau-Kui Hanyu Institute, K. K. Leung Architectural Building of Beijing's Tsinghua University, Guangzhou's Zhongshan University's Leung Kau-Kui Hall and Leung Lee Sau Yu Library, and The K. K. Leung Brain Research Centre of the Fourth Military Medical University in Xian, China. He also sponsored the Foundation of Zhongshan University Advanced Research Centre and the China Educational Exchange Association's Scholarships for Overseas Studies, both of which were promoted by Professor Yang Chen Ning. He also set up the Book Foundation of Dr. Leung Kau-Kui for Tsinghua University.

In Hong Kong, his other contributions were supports given to: Shun Tak Fraternal Association Leung Kau-Kui College, Shun Tak Fraternal Association Leung Lee Sau Yu Kindergarten (Tuen Mun), Shun Tak Fraternal Association Leung Lee Sau Yu Kindergarten (Shatin), The Endeavourers Leung Lee Sau Yu Memorial Primary School, Hang Seng School of Commerce, the assembly hall of Lok Sin Tong Chan Cho Chak Primary School, Lok Sin Tong Leung Kau-Kui Primary School, Lok Sin Tong Leung Kau-Kui College, Dr. Raymond Huang Foundation of the University of Hong Kong, S. T. F. A. Leung Kau-Kui Clinic of the Medical and Health Department, The Hong Kong Anti-Cancer Society, Queen Mary Hospital's Leung Kau-Kui Diabetes Centre and donations to upgrade the Radiology Library/Museum as well as teaching materials and staff welfare of the Hospital. He also contributed to the Department of Medicine of the University of Hong Kong to do research work on gastric cancer in Shandong Province, China. Dr. Leung also made generous contributions to the religions bodies, which included assisting the Christian Break-through Organization in establishing and donating to the Youth Village-Information Centre, redevelopment foundation of the Buddhist Chi Lin Nunnery, as well as the construction fund of the Buddha Statue at Po Lin Monastery on Lantau Island.

Dr. Leung was generous and zealous in promoting education in science and technology and medical services in his hometown, Shunde. In particular, he was the first donor working to improve the public amenities of his native Beitou Village. Notable projects which he supported in Shunde included multipurpose halls, hospitals, child care and nursery centres, schools, kindergartens, libraries, sports and recreational centres as well as welfare institutions.

Dr. Leung received an Honorary Degree of Doctor of Social Sciences from The Chinese University of Hong Kong in 1987 and became an Honorary Adviser to Guangzhou's Zhongshan University in 1990. In 1992, the government of Shunde named him an Honorary Citizen. He was conferred an Honorary Doctorate by Tsinghua University in 1994. In April 1994, Premier Li Peng praised him for his enthusiastic support of charitable causes and development of education in China.

Dr. Leung had also donated to overseas institutions such as the Oxford University of United Kingdom, the medical school of Aberdeen University in Scotland, and the Yee Hong Geriatric Centre in Toronto, Canada.

Dr. Leung passed away peacefully in Hong Kong on November 10, 1994 at the age of 91.

Brief Biography of Dr. Ho Tim

Dr. Ho Tim joined Hang Seng Bank Ltd (formerly Hang Seng Ngan Ho) in Hong Kong in 1933, was appointed its Director and General Manager in 1953 and Vice-Chairman from 1967 to 1979. In April 2004, he retired from the Board of Hang Seng Bank Limited and was named one of the Bank's Honorary Senior Advisers. Dr. Ho held directorships in a number of listed companies. He was the Chairman of Miramar Hotel and Investment Co. Ltd.; a Director of New World Development Co. Ltd., Sun Hung Kai Properties Ltd., Kumagai Gumi (Hong Kong) Ltd. and King Fook Holdings Ltd.

Dr. Ho was active in public service. He was a Permanent Member of the Board of Trustees of the United College of The Chinese University of Hong Kong, a Council Member of The Chinese University of Hong Kong, a Board Member of the Hang Seng School of Commerce, one of the founders of the Tang Shiu Kin and Ho Tim Charitable Fund, Permanent President of the Ho's Clansmen Association Ltd., Honorary President of the Panyu District Association of Hong Kong and Honorary Permanent President of the Chinese Gold & Silver Exchange Society.

In 1982, The Chinese University of Hong Kong conferred on Dr. Ho the Honorary Degree of Doctor of Social Science; in 1997, an Honorary Doctorate Degree of Business Administration by The City University of Hong Kong; and in 1999, an Honorary Degree of Doctor of Laws by The University of Hong Kong. He was made an Honorary Citizen of Guangzhou, Panyu, Shunde and Foshan in 1988, 1993, 1995 and 2004 respectively by the respective municipal governments. He was appointed a member of the Selection Committee of the First Government of the Hong Kong

Special Administrative Region of the People's Republic of China in November 1996.

Dr. Ho Tim passed away peacefully in Hong Kong on November 6, 2004 at the age of 95.

Brief Biography of Dr. Lee Quo-Wei

Dr. Lee Quo-Wei, the founder of Wei Lun Foundation Limited which donated to Ho Leung Ho Lee Foundation, joined Hang Seng Bank (formerly Hang Seng Ngan Ho) in Hong Kong in 1946. He was appointed a Director of the Bank in December 1959 and elected Vice-Chairman in January 1976. He became Executive Chairman of the Bank from 1983 until February 1996; non-executive Chairman from March 1996 to December 1997. He was appointed Honorary Senior Advisor of the Bank after his appointment as Honorary Chairman from January 1998 to April 2004.

Dr. Lee was well-known for his active involvement in public services. He had been Treasurer of the Chinese University of Hong Kong from 1963 to 1982, the Chairman of the Council of the University from 1982 to 1997 and a Life Member of the Council of the University since 30 November 1994. He was the Founding Chairman and later the Honorary Chairman of the Li Po Chun United World College of Hong Kong as well as the Honorary President of Jiangmen's Wuyi University.

He was a member of the Executive Council in Hong Kong for 7 years and a member of the Legislative Council for 10 years. He was also a member of the Banking Advisory Committee for 14 years, Chairman of the Board of Education for 7 years and Chairman of the Education Commission for 5 years.

Several universities in Hong Kong and overseas had conferred Honorary Doctorate Degrees on Dr Lee, including The Chinese University of Hong Kong in 1972, University of Hull (United Kingdom) in 1985, University of Birmingham (United Kingdom) in 1989, University of Hong Kong in 1990, City Polytechnic of Hong Kong (presently known as the City University of Hong Kong) in 1990, Hong Kong Polytechnic (now the Hong Kong Polytechnic University) and Hong Kong Baptist College (now the Hong Kong Baptist University) in 1972, London Guildhall University (United Kingdom) in 1993, Tsinghua University (Beijing of China) and the Open Learning Institute (now the Open University of Hong Kong) in 1995. Dr Lee was also elected to a fellowship of the Chartered Institute of Bankers, London in 1971 and Tufts University (USA) in 1995 as well as honorary fellowships of St Hugh's College, Oxford University; Royal College of Physicians of Edinburgh; Hong Kong College of Cardiology; and Hong Kong College of Physicians; and Needham Research Institute, Cambridge in 1991, 1993, 1995, 1996 and 2003 respectively. In 1993, he was made an Honorary Citizen of Guangzhou, Kaiping and Jiangmen by the three municipal governments. In the 1994 South China Morning Post/DHL Hong Kong Business Awards, he was awarded Businessman of the year. Dr Lee had been engaged Honorary President of

China Senior Professors Association from 1995 to 2003. In July 1997, he was awarded the Grand Bauhinia Medal by the Hong Kong Special Administrative Region Government. In 2006, he was elected Honorary Fellow for the year by the Hong Kong Securities Institute.

Over the years, Dr Lee had donated generously to his homeland Kaiping, helping to improve infrastructure, education and medical services. He had also made significant contributions to Jiangmen. In addition, he had made donations to Tsinghua University in Beijing and other institutions in the cities of Shanghai and Guangzhou.

Dr Lee Quo-Wei passed away peacefully in Hong Kong on August 10, 2013 at the age of 95.

何梁何利基金信托人简历

朱 丽 兰

朱丽兰，女，1935年8月出生于上海。教授，原科学技术部部长，现任全国人大常委会委员、全国人大教科文卫委员会主任委员。曾就读于上海中西小学，毕业于第三女中。1956年在苏联敖德萨大学高分子物理化学专业学习，1961年获优秀毕业生文凭。回国后在中国科学院化学研究所工作到1986年。长期从事高分子反应动力学、高分子材料剖析及结构表征研究。所承担的高分子材料剖析、性能结构形态关系的研究项目曾分别获国家级重大科研成果奖及应用成果奖，多次在国内外发表学术论文。曾任中国科学院化学研究所研究室主任和所长职务。

1979—1980年，在德国费拉堡大学高分子化学研究所做访问学者。在科研工作中，发展了一种新的染色技术用于制备样品，被称为一种突破，在国内外同行中享有较高声誉。

1986—2001年，曾任国家科委副主任、常务副主任、科学技术部部长。任国家科委、科技部领导期间，组织制定并实施了国家高技术研究发展计划（"863"计划）、国家发展基础研究的攀登计划以及高技术产业化的火炬计划等。倡导和推行新的专家管理机制，提出了一系列适应当代高技术发展规律并结合中国国情的管理理论与政策、方法，出版了专著《当代高技术与发展战略》《发展与挑战》等，并获中国材料研究学会成就奖。由于在推动国际科技合作以及促进中国国家高技术研究发展与产业化方面成绩卓著，1993年获美洲中国工程师协会颁发的杰出服务奖；1998年获德国联邦总统星级大十字勋章。

朱丽兰曾任中国工程院主席团顾问，中国科学院学部主席团顾问，国家科技领导小组成员，中央农村工作领导小组成员，国家信息化领导小组成员，国家奖励委员会主任委员等职。现任中国化学会常务理事会理事，中国对外友好协会常务理事，中国自然辩证法研究会理事，中国材料研究学会理事，并被聘为北京理工大学、国家行政学院、清华大学、中国科学院化学研究所兼职教授。

朱丽兰是国际欧亚科学院院士、亚太材料科学院院士。

孙　煜

　　孙煜自 2020 年 12 月起任中银香港（控股）有限公司及中国银行（香港）有限公司副董事长兼总裁。彼为战略及预算委员会和可持续发展委员会委员。调任前，于 2020 年 3 月—2020 年 12 月出任集团非执行董事和风险委员会委员。

　　孙煜于 1998 年加入中国银行，2012 年 7 月—2014 年 12 月任中银香港全球市场总经理，2015 年 3 月—2018 年 11 月任中国银行伦敦分行行长、中国银行（英国）有限公司行长，2015 年 12 月—2018 年 11 月兼任中国银行伦敦交易中心总经理。此前，先后担任中国银行全球金融市场部总监、金融市场总部总监（代客）、金融市场总部总监（证券投资）和上海市分行副行长。2018 年 9 月—2019 年 2 月任中国银行海外业务总监，2019 年 2 月—2020 年 12 月任中国银行副行长，并于 2019 年 2 月—2020 年 12 月兼任中银航空租赁有限公司（于香港上市）董事长，于 2019 年 11 月—2020 年 12 月兼任中国银行上海人民币交易业务总部总裁，于 2019 年 12 月—2020 年 12 月兼任中国银行北京市分行行长。

　　孙煜目前亦兼任多项职务，包括中国银行（英国）有限公司董事长、中银保险（国际）控股有限公司董事长、中银集团人寿保险有限公司董事长以及中银香港慈善基金董事局主席。孙煜现任多项公职，包括香港中资银行业协会会长、外汇基金咨询委员会委员、银行业务咨询委员会委员、财资市场公会议会委员、香港总商会理事会理事、香港贸易发展局"一带一路"及大湾区委员会委员、香港交易所风险管理委员会成员、香港印钞有限公司董事、香港银行学会副会长等。

　　孙煜于 1998 年毕业于南开大学，获经济学硕士学位。

钟　登　华

　　钟登华，1963 年 11 月出生。天津大学工学博士。现任教育部党组成员、副部长。曾任天津大学党委副书记、校长。2009 年当选中国工程院院士。

　　长期从事水利工程领域的人才培养和科学研究工作。提出了水利工程智能仿真与实时控制理论方法与技术、水利工程地质精细建模与分析理论方法与技术、水利工程建设智能控制数字大坝理论方法与技术。

先后承担并完成 10 余项国家重大工程的科技攻关或技术开发任务，研究成果在我国 80 多项水利水电工程中得到推广应用，在提高工程设计水平与效率、保证工程质量和节省工程投资方面发挥了重要作用。作为第一完成人获国家科技进步奖二等奖 2 项。

郑 慧 敏

郑慧敏女士为恒生银行副董事长兼行政总裁、恒生银行（中国）及恒生集团内若干附属公司之董事长、恒生指数顾问委员会主席、澳洲 Treasury Wine Estates Limited（富邑葡萄酒集团）独立非执行董事以及何梁何利基金信托委员会委员。郑慧敏亦为汇丰控股集团总经理。

郑慧敏于 1999 年加入汇丰集团，曾出任个人理财服务及市场推广业务多个要职。2007 年获委任为香港个人理财服务主管；2009 年为亚太区个人理财服务董事；2010 年为亚太区零售银行及财富管理业务主管。2014 年被委任为汇丰集团环球零售银行业务主管，至 2017 年出任恒生银行副董事长兼行政总裁。2017—2020 年出任香港上海汇丰银行董事。

郑慧敏目前亦出任下列机构职务：
- 香港恒生大学校董会主席
- 香港大学校董
- 江苏省港商投资企业服务协会荣誉会长
- 中国银联国际顾问
- 第十二届江苏省政协委员
- 中国（广东）自由贸易试验区深圳前海蛇口片区暨深圳市前海深港现代服务业合作区咨询委员会委员
- 香港银行学会副会长

其过往职务包括：
- 美国花旗银行市场总监
- 香港按揭证券有限公司董事
- 汇丰集团多间公司董事
- 香港公益金董事及执行委员会委员

郑慧敏毕业于香港大学并取得社会科学学士学位，为 Beta Gamma Sigma 香港大学分会终身荣誉会员。

沈 祖 尧

沈祖尧，1959 年出生。1983 年取得香港大学内外全科医学士学位，1992 年获得加拿大卡尔加里大学生命科学博士学位并于 1997 年获得香港中文大学医学博士学位。沈祖尧为中国工程院院士，英国爱丁堡、格拉斯哥及伦敦皇家内科医学院院士，美国肠胃病学学院院士，澳洲皇家内科医学院院士，香港内科医学院院士，香港医学专科学院院士及香港科学院创会院士。

曾任香港中文大学医学院内科学系讲师、内科及药物治疗学系系主任、医学院副院长、逸夫书院院长等职，并于 2010—2017 年担任香港中文大学校长。

为肠胃研究权威，研究对象包括肠道出血、幽门螺杆菌、消化性溃疡、乙型肝炎和大肠癌，其研究成果为世界肠胃病的防治带来了重大影响及改变。2004 年，他带领由 15 个亚太国家的专家组成的团队开展了大肠癌筛查研究，为筛查制定了清晰的规范，并在亚太地区推广大肠癌筛查。此外，他还积极开展科研，著作甚丰，在国际期刊发表逾千篇科研文章，写作逾 15 本书籍，并为逾 15 本著名期刊担任评审。

现任新加坡南洋理工大学李光前医学院院长及高级副校长（健康及生命科学）。同时为香港中文大学荣休讲座教授。

BRIEF INTRODUCTION TO THE TRUSTEES OF HO LEUNG HO LEE FOUNDATION

Brief Biography of Professor Zhu Lilan

Professor Zhu Lilan, female, born in Shanghai in August 1935, is the member of the Standing Committee of the National People's Congress, the director of the Science, Education, Culture and Health Commission of the National People's Congress, former minister of the Ministry of Science and Technology of China. From 1956 to 1961, Professor Zhu studied in the Aodesa University of former Soviet Union majoring in macromolecule physical chemistry. After graduated from the university as an excellent student, Professor Zhu worked in the Institute of Chemistry, Chinese Academy of Sciences till 1986. For a long time, Professor Zhu had been conducted the research of macromolecule reactivity dynamics, macromolecule material analysis and structure token. The research project had got the national award of Grand Research Achievements and Award of Application Achievements. During this period, Professor Zhu served as the director of the research department and the director of the Institute of Chemistry, Chinese Academy of Sciences.

From 1979 to 1980, Professor Zhu was a visiting scholar in macromolecule institute in Fleberg University in Germany. In her research, she developed a kind of new dyeing technique for the sample producing, which was considered a break through at that time and won high reputation in the research circle.

From 1986 to 2001, Professor Zhu was appointed vice-minister of the State Science and Technology Commission and minister of the Ministry of Science and Technology of China. During this period, Professor Zhu organized the formulating and implementation of the National High-Tech Development Plan (863 Plan), National Climbing Plan for the Basic Research, and Torch Program for the High-Tech Industrialization. Professor Zhu advocated and implemented the new expertise management mechanism, put forward a series of management theories and policies which suit to the development of high-tech and the situation of China, published her monograph *High-tech, Development Strategy in the Contemporary Era, Development and Challenge*. Owing to her outstanding contribution to promoting international science and technology cooperation and the development of China's high-tech research and industrialization, Professor Zhu was awarded the Outstanding Service Prize in 1993 by the American Association of Chinese Engineers, and the Germany Federal President Star Great Cross Medal in 1998.

Professor Zhu has been the counselor of Chinese Academy of Engineering Presidium, the counselor of Chinese Academy of Science Presidium, the member of State Science and Education Steering Group, member of Central Rural Work Steering Group, member of State Informationaliza-tion Steering Group, director–commissioner of State Award Commission. Professor Zhu is now the member of China Chemistry Society Administrative Council, the administrative member of the board of the Association of China Foreign Friendship Relations, the member of board of China Nat-ural Dialectic Seminar, the director of China Material Seminar. Professor Zhu is also the concurrent Professors of Beijing University of Science and Technology, National Administration College, Tsinghua University, Chemistry Institute of Chinese Academy of Sciences. Professor Zhu is the academician of International Europe and Asia Academy of Science, and the academician of Asian and Pacific Material Academy of Science.

Brief Biography of Mr. Sun Yu

Mr. Sun has been appointed as Vice Chairman and Chief Executive of BOC Hong Kong (Holdings) Limited and Bank of China (Hong Kong) Limited since December 2020. He is a member of each of the Strategy and Budget Committee and the Sustainability Committee. Prior to the re–designation, Mr.Sun was a Non–executive Director and a member of the Risk Committee of the Group from March 2020 to December 2020.

Mr. Sun joined BOC in 1998. He served as the Executive Vice President of BOC from February 2019 to December 2020, and as Chief Overseas Business Officer of BOC from September 2018 to February 2019. From March 2015 to November 2018, Mr.Sun served as General Manager of London Branch of BOC, CEO of Bank of China (UK) Limited, and also served as General Manager of London Trading Center of BOC from December 2015 to November 2018. Mr.Sun previously served as Director of Global Financial Markets Department, Director of Financial Markets Unit (Client Business), Director of Financial Markets Unit (Securities Investments) and Deputy General Manager of the Shanghai Branch of BOC. He served as General Manager of Global Markets of BOCHK from July 2012 to December 2014. He was also Chairman of the Board of Directors of BOC Aviation Limited (listed in Hong Kong) from February 2019 to December 2020, President of Shanghai RMB Trading Unit of BOC from November 2019 to December 2020 and General Manager of Beijing Branch of BOC from December 2019 to December 2020.

Mr. Sun holds other roles with the group, including Chairman of the Board of Directors of Bank of China (UK) Limited, Chairman of BOC Insurance (International) Holdings Company Limited, Chairman of BOC Group Life Assurance Company Limited and Chairman of BOCHK Charitable Foundation. Mr.Sun also holds a number of public offices in Hong Kong. He serves as Chairman of the Chinese Banking Association of Hong Kong, and sits on the Exchange Fund Advisory Committee, the Banking Advisory Committee, the Council of Treasury Markets Association, the General Committee of the Hong Kong General Chamber of Commerce, the Belt and Road and Greater Bay Area Committee of the Hong Kong Trade Development Council, and the Risk Management Committee of the Hong Kong Exchanges and Clearing Limited. He is also Director of Hong Kong Note Printing Limited, as well as Vice President of the Hong Kong Institute of Bankers, etc.

Mr. Sun graduated from Nankai University with a Master's Degree in Economics in 1998.

Brief Biography of Mr. Zhong Denghua

Zhong Denghua was born in November 1963. He earned a doctorate in engineering from Tianjin University. He is currently Vice Minister and member of CPC Leading Group of Ministry of Education. He served as the deputy secretary of the CPC committee and president of Tianjin University. He was elected a member of the Chinese Academy of Engineering in 2009.

Zhong Denghua has long been engaged in the training of talents and scientific research in the field of hydraulic engineering. He put forward theories, methodologies and developed technologies in the following areas: intelligent simulation and real−time control of hydraulic projects, precision modeling and analysis of the geological conditions of hydraulic projects, and intelligent control in the construction of hydraulic projects and digital dam.

Zhong Denghua has undertaken and completed the tasks of tackling hard−nut problems or technological development in more than 10 national major projects. The research achievements he has scored have been applied in more than 80 hydraulic and hydroelectric power projects in China, and have played important roles in improving the level and efficiency of project design, guaranteeing project quality and saving project investment. He was presented with 2 second−prizes of the State Science and Technology Advancement Award as the first complete person.

Brief Biography of Ms Louisa Cheang

Ms Louisa Cheang is Vice−Chairman and Chief Executive of Hang Seng Bank, and Chairman of Hang Seng Bank (China) and various subsidiaries in Hang Seng Group. She is Chairman of Hang Seng Index Advisory Committee of Hang Seng Indexes, an Independent Non−executive Director of Treasury Wine Estates Limited, Australia and a Member of the Board of Trustees of the Ho Leung Ho Lee Foundation. She is also a Group General Manager of HSBC.

Ms Cheang joined HSBC in 1999, and has worked across a wide range of Personal Financial Services and Marketing positions. She was appointed Head of Personal Financial Services, Hong

Kong in 2007; Regional Director of Personal Financial Services, Asia Pacific in 2009; and Regional Head of Retail Banking and Wealth Management, Asia Pacific in 2010. Ms Cheang became Group Head of Retail Banking, HSBC in 2014 prior to her appointment as Vice-Chairman and Chief Executive of Hang Seng Bank in 2017. She was also a Director of The Hongkong and Shanghai Banking Corporation from 2017 to 2020.

Ms Cheang currently also holds the following appointments:

- Chairman of the Board of Governors of The Hang Seng University of Hong Kong
- Member of the Court of The University of Hong Kong
- Honorary President of Jiangsu Service Association for Hong Kong Enterprise Investment
- International Advisor of China Union Pay
- Member of The Twelfth Jiangsu Provincial Committee of the Chinese People's Political Consultative Conference
- Member of the Consulting Committee of Qianhai & Shekou Area of Shenzhen, China (Guangdong) Pilot Free Trade Zone, and Qianhai Shenzhen-Hong Kong Modern Service Industry Cooperation Zone of Shenzhen
- Vice President of The Hong Kong Institute of Bankers

Her previous appointments include:

- Marketing Director of Citibank N.A.
- Director of The Hong Kong Mortgage Corporation Limited
- Director of various subsidiaries in HSBC
- Board Member and Member of Executive Committee of The Community Chest of Hong Kong

Ms Cheang graduated from The University of Hong Kong receiving a Bachelor of Social Sciences degree. She was made a Chapter Honoree of Beta Gamma Sigma of The University of Hong Kong Chapter.

Brief Biography of Joseph Jao-Yiu Sung

Joseph Jao-Yiu Sung was born in 1959. He received his medical degree (MB BS) from The University of Hong Kong in 1983, and conferred Ph.D in biomedical sciences by the University of Calgary in 1992 and MD by The Chinese University of Hong Kong (CUHK) in 1997. He is an Academician of the Chinese Academy of Engineering of the People's Republic of China and holds fellowships from the Royal Colleges of Physicians of Edinburgh, Glasgow, London, and Australia, the American College of Gastroenterology, the American Gastroenterological Association, the Hong Kong College of Physicians, the Hong Kong Academy of Medicine and Hong Kong Academy of Sciences (ASHK).

He joined the CUHK's Department of Medicine as Lecturer in 1992, and became Chairman of Department of Medicine and Therapeutics (1999—2010), Associate Dean (Clinical)(2002—2004), Associate Dean (General Affairs) (2004—2009) of the Faculty of Medicine, Head of Shaw College (2009—2010) and the Vice-Chancellor and President of CUHK (2010—2017) .

A world-renowned scientist in Gastroenterology and Hepatology, Professor Sung's research interests include intestinal bleeding, Helicobacter Pylori, peptic ulcer, hepatitis B, and colorectal cancer. Professor Sung, together with his research team, has pioneered several projects, the results of which have a major impact on and have changed the practice of gastroenterology worldwide. He led a group of 15 Asia-Pacific countries to launch colorectal cancer screening research in 2004 and laid down clear guidelines and promoted colorectal screenings in the region. A tireless prolific researcher, Professor Sung has published over 1000 scientific articles in international journals, authored more than 15 books, and refereed for more than 15 prestigious journals.

He is currently the Senior Vice-President (Health & Life Sciences) and Dean of Lee Kong Chian School of Medicine of Nanyang Technological University, Singapore. He is also the Emeritus Professor of Medicine at The Chinese University of Hong Kong.

何梁何利基金评选委员会成员简历

评选委员会主任
朱 丽 兰

　　朱丽兰，女，1935年8月出生，浙江湖州人，教授。现任中国发明协会理事长，澳门特别行政区科技奖励委员会主任。曾任国家科委副主任（1986年）、国家科学技术部部长（1998年），全国人大常委会教科文卫委员会主任委员（2001年），中国工程院主席团顾问，中国科学院学部主席团顾问，国家科教领导小组成员，国家科技奖励委员会主任委员，澳门特别行政区科学技术委员会顾问等职。

　　在中国科学院化学所从事高分子材料剖析及结构形态表征、反应动力学研究期间，承担了多项国家、国防重点科研攻关项目，曾获国家级、省部级重大科研成果奖及应用成果奖。担任全国人大常委会教科文卫委员会主任委员期间，负责组织完成《科技进步法》《义务教育法》的修订和实施；组织实施一批关系到社会、民生、科技、文化、卫生等重要法律的立法调研与修法任务，为法制建设奠定重要基础。

　　发表了多篇有关高技术发展现状及对策和管理方面的文章，出版了《当代高技术与发展战略》《发展与挑战》等专著。曾获中国材料研究学会成就奖。由于在推动中国高技术发展及国际科技合作方面成绩显著，获美洲中国工程师协会颁发的杰出服务奖、德国总统颁发的德意志联邦共和国大十字勋章、乌克兰总统二级勋章。

评选委员会副主任
钟 登 华

　　钟登华，1963年11月出生。天津大学工学博士。现任教育部党组成员、副部长。曾任天津大学党委副书记、校长。2009年当选中国工程院院士。

长期从事水利工程领域的人才培养和科学研究工作。提出了水利工程智能仿真与实时控制理论方法与技术、水利工程地质精细建模与分析理论方法与技术、水利工程建设智能控制数字大坝理论方法与技术。

先后承担并完成10余项国家重大工程的科技攻关或技术开发任务，研究成果在我国80多项水利水电工程中得到推广应用，在提高工程设计水平与效率、保证工程质量和节省工程投资方面发挥了重要作用。作为第一完成人获国家科技进步奖二等奖2项。

评选委员会副主任
沈 祖 尧

沈祖尧，1959年出生。1983年取得香港大学内外全科医学士学位，1992年获得加拿大卡尔加里大学生命科学博士学位并于1997年获得香港中文大学医学博士学位。沈祖尧为中国工程院院士，英国爱丁堡、格拉斯哥及伦敦皇家内科医学院院士，美国肠胃病学学院院士，澳洲皇家内科医学院院士，香港内科医学院院士，香港医学专科学院院士及香港科学院创会院士。

曾任香港中文大学医学院内科学系讲师、内科及药物治疗学系系主任、医学院副院长、逸夫书院院长等职，并于2010—2017年担任香港中文大学校长。

为肠胃研究权威，研究对象包括肠道出血、幽门螺杆菌、消化性溃疡、乙型肝炎和大肠癌，其研究成果为世界肠胃病的防治带来了重大影响及改变。2004年，他带领由15个亚太国家的专家组成的团队开展了大肠癌筛查研究，为筛查制定了清晰的规范，并在亚太地区推广大肠癌筛查。此外，他还积极开展科研，著作甚丰，在国际期刊发表逾千篇科研文章，写作逾15本书籍，并为逾15本著名期刊担任评审。

现任新加坡南洋理工大学李光前医学院院长及高级副校长（健康及生命科学）。同时为香港中文大学荣休讲座教授。

评选委员会秘书长
段 瑞 春

段瑞春，1943年2月出生。上海交通大学工学学士，中国科学院研究生院理学硕士，北京大学法学硕士；20世纪90年代，任国家科委政策法规与体制改革司司长、国务院知识产权办公会议办公室主任，2000—2007年任国务院国有重点大型企业监事会主席。现任中国科学技术法学会会长、中国产学研合作促进会常务副会长。

我国知识产权、科技政策和企业创新领域著名专家，具有自然科学、经济管理和法律科学复合型知识结构。曾主持起草我国《技术合同法》《科学技术进步法》《国家科技奖励条例》等法律法规，参加多项知识产权法律的制定和修改工作；担任中美、中欧、中俄科技合作知识产权谈判首席代表、中国"入世"知识产权谈判主要代表；《国家知识产权战略》总报告评审组组长；何梁何利基金《信托契约》《评选章程》主要制定者之一。

其研究成果于1992年获得国家科委科技进步奖一等奖、1993年获得国家科技进步奖二等奖，均为第一完成人。2004年获我国技术市场建设功勋奖，2008年获中国科技法学杰出贡献奖。撰写出版《国际合作与知识产权》《技术合同原理与实践》《技术创新读本》《科技政策多维思考》等多部著作。

评选委员会委员
马 永 生

马永生，1961年10月出生于内蒙古自治区呼和浩特市。石油地质学家、沉积学家。1980年至1990年先后就读于中国地质大学（原武汉地质学院）和中国地质科学院，获博士学位。现任中国石化集团公司副总经理、总地质师。2009年当选中国工程院院士。

长期从事中国油气资源勘探理论研究和生产实践，在中国海相碳酸盐岩油气勘探理论和技术方面取得了多项创新性成果，成功指导发现了普光、元坝等多个大型、特大型天然气田，为国家重大工程"川气东送"提供了扎实的资源基础。他在非常规天然气领域的前瞻性研究，为中国第一个页岩气田——涪陵页岩气田的发现做出了重要贡献。他的科研成果对缓解我国天然气供需矛盾、发展地区经济与环境保护起到了重要的促进作用。

获国家科技进步奖一等奖 2 项；2007 年获何梁何利科学与技术成就奖，同年获第十次李四光地质科学奖；2013 年被评为国家首批"万人计划"杰出人才。由于他在石油工业界的杰出成果，2017 年国际小行星中心将国际编号为 210292 号小行星命名为"马永生星"。

评选委员会委员
王 小 凡

王小凡，著名癌症生物学家。1955 年出生于乌鲁木齐市，1982 年毕业于武汉大学生物化学专业，同年考入中国科学院遗传研究所，并在当年举办的首届"中美生物化学联合招生项目"（CUSBEA）中取得第一名的成绩赴美留学。1986 年获加州大学洛杉矶分校博士学位，之后在麻省理工学院师从癌症生物学家 Robert A. Weinberg 从事博士后研究。1992 年被聘为杜克大学药理学和肿瘤生物学系助理教授，成为最早在杜克大学执教的华人教授之一。1998 年成为终身教授，2003 年晋升为正教授。现任杜克大学医学中心药理学和肿瘤生物学 Donald and Elizabeth Cooke 终身讲席教授。

王小凡在细胞信号转导、DNA 损伤与修复、癌症转移分子机制、肿瘤微环境等多个领域均有重要学术贡献，尤其在 TGF-β 相关研究领域取得了令人瞩目的成绩。先后发表了 100 多篇学术论文，其中在 *Cell*、*Nature*、*Science*、*Cancer Cell*、*Nature Cell Biology* 等高水平杂志上发表论文 20 余篇。王小凡长期坚持通过多种渠道为中国的教育科技事业建言献策，推动、促成了一系列改善中国教育科研环境的政策制度，目前担任中国国务院侨办海外专家咨询委员会委员。

评选委员会委员
朱 道 本

朱道本，1942 年 8 月出生于上海，原籍浙江杭州。有机化学、物理化学家，中国科学院化学研究所研究员，1997 年 10 月当选为中国科学院院士。

1965 年毕业于华东化工学院，1968 年华东化工学院有机系研究生学习后到中国科学院化学研究所工作。曾任中国科学院化学研究所副所长、所长、中国化学会理事长、国家自然科学基金会副主任。现任中国科学院学术委员会副主任、中国科学院有机固体重点实验室主任等职。

20 世纪 70 年代开始有机固体领域的研究，在有机晶体的电导、铁磁性、分子薄膜与器件、C60 及其衍生物的结构性能等研究都引起了国际同行的关注。发表论文 500 余篇，研究成果曾获国家自然科学奖二等奖 4 项，中国科学院自然科学奖二等奖 2 项。

评选委员会委员
杨 祖 佑

杨祖佑，1940 年出生。获美国康奈尔大学博士学位。先后任普度大学航空宇宙工程系主任，工学院院长；曾兼任美国国家科学基金会智能制造工程中心共同主任，同时任阿姆斯特朗（首位登陆月球者）杰出宇航讲座教授。现任美国圣塔芭芭拉加州大学校长（1994 年始任），美国国家工程院院士，美国航天、机械学会 Fellow，中国工程院海外院士。兼任美、中、印、日、加"三十米望远镜"计划（简称 TMT 计划）主席，太平洋滨 42 所大学联盟主席（包括北大、清华、复旦、科大、浙大、南京），美国总统科学奖章评委，科维理科学基金会理事，曾任美国大学联盟（AAU，包括 62 所顶尖研究型大学）主席，芬兰千禧科技奖评委。共获 7 所大学荣誉博士。

长期致力于教学及科研。从事宇航结构、颤振、控制转型至地震、制造、材料（LED）及生物工程等方面的研究，亲任博士论文主席指导 60 篇，发表期刊论文 200 余篇，学术会议论文 200 余篇，有限元教科书 1 本（被 40 余所美国大学采用，有中文、日文版）。

曾获 2008 年美国航天学会结构、振动、材料奖（SDM Award），美国工程教育学会最高李梅金质奖章以及十余次最佳教学奖。

评选委员会委员
杨 纲 凯

杨纲凯，1948 年 7 月出生于上海市。自 1973 年起任职香港中文大学，曾任物理系主任、理学院院长、研究院院长、副校长。现任香港中文大学敬文书院院长、物理系教授，香港特别行政区教育统筹委员会委员、课程发展议会主席。曾任香港特别行政区大学教育资助委员会委员及香港研究资助局主席，亚太物理联会秘书长、副会长。1965—1972 年就读于美国加州理工学院，主修物理，1969 年获学士学位，1972 年获博士学位。1972—1973 年在美国普林斯顿大学从事教学及研究。

长期从事理论物理学研究，包括基本粒子、场论、高能唯象、耗散系统及其本征态展开，对光学、引力波等开放系统的应用做出贡献，其主要研究成果载于有关国际杂志，包括 Microscopic derivation of the Helmholtz force density, Phys Rev Lett 47, 77; Late time tail of wave propagation on curved spacetime, Phys Rev Lett 74, 2414; Quasinormal mode expansion for linearized waves in gravitational systems, Phys Rev Lett 74, 4588; Quasinormal modes of dirty black holes, Phys Rev Lett 78, 289 等。1999 年被选为美国物理学会院士，2004 年被选为国际欧亚科学院院士。

评选委员会委员
吴 伟 仁

吴伟仁，1953 年出生，中国探月工程总设计师，航天测控通信和深空探测工程总体技术专家。中国工程院院士，国际宇航科学院院士，全国政协常委。我国深空探测领域主要开拓者之一和航天战略科学家。

先后获国家科技进步特等奖 3 项，一等奖 2 项；获首届全国创新争先奖章，何梁何利科学与技术成就奖，钱学森最高成就奖等。2020 年获国际宇航联合会最高奖——世界航天奖。鉴于他在航天领域的杰出贡献，国际天文学联合会将国际永久编号 281880 小行星命名为"吴伟仁星"。

评选委员会委员
张 立 同

张立同，女，1938 年 4 月出生于重庆，著名航空航天材料专家。1961 年毕业于西北工业大学。1989—1991 年在美国 NASA 空间结构材料商业发展中心作高级访问学者。现任西北工业大学教授、博士生导师、超高温结构复合材料技术国家重点实验室学术委员会副主任。1995 年当选中国工程院院士。

致力于航空航天材料及其制造技术研究，在薄壁复杂高温合金和铝合金铸件的无余量熔模精密铸造技术及其理论基础研究中取得丰硕成果。揭示了叶片变形规律、粗糙度形成规律和陶瓷型壳中温和高温软化变形机理。创新发展了高温合金无余量熔模铸造技术、铝合金石膏型熔模铸造技术、高温合金熔模铸造用中温和高温抗蠕变陶瓷型壳材料、高温合金泡沫陶瓷过滤净化材料技术等。相关成果成功用于航空发动机和飞机构件生产中。

突破大型空间站用陶瓷基复合材料技术，建立了具有自主知识产权的制造工艺、制造设备与材料环境性能考核三个技术平台，打破了国际技术封锁。

获国家技术发明奖一等奖 1 项，国家科技进步奖一、二、三等奖 4 项，国家级教学成果奖二等奖 1 项，获授权国家发明专利 64 项。

评选委员会委员
张 恭 庆

张恭庆，1936年5月29日出生于上海。1959年毕业于北京大学数学系，毕业后留校工作至今。1978年作为我国改革开放后第一批赴美访问学者赴美进修。现为北京大学教授、中国科学院院士、发展中国家（第三世界）科学院院士、高校数学研究与人才培养中心主任，还担任多个国际核心刊物的编委。

著名数学家。发展无穷维 Morse 理论为临界点理论的统一框架，并首次将其应用于偏微分方程的多解问题，其著作成为该领域的基本文献。发展了集值映射的拓扑度理论以及不可微泛函的临界点理论，使之成为研究数学物理方程以及非光滑力学中的一类自由边界问题的有效方法。

曾荣获全国科技大会奖（1978）、国家自然科学奖三等奖（1982）、国家自然科学奖二等奖（1987）、陈省身数学奖（1986）、有突出贡献的中青年科学家（1984）、第三世界科学院数学奖（1993）、华罗庚数学奖（2009）、北京大学国华奖、方正教学特等奖（2011）等。

评选委员会委员
陈 佳 洱

陈佳洱，1934年10月1日出生于上海。中国科学院院士、第三世界科学院院士。现任北京大学物理学教授，国家重点基础研究计划（"973"计划）专家顾问组副组长，国际科联中国协调委员会副主席等职。

曾任北京大学校长和研究生院院长、国家自然科学基金委员会主任、中国科学院数理学部主任和中科院主席团成员以及中科院研究生院物理科学学院院长等职。

长期致力于低能粒子加速器及其应用的教学与科研工作，善于把握学科前沿发展与国家需求的结合，前瞻性地部署物理研究与人才培养，开拓发展我国的射频超导加速器、超灵敏加速器质谱计、射频四极场加速器、高压静电加速器等，是我国低能粒子加速器的奠基者和领头人之一。

陈佳洱长期在北京大学和国家自然科学基金委等单位担任领导工作，并曾担任国家中长期科技规划领导小组成员等职，为我国科学技术中长期规划的制订与相关的科教事业的发展做出了重要贡献。

评选委员会委员
郝 吉 明

郝吉明，1946年8月出生于山东省，著名环境工程专家。1970年毕业于清华大学，1981年获清华大学硕士学位，1984年获美国辛辛那提大学博士学位。现任清华大学教授、博士生导师、教学委员会副主任、环境科学与工程研究院院长，兼任国家环境咨询委员会委员、中国环境与发展国际合作委员会委员。2005年当选中国工程院院士，2018年当选美国国家工程院外籍院士。

致力于中国空气污染控制研究40余年，主要研究领域为能源与环境、大气污染控制工程。主持全国酸沉降控制规划与对策研究，划定酸雨和二氧化硫控制区，被国务院采纳实施，为确定我国酸雨防治对策起到主导作用。建立了城市机动车污染控制规划方法，推动了我国机动车污染控制进程。深入开展大气复合污染特征、成因及控制策略研究，发展了特大城市空气质量改善的理论与技术方法，推动我国区域性大气复合污染的联防联控。长期开展大气污染控制关键技术研究，在燃煤烟气除尘脱硫脱硝、机动车污染控制等领域做出贡献。

获国家科技进步奖一等奖1项、二等奖2项，国家自然科学奖二等奖和国家技术发明奖二等奖各1项，国家教学成果奖一等奖2项。2006年获国家教学名师称号，获2015年度哈根–斯密特清洁空气奖及2016年IBM全球杰出学者奖。

评选委员会委员
钱 绍 钧

钱绍钧，1934 年出生于浙江平湖。1951 年考入清华大学物理系，后在北京俄语专科学校和北京大学物理系、物理研究室（现技术物理系）学习。现任原总装备部科技委顾问，研究员，中国工程院院士。曾任核试验基地副司令员、司令员，国防科工委科技委常任委员。

长期从事核试验放射化学诊断工作，参与了由原子弹到氢弹、由大气层到地下的一系列核试验，建立完善多项诊断方法和技术，显著提升测量精度。多次参加国防科技和武器装备发展战略研究，参与组织国家中长期科学技术发展规划专题研究。指导开展国防应用基础研究，努力促进与国家基础研究的协调链接。指导军用核技术发展，长期跟踪研究国际态势及主要国家政策演变，参与军备控制研究和"全面禁止核试验条约"谈判。

出版译著 1 部，主编专著 2 部，撰写科技论文和重要科技档案多篇，获国家科技进步奖特等奖、二等奖各 1 项，国家发明奖二等奖、三等奖各 1 项，军队科技进步奖多项。

评选委员会委员
倪 军

倪军，1961 年 11 月出生于青海，著名制造科学专家。1982 年获上海交通大学学士学位。1984 年和 1987 年分别获得美国威斯康星大学硕士和博士学位。1987 年起在美国密歇根大学任教至今。现为美国密歇根大学吴贤铭制造科学冠名教授及机械工程系终身教授；上海交通大学校长特聘顾问、交大密西根学院荣誉院长，并同时担任美国密西根大学吴贤铭制造研究中心主任及美国国家科学基金会产学研"智能维护系统中心"共同主任。倪军教授目前担任世界经济论坛（达沃斯论坛）未来制造委员会主席。

曾担任美国国家科学基金会"可重组制造系统中心"执行主任及美国国家科学基金会产学研"制造质量测量与控制中心"主任。倪军教授主要从事先进制造科学领域中智能制造技术的研究，包括基于工业大数据分析和人工智能技术在精密质量控制、制造过程效率优化、重大装备的可靠性和健康预测管理、智能维护系统等研究。他的研究成果在众多工业领域得到成功应用。

倪军教授获得 40 多项学术成就奖。2013 年获中华人民共和国国际科技合作奖；1994 年获克林顿颁发的美国总统教授奖；2013 年获国际制造工程师协会金奖，是该奖 1955 年设立之后首位获此殊荣的华人学者；2009 年获美国机械工程学会 William T. Ennor 最高制造技术奖；2002 年当选为美国制造工程师学会 FELLOW；2004 年当选为美国机械工程学会 FELLOW；1991 年获国际制造工程师学会杰出制造工程师奖。

评选委员会委员
桑 国 卫

桑国卫，1941 年 11 月出生，浙江湖州人。临床药理学家，中国工程院院士。中国药学会理事长，"十一五""十二五""十三五"国家"重大新药创制"重大专项技术总师，工信部"医药工业'十三五'发展规划"专家咨询委员会主任，中国药品生物制品检定所资深研究员，上海中医药大学名誉校长。曾任十一届全国人大常委会副委员长、农工民主党中央主席。

对长效注射与口服甾体避孕药及抗孕激素的药代动力学、种族差异及临床药理学做了系统研究，取得多项重大成果。近年来，在新药的安全性评价、质量控制和临床试验等方面进行了卓有成效的工作，为加强我国 GLP、GCP 平台建设做出了重要贡献。

获全国科技大会奖 2 项，国家科学技术进步奖二等奖 3 项，部委级科技进步奖一等奖 1 项、二等奖 4 项。1997 年获何梁何利科学与技术进步奖（医学药学奖）。2008 年获吴阶平—保罗·杨森奖特殊贡献奖。2014 年获国际药学联合会药学科学终身成就奖。

评选委员会委员
曹 雪 涛

曹雪涛，1964 年 7 月出生，山东济南人。1990 年毕业于第二军医大学。现为中国医学科学院院长、中国工程院院士、医学免疫学国家重点实验室主任，兼任中国免疫学会理事长、全球慢性疾病防控联盟主席、亚洲大洋洲免疫学会联盟主席等。担任 *Cell* 等杂志编委。

主要从事天然免疫识别及其免疫调节的基础研究、肿瘤免疫治疗应用性研究。发现了具有重要免疫调控功能的树突状细胞新型亚群；独立发现了 22 种免疫相关分子；系统研究了天然免疫识别与干扰素产生调控的新机制；探讨了表观分子在炎症与肿瘤发生发展中的作用；建立了肿瘤免疫治疗新途径并开展了临床试验。

以第一完成人获国家自然科学奖二等奖 1 项，中华医学科技奖一等奖 1 项，军队科技进步奖一等奖 1 项，上海市自然科学奖一等奖 3 项，已获得国家发明专利 16 项，获得 2 个国家 II 类新药证书。研究成果入选 2011 年中国十大科技进展。获得光华工程奖、长江学者成就奖、中国青年科学家奖、中国十大杰出青年等。以通讯作者发表 SCI 收录论文 220 余篇，包括 *Cell*、*Science*、*Nature Immunology*、*Cancer Cell*、*Immunity* 等。论文被 SCI 他引 5600 多次；编写和共同主编专著 8 部；培养的博士生中有 11 名获得全国百篇优秀博士论文。

评选委员会委员
程　　序

程序，1944 年出生，江苏无锡人。1965 年毕业于北京农业大学（现中国农业大学）农学系，后入中国农业科学院作物育种栽培研究所从事研究工作。现为中国农业大学教授，博导。曾就职于北京市农科院、农业部等单位。主要研究方向为可持续农业与农村发展、农业生态与生态农业以及生物能源等。

曾主持农业现代化规律和实验基地建设（实验基

地：北京市房山区窦店村）以及生态农业两个研究项目。1985年率先引进农业可持续发展的理论，此后开始研究中国条件下农业可持续发展的途径。重点放在农牧交错生态脆弱带的生态恢复途径，以及探索可持续的集约化农业模式的研究两个方面。

作为第一完成人，先后被授予北京市科技进步奖一等奖及国家星火科技奖（等同科技进步奖）一等奖。累计获省部级科技进步奖二、三等奖7项，1988年被批准为国家级有突出贡献的中青年专家。

著有《可持续农业导论》和《中国可持续发展总纲第13卷：中国农业与可持续发展》两部专著。

评选委员会委员
曾 庆 存

曾庆存，1935年5月出生于广东省阳江市（原阳江县）。1956年毕业于北京大学物理系。1961年在苏联科学院应用地球物理研究所获副博士（现称博士即Ph.D）学位。回国后先后在中国科学院地球物理研究所和大气物理研究所工作。1980年当选中国科学院院士。现为中国科学院大气物理研究所研究员。

主要研究领域为大气科学和地球流体力学。致力于大气环流和地球流体动力学基础理论和数值模式及模拟、地球系统动力学模式、数值天气预报和气候预测理论、气候动力学和季风理论、大气边界层动力学、卫星遥感理论方法、应用数学和计算数学以及自然控制论等的研究工作。在国际上最早提出半隐式差分法和平方守恒格式，最早成功将原始方程应用于实际数值天气预告（1961）和研制成大气海洋耦合模式并用作跨季度气候预测（1990，1994），提出系统的卫星大气遥感理论（1974）以及自然控制论理论方法（1995）。

曾获国家自然科学奖二等奖2项和三等奖1项，中国科学院自然科学奖一等奖6项和杰出贡献奖1项。出版专著包括《大气红外遥测原理》《数值天气预报的数学物理基础》《短期数值气候预测原理》《千里黄云——东亚沙尘暴研究》等。发表学术文章约百篇。

BRIEF INTRODUCTION TO THE MEMBERS OF THE SELECTION BOARD OF HO LEUNG HO LEE FOUNDATION

Zhu Lilan, Director of the Selection Board

Zhu Lilan, female, was born in August 1935 and is of the origin of Huzhou, Zhejiang Province. At present, she is the Chairman of the China Association of Inventions and the Chairman of the Committee of Science and Technology Awards of Macau Special Administrative Region. She was the vice-minister of the State Science and Technology Commission (1986), the Minister of the Ministry of Science and Technology (1998), the Director of the Education, Science, Culture and Public Health Committee of the National People's Congress (2001), the counselor of Chinese Academy of Engineering Presidium, the Advisor of the Presidential Committee of CAS Academic Board, the Member of the State Leading Group of Science, Technology and Education, the Director of the State Committee of Science and Technology Awards and the Advisor of the Macao Science and Technology Council.

When analyzing polymer materials and researching morphological structure and reaction dynamics in the Institute of Chemistry of the Chinese Academy of Sciences, Zhu Lilan undertook several national and national defense key science and technological projects and was granted the statelevel and provincelevel significant scientific and technological result awards and application result awards. When being the Director of the Education, Science, Culture and Public Health Committee of the National People's Congress, she organized the amendments to and implementation of the Science and Technology Progress Law and the Compulsory Education Law; and organized a series of investigations for making the laws and amending the important laws concerning such matters as society, people's life, science and technology, culture and health, which has provided an important basis for legal construction.

Zhu Lilan has published several articles and books on the status quo of hi-tech development and the corresponding strategies and management measures, including *Modern Hi-tech. Development Strategy in the Contemporary Era* and *Development and Challenge*. She was granted the Achievement Award by the Chinese Materials Research Society. Thanks to her significant contribution to the development of China's hi-tech development and international scientific and technological cooperation, Zhu Lilan obtained the Distinguished Service Award granted by the Chinese Institute of Engineers, USA, the Grand Cross Medal of the Federal Republic of Germany granted by German President and the Medal No. 2 of Ukraine President.

Zhong Denghua, Deputy Director of the Selection Board

Zhong Denghua was born in November 1963. He earned a doctorate in engineering from Tianjin University. He is currently Vice Minister and member of CPC Leading Group of Ministry of Education. He served as the deputy secretary of the CPC committee and president of Tianjin University. He was elected a member of the Chinese Academy of Engineering in 2009.

Zhong Denghua has long been engaged in the training of talents and scientific research in the field of hydraulic engineering. He put forward theories, methodologies and developed technologies in the following areas: intelligent simulation and real—time control of hydraulic projects, precision modeling and analysis of the geological conditions of hydraulic projects, and intelligent control in the construction of hydraulic projects and digital dam.

Zhong Denghua has undertaken and completed the tasks of tackling hard—nut problems or technological development in more than 10 national major projects. The research achievements he has scored have been applied in more than 80 hydraulic and hydroelectric power projects in China, and have played important roles in improving the level and efficiency of project design, guaranteeing project quality and saving project investment. He was presented with 2 second—prizes of the State Science and Technology Advancement Award as the first complete person.

Joseph Jao-Yiu Sung, Vice Director of the Selection Board

Joseph Jao—Yiu Sung was born in 1959. He received his medical degree (MB BS) from The University of Hong Kong in 1983, and conferred Ph.D in biomedical sciences by the University of Calgary in 1992 and MD by The Chinese University of Hong Kong (CUHK) in 1997. He is an Academician of the Chinese Academy of Engineering of the People's Republic of China and holds fellowships from the Royal Colleges of Physicians of Edinburgh, Glasgow, London, and Australia, the American College of Gastroenterology, the American Gastroenterological Association, the Hong Kong College of Physicians, the Hong Kong Academy of Medicine and Hong Kong Academy of Sciences (ASHK) .

He joined the CUHK's Department of Medicine as Lecturer in 1992, and became Chairman of Department of Medicine and Therapeutics (1999 — 2010), Associate Dean (Clinical)(2002 — 2004), Associate Dean (General Affairs) (2004 — 2009) of the Faculty of Medicine, Head of Shaw College (2009 — 2010) and the Vice—Chancellor and President of CUHK (2010 — 2017) .

A world—renowned scientist in Gastroenterology and Hepatology, Professor Sung's research interests include intestinal bleeding, Helicobacter Pylori, peptic ulcer, hepatitis B, and colorectal cancer. Professor Sung, together with his research team, has pioneered several projects, the results of which have a major impact on and have changed the practice of gastroenterology worldwide. He led a group of 15 Asia–Pacific countries to launch colorectal cancer screening research in 2004 and laid down clear guidelines and promoted colorectal screenings in the region. A tireless prolific researcher, Professor Sung has published over 1000 scientific articles in international journals, authored more than 15 books, and refereed for more than 15 prestigious journals.

He is currently the Senior Vice–President (Health & Life Sciences) and Dean of Lee Kong Chian School of Medicine of Nanyang Technological University, Singapore. He is also the Emeritus Professor of Medicine at The Chinese University of Hong Kong.

Duan Ruichun, Secretary-General of the Selection Board

Duan Ruichun, born in February 1943, is a bachelor of engineer from Shanghai Jiaotong University, a master of science from Graduate University of Chinese Academy of Science and a master of law from Peking University. In the 1990s, he was the Director of the Policy, Law and System Reform Department of the State Science and Technology Commission and the Director of the Intellectual Property Working Meeting Office of the State Council. From 2000 to 2007, he was the Chairman of the Board of Supervisors for Key Large State–Owned Enterprises of the State Council. At present, Duan Ruichun is the Chairman of the China Association for Science and Technology and the permanent vice chairman of the China Association for Promotion of Cooperation among Industries, Universities & Research Institutes.

As a famous expert in China's intellectual property rights, scientific and technological policies and enterprise innovation, Duan Ruichun possesses interdisciplinary knowledge in natural science, economic management and legal science. He has led the drafting of many Chinese laws and regulations such as the Technology Contract Law, the Scientific and Technological Progress Law and the Regulation on National Awards for Science and Technology; he has participated in drafting of and amendments to many laws on intellectual property rights; he was the chief representative of the Intellectual Property Negotiations for Scientific and Technological Cooperation between China and the United States and the main representative of intellectual property negotiations in the process of China's entry into WTO; he was the Leader of the Review Team of the general report of the National IP Strategy; and he was one of the main person formulating the Trust Deed and the Selection Articles of the Ho Leung Ho Lee Foundation.

Due to his research results, Duan Ruichun was granted the first prize of the Science and Technology Progress Award by the State Science and Technology Commission in 1992 and granted the second prize of the Science and Technology Progress Award in 1993. He was granted the recognition award of China's technology market in 2004 and the significant contribution award of the China Law Association on Science and Technology in 2008. He has written and published several books such as *International Cooperation and Intellectual Property Rights*, *Principles and Practice of Technology Contracts*, *Guidelines on Technology Innovation* and *Multi-Dimensional Thinking of Scientific and Technological Policies*.

Ma Yongsheng, Member of the Selection Board

Ma Yongsheng, a petroleum geologist and sedimentologist, was born in Hohhot City of Inner Mongolia in October 1961. He obtained his bachelor's and master's degrees from China University of Geosciences (previously known as Wuhan College of Geology) and received his Ph.D from Chinese Academy of Geological Sciences in 1990. He is now the Vice President and Chief Geologist of China Petroleum & Chemical Corporation (Sinopec Group). He has been elected as academician of Chinese Academy of Engineering in 2009.

Over the past few decades, he devoted his career to the research and application of the petroleum and natural gas exploration theory. He has made great contributions to the marine carbonates hydrocarbon exploration theory with a number of leading technological and theoretical achievements. For instance, he led the successful discovery of several giant natural gas reservoirs in China, such as the Puguang and Yuanba gas fields, establishing solid foundations for the Sichuan-to-East China Gas Transmission Project. His pioneering research in unconventional natural gas contributed significantly to the discovery of Fuling shale gas field in Chongqing, China's first large-scale shale gas field. His research accomplishments have also remarkably facilitated the mitigation of natural gas supply-demand imbalance, as well as the promotion of regional economy and environmental protection in China.

Ma has won the 1st Prize of the National Science & Technology Progress Award twice. In 2007, he won the Scientific & Technological Achievements Award granted by the Ho Leung Ho Lee Foundation. In the same year, he won Li Siguang Geoscience Prize for the 10th time. In 2013, he was selected as one of China's first six outstanding scientists supported by the National Ten-Thousand Talents Program. For his distinguished achievement in the petroleum industry, the Minor Planet Center named No. 210292 asteroid officially after him as "Ma Yongsheng Planet" in 2017.

Wang Xiaofan, Member of the Selection Board

Wang Xiaofan is a renowned cancer biologist. He was born in Urumqi in 1955.

In 1982, he graduated from Wuhan University after completing an undergraduate program in biological chemistry, and was admitted into the Institute of Genetics, the Chinese Academy of

Sciences.

In the same year, he ranked the highest in the first China–United States Biochemistry Examination and Application (CUSBEA) and went to the U.S. to pursue further studies.

In 1986, he obtained the doctoral degree from the University of California, Los Angeles (UCLA) . Later he engaged in post–doctoral study by following Robert A. Weinberg, an eminent cancer biologist, at Massachusetts Institute of Technology (MIT) .

In 1992, he was engaged as an assistant professor by the Department of Pharmacology and Tumor Biology at Duke University, becoming one of the earliest Chinese professors who taught at Duke University.

He became a tenure–track professor in 1998 and was promoted to be a full professor in 2003.

He is the Donald and Elizabeth Cooke Professor of Cancer Research at the Department of Pharmacology and Cancer Biology, School of Medicine, Duke University.

Professor Wang Xiaofan has made important academic contributions in many fields including cell signal transduction, repair of DNA damage, molecular mechanism of cancer metastasis and tumor microenvironment. In particular, he has made eye–catching achievements in the field related to TGF–β. He has published more than 100 academic papers, of which more than 20 were published in high–level academic periodicals such as *Cell*, *Nature*, *Science*, *Cancer Cell* and *Nature Cell Biology*.

Over a long period of time, professor Wang Xiaofan has insisted on offering advice and putting forward suggestions on education and science and technology undertakings in China through various channels. He has promoted or brought about a series of policies and systems for improving the environment of education and scientific research in China. He currently serves as a member of the Overseas Expert Consultant Committee of Overseas Chinese Affairs Office of the State Council.

Zhu Daoben, Member of the Selection Board

Zhu Daoben, born in Shanghai in August 1942, came from Hangzhou, Zhejiang Province. As an organic and physical chemist, he is a researcher from the Institute of Chemistry of the Chinese Academy of Sciences. In October 1997, He was elected as an academician of the Chinese Academy of Sciences.

He graduated from East China Institute of Chemical Technology in 1965 and completed his postgraduate program at the Organic Chemistry Department of the Institute in 1968. Then he began his career at the Institute of Chemistry of the Chinese Academy of Sciences. Throughout his career, he has served as Deputy Director and Director of the Institute of Chemistry, Director–general of Chinese Chemical Society and Deputy Director of the National Natural Science Foundation. Currently, he is Vice Director of the Academic Committee of the Chinese Academy of Sciences and Director of the Key Laboratory of Organic Solids.

Since 1970s, Zhu has been involved in the research of organic solids and attracted international attention in the fields of conductance of organic crystal, ferromagnetism, molecular membranes and devices, structure performance of C60 and its derivatives. He has published over 500 papers. His research findings have won four National Natural Science Awards (Grade II) and two Natural Science Awards (Grade II) of the Chinese Academy of Sciences.

Henry T. Yang, Member of the Selection Board

Henry T. Yang was born in 1940. He obtained a Ph.D from Cornell University. He has served as Dean of the Aerospace Engineering Department and Head of the Engineering College of Purdue University. He used to be a co-director of the Smart Manufacturing Engineering center of the National Science Foundation (U. S.) and an outstanding professor of Armstrong (the first Moon lander) Astronautics Lectures. Currently, he is President of University of California Santa Barbara (since 1994), an academician of American Academy of Engineering, a fellow of both American Institute of Aeronautics and Astronautics and American Society of Mechanical Engineers, an overseas academician of Chinese Academy of Engineering and an academician of the Taiwan Academia Sinica. He is the chairman of the Thirty-metre Telescope Program (TMT Program) jointly sponsored by the United States, China, India, Japan and Canada. He is the chairman of the Association of Pacific Rim 42 Universities (including Peking University, Tsinghua University, Fudan University, University of Science and Technology of China, Zhejiang University and Nanjing University), a member of the Selection Board of the United States Presidential Medal of Science and a member of council of the Kavli Foundation. He used to be the Chairman of Association of American Universities (AAU) that consists of 62 top universities and a member of the Selection Board of Finnish Millennium Technology Grand Prize. He has been conferred seven honorary doctoral degrees.

He has been involved in teaching and research in aerospace structure, oscillation, control transition to earthquake, manufacturing, material (LED) and biological engineering. He has served as doctoral supervisor for sixty dissertations. He has published over 200 papers in journals, over 200 papers for academic conferences and one textbook on finite element (used by over forty American universities and translated into Chinese and Japanese).

He won the SDM Award granted by the American Institute of Aeronautics and Astronautics in 2008. He won Benjamin Garver Lamme Gold Metal, the highest one granted by the American Society for Engineering Education, and over ten excellent awards for education.

Kenneth Young, Member of the Selection Board

Born in July 1948 in Shanghai, Kenneth Young has been working at The Chinese University of Hong Kong (CUHK) since 1973, and has held the position of Chairman of the Department of Physics, Dean of the Faculty of Science, Dean of the Graduate School and Pro-Vice-Chancellor/Vice-President. At present, Kenneth Young is Master of the CW Chu College and professor of physics at CUHK. He is also a member of the Education Commission (EC) and the Chairman of the Curriculum Development Council of the Hong Kong SAR. He was a member of the Hong Kong University Grants Committee and Chairman its Research Grants Council. He was the Secretary and later Vice-President of the Association of Asia Pacific Physical Societies. Kenneth Young studied at the California Institute of Technology from 1965 to 1972 and obtained the BS in physics in 1969 and the Ph.D in physics and mathematics in 1972. He was engaged in teaching and research at Princeton University from 1972 to 1973.

Kenneth Young has been engaged in physics research for a long time, on topics including elementary particles, field theory, high energy phenomenology, dissipation system and their eigenfunctions expansion, with applications to such open systems as optics and gravitational waves. Some of his publications include "Microscopic derivation of the Helmholtz force density", Phys Rev Lett 47, 77; "Late time tail of wave propagation on curved spacetime", Phys Rev Lett 74, 2414; "Quasinormal mode expansion for linearized waves in gravitational systems", Phys Rev Lett 74, 4588; "Quasinormal modes of dirty black holes", Phys Rev Lett 78, 289. Kenneth Young was elected as a Fellow of the American Physical Society in 1999 and an academician of International Eurasian Academy of Science in 2004.

Wu Weiren, Member of the Selection Board

Wu Weiren was born in 1953. He is the designer-in-chief of China's Lunar Exploration Program, expert in aerospace TT&C and communication area and overall design technology in deep space exploration program; Prof. Wu is the academician of Chinese Academy of Engineering (CAE) and the member of International Academy of Astronautics (IAA), member of the standing committee of the National Committee of the Chinese People's Political Consultative Conference (CPPCC). He is also one of the main pioneers in the Chinese deep space exploration area and aerospace strategy scientist in China.

Prof. Wu has won 3 special awards and 2 first awards of national science and technology progress award, the first national innovation award, Ho Leung Ho Lee foundation for scientific and technological achievement award and Qian Xuesen's highest achievement award, etc. Also, Prof.

Wu has been given the World Space Award, the highest award of the International Astronautical Federation (IAF) in 2020. For his outstanding contributions to the field of aerospace, the International Astronomical Union (IAU) approved the official name of the asteroid numbered 281880 as "Wu Weiren star".

Zhang Litong, Member of the Selection Board

Zhang Litong, female, born in Chongqing in April of 1938, is a famous expert in aerospace materials. She graduated from Northwestern Polytechnical University in 1961. She was a senior visiting scholar in the Business Development Center of Spatial Structure Materials of NASA of the US from April 1989 to January 1991. Now, she acts as a professor and doctoral supervisor of Northwestern Polytechnical University and the deputy director of the Academic Committee of National Key Laboratory on Ultra-temperature Structure Composite Material Technology. She was elected as an academician of the Chinese Academy of Engineering in 1995.

She has been devoting himself to the research of aerospace materials and the technologies of manufacturing aerospace materials for many years and has achieved abundant research results in marginless melted module precise casting technologies and their fundamental theory research of thin-wall complex high-temperature alloy and aluminum alloy castings. She reveals the blade deformation rules, roughness generation rules and middle/high-temperature softening deformation mechanism of ceramic shells. Through independent innovation, she develops marginless melted module casting technology of high-temperature alloy, plaster-mold melted module casting technology of aluminum alloy, technology of middle/high-temperature creep-resisting ceramic shell materials for melted module casting of high-temperature alloy, and technology of foamed ceramic filtering and purifying materials for high-temperature alloy. Relevant achievements have been applied to production of aero-engines and aircraft components successfully.

After returning to China, she establishes three technology platforms with independent intellectual property rights (manufacturing process, manufacturing equipment and material and environment performance assessment), breaking international blockade on technologies.

She was awarded with one first-class prize of National Award for Technological Invention, four first-class, second-class and third-class prizes of National Award for Scientific and Technological Progress, one second-class prize of State-level Teaching Award. She is authorized with 64 national invention patents.

Zhang Gongqing, Member of the Selection Board

Zhang Gongqing was born on May 29, 1936 in Shanghai. After he graduated from the Department of Mathematics of Peking University in 1959 he worked in his university. In the year of 1978, as one of the first visiting scholars since the reform and opening-up, he made further study in the United States. Now he is a professor of Peking University, an academician of Chinese Academy of Sciences, an academician of the Academy of Sciences for the Developing World, the Director of the Research and Talent Training Center for Teaching and Learning Mathematics in Universities and Colleges, and he also serves as a member in the editorial board of many international core academic journals.

As a famous mathematician, he develops infinite dimensional Morse theory into a unified framework of the critical point theory, and is the first one to employ Morse theory as a tool to study multiple solutions to partial differential equations. His monograph is the fundamental literature of the related field. He also develops the topological degree theory of set-valued mappings and the critical point theory of non-differential functional, making them a kind of free boundary problem in the study on equations of mathematical physics and on non-smooth mechanics.

He won the Award of National Science & Technology Conference (1978), the third prize of the State Natural Sciences Award (1982), the second prize of the State Natural Sciences Award (1987), Chen Xingshen Mathematics Prize (1986), the title of the Young Scientist with Outstanding Contributions (1984), the Third World Academy of Sciences Award in Mathematics (1993), Hua Luogeng Mathematics Prize (2009), Guohua Award of Peking University, and Special Award for Teaching presented by Founder Group (2011), etc.

Chen Jiaer, Member of the Selection Board

Chen Jiaer, born on October 1, 1934 in Shanghai, is an academician of Chinese Academy of Sciences, an academician of the Academy of Sciences for the Developing World. He is currently a professor of physics at Peking University, the vice director of the Advisory Group of the National Basic Research Program of China (or 973 Program), and the vice chairman of the China Coordination Committee of the International Council of Scientific Unions.

He was the president of the Peking University and the dean of the Graduate School of Peking University, the director of the Committee of the National Natural Sciences Foundation, the director of the Division of Mathematics and Physics of the Chinese Academy of Sciences (CAS), a member of the CAS presidium, and the dean of the School of Physics of the Graduate University of CAS.

For a long time he has been devoting himself to the teaching and scientific research of the low-energy particle accelerator and its application. He is good at combining the cutting-edge development of an academic subject with national demands and planning the research in physics and talent training in a forward-looking way. He pioneered the development of RF superconducting accelerator, ultra-sensitive accelerator mass spectrometry, RF quadrupole field accelerator and electrostatic accelerator in China. He is a founder and one of the leaders in researching and developing low-energy particle accelerator in China.

Chen Jiaer was a long-time leader in Peking University and the Committee of the National Natural Science Foundation, and was also a member of the Leadership Group of Medium and Long Term Planning for Development of Science and Technology. He made important contribution to the formulation of the National Medium and Long Term Planning of Development of Science and Technology and the development of relevant science and education causes in China.

Hao Jiming, Member of the Selection Board

Hao Jiming, a well-known expert in environmental engineering, was born in Shandong Province in August 1946. He graduated from Tsinghua University in 1970. He earned a master degree from Tsinghua University in 1981, and obtained a Ph.D from University of Cincinnati in 1984. At Tsinghua University, he is a professor, tutor for doctoral candidates, deputy director of the teaching committee, and director of the Research Institute of Environmental Science and Engineering. He is also a member on the National Environmental Consultation Committee and China Council for International Cooperation on Environment and Development. He was elected as academician of the Chinese Academy of Engineering in 2005, and was elected as foreign academician of the National Academy of Engineering in the U.S. in 2018.

Hao Jiming has dedicated himself to the research in controlling air pollution in China for more than 40 years. His main fields of research include energy and environment, and air pollution control engineering. He is in charge of national acid deposition control planning and the research in countermeasures against acid deposition. His research result on dividing the areas for controlling acid rain and carbon dioxide has been adopted by the State Council, playing a guiding role in formulating China's policies on preventing and treating acid rain pollution. He has developed the planning and methods for controlling pollution caused by motor-driven vehicles in urban areas, promoting the control of the pollution caused by motor-driven vehicles in China. He has conducted in-depth research in the characteristics, causes and control policy on air compound pollution, further developed the theoretical and technological methods on improving the air quality in mega cities, and promoted the joint efforts to prevent and control the regional air compound pollution in China. He has conducted the research in the key technologies for controlling air pollution for a long period of time, and has made contributions in the fields such as dust control, desulfurization and denitration in coal-fired flue gas, and control of the pollution caused by motor-driven vehicles.

Hao Jiming won one first-prize and two second prizes of National Award for Scientific and Technological Progress, one second prize of National Award for Natural Science and two second prizes of National Award for Technical Invention, and two first prizes of National Award in Teaching Achievement. He was granted the title of national famous teacher in 2006. He won the Haagen-Smit Clean Air Award in 2015, and the IBM Global Faculty Award in 2016.

Qian Shaojun, Member of the Selection Board

Qian Shaojun was born in 1934 in Pinghu, Zhejiang Province. In 1951, he was admitted to the Department of Physics of Tsinghua University, and later studied Beijing Russian Language College, Department of Physics and the Research Section of Physics (now the Department of Technical Physics) of Peking University. He currently works as a consultant and research fellow of the Committee of Science and Technology of General Armament Department of the PLA, a research fellow and an academician of the Chinese Academy of Engineering. He used to be the deputy commander and the commander of the Nuclear Test Base, and was a standing member of the Committee of Science and Technology in the State Commission of Science and Technology for National Defense Industry.

He has been long engaged in the radiochemical diagnostic work of nuclear test and participated in a series of atomic bomb and hydrogen bomb nuclear tests conducted in the atmosphere or underground, in which he remarkably enhanced the measurement accuracy by establishing and improving many diagnostic approach and technology. For many times he took part in the study on the development strategy of science and technology and weaponry and equipment for national defence and participated in organizing the special research in national medium and long term scientific and technical development planning. He guided the basic study on applying research results in national defense, and worked hard to make such basic study consistent with the national basic research programs. He was put in charge of developing nuclear technology for military use, kept track of long-term changes with international situations and the policy evolvement of some leading nations, and instructed and took part in the study of arms control. He participated in the negotiation of the Comprehensive Nuclear Test Ban Treaty and guided the preparatory work for the performance of the treaty after it was signed.

His published works include a translated work, two monographs, wrote many scientific and technical papers and important scientific and technical articles for archival purpose. He won the

Top Prize of the State Scientific and Technological Progress Award and the second prize of the State Scientific and Technological Progress Award once, the second prize of the State Award for Inventions and the third prize of the State Award for Inventions once, and the Military Progress Prize in Science and Technology many times.

Ni Jun, Member of the Selection Board

Ni Jun was born in Qinghai Province in November 1961. He is the Shien-Ming (Sam) Wu Collegiate Professor of Manufacturing Science and Professor of Mechanical Engineering at the University of Michigan, USA. He is the director of the Wu Manufacturing Research Center and the co-director of a National Science Foundation sponsored Industry/University Cooperative Research Center for Intelligent Maintenance Systems at the University of Michigan. Professor Ni served as the founding Dean of the University of Michigan – Shanghai Jiao Tong University Joint Institute located in Shanghai, China and is currently the Honorary Dean and Special Advisor to the President of Shanghai Jiao Tong University. Professor Ni is currently the Chairman of Global Future Council on Production at the World Economic Forum. Professor Ni served as the Deputy Director of the National Science Foundation Engineering Research Center for Reconfigurable Manufacturing Systems, and the Director of a National Science Foundation sponsored Industry/University Cooperative Research Center for Dimensional Measurement and Control in Manufacturing.

Professor Ni's research covers many topics in advanced manufacturing, including smart manufacturing technologies, and applications of industrial big data analytics and artificial intelligence in quality assurance, precision manufacturing, and intelligent maintenance systems. His research has been successfully applied by various industrial companies.

Selected honors and awards that Professor Ni received are 2013 International Science and Technology Cooperation Award from the President of People's Republic of China, 2013 Gold Medal from Society of Manufacturing Engineers, 2009 Ennor Manufacturing Technology Award from American Society of Mechanical Engineers, and 1994 Presidential Faculty Fellows Award from President Clinton. He is an elected Fellow of International Society of Engineering Asset Management, International Society for Nano-manufacturing, American Society of Mechanical Engineers, and Society of Manufacturing Engineers.

Sang Guowei, Member of the Selection Board

Sang Guowei was born in Huzhou, Zhejiang in November 1941. He is a clinical pharmacologist, an academician of the Chinese Academy of Engineering, Chairman of Chinese Pharmaceutical Association, Chief Engineer for the important specific techniques for the national "development of important new medicines" in the "11th Five-Year Plan", "12th Five-Year Plan" and "13th Five-Year Plan". He is also the director of the Expert Consultation Committee of the "Development Program of the Pharmaceuticals Industry in the 13th Five-Year Plan" of the Ministry of Industry and Information Technology, senior research fellow of National Institute for the Control of Pharmaceutical and Biological Products (NICPBP), honorary president of Shanghai University of Traditional Chinese Medicine (SHUTCM), and was the vice chairman of the 11th National People's Congress Standing Committee, and chairman of Chinese Peasants' and Workers' Democratic Party.

He has systematically studied the pharmacokinetics, race differences and clinical pharmacology of steroidal contraceptives and antiprogestogens for long-acting injection and for oral taking, and made a number of important achievements. He has done fruitful work in terms of safety evaluation, quality control and clinical trial etc. for new drugs in recent years, and has made great contributions in strengthening China's construction of the GLP and GCP platforms.

He has won two National Scientific Conference Awards (in 1978), three Second Prizes of National Science and Technology Progress Award (in 1987, 1997 and 2008), one First Prize and four Second Prizes of Science and Technology Progress Award at the ministerial and commission levels, the Science and Technology Awards of the Ho Leung Ho Lee Foundation in 1997 (Medical-Pharmaceutical Award), the Special Contribution Award of the Wu Jieping-Paul Janssen Medical-Pharmaceutical Award in 2008, and the Lifetime Achievement Award in Pharmacy Science of the Federation International Pharmaceutical (FIP) in 2014.

Cao Xuetao, Member of the Selection Board

Cao Xuetao, was born in July 1964 in Jinan City, Shandong Province. In 1990, he graduated from the Second Military Medical University. He is the President of Chinese Academy of Medical Sciences (CAMS), member of the Chinese Academy of Engineering, and the Director of National Key Laboratory of Medical Immunology. Concurrently he is the President of the Chinese Society for Immunology, Chairperson of Global Alliance of Chronic Diseases (GACD), and President of the Federation of Immunological Societies of Asia-Oceania (FIMSA). He also serves as a member of the editorial board of magazines including Cell.

He is mainly engaged in fundamental research on innate immune recognition and relevant immune regulation, and applicability research on tumor immunotherapy. He has found a new dendritic cell (DC) subset with an important immune regulation function, independently identified 22 immune-related molecules, systematically studied innate immune recognition and the new mechanism for interferon production regulation, explored apparent molecular action on inflammation and cancer development and progression, established new approaches for tumor immunotherapy, and carried out relevant clinical trials.

He won the second-class prize of National Science and Technology Awards as the primary participant of a research project, a first-class prize of Chinese Medical Science and Technology Awards, a first-class prize of Military Science and Technology Progress Awards, three first-class prizes of Shanghai Science and Technology Progress Awards. He has obtained 16 national invention patents and two national category-II new medicine certificates. His research result was selected as one of the top ten results representing the scientific and technological progress in China in 2011. He was presented with Guanghua Engineering Science and Technology Award, Cheng Kong Scholar Achievement Award, China Young Scientist Award, and others. As corresponding author, he published over 220 papers in SCI-cited journals including Cell, Science, Nature Immunology, Cancer Cell, Immunity and others. His papers have been non-self-cited for over 5600 times in SCI-cited journals; he has written and served as a co-chief-editor for eight monographs. Of all the doctoral candidates under his tutorship, 11 have been presented with the awards of "national 100 excellent dissertations for doctoral degrees."

Cheng Xu, Member of the Selection Board

Cheng Xu, born in 1944, is of the origin of Wuxi, Jiangsu Province. He graduated from the Department of Agronomy of Beijing Agricultural University (Now China Agricultural University), later he worked in the Institute of Crop Breeding and Cultivation of the Chinese Academy of Agricultural Science. He is currently a professor of the China Agricultural University, and a tutor for doctoral candidates. He worked in the Beijing Academy of Agricultural Science and the Ministry of Agriculture. His major fields of research include sustainable agriculture and rural development, agricultural ecology and ecological agriculture.

He was put in charge of two research projects: one is the construction of the Agricultural Modernization and Experimental Base (location: Doudian village, Fangshan County, Beijing) and the other is Ecological Agriculture Program. In 1985, he took the lead in introducing the theory of sustainable agricultural development. From then on he started to study the way to realize sustainable agricultural development in China. He focused his research on the ecological restoration in the fragile farming-pastoral transitional zones and the exploration of the sustainable intensive agriculture.

As the main participant in completing the research project, he won the first prize of the Beijing Science and Technology Progress Awards and the first prize of the National Sparkle Technology Award (equivalent to Science and Technology Progress Award). He was totally presented with seven second or third prizes of science and technology progress awards at provincial and ministerial level. In 1988, he was approved as a National Young & Middle-Aged Expert with Outstanding

Contribution.

His works include *An Introduction to Sustainable Agriculture* and *General Program on Sustainable Development in China Volume* 13: *Agriculture in China and the Sustainable Development.*

Zeng Qingcun, Member of the Selection Board

Zeng Qingcun, born in May 1935 in Yangjiang County of Guangdong Province, graduated from the Department of Physics of Peking University in 1956. In 1961, he completed his Licentiate (namely Ph.D now) in the Institute of Applied Geophysics of the Soviet Academy of Science. After he returned to China he worked in the Institute of Geophysics and then the Institute of Atmospheric Physics of the Chinese Academy of Sciences (CAS) . He was elected as an academician of the Chinese Academy of Sciences in 1980. Currently he is a research fellow of the Institute of Atmospheric physics of the CAS.

His major research field includes atmospheric sciences and geophysical fluid dynamics. He has been devoting himself to the study of the basic theory and numerical model and simulation of general atmospheric circulation and fluid dynamics, earth system dynamics model, numerical weather prediction and climatic prediction theory, climate dynamics and monsoon theory, dynamics of atmospheric boundary layer, theoretical method of satellite remote sensing, applied mathematics and numerical mathematics, and natural cybernetics. He is the first one in the world to put forward half–implicit difference scheme and square conservative scheme, applied the original equation into the actual numerical climate prediction (1961), developed the marine–atmosphere coupled mode for the extra–seasonal climate predictions (1990, 1994), and put forward the systematic theory of satellite remote sensing (1974) and the Theoretical method of natural control (1995) .

He won the second prize of the State Natural Sciences Award twice and the third prize of the State Natural Sciences Awards once, the first prize of the Natural Science Award of the CAS six times and Outstanding Contribution Award once. His monographs include *Principles of the Atmospheric Remote Sensing in Infrared*, *Mathematical Physics Foundations of the Numerical Weather Prediction*, *Principles of the Short–term Numerical Climatic Prediction*, *Yellow Clouds Stretching Thousands of Miles— The research on Dust–storm in East Asia.* He has also published hundreds of academic articles.